FLEXIBLE EXCHANGE RATES AND STABILIZATION POLICY

FLEXIBLE EXCHANGE RATES AND STABILIZATION POLICY

Edited by

JAN HERIN, ASSAR LINDBECK
AND JOHAN MYHRMAN

Routledge
Taylor & Francis Group
LONDON AND NEW YORK

First published 1976,1977 by Westview Press

Published 2018 by Routledge
52 Vanderbilt Avenue, New York, NY 10017
2 Park Square, Milton Park, Abingdon, Oxon OX14 4RN

Routledge is an imprint of the Taylor & Francis Group, an informa business

Library of Congress Cataloging in Publication Data
Main entry under title:
Flexible exchange rates and stabilization policy.
Proceedings of a conference held at Saltsjöbaden, Stockholm, August 26–27, 1975.
"Originally published in The Scandinavian journal of economics, vol. 78, no. 2, 1976."
1. Foreign exchange problem—Congresses. I. Herin, Jan. II. Lindbeck, Assar. III. Myhrman, Johan, 1937–

HG3821.F56 332.4'5 76–30881

ISBN 13: 978-0-367-02195-5 (hbk)

ISBN 13: 978-0-367-17182-7 (pbk)

CONTENTS

PREFACE

The shift to greater exchange-rate flexibity during the early 1970s has created a need to strengthen the theory of flexible exchange rates and to improve its integration with macro theory and stabilization policy analyis.

This volume consists of the papers, comments and, in summary form, the discussion at a conference on "Flexible Exchange Rates and Stabilization Policy", held at Saltsjöbaden, Stockholm, August 26–27, 1975. The conference was organized by the Institute for International Economic Studies at the University of Stockholm, and arrangements and financing were carried out by the Bank of Sweden Tercentenary Foundation, under the guidance of its Director, Dr. Nils-Eric Svensson. A special committee, appointed by the Foundation, was formed to plan the conference. The members of the committee were Ragnar Bentzel, Erik Lundberg, Assar Lindbeck (Chairman) and Nils-Eric Svensson. Birgitta Eliason of the Institute for International Economic Studies carried the main burden of organization during the conference.

These proceedings were originally published in *The Scandinavian Journal of Economics*, Vol. 78, No. 2, 1976.

Institute for International Economic Studies
Stockholm

Jan Herin
Assar Lindbeck
Johan Myhrman

APPROACHES TO EXCHANGE RATE ANALYSIS—AN INTRODUCTION

Assar Lindbeck

Institute for International Economic Studies, Stockholm, Sweden

It is the fate of social scientists to shoot at moving targets. At about the time when macro economists started to understand the operations of a world economy with fixed exchange rates, or adjustable pegs, the system was replaced with a regime with considerable exchange rate flexibility, occasionally even floating rates. As a consequence, prevailing "embryos" to a theory of the balance of payments for a regime of flexible rates—as formulated by Milton Friedman, James Meade, Egon Sohmen and others—were suddenly put into empirical test and found to be in need of some modification. The same can be said about theoretical suggestions concerning the performance of stabilization policy under alternative exchange rate regimes, as formulated *inter alia* by Marcus Fleming and Robert Mundell.

When approaching the theory of the balance of payments, exchange rates and stabilization policy, it is easy to agree that the analysis ideally should be pursued in the context of a complete macro model *with full consideration to the interaction of various markets*, i.e. by way of a general equilibrium, or a "general disequilibrium" (without market-clearing) model. In practical applications, drastic simplifcations are, of course, necessary both to make the analysis manageable and to reach unambiguous conclusions. It is about the choice of such simplifications and shortcuts that the analytical controversies rage. This is evident also from most of the papers in this conference volume.

Among the various controversies, a rather technical one concerns the celebrated issue of (I) the choice between stock and flow formulations for the financial markets. A more fundamental controversy refers to (II) the choice between partial and total equilibrium analysis, or rather the *degree* of "partiality", as well as the related issues of the specification of endogenous and exogenous variables, and the length of the time perspective (short-run versus long-run analysis). A third basic controversy concerns (III) the relative speed of reaction and market-clearing in various markets.

The purpose of this introductory paper is to take a brief look at these three, highly interrelated issues, and then to try relating some of the major contributions of the conference to earlier and contemporary doctrinal development of those issues.

I. Stocks versus Flows

Perhaps the main advances in theoretical and empirical analysis of the balance of payments and exchange rates in recent years have been (1) an increased understanding of the analytical advantages of formulating the financial markets in terms of demand and supply of *stocks* of assets in various currency denominations, and not just the *flow* of funds; and (2) a realization that *expectations* about the variables which influence asset behavior should be a crucial consideration in the analysis.

These points are developed in several of the papers in this volume. More specifically, the exchange rate is seen as a consequence of the requirements of equilibrium in the market of financial assets with different currency denominations. Moreover, changes in the stock-supply and stock-demand of assets are regarded as an important part of the adjustments of the balance of payments and the exchange rate over time.[1]

It is well known from the celebrated controversy about the loanable funds and the liquidity preference approaches to interest rate theory that "flow models" and "stock models" under certain conditions can be formulated in such a way that the two approaches may be regarded as consistent, or perhaps even equivalent. However, as in the case of interest rate analysis, an explicit formulation of the financial markets in stock-terms has obvious advantages as compared to flow formulations only. In the case of exchange-rate and balance-of-payments analysis, perhaps three advantages of a stock formulation are particularly worth emphasizing:

(1) A stock formulation reminds us that flows can fruitfully be seen as adjustments to desired stocks, and that the flows become zero when desired stocks have been reached (if net wealth is constant). Thereby a stock formulation helps to clarify when a flow is temporary and permanent, respectively. Then we can also easily dispel the theoretically dubious, but rather usual, assumption that capital movements (rather than desired stocks of foreign assets) are functions of interest rate differentials between nations.

(2) An explicit asset approach also helps us realize that even a rather moderate percentage change in stock-demand or stock-supply may generate a large percentage change in the flow of funds because of the large size of stocks relative to flows during a short period (for instance a few months).

(3) Moreover, an explicit introduction of *both* stocks and flows (of financial and monetary variables) helps focus on the basic macroeconomic adjustment mechanism, which may otherwise easily be "forgotten", by highlighting changes

[1] Harry Johnson made a rather prophetic statement some ten years ago about the likely "future" role of asset (portfolio) considerations in exchange-rate and balance-of-payments analysis, when commenting on a pioneering article in this field by Ronald McKinnon: "I should not be surprised if in ten years time most of us will be talking McKinnon's language (i.e. portfolio analysis) as a matter of course." *Monetary Problems of the International Economy*, ed. by R. A. Mundell and A. K. Swoboda, University of Chicago Press, 1969, p. 399.

in net wealth via the flow of saving through a surplus (or deficit) in the current account of the balance of payments or in the government budget. We are thus reminded that a full (stationary) equilibrium, *ceteris paribus*, is not reached until the sum of the current account and the government budget is zero.[1] (This argument implicitly assumes that the private sector does not regard the capital value of future taxes, needed to finance the public debt, as a liability of the private sector.)

II. Partial versus Total Analysis

If we choose a continuous treatment of time in our model, it follows as an "analytical triviality" that the exchange rate *at every movement of time* is determined *only* by the conditions of instantaneous stock equilibrium—without any influence whatsoever from the rate of the flow on the current account (except in the sense that the rate of the flow of the current account may influence *expectations* and hence stock-demand for assets).

Controversies start when we choose a discrete treatment of time, as in empirical studies. In a very short-run time perspective, such as a few weeks, an isolated *partial equilibrium* stock analysis, without explicit connections to the flows in the current account, may often be quite appropriate as a rough analysis of the balance of payments and/or exchange rates. The reason is, of course, the short-run "stickiness" of the flows on the current account, and the often dominating influence of portfolio shifts upon the exchange rate (unrelated to the development on the current account) in the short run, for instance in response to changes in interest rate differentials, exchange rate expectations or political circumstances.

---

[1] Some other often asserted "advantages" of a stock approach are more doubtful, as they do not *logically* seem to be tied more to stock formulations than to flow formulations. For instance, it is sometimes claimed that the emphasis on portfolio behavior quite automatically leads us to assign a crucial role to expectations. However, there is hardly any reason why expectations should play a more important role in an analysis built on stock formulations than in analyses in terms of flows.

Another alleged advantaged of stock formulations is that the correlation between the size of flows during a period (*ex post*) and actual or expected exchange rate changes is weak. The reason would be that financial flows are largely a function of the *dispersion* and *accuracy* of exchange rate expectations rather than of the size of the actual or ("on the average") expected change in the rate. However, this correct observation by itself is no ground for preferring "stock formulations" to "flow formulations", as the same weak correlation holds between exchange rate changes and stock-demand shifts (*ex post*). The point is rather that it is important to distinguish between, on the one hand, *desired* flows and stocks (*ex ante*) and, on the other hand, actual flows and stocks (*ex post*), and that exchange rate changes should be explained by the former types of variable rather than the latter.

For instance, if *everybody* operating in the market for assets correctly expects the exchange rate to shift by α percent, a given (*ex post*) change in the spot rate may take place with rather small shifts in assets, and hence with rather small financial flows, even though desired (*ex ante*) asset holdings and flows may have changed quite a lot. If, by contrast, some people expect large exchange rate changes whereas others expect small ones, or even changes in the opposite direction, large reshufflings of assets, and hence large financial flows, will usually take place *ex post*.

The reason for the words "usually" and "as a rough analysis" in these formulations is that actual and expected changes in the current account may *occasionally* have quite strong effects even in a rather short time perspective, such as a few months. For instance, a sudden dramatic change in the terms of trade may within a rather short period of time considerably influence both the supply and demand side of assets via the actual and expected flows on the current account. An illustration is probably provided by the events in the world economy during the 1973–75 period, in connection with violent changes in the price of oil and certain other raw materials. In cases like these, some useful information is lost—even in a rather short-run perspective—if stock equilibrium in the asset markets is analyzed without considering the influence from, and perhaps also the interaction with, the actual and expected future current account. Moreover, for large countries for which the exchange rate influences world market prices—with a feedback on the exchange rate via the *value* of the current account—"stickiness" of the *volume* of trade (during perhaps several months) is no reason to neglect the interdependence between the exchange rate and the *value* of the current account, even in a rather short-run analysis.

It should perhaps be added that the current account has an important information value "by itself" for policy purposes, as many governments seem to be much concerned with the *composition* of the balance of payments, and not just its total value (at fixed rates) or the exchange rate (at floating rates).

In spite of these reservations, and without ambitions to deal with the *composition* of the balance of payments, it is probably reasonable to argue, as Michael Mussa does, that in a short-run perspective (a few weeks or perhaps even a few months) "the proximate determination of exchange rates and the balance of payments are the demand and supply of various monies". However, then the term "monies" has to be liberally interpreted as "financial assets" rather than "money" in the literal sense. For there is hardly any theoretical presumption that shifts in the market for money are "more important" (for the exchange rate and/or the balance of payments) than shifts in the markets for interest-bearing financial assets. Empirical evidence in recent years suggest, in fact, that portfolio shifts have often taken place between *earning assets* of different denominations (bonds, bills and time deposits of various types) rather than just money. Thus, there is hardly any reason to turn an "asset theory" (of the balance of payments and exchange rates) into a "monetary theory". I understand that the emphasis on a "monetary approach" to the balance of payments and exchange rates in some of the papers in this volume—such as the papers by Michael Mussa, Rudiger Dornbusch and Pentti Kouri—is simply a "pedagogical simplification" of what is basically an asset approach. "Money" should then perhaps be read "financial assets" in all these papers.

As soon as the time perspective is lengthened (over several months or years) it is probably important that the determination of the exchange rate, the price level, and the current and capital accounts is analyzed in the context of a "complete", general equilibrium macro model. In such a long-run framework, the exchange rate tends to be not only a relative price between two "national monies" (which is true by definition) but also, when purchasing power parity holds, a relative price between two "national outputs". More specifically, whereas the short-term behavior of the exchange rate can be seen as a consequence of the requirements of instantaneous equilibrium in the market of financial assets, the long-run development probably has to be explained by reference to the relative commodity-price levels in the countries concerned. The short run and the long run may then be tied together via the interaction over time between the flows in the current account, the accumulation of financial assets in different denominations, and the price trends in various countries, which presupposes a realistic treatment also of the labor market and wage formation.

III. Speed of Reaction and Market Clearing

One conceivable simplification of such a macro analysis is to exploit the different speeds of adjustment between markets, which may make it possible to operate with recursive relations between various blocks in the macro model. For instance, based on the assumption that the market for financial assets clears rapidly, whereas the markets for commodity flows (including imports and exports) clear slowly, a partial equilibrium "asset block" may be used to determine exchange rates (or the balance of payments) at every point of time, whereas the current account is asserted to be affected by the exchange rate "later on", with an over time accumulating "feedback" on the asset markets via the accumulation of assets. This is, in fact, the way Pentti Kouri in his paper integrates the markets for financial assets (and hence the capital account) with the markets for commodity flows (and hence the current account). On the basis of this approach, Kouri can claim that "the exchange rate is determined to equilibrate the demand for foreign assets with the existing stock of foreign assets", and that "a shift in absorption [i.e. in the current account] that does not affect asset demand has no effects on the exchange rates in the short run" (*ceteris paribus*, including "stationary expectations").

Another important consequence of slowness of market-clearing for "real markets"—commodities and labor—is, of course, the emergence of short-run variations in the volume of output and employment in response to fluctuations in aggregate demand. In fact, it would seem to me that the most important task for the immediate future in exchange-rate and balance-of-payments theory is to elaborate the consequences of short-term stickiness not only of nominal prices and wages, in particular downwards, but also of real wages (as emphasized by Max Corden)—mainly for the purpose of explaining fluctuations in "involuntary" unemployment of the Keynesian type. Thereby we would perhaps also be able to avoid "the obsession", to be found in most monetarist models, with *long-term, full-employment stationary equilibria*, which certainly is not the appropriate context for an analysis of short-run stabilization policy, where short-run fluctuations in output and employment, including "involuntary unemployment", certainly are crucial aspects.

A concentration on long-run stationary equilibria tends to "define away" exactly the situations in which stabilization policy is potentially *useful*. In such models the effects of stabilization policy are in fact often studied in a context when stabilization policy *is not even needed*, since long-run adjustments in prices and wealth anyway will move the economy to a stationary full-employment equilibrium regardless of the policy pursued—a point mentioned by Richard Cooper. It is therefore no surprise that many long-run models of this type have generated the conclusions that both exchange rate changes and stabilization policy in general are not very effective.

The purpose of stabilization policy is, of course, to influence the economy exactly when it is *outside* such states, and then policy can certainly have effects. This has, in fact, always been indirectly admitted even by the "enemies" of stabilization policy when they, not without empirical support, often assert that stabilization policy is often *destabilizing* the economy.

A Historical Perspective

To some extent, the "advances" in recent years in the theory of the balance of payments and exchange rates simply mean that economists are "catching up" with the long-run analysis of classical economists such as Hume, Thornton, Ricardo and Cassel, as shown in the papers by Johan Myhrman and Jacob Frenkel. However, a difference is that whereas these classical authors, combining asset-formulations and the purchasing power parity theory, were concerned mostly with the effects of monetary changes on exchange rates *via domestic commodity prices*, contemporary versions of the "monetary approach" have a tendency to emphasize the *direct* effects, at given prices and interest rates, on the balance of payments and exchange rates. The main analytical explanation for this difference is that external commodity and asset prices (interest rates) in contemporary monetarist models are usually assumed to be parametrically given for the individual country, and therefore that domestic excess supply for money is reflected either in excess demand for commodities, which spills over into the current account, or excess demand for financial claims, which spills over into the capital account.

The classical economist, by contrast, usually assumed that domestic excess supply for money also influences domestic commodity and asset prices, with *indirect* effects on the balance of payments and/or the exchange rate—along the lines of the purchasing power theory. This approach can be specified more explicitly by assuming that some commodities are non-tradables, and/or that domestic and foreign tradables are not perfect substitutes, and that also a labor market is introduced. Thereby it is possible to consider explicitly the importance of relative prices between tradables, non-tradables, and labor, and hence to put demand and supply elasticities into place. The importance of these considerations is illustrated by the empirical observation that *both* the current account *and* the employment level are strongly related to the real wage rate in various sectors of the economy.

The postulated relations between the current and the capital account have changed considerably over time in "dominating" models of balance-of-payments adjustment. In traditional analysis before the Second World War, long-term capital movements were usually assumed to be determined by differences in real rates of return on physical assets, to which the current account was asserted to adjust via changes in relative prices, stocks of assets, exchange rates and possibly income. In analytical expositions during the first decades after World War II—in fact a period when capital flows were regulated, currencies were largely inconvertible, and the stock of foreign claims was small relative to the flows of trade—the emphasis in analyses of the balance of payments and the exchange rate was on the development of the current account. In fact, perhaps we can say that the capital account was asserted to adjust to the state of the current account, via politically controlled capital flows and interest rate induced capital flows—with obvious risk of "distortions" in the global allocation of investments in physical assets (as pointed out many years ago by Friedrich Lutz and Harry Johnson).

The increased size of the stock of foreign financial assets and capital flows during the last decade has once again changed the "dominating" notion of the interaction between the current and the capital account. Now the most important short-run effects on the balance of payments and exchange rates are, as already mentioned, asserted to come from shifts (unrelated to the current account) in stock-demand and stock-supply for financial assets, with accumulating effects over time on the current account, and with "later" feedbacks on the markets for assets and exchange rates.

Some of these various approaches to exchange rate analysis could perhaps be schematically summarized in Fig. 1, where A^d and A^s denote the demand and supply for the stock of financial assets (in several models expressed as money), P the domestic price level, C the current account, K the capital account, B the balance of payments (zero in a freely floating system) and E the exchange rate. The classical school (Thornton, Ricardo, Hume and Cassel) concentrated on the *three* recursive links denoted (1), (2) and (3) in the chart—often perhaps also disaggregating the effects on the balance of payments as illustrated by links (4) and (5). However, sometimes the traditional analyses of the balance of payments "started" with a shift in K, generated by for

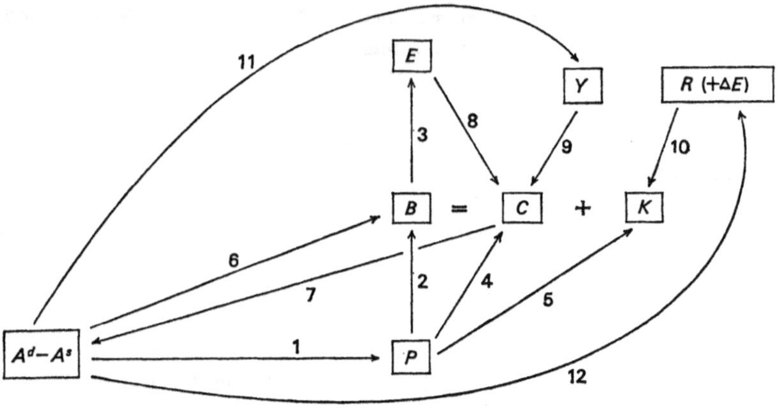

Fig. 1. Mechanisms of exchange rate determination.
$A^d - A^s$ = excess demand for assets in various currency denominations
P = domestic price level
C = current account
E = exchange rate
R = interest rate differential
B = the balance of payments
K = capital account
Y = real national income

instance a difference in the rate of return on physical assets or war reparations, and derived the effects on E and C via links (3) and (8), respectively.

Some contemporary monetarists, such as Mussa, by contrast, seem to concentrate on the "shortcuts" denoted by links (6) and (3), while others, such as Dornbusch, rather emphasize links (12) and (10), expressing an interest rate and exchange rate arbitrage mechanism $[R(+\Delta E)]$ influencing the capital account; for more long-run developments Dornbusch also stresses links (1) and (4), reflecting the purchasing parity mechanism.

It is also typical of some contemporary monetarists to let aggregate demand (Y), and hence also the C-variable, shift as a response to a non-zero situation for the current account, by way of a wealth effect on aggregate demand—as indicated by the "loop" expressed by the links (7), (11), (9). In Kouri's paper in this volume the emphasis is on the recursively formulated "loop" denoted by the links (6), (3) and (8), (7) expressing what happens when the stock of assets changes as a result of a non-zero current account. Thus, whereas Dornbusch lets the short-run analysis converge to a long-term equilibrium by way of a gradual adjustment to purchasing power parity, Kouri emphasizes the long-term relation between the exchange rate and the accumulation of wealth via the current account.

The most usual approach during the first decades after the Second World War, by contrast, was perhaps to emphasize *separately* the effects on the *current account* of variations in aggregate demand (Y), as illustrated by link (9) in the chart, and the effects on the *capital account* via interest rate differentials (R)

and possibly expectations about exchange rate changes (ΔE), as illustrated by link (10).

In more complete macro models, all these variables should probably be endogenously determined together with variables such as real wage rates, prices of tradables and non-tradables, profits and investment—with properly specified time-lags. Which of these variables and links that can be neglected in a *specific analysis* depend, of course, largely on the type of disturbance we are studying, the question we are trying to answer, the time perspective, and the country we are considering.

The Papers in this Volume

Several of the problems discussed above are analyzed in the various papers in this volume. *Richard Cooper* opens by presenting the states of the arts of the theory of stabilization policy in alternative exchange rate regimes. Cooper also suggests a number of further advances of the research frontier, such as more explicit considerations to the effects of changes in exchange rates on nominal factor prices, the implications for the *need* for stabilization policy in alternative exchange rate regimes, and the consequences of the holdings of foreign money.

However, before further attempts are made to advance the research frontier in this field, it is perhaps worthwhile to look at the experiences and debates during previous periods of floating exchange rates. This task is undertaken by *Johan Myhrman* and *Jacob Frenkel*, who discuss and illustrate empirically the purchasing power parity doctrine of exchange rate determination in the context of an explicit asset approach. These papers clearly bring out, not unexpectedly perhaps, a long-run historical regularity for the relations between the trend values of the money stock, prices and the exchange rate. It is my understanding that Myhrman—in his study of the experiences in Sweden in the 18th century and Britain in the early 19th century—finds the "first" link in the purchasing power parity theory (the link between money and prices) less tight than the "second" link (the one between prices and exchange rates). It was to be expected that Frenkel in his study of hyperinflation in Germany in the nineteen-twenties would find a much tighter link between money and prices.

The papers by Michael Mussa. Rudiger Dornbusch and Pentti Kouri undertake the task of developing the macro theory of flexible exchange rate regimes with the emphasis on asset equilibrium, though Mussa and Kouri simplify the asset side drastically by concentrating on one kind of financial asset, money.

Michael Mussa employs the simplest approach by concentrating entirely on asset equilibrium in the money market, without considerations to relative commodity prices and the real wage rate. Formally, the analysis looks like a partial equilibrium analysis for the money market, but the applications suggest that it is rather a reduced form equilibrium equation reflecting an implicit macro model.[1] However, it would seem that here the theory of exchange rates is largely removed from the purchasing parity doctrine. Short-term and long-term asset equilibrium for *one* type of asset (money), is alleged to tell the whole (or at least the important part of the) story.

Rudiger Dornbusch's model is considerably richer than Mussa's as it considers explicitly not only asset equilibrium (in the money market) but also the trend for the exchange rate, determined by a purchasing power parity path, along which portfolio shifts may exert a short-run influence on the exchange rate. Thus, Dornbusch takes an explicit step in the direction of a general equilibrium approach, as compared to Mussa's partial equilibrium, or reduced form, model. A crucial feature of the Dornbusch model is that short-run changes in the forward premium allow interest rates, and hence velocity, to change, which both tend to reduce the impact on the domestic economy of monetary policy and to allow an impact of fiscal policy. Technically, this is achieved by assuming that the asset market in the short run is not characterized by homogeneity properties, since the elasticity of expectations is assumed to be smaller than unity. Similarly, it is shown how incorrect exchange rate expectations may result in an overshooting of the exchange rate, relative to the long-term equilibrium path as defined by purchasing power parity. This assertion is quite consistent both with Cooper's and Kouri's theoretical analysis, and with the empirical finding in Frenkel's paper that the elasticity of the exchange rate with respect to the supply of money seems to be larger than unity.

The general equilibrium character of the problem is stressed also in *Pentti Kouri's* paper, where the interaction between the capital and current accounts is highlighted. In contrast to the analysis that dominated during the forties and fifties, when the capital account was often assumed to accommodate to the current account—at the fixed exchange rate regimes then prevailing—Kouri lets rather the current account adjust over time to the exchange rate that is determined on the market for assets (in fact money). Thereby a recursive interaction over time between the exchange rates, the balance of payments and net financial wealth is highlighted—under alternative assumptions about exchange rate expectations.

Of course, neither of these three papers should be interpreted as statements about all important facets of exchange rate determination in the real world but rather as attempts to follow the logic of one or a few specified mechanisms, under alternative assumptions about the formation of expectations. A richer specification of markets, and of the channels of transmission could largely modify the conclusions in all three papers, for instance by the explicit introduction of earning assets with flexible prices, capital goods, inventories, as

[1] Perhaps we should rather talk about a "quasi-reduced form", as Mussa's equation seems to include more than one endogenous variable.

well as by an elaboration of the importance of price and wage rigidities and therewith connected possibilities of involuntary unemployment.

In the general discussion about the practical implications of flexible exchange rates during recent decades, three basic issues seem to have been particularly stressed: (1) the consequences of alternative exchange rate regimes for the risk of foreign transactions and therefore also the implications for the volume of international trade; (2) the consequences of the exchange rate regime for the need of reserves and reserve use; and (3) the implication for the trade-off between unemployment and inflation. In this volume, the first issue is dealt with by Robert Aliber, the second by John Williamson, and the third by Emil-Maria Claassen and Max Corden.

In an empirical study of the exchange risks connected with flexible rates, *Robert Aliber* finds evidence that the short-term risk in the exchange market, as reflected by the bid-ask spread and by the deviation of exchange rates from purchasing power parity, has increased after the introduction of more flexible exchange rates. However, in evaluation of this result, it is important to emphasize that *the ceteris paribus lines* in Aliber's paper are drawn rather narrowly—in fact too narrowly to provide evidence about the "total" risks of foreign transactions under alternative exchange rate regimes (as explained below).

John Williamson asks if there is a trade-off between exchange rate variability and reserve use. His starting point is the empirical observation that changes in exchange reserves (deflated by the value of international trade) have hardly been smaller during the period of managed float than during the period of adjustable pegs. He also shows that there is indeed a theoretical *possibility* that the allowance of increased exchange rate flexibility, by way of managed float, generates larger reserve use than a system of more fixed exchange rates—if there is a specific combination of lags structures, formation of expectations and types of official interventions.

However, it is important to point out that the empirical data generated during the early seventies in the exchange market may be dominated by two special features which are not logically connected to a system of *permanently* managed floating: (1) The large observed reserve use may have been a result of unusually great disturbances of the balance of payments during this period. In fact, the shift to floating rates may perhaps be seen as a *response* to greater fluctuations in reserve use rather than as a *cause* of it. (2) The shift to floating rates may have created a period of large *temporary* reserve use as countries reshuffled reserves to fit the new levels of desired reserves during the floating rate system.

Finally, *Claassen* and *Corden* try to show that flexible rates are *in principle* neither more nor less inflationary than fixed rates. A general reflection in both papers is that flexible rates create a possibility for inflation-prone countries to inflate more and for inflation-shy countries to inflate less than at fixed rates—the effects on the average rate of inflation in the world as a whole being uncertain. The papers also illustrate the important point that an analysis of the effects of alternative exchange rate regimes presupposes that the effects *on politicians* of a shift in the exchange rate regime are specified, i.e. that behavior functions for politicians are explicitly, or at least implicitly, assumed. In fact, most of the usually asserted differences in the performance of the economy at alternative exchange rate regimes seem to depend on assumed differences in economic policy in two systems, due largely to differences in trade-off opportunities.

Policy Implications

The emphasis in most papers at the conference is largely on analytical issues, i.e. on the theoretical foundations of macro analysis in a flexible exchange rate regime, rather than on policy issues. This emphasis is perhaps quite proper at the present state of knowledge, in order to avoid premature policy conclusions. However, the theoretical foundations are now becoming good enough for future investigations of the policy implications of recent theoretical developments. For instance, one policy implication seems to be that monetary policy is potentially rather effective at floating exchange rates, *even if the interest rate elasticity of spending is low*. The reason for this is that the exchange rates, in the short run, are dominated by stock-demand and stock-supply for financial assets, which means that monetary policy creates repercussions on excess demand for domestic output *via changes in exports and imports* by way of policy-induced changes in exchange rates. Against this background, demand and supply elasticities for imports and exports become, in a floating rate regime, at least as important for the efficacy of monetary policy as the interest rate elasticity of domestic spending. However, more definite conclusions about the efficacy of monetary and fiscal policy in floating exchange rate regimes must await better specifications of the mechanisms of fluctuations in output and employment, and hence of the role of stickiness of wages and prices.

Another policy implication of the analytical emphasis on asset equilibrium and expectations is that exchange rates in reality may fluctuate rather substantially—if expectations or economic policy abroad and at home fluctuate much. This also means that the ability of floating rates to shield the domestic economy from foreign disturbances is far from perfect. In fact, the analytical approaches chosen in most papers in this volume make the forces operating on exchange rates rather similar to the forces affecting the prices in the stock market, which is notoriously rather unstable. There is therefore hardly any presumption that the exchange rate market should be highly stable in floating rate regimes. However, this does *not* necessarily mean that the risks for agents in foreign transactions are greater in flexible than in fixed rate (or adjustable peg) systems. For it is certainly not appropriate to compare fixed rates and floating rates *ceteris paribus* for all other circumstances, as a number of other features are logically connected with the exchange rate system. The most obvious example is perhaps the degree of development of the forward markets. However, a more important point is that fixed rates too are connected with obvious uncertainties—not only because of the risks of discretionary exchange rate changes (in systems with adjustable pegs), but also the risks of other policy actions induced by balance-of-payments disequilibrium, such as changes in tariffs, import controls, export subsidies, as well as in aggregate demand management, as mentioned by Per Meinich in his comment.

In principle, *the entire package* of circumstances that is characteristic of a given exchange rate system has to be considered, and not just one element in such a package (such as the risks of market-induced exchange rate changes in a system with floating rates, and the risks of demand-reducing policies in a system with fixed rates). Thus, it is important that the *ceteris paribus* clause is drawn properly when the two systems are compared.

MONETARY THEORY AND POLICY IN AN OPEN ECONOMY*

Richard N. Cooper

Yale University, New Haven, Connecticut, USA

Abstract

This paper identifies several respects in which analysis of the macro-economics of small open economies has to be modified beyond its development a decade ago, with special reference to the effectiveness of monetary and fiscal policies under alternative exchange rate regimes. Capital movements must be viewed in the context of portfolio equilibrium rather than as continuous flows. Room must be made in monetarist formulations for holdings of foreign money. The impact of changes in exchange rates on nominal factor prices should be taken into account. And the effect of the exchange rate regime on the magnitude of the stabilization task must figure in any evaluation of alternative exchange rate regimes. Suggestions are made along each of these lines.

Two developments in the world economy in recent years have created an immediate and practical interest in certain propositions which only a few years ago seemed to be merely of theoretical interest. The first development has been the great increase in the international movement of capital, with the presumption that this increased movement reflects increased mobility in response to given economic incentives. The second development is the movement for many currencies, since March 1973, from fixed to flexible exchange rates. Both of these developments raise important questions concerning (1) the frequency and amplitude of disturbances to macro-economic stability in national economies and (2) the effectiveness of various instruments of stabilization policy, notably fiscal and monetary measures, at stabilizing national income and output under the new circumstances.

Relatively little systematic attention has been addressed to the first of these questions. The second was dealt with in theoretical terms by Mundell (1960–1964, collected in *International Economics*, 1968) and by Fleming (1962) in the early sixties. This paper will use the Fleming analysis as a starting point for a discussion of how their now widely taught results might have to be modified in the interests of better theory and of greater realism. The paper will not offer a systematic review of the rapidly growing professional literature

* This paper was first presented at the Reserve Bank of Australia's Conference in Monetary Economics, Sydney, July 10–11, 1975.

on the subject of the title, but rather it will focus on several facets of what turns out to be an extraordinarily difficult set of related problems to deal with satisfactorily from a theoretical point of view while still retaining practical relevance. In a later section it will also address briefly the first question identified above, the impact of capital mobility and alternative exchange rate regimes on the disturbances with which national monetary authorities may have to deal.

I. Monetary Policy in a Closed Economy

It is useful first to review briefly how monetary measures supposedly influence the aggregate demand for goods and services in a closed economy. It is now customary to identify three channels whereby monetary measures—specifically, an increase in the money supply—may be expected to influence aggregate monetary demand. The first is through at least a temporary reduction in real interest rates—or, equivalently, an increase in the market value of physical assets relative to their reproduction costs or supply price. Expenditure on all forms of durable goods, especially housing and plant and equipment, will be stimulated by this discrepancy in prices, and in the process money income, output, and prices will also rise, the output–price division depending on the degree of utilization of the economy at the time of monetary expansion.

The second and third channels operate through changes in wealth and the influence which such changes in turn have on demand for goods and services. By reducing nominal interest rates, an increase in the supply of money will raise the market value of all assets whose yield is fixed in nominal terms and of close substitutes for such assets. By so doing, wealth-holders presumably find themselves with more wealth than they desire to hold, and they therefore increase their spending on goods and services.

The third channel also operates through its effect on wealth, and arises when the increase in money has come about in such a way as to increase total wealth held by the public even at unchanged interest rates, e.g. through a deficit in the government budget financed by money creation.

All of these channels may also be expected to operate in an open economy, but with some important modifications. First, changes in the exchange rate, like changes in interest rates, will in general alter wealth held by the public, especially if they hold foreign securities. Moreover, changes in the exchange rate, like changes in interest rates, can create discrepancies between the current price of goods and services and their long-run supply prices, thereby stimulating or retarding demand. On both counts the influence of monetary actions on the exchange rate must therefore be taken into account. Thirdly, the balance of payments offers another route whereby increases in the money supply will also increase wealth, a so-called "outside" source of new money.

II. Early Theory for an Open Economy: the Fleming Model and Results

Fleming deals with an open economy that is too small to influence world interest rates, world prices, or world incomes, so that the rest of the world can be treated parametrically. He excludes changes in the terms of trade from his analysis, but he allows for discrepancies between home country interest rates and rest-of-the-world interest rates by permitting less than complete mobility of capital between the home country and the rest of the world. These "small country" assumptions will be retained throughout this paper.

The model is a simple Keynesian one and adapted to standard notation is as follows:

$$Y = E(Y, i, r) + X(Y, r) + G \tag{1}$$

$$L(Y, i) = M = H + R \tag{2}$$

$$X(Y, r) + K(i) = B \tag{3}$$

Here Y is national income (assumed equal to output), E is national expenditure, X is *net* exports, G is government expenditure on goods and services, L is the demand for high-powered money, M is the supply of high powered money, H is central bank holdings of domestic securities, R is central bank holdings of international reserves, K is international capital movements, B is the balance of payments, i is the domestic rate of interest on government securities, and r is the exchange rate (domestic currency price of a unit of foreign currency). All variables (except i and r) are measured in domestic currency, and prices of domestic output are assumed to be fixed. The terms in parentheses indicate the variables that influence the variable they follow. Differentiating this system of equations and reorganizing terms leads to:

$$\begin{bmatrix} s+m & -E_i & -X_r \\ L_y & L_i & 0 \\ -m & +K_i & +X_r \end{bmatrix} \begin{bmatrix} dY \\ di \\ dr \end{bmatrix} = \begin{bmatrix} dG \\ dM \\ dB \end{bmatrix} \tag{4}$$

where T_v indicates the partial derivative of T with respect to v, $s = 1 - E_y$, the marginal propensity not to spend, and $m = -X_y$, the marginal propensity to import. It is assumed that all of these structural parameters are non-negative except E_i and L_i, which are negative.

Within this framework, a system of fixed exchange rates can be depicted by setting $dr = 0$, and a system of freely flexible exchange rates by $dB = 0$. Under a system of fixed exchange rates the balance of payments, B, need not be zero, and as a result central bank reserves will be changing. It is assumed that the central bank automatically sterilizes these reserve changes through offsetting domestic open market operations (or in some other way), so that the balance of payments position does not directly affect the money supply. In other words, the monetary authorities are assumed to have full control over M, no matter what is happening to reserves. An act of pure monetary policy will therefore be a change in M, a stock variable, with G held unchanged. An act of pure fiscal policy, by the same token, is a change in G, a flow variable, with M held unchanged. We are interested in the impact of these two measures on Y under alternative exchange rate regimes and as a function of K_i, the interest-sensitivity of international capital movements.

The above system of equations can be solved for the policy multipliers $(dY/dG)_j$ and $(dY/dM)_j$, where j indicates the exchange rate regime. The well-known conclusions from this analysis are three:

(1) $(dY/dM)_{\text{flexible}} > (dY/dM)_{\text{fixed}}$

(2) $(dY/dG)_{\text{flexible}} \gtrless (dY/dG)_{\text{fixed}}$ as $K_i \lesseqgtr -mL_i/L_y$

(3) $[(dY/dG)/(dY/dM)]_{\text{flexible}} < [(dY/dG)/(dY/dM)]_{\text{fixed}}$ for $K_i > 0$

These results can be readily interpreted and have intuitive appeal. The first says that a given expansion in the money supply will be more effective at stimulating money income under a regime of flexible rates than under a regime of fixed exchange rates because under the latter some of the stimulus will leak away to other countries, whereas under the former the induced depreciation in the exchange rate will prevent this leakage on trade account. Moreover, a high mobility of capital will cause an even greater depreciation of the currency, thus stimulating domestic demand further.

The second result arises from the fact that under fixed exchange rates some of the fiscal stimulus will leak abroad, and this leakage is prevented with flexible rates by a depreciation of the currency. On the other hand, a fiscal stimulus without monetary support, as here, will tend to raise interest rates within the country. Under flexible rates, the resulting inflow of capital will tend to appreciate the currency, thus restricting demand. The inequality shows the conditions under which the second influence will outweigh the first. It is equivalent to fiscal stimulus leading to a deterioration or an improvement to the balance of payments under fixed exchange rates. In the limiting case of infinitely large sensitivity of capital movements to interest rate changes, the influence of fiscal policy on domestic demand disappears altogether, for the induced currency appreciation fully offsets an initiating fiscal stimulus.

The third result clearly follows from the first two for sufficiently high mobility of capital. In the absence of capital mobility, equality holds between the two ratios; but any interest sensitivity of capital will give monetary policy a "comparative advantage" under a regime of flexible exchange rates because of capital-induced movements in the exchange rate. By the same token, with any capital mobility monetary policy under a regime of fixed exchange rates has a comparative advantage over fiscal policy in dealing with the balance

Table 1

	After one quarter	After six quarters
Impact on income of $100 in bond-financed government expenditure (dollars)		
Fixed exchange rate	101	171
Altered exchange rate	77	173
Impact on income of 1 percent increase in the rate of growth of the money supply ($ million)		
Fixed exchange rate	4.3	4.4
Altered exchange rate	63.8	19.0

Source: Caves & Reuber, 1969, p. 69.

of payments as compared with influencing aggregate demand, as has been emphasized by Mundell (1968).

The money supply in this framework has been assumed to be completely exogenous, so the frequently-cited result that high mobility of capital will undercut the effectiveness of monetary measures under a regime of fixed exchange rates cannot be derived. Removal of the assumption of complete sterilization of reserve changes will yield this result.

A certain amount of empirical work on the Canadian economy provides general support for these results. Rhomberg (1964) confirmed the first result and found that capital mobility was sufficiently high that fiscal policy was more effective under fixed exchange rates. Caves & Reuber (1969), using a different method, got qualitatively similar results. Choudry et al. (1972) confirmed the first result but found capital mobility sufficiently low that fiscal measures would be stronger under flexible exchange rates. In each case, the modelling incorporated response lags, so impact effects differ from subsequent effects. The Caves–Reuber results, shown in Table 1, suggest the pattern.

III. Stock Equilibrium and Balance-Sheet Requirements

Unfortunately there are several important conceptual weaknesses in the kind of analysis represented by the Fleming model. The remainder of this paper will be devoted to a discussion of some of these weaknesses and to suggestions on how they might alter the conclusions of the analysis.

The first problem is that capital movements have been cast exclusively in terms of flows, and the related point that no balance sheet constraints have been imposed either on the public or on the monetary authorities of the country under examination. Under these circumstances, a given interest rate may lead to capital flows of a given magnitude for an indefinite period of time, and the country can run a balance of payments surplus or deficit for an indefinite period of time, without having it affect the money supply.

It would be equally and for some purposes more appropriate to depict capital movements as changes in portfolio positions held by residents or non-residents, and capital movements would cease when portfolio equilibrium was restored (or, in the context of a growing domestic and world economy, when all portions of the portfolio are growing at the same rate). Portfolio positions could be expected to change whenever there were changes in asset yields or in wealth. In addition, the monetary authorities would have a portfolio of domestic and foreign assets, and they could not sell either without limit. The major contribution of the "monetary" approach to balance-of-payments analysis is to focus attention on stock equilibrium and balance-sheet requirements, and to make the point that "equilibrium" is not reached so long as central bank reserves or the public's holdings of bonds are changing in a non-growing economy (or are changing in a way other than dictated by steady-state growth in a growing economy). This is fundamentally an old idea: David Hume's analysis (1748) contained an endogenous money supply, changes in which were linked to balance-of-payments flows. Thus, according to this approach, Fleming has not provided an adequate characterization of the impact of policy measures so long as $dB \neq 0$. Moreover, by defining dG as a continuing change in government expenditure financed by sale or retirement of bonds, he has assured continuing portfolio disequilibrium.

Equally important, formulation of the problem in terms of portfolio equilibrium draws attention to the transitional dynamics, since exogenous (or policy) changes lead to transitory stock adjustments in portfolios, plus continuing debt service payments.

Unfortunately, it is very difficult to model portfolio equilibrium and stock adjustment satisfactorily without shedding much of what is of interest for stabilization policy. To avoid stock-flow complications and to emphasize the implications of full stock equilibrium, a number of authors have either required continuous equilibrium in the balance of payments even in a regime of fixed exchange rates or have assumed a stationary state or both (McKinnon in Mundell & Swoboda (1969); Swoboda, 1972; Swoboda in Claassen & Salin (eds.), 1972; Kenen, 1976). As a consequence of these assumptions, a small country has no control at all over its money supply under fixed exchange rates, regardless of the degree of capital mobility, for any attempt to achieve a money supply differing from that required for total portfolio balance will evoke offsetting inflows or outflows from abroad. (Indeed, using basically the same kind of framework, Mundell (1969) has argued that a small, growing economy must have a balance-of-payments surplus to satisfy its growing demand for money if the monetary authorities are not increasing their purchases of domestic assets rapidly enough.) A commitment to fix the exchange rate ipso facto leads to loss of monetary autonomy, and the central bank can merely alter the composition of its domestic and foreign assets.

Kenen's model is illustrative of this approach. His system defines household wealth, requires that demand for money equal supply of money, stipulates that savings will occur only when actual wealth differs from desired wealth and that any such discrepancy must equal the trade balance, and defines the change in international reserves as equal to the balance of payments. Households cannot hold foreign bonds, but foreigners can (in the case of perfect capital mobility) hold our country's bonds and will do so at a constant yield. In equilibrium neither wealth nor reserves can be changing, and as a result the trade balance and the government budget must both be balanced. (Kenen's model is modestly flawed by failing to allow for service payments on external debt.) Fiscal policy must be defined in terms of a balanced-budget change in government expenditures or a once-for-all increase in bond-holdings by the public, in order to preserve the stock equilibrium constraint.

Under these assumptions, monetary measures cannot influence domestic output at all under fixed exchange rates, but they can influence aggregate money demand under flexible rates. Thus, in a rough way Fleming's first conclusion is confirmed, but with further restrictions. Fiscal action, as defined by Kenen, cannot influence aggregate demand under flexible rates if capital is perfectly mobile, but it can with immobility of capital—the same result as Fleming got—but in contrast fiscal action cannot influence aggregate demand at all under fixed exchange rates in Kenen's world. (In Fleming's model the influence of fiscal action as defined by Kenen would remain positive.)

These kinds of results are not especially helpful to those concerned with stabilization policy. The need for stabilization policy is predicated on the assumption that from time to time the economy will be jostled off its full employment equilibrium, perhaps with cumulative effect. Stabilization policy is designed to offset or at least to mitigate these disturbances. But if stabilization policies will not work under fixed exchange rates, as indicated by this class of stock equilibrium models, neither will they be necessary, for exogenous disturbances will also lose their ability to affect aggregate demand. Adjustment of the economic system will automatically nullify them. Unfortunately, while a system of fixed exchange rates does under usual circumstances help to reduce the disturbances that impinge on an economy (as discussed below), the day is not yet at hand when we can rely on the economy to absorb them without effect. However good the adjustment of the system might be, in practice disturbances have important transitory effects—and so do stabilization measures. Short recognition and response lags are of course essential if stabilization measures are to help reduce variations in aggregate demand arising from exogenous disturbances.

An alternative to the stock equilibrium models is to require only flow equilibrium, but subject to balance-sheet consistency, as Borts & Hanson (1975) have done for the private sector. But that leaves the possibility of unresolved stock disequilibria. A complete model cannot avoid having both stock and flow equilibria, with explicit stock adjustment responses to disequilibria. This inevitably greatly complicates the model, and the results that are crucial for assessing the stabilization impact of monetary and fiscal measures depend critically on assumptions that are made about which markets clear instantaneously and which do not, and which markets clear in the short run by price adjustment as opposed to quantity adjustment. From the viewpoint of scientific analysis these "dynamic" specifications, and tests of their validity, are of course desirable, however difficult they may be, for that is what economic stabilization is all about. With these more complicated models, the qualitative character of some of Fleming's results are likely to survive, for example that national monetary autonomy in the short or even medium run exists even under fixed exchange rates, provided that capital is not highly mobile.

Dornbusch (1973) has emphasized the desirability of wedding flow equilibrium analysis to stock equilibrium through explicit stock adjustment in connection with assessing the impact of currency devaluation on an economy. More recently, Genberg & Kierzkowski (1975) have applied the "new" approach to devaluation to a model of employment and price fluctuations under flexible exchange rates. In this model, unlike Kenen's, the public is allowed to hold foreign bonds; but like Kenen's in equilibrium it allows no saving and no government deficit. Flexible exchange rates assure that payments are always in balance, and in addition equilibrium requires no new acquisition of foreign assets, so the trade balance must equal any interest earnings on foreign investment. The economy is divided into two sectors, tradable and non-tradable goods; labor is effectively the only factor of production (capital goods being specific to each sector and playing no role in the analysis), and the labor market always clears. But variations in employment, and hence in voluntary unemployment, occur through variations in the real wage rate.

An increase in the money supply through an open market purchase of domestic bonds creates portfolio disequilibrium in this model both because of a reduced interest rate on domestic bonds and because the lower interest rate has raised the market value of the bonds, thus initially increasing total wealth. Provided that the elasticity of demand for foreign bonds with respect to the domestic interest rate is higher than the interest elasticity of demand for money, the percentage increase in demand for foreign bonds will be higher than the percentage increase in demand for money. And since the public holds neither stocks of tradable goods nor stocks of foreign money, the increased demand for foreign bonds can be "satisfied" in the short run only through a depreciation of the currency proportionately greater than the increase in the money supply. This is required to rebalance the portfolio in the short run. But at the newly depreciated rate, there will be an excess supply of tradable goods, a trade surplus will emerge, and gradually the currency will appreciate back toward (but not to) its initial level, as the public now adjusts its portfolio by purchasing new foreign bonds with the proceeds of its trade surplus. Employment during this process of adjustment to new stock equilibrium will at first fall, since the depreciation-induced increase in domestic prices will reduce total wealth and thereby induce net saving (the equivalent of the trade surplus), but then will gradually rise as portfolio balance is restored and in the final equilibrium will be above the initial level of employment prevailing before the increase in the money supply. Thus in this model the initial impact on employment of an open market operation is the opposite of the ultimate effect, and while the impact effect on the exchange rate is in the same direction as the ultimate effect, the exchange rate overshoots its final equilibrium position.

An increase in the money supply does not result in an equiproportionate increase in prices even in the long run in this model because, as Patinkin (1965) showed in connection with government bonds, the existence of an outside asset other than money will break the proportionality. Here foreign bonds play the role of the second outside asset. Their presence causes real employment and output effects, and even leads to changes in *relative* prices between the two sectors.

One has in the exchange rate of this model a variable that is analogous to the market valuation of physical assets in Tobin's analysis of incentives to invest. Movements in the exchange rate alter the real value of wealth and create discrepancies between the market valuation of foreign bonds in the bond-holding country and the long-run cost of foreign bonds purchasable through the net sale of tradable goods. So the market for foreign bonds clears in the first instance through an adjustment of the exchange rate, but in the longer run quantities can adjust and the market price in domestic currency reverses course.

If this is the pattern, why is it not smoothed by currency speculation? Genberg–Kierzkowski do not allow foreign currencies to be held in anyone's portfolio, so in their model this complication is ruled out. But the possibility of speculation draws attention to the crucial role in dynamic adjustment processes that can be played by expectations. Speculation that is "stabilizing" in the sense of avoiding over-reaction of the exchange rate would also greatly smooth the path of employment from its initial to its new equilibrium.

Before this type of portfolio equilibrium model is accepted, however, we must explore more fully the reasons why households hold wealth, to ascertain what are sensible behavioral assumptions when it comes to adjustments in portfolios. In particular, under what circumstances is it plausible to assume that changes in the market valuation of households' wealth caused by changes in market interest rates will influence expenditure, as in Kenen's model, or that caused by changes in the exchange rate will influence expenditure, as in the Genberg–Kierzkowski model? If either change is regarded as temporary, there has been no change in "permanent" (expected) wealth, and there may be no change in consumption (although expenditures on durable goods may be influenced even by the temporary change in relative prices).

Even if the change in interest rate or exchange rate is regarded as permanent, the pattern of desired *future* consumption may also be influenced in such a way as to neutralize or even to reverse any apparent ceteris paribus effect of changes in wealth on current consumption. Thus we need to know more about the formation of expectations and we need to combine portfolio balance models with lifetime saving–consumption models to discover under what circumstances and in what ways changes in the market valuation of wealth will alter expenditure. If, for example, foreign bonds are held in part to backstop future anticipated consumption of foreign goods, the influence of a change in the exchange rate (regarded as permanent) on portfolio and consumption behavior will be quite different from the case in which foreign bonds are held merely as a yield-diversifying alternative to domestic bonds.

The latter motive would lead to results such as those in the Genberg–Kierzkowski model. But that is not the only possible outcome. A depreciation of the currency that reflects a "permanent" worsening in the country's terms of-trade would increase the local currency value of resident holdings of foreign assets, but it would generally lower the value of foreign assets in terms of imported goods. Under the former motive for holding foreign assets, therefore, domestic spending might fall rather than rise in response to the effects of depreciation on the "wealth" embodied in foreign bonds, to preserve its command over imports. If however the change in relative prices substantially reduces the public's desire to consume imported goods in the future, the public may instead decide to spend more by liquidating some of its now redundant holdings of foreign bonds.

IV. Flow Models of Capital Movements

A second weakness of the Fleming-type model concerns its specification of international capital movements even when they are cast in terms of flows and stock adjustment considerations are deliberately neglected. The influence of changes in the exchange rate under flexible exchange rates is wholly neglected, and comparisons between regimes implicitly assume that the character of the regime itself does not influence the values of the structural parameters of the economy.

With the exchange rate free to move, capital movements should be specified to allow for (1) a possible price effect, since foreign securities purchased or sold against domestic currency are done at different prices at different times, and (2) a speculative effect, since claims on foreigners may be held in anticipation of future increases in prices rather than just for current yield. In the latter instance it is of course necessary to specify how exchange rate expectations are formed. If expectations are highly inelastic, a regime of flexible exchange rates differs little from a regime of fixed exchange rates: private speculative capital movements perform the function of official reserve movements under a fixed exchange rate regime. There is some evidence that this was the case in Canada during the 1950s: private speculation was strongly "stabilizing" around a one-for-one rate between the U.S. and the Canadian dollars. But of course expectations might also be strongly elastic. In either case, $K_r dr$ might dominate $K_i di$ under a regime of flexible exchange rates, and this could either weaken (in the case of inelastic expectations) or strengthen (in the case of elastic expectations) the influence of monetary measures on aggregate demand under such a regime.

Moreover, alteration of regimes would in general be expected to alter the values of the parameters. In particular, both the marginal propensity to import (m) and the interest-sensitivity of capital movements (K_i) might be expected to fall in value in moving from fixed to flexible exchange rates, because of the greater short-run uncertainty in foreign currency dealings associated with flexible exchange rates. (Long-run uncertainty will be no greater, and possibly less, than under an adjustable peg regime of exchange rates.) If businesses are risk averse, at least as far as foreign currency transactions are concerned, the possibility of wide week-to-week variations in rates will tilt transactions toward domestic customers and suppliers and away from foreign ones. (The Fleming analysis assumed that a change in interest rates will induce uncovered capital movements. The exchange risk argument does not apply to covered movement, but changes in forward exchange rates may be assumed to eliminate any net covered interest incentive quickly.)

Making allowance for this likelihood does not alter the Fleming results formally, since the marginal propensity to import does not appear in the multipliers under flexible exchange rates and the interest sensitivity of capital movements, K_i, does not appear in the multipliers under fixed exchange rates because of the assumption of complete sterilization. But if sterilization is incomplete, that is, if reserve movements do have some effect on the money supply, then K_i will appear in the fixed exchange rate multipliers and if initially $K_i > -mL_i/L_y$ under fixed exchange rates (so that fiscal expansion will produce a payments surplus), then a switch to flexible exchange rates which also lowers K_i may either increase or reduce the fiscal impact on income, depending on the extent of reduction of K_i. This is contrary to Fleming's second result.

V. Specification of the Demand for Money

The specification $L(Y, i) = M$ is a common one in simple macro-economic models. But if the public can hold *foreign* money, what role should that play in the money stock equation? Under what circumstances does foreign money satisfy the demand for money? If money were held only for transactions purposes, and all transactions were denominated in the currency of the selling country, then one need not be concerned about holdings of foreign money in this context so long as trade is balanced. All holdings of domestic money, non-resident as well as resident, would be appropriate for the home country.

But if money is held for precautionary and speculative purposes, including precautions and speculation with respect to the exchange rate and the price of foreign bonds, then the appropriate concept of "money" is even less clear than it is in closed economies. Indeed, McKinnon (1963) has argued that the more open the economy, the more likely it is that residents will switch to the regular use of foreign money under a regime of flexible exchange rates, thereby denying the country the seigniorage gains arising from the issuance of money and denying it monetary control over aggregate demand, even under flexible exchange rates.

The question of holdings of foreign money has ceased to be of merely academic interest now that the euro-currency market contains over $200 billion in liabilities, mostly but by no means exclusively in U.S. dollars. To the extent that these liabilities represent money (the same controversy surrounds that as surrounds the appropriate classification of various highly liquid assets in domestic economies), whose money are they?—that is, in what country's model of financial and macro-economic equilibrium should they be placed?

Whether or not allowance is made for the holding of foreign monies to satisfy the demand for money, in a regime of changeable exchange rates the demand for money surely should include the exchange rate as an argument, just as the demand for bonds does. (This has been done by Dornbusch, 1973, in his analysis of devaluation.)

VI. Macro-economic Disturbances

In assessing the impact of openness and of exchange rate regimes on stabilization policy, it is not sufficient to look only at the influence of policy instruments on aggregate demand; one must also look at the magnitude of the stabilization task. In general that magnitude will be sensitive both to the degree of openness and to the exchange rate regime. Openness of an economy exposes it to disturbances originating in the rest of the world, for example through variations in world demand for its export products. But openness also disperses disturbances originating at home, for example by permitting imports to satisfy a temporary boom in demand for goods and services. Thus the choice for an economy with respect to the desired degree of openness is not a straightforward one of simply weighing the gains from trade against the losses with respect to stability.

In fact, the insurance principle is at work: if disturbances are widely distributed around the world with less than perfect correlation in their timing, the stability of the world economy will be enhanced by distributing them as widely as possible, so much offsetting of disturbances will occur and the task of stabilization policy will generally be reduced. But of course in "nature" some economies are more stable than others, so the stabilization gains from wide distribution of disturbances will be spread unevenly among countries, and some individual countries will find themselves experiencing greater instability than under autarky or with a lower exposure to the world economy. Moreover, an important source of disturbance is government policies, so if ineptitude in economic policy is greater abroad than at home, this too may increase the stabilization task for the domestic authorities in an open economy and tilt the balance of gains and losses toward greater autarky.

The main point can be made with a simple illustration. Consider a small economy in a Keynesian framework in which non-policy disturbances affect aggregate demand linearly, through shifts in home demand or shifts in export demand, with zero means and with standard deviations of w and w' respectively (see Cooper, 1974). Then the standard deviation of aggregate demand (u) in the absence of stabilizing action (one measure of the task facing the stabilization authorities) will be w/s in a closed economy, and

$$u^* = (w^2 + w'^2 + 2ww'\varrho)^{\frac{1}{2}}/(s+m) \tag{5}$$

in a small open economy. Here s is the marginal propensity not to spend, m is the marginal propensity to import, and ϱ is the correlation between disturbances at home and disturbances abroad in the presence of trade. The asterisk stands for the open economy. If the disturbances are perfectly correlated ($\varrho = 1$), then $u > u^*$ if $w/s > w'/m$. That is, the unstabilized variation in aggregate demand will be reduced in moving from a closed to an open economy if the leakages through imports (as measured by m) exceed the imported disturbances (w'), relative to the multiplier effect on domestic disturbances in a closed economy. For $\varrho < 1$ the conditions for a reduction in income variation in moving from a closed to an open economy will be less stringent.

A regime of flexible exchange rates is not the same as autarky, but it does reduce both the impact of disturbances abroad on domestic income and the leakage of domestic disturbances abroad. Thus it is not obvious what the net impact will be: in general, the higher w' is relative to w, the more attractive will be some form of insulation from the world economy.

How much insulation does a floating exchange rate provide? The answer depends on the nature of the disturbance. In some cases a flexible exchange rate can neutralize completely a disturbance to aggregate demand that would take place under a fixed exchange rate; in others it can reduce but not eliminate the impact; and in still others a flexible rate may aggravate the impact of the disturbance as compared with a fixed exchange rate.

An example of complete neutralization is provided by a general rise in the world price level, which under a fixed exchange rate would stimulate demand in our small economy. But an appreciation of the currency proportionate to the increase in foreign prices will compensate at the border, preventing either relative price or wealth effects.

An example of mitigation is provided by a world increase in demand for our country's export products, which will raise incomes and stimulate domestic demand. With a flexible rate, the currency will appreciate and partially damp the sale of exports; it will also encourage a larger volume of imports, on both counts relieving pressure on the domestic economy. But relative prices will have changed, unlike in the first example, resources will be reallocated, and total wealth will have been increased. So the insulation is incomplete.

An example of aggravation is provided by an increase in foreign demand for our country's securities (at constant interest rates), which will lead to appreciation of the currency. That in turn will both diminish aggregate demand and will call for a reallocation of resources away from tradable goods to non-tradable goods, possibly with transitional unemployment. Large movements of capital, in the absence of speculative counter-movements, may therefore result in greater disturbance to aggregate demand than would be the case under fixed exchange rates, even when the monetary authorities cannot sterilize such flows and they result in changes in the money supply. Aggravation is especially likely if exchange rate expectations are elastic and the exchange rate (rather than local-currency prices) represents the principal price which clears the market for holdings of foreign securities in the short run. Changes in exchange rates would be large under these circumstances, and they would play havoc with profitability of foreign trade transactions. Firms could be thrown into bankruptcy on a wide swing of the exchange rate, both creating damage to the economy and provoking risk-averting actions which increase costs. A movement in the exchange rate that persists will eventually evoke a corrective change in the trade balance, but only with a lag. Indeed, the "*J*-curve" effect of movements in the exchange rate on earnings from trade might in the short-run (for a country that is not a price-taker in its export markets) aggravate the swing. Under these circumstances, official stabilizing speculation, i.e. management of the exchange rate, will help stabilize aggregate demand (but of course it may increase the movement of capital). Part of the debate between fixers and flexers involves differing assessments of the importance of capital movements as a source of disturbance to the exchange rate and, through it, to the economy, on the one hand, and the ability and willingness of private wealth holders to adopt speculative positions with the proper timing and magnitude to mitigate such disturbances on the other.

All of these categories have their counterparts in dealing with disturbances of domestic origin. Movements in a flexible exchange rate will offset fully a general monetary inflation, "bottling it up" in the originating economy and preventing both the relative price change between tradables and non-tradables and the exportation of excess demand that would occur if the exchange rate were fixed. There is complete neutralization. But with a shift in the composition of demand, e.g. toward imports, currency depreciation will only mitigate the aggregate demand and relative price effects. And if residents want more foreign securities and the exchange rate is the short-run equilibrator of shifts in preference between foreign and domestic securities, its movement (in the absence of currency speculation) will aggravate domestic instability. If the shift in preference is durable, it will in time evoke the reallocation of resources toward tradables that will make the real transfer; but even then the rate may overshoot, as in the Genberg–Kierzkowski model.

Thus contrary to claims that have been made for it, a flexible exchange rate cannot insulate an economy completely from external disturbances, or even from purely "monetary" disturbances if by that term we encompass switches among financial assets. An open economy is open, no matter what its exchange rate regime.

Flexible exchange rates do, however, have one further effect which may mitigate disturbances; they may reduce the correlation in timing between disturbances in different countries as compared with a regime of fixed exchange rates. Shifts in demand for goods or securities may be partly expectational in nature, and business activity is less likely to move in tandem in the presence of even the partial insulation provided by flexible exchange rates. (Canada's experience in the 1950s does not support this view, but in that case there was strongly stabilizing currency speculation plus a certain parallelism between Canadian and U.S. policies, i.e. the Canadian authorities did not use fully what autonomy a flexible exchange rate would have afforded them.)

VII. Factor Price Responses and "Money Illusion"

The Fleming analysis and much that has followed it assumes no change in the general level of factor prices, i.e. changes in exchange rates are assumed to affect real incomes, and indeed it is from this that they derive most of their influence. It has recently been argued that currency depreciation requires "money illusion" in order to influence real variables. This is not strictly true, since wealth effects will remain even if factor prices adjust to restore real income. But clearly the presence of "money illusion" helps the process of adjustment by introducing some flexibility into real factor prices. There may be sound reasons why an increase in goods prices brought about by currency devaluation will be accepted even while a general reduction in money incomes would not be acceptable. The first will be perceived as relatively impartial in its effects, whereas reductions in money incomes would be the subject of suspicions that some incomes were reduced more than others (e.g. because of differential protection through contracts), i.e. that the wage structure or the *distribution* of income would be altered. Thus "money illusion" may be present without any illusion about it at all.

If money illusion is present, it is useful in facilitating adjustment. Hoarding or dishoarding to adjust actual to desired wealth following a change in the exchange rate is bound to be a prolonged process; and since it involves shifts in aggregate demand, the adjustment may be frustrated by official action aimed at stabilizing employment. At best, therefore, exchange rate flexibility may introduce some real factor price flexibility into economies where nominal flexibility, at least in a downward direction, is rare. At worst, however, exchange rate movements might trigger factor price adjustments to compensate for them. Indeed, nominal factor prices might respond to a depreciation of the currency even more quickly than to other price changes because of the generality and wide diffusion of the consequences of movements in the exchange rate. Moreover, if the exchange rate depreciates in response to shifts in portfolio preference, it may generate a price–wage–price spiral where none existed before, thereby confronting the monetary authorities with the difficult choice between validating the increase in prices and wages through monetary expansion or letting unemployment rise. It is thus possible that via this route inflation can be "imported" as much under flexible rates as it can under fixed rates.

Factor price responses to changes in exchange rates, if they exist, may well not be symmetrical: a depreciation is more likely to trigger demands for increases in wages than an appreciation is for reductions in wages. Response may be rapid to depreciations, slow to appreciations. If so, fluctuating exchange rates will have an inflationary bias for the world economy as a whole. We have too little evidence so far to judge the presence or the extent of any such asymmetry, although it is noteworthy that wage settlements in recent years have been much more moderate in Germany and Switzerland, where currencies have appreciated, than in other European countries, where they have not. The causation between movements in wages and movements in exchange rates can of course run both ways, from wages to exchange rates as well as from exchange rates to wages, but at least a superficial look at the evidence offers no support for strong asymmetry in the response of money wages to changes in exchange rates.

We also have too little evidence on the presence and extent of money illusion with respect to movements in the exchange rate, but various estimates of the response of wages to increases in prices in the United States and Britain (summarized in Kwack, 1974) suggest that other things being equal wages respond only partially to increases in expected prices (35 to 77 percent, averaging around 50 percent), where "expected" prices are a geometric weighted average of present and past price changes. Thus an increase in price leaves a ceteris paribus reduction in real wages. Of course, Britain and the United States are rather large economies, and might not be representative of small ones.

The problem of factor price response suggests another reason, in addition to the increase in certain kinds of disturbances, for managing a flexible exchange, at least to the extent of preventing large sudden changes in the rate except when they are clearly needed. The price to be paid for such management is some loss of monetary autonomy, but it may reduce the load on the monetary authorities more than enough to compensate for that loss.

VIII. Controls on Capital Movements

A principal source of difficulty under either fixed or flexible exchange rates seems to be capital movements. Movements of liquid funds can play havoc with domestic monetary control under a fixed rate and with the exchange rate under a flexible rate. This suggests that capital movements should be subject to direct control, and indeed many countries have some system of control. But direct controls confront three difficulties. First, it is difficult to separate socially desirable capital movements from potentially disruptive capital movements. Second, any limited set of controls is likely to prove temporary in its effectiveness, for one consequence of the increasing mobility of capital is its ability to discover new channels for movement. To be effective, therefore, controls must be extended to cover all capital movements and even trade transactions, since credit has become an inseparable part of much trade and changes in the terms of credit can move large amounts of capital from one country to another. Third, however, such a comprehensive set of controls, covering intra-corporate transactions and trade, is bound to lead to major distortions in the allocation of resources and in many countries to foster corruption of the controlling officials and those who must deal with them.

The general move toward flexible exchange rates is motivated largely by a desire to provide some insulation without controls, but as noted above official management of the rates may be desirable if private speculation does not perform a stabilizing function.

IX. Considerations on the Choice of Exchange Rate Regime

Countries now face a choice: to float or not to float? And if not, they must choose what currency or group of currencies to which they want to tie their own currency. The theoretical work on flexible exchange rates is not well enough developed to answer these questions, even in principle. But the observations in this paper, in addition to pointing to areas where more extensive analysis is needed, suggest that the choice of exchange rate regime for a small country should be influenced by:

(1) the magnitude of external economic disturbances relative to internal ones, and the difficulty (e.g. in timing) the authorities have in coping with disturbances;

(2) the responsiveness of nominal factor incomes to changes in the exchange rate;

(3) the extent to which capital movements can be controlled successfully, and the costs of controlling them; and

(4) the remaining trade-off between the average level of real income and the stability of real income afforded by the relationship of the country to the world economy, and public preferences regarding this trade-off.

References

Borts, G. & Hanson, J.: The Monetary Approach to the Balance of Payments. In Jere Behrman (ed.), *Short Run Macroeconomic Policy in Latin America*, National Bureau fnr Economic Research (forthcoming).

Caves, R. & Reuber, G.: *Canadian Economic Policy and the Impact of International Capital Flows*. University of Toronto Press, 1969.

Choudry, N., Kotowitz, Y., Sawyer, J. A. & Winder, J. W. L.: *The TRACE Econometric Model of the Canadian Economy*. University of Toronto Press, 1972.

Claassen, E. & Salin, P. (eds.), *Stabilization Policies in Open Economies*. North-Holland, Amsterdam, 1972.

Cooper, R. N.: *Economic Mobility and National Economic Policy* (The Wicksell Lectures, 1973). Almqvist & Wiksell, Stockholm, 1974.

Dornbusch, R.: Currency depreciation, hoarding and relative prices. *Journal of Political Economy 83*, July/August 1973.

Fleming, M.: Domestic financial policies under fixed and under floating exchange rates. IMF *Staff Papers*, 1962, reprinted in R. N. Cooper (ed.), *International Finance*. Penguin Books, 1969.

Genberg, H. & Kierzkowski, H.: Short run, long run and dynamics of adjustment under flexible exchange rates. Discussion Paper, GIIS-Ford Foundation International Monetary Research Project, Graduate Institute of International Studies, Geneva, June 1975.

Hume, D.: On the balance of trade. Reprinted in Cooper (1969).

Kenen, P. B.: International capital movements and the integration of capital markets. In Fritz Machlup (ed.), *Economic Integration: Worldwide, Regional, Sectional*, Proceedings of the Fourth World Congress of the International Economic Association. St. Martin's Press, New York, 1976.

Kwack, S. Y.: The Effects of Foreign Inflation on Domestic Prices and the Relative Price Advantage of Exchange Rate Changes. 1974, Mimeo.

McKinnon, R. I.: Optimum currency areas. *American Economic Review 53* (Sept. 1963), reprinted in Cooper (1969).

Mundell, R. A.: *International Economics*. Macmillan, New York, 1968.

Mundell, R. A.: *Monetary Theory*. Pacific Palisades, 1969.

Mundell, R. A. & Swoboda, A. (eds.), *Monetary Problems of the International Economy*. University of Chicago Press, 1969.

Patinkin, D.: *Money, Interest and Prices*, 2nd ed. Harper and Row, 1965.

Rhomberg, R.: "A model of the Canadian Economy under Fixed and Fluctuating Exchange Rates", *Journal of Political Economy 72*, February 1964.

Swoboda, A.: Equilibrium and macro policy under fixed exchange rates. *Quarterly Journal of Economics 86*, February 1972.

COMMENT ON R. N. COOPER, "MONETARY THEORY AND POLICY IN AN OPEN ECONOMY"

Per Meinich

University of Oslo, Oslo, Norway

My impression is that Richard Cooper has given a very clear and good survey of questions concerning the effectiveness of various instruments of stabilization policy and the frequency and amplitudes of disturbances to macroeconomic stability in national economies under alternative exchange rate regimes. However, it might be argued that the paper raises more problems than it solves.

My critical comments will be rather few.

My main point concerns some critical comments to the reasoning on p. 156.

First, Cooper accepts the usual assertion that there will be greater short-run uncertainty in international trade transactions with flexible exchange rates than with fixed exchange rates. The usual counter-argument is that the uncertainty in the case with flexible exchange rates can be reduced by forward exchange contracts. In addition to this, it can be argued that a system with fixed exchange rates might mean more uncertainty with respect to other conditions which are of relevance for exporters and importers. Exporters and importers are primarily interested in prices, in terms of their own currency, of the goods bought and sold. Further, exporters and importers are interested in having easy access to all kinds of foreign exchange and international trade transactions.

(*a*) Circumstances which under a regime of flexible exchange rates lead to a change in the exchange rate, will under a regime of fixed exchange rates lead to variations in other prices of relevance for exporters and importers.

(*b*) Circumstances which under a regime of flexible exchange rates lead to a reduction in the exchange rate for a currency, will under a system of fixed exchange rates lead to a reduction in international reserves of the country under consideration. Such a reduction in international reserves may lead to a restrictive economic policy—for example increased control of dealings in foreign currencies, import duties or import quotas—which will change the economic conditions for exporters and importers.

Thus, all in all, it is not easy to say whether the total degree of short-run uncertainty for exporters and importers will be greater under a system of flexible exchange rates than under a system of fixed exchange rates.

I also have some critical comments to the second part of Cooper's reasoning on p. 24. Even if the assertion that short-run uncertainty in foreign currency dealings will be greater under flexible exchange rates is accepted, this does not necessarily mean a lower marginal propensity to import. Here it is crucial to distinguish between the *marginal* propensity to import and the *average* (or total) propensity to import.

If businesses are risk averse concerning foreign currency transactions, then it is obvious that the *average* (and total) propensity to import will be reduced under a flexible exchange rate regime if the assertion of greater uncertainty in this case is accepted.

Let us now consider the effect upon the *marginal* propensity to import. According to the principle of decreasing absolute risk aversion, people will take more risk the larger the income. Given the assumption of a higher degree of uncertainty for international transactions under the regime of flexible exchange rates, this means that an increase in income will lead to a greater tendency toward foreign customers and suppliers and away from domestic ones under a regime of flexible exchange rates. Consequently, under these assumptions the *marginal* propensity to import will be *greater* under a system of flexible exchange rates than under a system of fixed exchange rates.

Using the same kind of argument, it is clear that one also has to distinguish between the effect on the absolute level of international capital movements (K) and the effect on the interest-sensitivity of capital movements (K_i). It is reasonable to say that K will be reduced in the case of greater uncertainty, but as far as I can see, it is difficult to determine the direction in which K_i will move.

If my conclusion regarding the marginal propensity to import is accepted, then the ambiguous result in the second paragraph following equation (5) in Section VI (Macro-economic Disturbances) of Cooper's paper can be replaced by: A move to a regime of flexible exchange rates will unambiguously reduce variability of income in the home country.

Further, I have two minor points.

On p. 19, Cooper writes: "Moreover by defining dG as a continuing change in government expenditure financed by sale or retirement of bonds, he has assured continuing portfolio disequilibrium." However, in the Fleming model, an increase in G will lead to a higher domestic rate of interest. Thus, the increase in private holdings of government securities implied by an increase in G, might have been induced by the increase in the rate of interest.

On p. 24, Cooper asks the following question: "But if the public can hold *foreign* money, what role should that play in the money stock equation?" I would answer this question by introducing separate supply, demand and market-clearing equations for foreign money in the model.

COMMENT ON R. N. COOPER, "MONETARY THEORY AND POLICY IN AN OPEN ECONOMY"

Stanley W. Black

Vanderbilt University, Nashville, Tenn., USA and Institute for International Economic Studies, Stockholm, Sweden

Since Professor Meinich has given us such a good summary of Dick Cooper's paper, I will confine myself to making several points that either were omitted in the paper or that I think require some further discussion and clarification. Let me say in the beginning that the paper is a very useful introduction to one of the basic problems with which this Conference is dealing: the theoretical analysis of macro-economic behavior under flexible exchange rates. My critical remarks are intended mainly to sharpen Cooper's discussion of the analytical questions.

One small point is that his discussion on page 15 of the three channels of monetary policy omits the important *credit-rationing* channel, which has been shown to be even more important in the smaller industrialized countries than in the United States. A related and more important point is that Cooper's discussion of the short-comings of the Fleming–Mundell model fails to note that the model casts open market operations as the sole instrument of monetary policy. We know that, for many countries with relatively small or nonexistent markets for domestic government securities, open market operations are not possible and hence sterilization of reserve movements cannot take place in the usual way. This should *not* lead to the Mundellian conclusion, shared by McKinnon and Swoboda, that such countries cannot have an independent monetary policy under pegged exchange rates. Rather, as Dornbusch and others have argued, non-traded assets can provide the leverage required. The use of credit-rationing and capital controls can then be explained as devices to establish non-tradability of domestic assets and to conduct monetary policy in the absence of open market operations and sterilization.

After noting the flow nature of the Fleming model, Cooper provides us with a useful discussion of the full stock equilibrium models of McKinnon, Swoboda, and Kenen. One must distinguish between full long-run stock equilibrium in a stationary state with zero saving required by these models and the more limited concept of short-run portfolio equilibrium, which merely implies that the existing stocks of assets are willingly held. Cooper points out that the long-run context of full stock equilibrium is *not* appropriate for analysis of stabilization policies. "The need for stabilization policy is predicated on the assumption that from time to time the economy will be jostled off its full employment equilibrium, perhaps with cumulative effect." But the full stock equilibrium models ignore this possibility, which we know to be very real.

Cooper concludes correctly that complete models must include stock and flow elements, with speculative expectations affecting stock demands, but he believes this will be quite difficult to accomplish. A simple framework showing the relationship of stocks and flows is the familiar balance of payments identity, which under flexible exchange rates requires the (flow) current account and the (change in stock) capital account to sum to zero. In the short run, the current account is predetermined by previous orders for goods and earnings on existing stocks of assets. Therefore the stock equilibrium in the capital account must adjust to determine the exchange rate. But as time passes, the current account responds to changes in the exchange rate, giving rise to a stock adjustment process. Speculative expectations affect the capital account as shown in my comment on the Williamson paper or in the papers by Kouri and Dornbusch for this Conference.

There follows an extended discussion of the Genberg–Kierzkowski stock-flow model with variable employment but excluding speculative behavior. In this model an increase in the money supply lowers the domestic interest rate, increases the demand for foreign bonds, and causes a capital outflow. The exchange rate depreciates *more* than in proportion to the increase in the money supply, then appreciates back as the flow response of the current account surplus adds holdings of foreign securities to allow portfolio rebalancing. This "whiplash" effect on the exchange rate is also found in the papers of Dornbusch and Mussa for this Conference, and is reminiscent of the "whiplash" effect of domestic short rates of interest in response to an increase in the money supply. Dornbusch's paper shows how the decline in the domestic rate of interest relative to the foreign rate creates a forward discount on foreign currency.

Cooper seems to think that results of this type must assume no speculation on changes in the exchange rate. But in fact, the larger the speculative response, the smaller will be the movement in the exchange rate required to compensate for the fall in the interest rate and the smaller will be the fall in the interest rate.

A very useful remark made by Cooper is that the assumptions on portfolio behavior are crucial in such models. In dealing with domestic money, we recognize its buffer stock role and do not require that *temporary* changes in the money supply be compensated by changes in interest rates. We shoul follow the same procedure for foreign money holdings.

There is also a suggestive argument as to *why* foreign assets are held. If it is to protect real wealth in order to maintain consumption of foreign goods, then devaluation will have a different effect than if it is just for diversification of yield risk. For example, Solnik's model assumes that investors only consume *domestic* goods, in order that domestic assets may be regarded as riskless. But in the real world, safety lies in diversification.

Cooper notes briefly that the money demand function should properly include both the foreign rate of interest and the exchange rate as well as the domestic rate of interest. This proposition follows from the adding-up constraints in a portfolio model, especially if there are wealth effects of exchange rate changes, as pointed out by Mundell.

Cooper reviews the arguments on the types of disturbances affecting open economies and shows that floating exchange rates offer incomplete insulation from "real" external disturbances. He argues that disturbances arising from portfolio shifts will be *aggravated* by floating exchange rates. But if we have learned anything from portfolio theory, it is that such shifts must be temporary, or one-shot adjustments. Therefore speculation will tend to offset their effects and prevent or attenuate destabilizing effects on real variables. The J-curve argument that he gives may be correct for the trade account, but it is wrong for the balance of payments, since speculators who are aware of the turnaround in the J will act to offset its effects on the exchange rate.

It is my feeling that Cooper's comment on capital movements as "a principal source of difficulty under fixed or flexible exchange rates" reflects a misunderstanding of the role of capital flows. Far from being a source of "difficulty", they are essential to the proper functioning of the exchange market. Improvements in the mobility of capital can be expected to improve the efficiency and stability of exchange markets, if expectations are rational.

In closing, let me reiterate that my choice of points of discussion is intended to sharpen or illuminate certain aspects of Cooper's valuable review of the analytical situation with respect to floating exchange rates.

EXPERIENCES OF FLEXIBLE EXCHANGE RATES IN EARLIER PERIODS: THEORIES, EVIDENCE AND A NEW VIEW

Johan Myhrman

Institute for International Economic Studies, Stockholm, Sweden

Abstract

Flexible exchange rates in earlier periods have usually meant that one or more countries left a metallic standard for some time. Three episodes dominate the historical material in this article: Sweden in the 18th century, England in the early 19th century and the period during and immediately after World War I. In all three cases there was a serious economic debate about the causes of the fluctuations in exchange rates. Two main views on this issue can be distinguished. One is that the fluctuations were caused by exogenous shifts in different items of the balance of payments. The other view attributes this role to the money supply. It is shown that theoretically both are possible, but that changes in the money supply probably predominate. This conclusion seems to be consistent with the empirical evidence.

1. Introduction*

When the First World War broke out, exchange rates began to change in most countries in the Western part of the world. As time went on, people started asking why exchange rates moved so much. Many economists did not have any ready answer to this problem. The long period of a gold standard system of international payments had allowed the knowledge of a hundred years earlier to sink further and further back in the memories of economists. Cassel was the first to rediscover Ricardo's writings on this subject, but others followed and in the 1920's there was an intensive study of "paper standards", especially in Harvard under Taussig's initiative. All this work seems to have culminated and ended with Viner's (1937) magnificent book.

There is something strange about economics because things get lost. After the Second World War, the economics of exchange rates seemed to consist of

* The spirit of this study was greatly inspired by my exposure to Harry G. Johnson's views on international monetary problems and to his encouragement. I have also been influenced by Rudiger Dornbusch and Jacob Frenkel. Many discussions with my colleagues Pieter Korteweg, Allan Meltzer, and Jeffrey Shafer, during a year at Carnegie-Mellon have also been very helpful. Any errors are due solely to the author. The article by Jacob Frenkel in this volume is a complement to this article because it deals with the period of flexible exchange rates in Germany which is not mentioned here

elasticities with respect to relative prices and/or foreign trade multipliers. Money and price levels were once again put back into the shadows to be neglected and forgotten. Finally, with Harry Johnson and Robert Mundell, money and prices were brought back to the scene in the 1960's and a new period of rediscovery has begun.

This development, or lack of development, is really odd because it does not follow Karl Popper's tetradic schema:

"$P_1 \rightarrow TT \rightarrow CD \rightarrow P_2$

We may start from some problem P_1—whether theoretical or historical —we proceed to a tentative solution—a conjectural or hypothetical solution, a *tentative theory*—which is submitted to critical discussion in the light of evidence, if available, with the result that new problems, P_2, arise."[1]

The same problem—inflation and flexible exchange rates—is now with us again, giving rise to the third scientific discussion in 175 years and we do not seem to be able to go beyond the "tentative theory" stage. What is lacking, it seems to us, is a systematic confrontation of our theories with evidence from different periods and different countries. We have chosen to write a short survey. It is not an exhaustive survey of the theory of flexible exchange rates. Instead we want to survey the *major* theoretical arguments and controversies and try to evaluate them. This led us to the formulation of a new view of the problem which we call the Monetary Impulse Theory. Finally, we have gathered what empirical evidence is still available from earlier times to see whether it has anything to tell us. It has not been possible to collect data for every country and every period with flexible exchange rates. Therefore we will rely to some extent on the work of other economists and try to collect it here in a systematic way.

The next three sections review the earlier theoretical discussions.[2] Section V contains a model which is constructed to help us evaluate some earlier controversies and we also develop the Monetary Impulse Theory. Section VI deals with empirical evidence and the paper ends with Section VII on the main conclusions.

II. The Bullion Debate

In 1793 a war broke out between England and France. The first two years of the war did not lead to any major financial disturbances for England. But by 1797, the Bank of England was forced to abandon convertibility and another twenty-four years elapsed before it could return to convertibility. Immediately after the suspension of specie payments, two Parliamentary committees were

[1] Popper (1969).

[2] For valuable information on some aspects of earlier theories, see Frenkel (1976).

taking extensive evidence from different experts. One of them was Henry Thornton, a private banker, and his evidence immediately made him one of the leading authorities on the subject. This position was considerably strengthened by the publication of his book "*An Enquiry into the Nature and Effects of the Paper Credit of Great Britain*" in 1802.

During the following years the price of gold increased steadily and, at the same time, the exchange rates were going against Great Britain. The Great Debate was gaining momentum and in 1810 a select committee was appointed and later the same year delivered a report, called the Bullion Report. This report led to an intense discussion of the problems it raised and the debate received the name of the Bullionist Controversy. Thornton's weakening health and early death in the beginning of 1815 led, among other things, to Ricardo becoming the leading personality in the debate.

This debate has been described and analyzed in detail in a number of articles and books and this is not the place to repeat it. Instead, we will try to bring out the major theoretical contributions because they form the foundation for later developments and controversies in the theory of flexible exchange rates.

There were basically two groups of participants in the debate, the Bullionists and the Anti-Bullionists. All the members of each group did not have exactly the same opinion about every detail but they were united on the main issue. This issue, as it is usually stated, was "whether the rise in prices in Britain was the cause or the effect of the high price of bullion and the depreciation of sterling abroad".[1] Now, this is not quite accurate because, more precisely, the issue really concerned two intertwined problems. First there was the problem of whether the paper pound had depreciated or not during the Restriction period. This is the same as asking whether there had been an inflation or not, and most people would say that there had. But because there was no general price index available, some indirect measure had to be used and the Bullionists proposed the price (or the premium) on gold and the foreign exchange rates as the best measures. The second question was what could be the reason for a depreciation of the paper pound. The Bullionists claimed that it was due to an excessive note issue by the Bank of England. As will be seen later on these two issues have continued to be mixed together on many other occasions, especially in discussions of the purchasing power parity theory. One problem is the relation between price levels and exchange rates and the other is the problem of determining the price level.

The Anti-Bullionists, on the other hand, argued "that under inconvertibility this limit to the fall in the exchanges did not exist; that the exchanges and the premium on bullion would be governed solely by the state of the balance of international payments; and that in a period when heavy military remittances and extraordinary importations of grain because of deficient

---

[1] Einzig (1970), p. 203.

English harvests had to be made, there was no definable limit beyond which the exchanges could not fall or the premium on bullion rise without demonstrating that the currency was in excess".[1]

The stage is now ready for our play. The actors are the Bullionists and their forerunners and followers who had a monetary approach to the determination of the exchange rates and the Anti-Bullionists with predessors and epigones who had a balance of payments view of the determination of the exchange rates. We interpret this view as asserting that the exchange rates are determined by exogenous shifts in different parts of the balance of payments (exogenous in this context means relative to the money supply).

Let us now study briefly the arguments used by the Bullionists to reject the Anti-Bullionists' claims. On the question of the effects of foreign remittances on foreign exchange rates, Ricardo and Wheatley clearly denied any such effects while the other Bullionists were willing to concede that there was some effect, although a minor one, and that the quantity of note issue would dominate. According to Viner,[2] Ricardo's position was most likely due to his absolute unwillingness to analyze or even to acknowledge any importance of short-run adjustment processes. He went directly from one stationary state to another. Later on, Ricardo seems to have modified his argument slightly and surrounded it with qualifications. However, the best refutation of this argument comes from Viner himself. He first states that extraordinary remittances would tend to affect the foreign exchange rates in the same way under both an inconvertible and a convertible currency, but in the latter case they could only fall to the gold export point and after that currency would leave the country. He further argued that if under a paper standard the note issue would be diminished to the same extent as the foreign remittances there would be no change in the money supply and the effect on foreign exchange rates would be approximately the same in both cases.[3]

In the case of crop failures and the related increase in imports Ricardo was just as emphatic as before; this had absolutely no influence on the balance of payments under a gold standard. Therefore we also conclude that he would agree it had no effect on the exchange rates under a paper standard. The reason for this attitude is once again concentration on the long-run stationary state equilibrium. In this perspective, everyone would anticipate that the disturbance would just be temporary and that in the end everything would be back in the original equilibrium.

If the Bullionists, and especially Wheatley and Ricardo, could be accused of pressing their arguments somewhat too far, this was true to an even larger extent with respect to the Anti-Bullionists. Or as Viner says: "The anti-bullionists insisted rightly that under inconvertibility the exchanges were

[1] Viner (1937), p. 138.
[2] Viner (1937), pp. 139–40.
[3] Viner (1937), p. 145.

immediately determined solely by the demand for and supply of foreign bills, but failed to see that this was equally true of a metallic standard and that a very important factor determining the relative demand for and supply of foreign bills was the relative level of prices in the two countries, which in turn was determined largely by the relative amounts of currency."[1]

In hindsight, and with knowledge of the 1930's, Viner raises a few extra objections to the Bullionists' beliefs. First, he brings up the problem of the definition of money. Was it sufficient to look only at Bank of England notes? What about bank deposits? And the notes issued by the country banks? This is a problem that we have lived with since then and it has still not been settled. Second, he discusses the possibility of changes in velocity, but aside from other factors such as improvements in the means of communication or the development of a clearing-house, the question is whether velocity would change simply because of the suspension of specie payments. Viner argues that there is some presumption that it should rise, but probably not very much. Third, there is the whole complex of speculation and expectations formation and their effects on the economy. We note the problem, but leave it until later in the text.

Before going on to the next section it should be pointed out that a great deal of the best that was written during this period is in Henry Thornton's book.[2] Because of his poor health and early death, he never became a prominent name in the public debates in England between Bullionists and Anti-Bullionists, although he did take an active part in the preparation of the Bullion Report. But on such questions as the determinants of velocity, the role of interest rates, the importance of country bank notes and the dangers of too rapid a reduction in the money supply, he was often superior to Ricardo in his analysis. It is worth pointing out, in particular, that he viewed the wage rate as adjusting slower than prices and with the resulting increase in unemployment when money was reduced.

> "The tendency, however, of a very great and sudden reduction of the accustomed number of bank notes, is to create an *unusual* and *temporary* distress, and a fall of price arising from that distress. But a fall arising from temporary distress, will be attended probably with no correspondent fall in the rate of wages; for the fall of price, and the distress, will be understood to be temporary, and the rate of wages, we know, is not so variable as the price of goods. There is reason, therefore, to fear that the unnatural and extraordinary low price ... arising from the sort of distress of which we now speak, would occasion much discouragement of the fabrication of manufactures."[3]

Quite similar to today's thinking!

---

[1] Viner (1937), pp. 145–146.
[2] Thornton (1802).
[3] Thornton (1802), p. 119.

III. The Swedish Debate[1]

We have presented the Bullion debate in Britain before the Swedish debate because it is more familiar to economists, but the same kind of events actually took place in Sweden fifty to sixty years earlier. The most amazing thing about the Swedish episode is the incredible degree of similarity to the later British experience, to the discussions initiated by these events and to the development of economic theory.

In Swedish history the period from 1719–1772 is called the Age of Freedom because the kings and queens of this period were so weak that the Swedish Parliament, the *Rikets Ständer*, had all the power. The Parliament contained four representative groups, Nobles, Clergy, Burghers and Peasants. This was also a time of early economic development and it witnessed the establishment of the first factories in Sweden. As a reflection of the lively economic activity, mercantile interests were widely represented in the Parliament and the work and discussions there were to a very large extent concerned with economic problems.

It also had its own bank. This bank was first opened as a private bank in 1657 but was in fact closely affiliated with the government. In 1661 it issued the first modern banknote in the world but was forced to close down in 1663 after an over-issue and a run on the bank. It was taken over by the Swedish Parliament in 1668, but the note issue was stopped.

In addition to gold and silver coins, there were also copper coins in Sweden. After several decreases in value the copper coins had become so big and clumsy that, by the 1720's, a horse and cart were necessary for many payments. The bank then introduced "bank transport notes" in 1726. They were only a receipt for copper deposited in the bank but they were equal to the copper coin in value and acceptability. Bank credit was liberalized in the 1730's in order to promote industry and the cultivation of land as well as to aid factories. Sweden had converted to a pure paper standard. During the next two decades there was a moderate increase in banknotes but in 1755 and 1756 there were crop failures and the bank lowered its interest rate from 4 1/2 or 5 % to 3 or 4 %. More important, Sweden entered the Seven Years' War in 1757. Now, from 1755 to 1762, the exchange rate on Hamburg went from 38.6 Swedish marks to 85.3 marks, an increase by 120 %. At the same time the bank notes increased by 189 %.

Concurrently with the increases in the exchange rate the debate in Sweden about the reasons for the higher exchange rates was expanding rapidly. Newspaper articles, pamphlets and books showed an incredible intellectual activity reminiscent of the development in Britain some fifty years later. In Parliament there were two political parties, the Hats and the Caps. The Hat party was in

[1] See the excellent work which brought this story to the English-speaking public; Eagly (1971).

the majority from 1739 to 1765. The economic program of this party was mercantilistic and the export industries were encouraged by favorable loans and subsidies, imports were held back by tariffs and on the whole the party pursued a very expansionary policy. They regarded increases in the supply of bank notes as a good way to stimulate production.

They explained the increase in exchange rates by a reference to the deficit in the balance of payments. The import surplus led to higher prices for foreign exchange and they also believed that the higher exchange rate caused an increase in Swedish prices. Consequently they tried to meet the inflation with further restrictions on imports and stimulation of exports.

Finally, in 1765, the continuous inflation had become intolerable to most people and the Hat party lost its majority to the Cap party. The Cap party had a more liberal economic program and it also attacked the Hat policies on the grounds that their economic policy benefited the rather wealthy owners of export industries and factories. With respect to the exchange rate the Cap party constituted the Bullionists of Sweden. The Caps explained the increase in foreign exchange rates by the over-issue of banknotes. This was not the only explanation, but it was the main one. The Cap party now started a period of deflation until 1768 and the exchange rate fell back to 42 Swedish marks on Hamburg and the note issue declined by 5–6 per cent per year. However, this resulted in deflation and increased unemployment. According to one estimate[1] the annual value of output (in specie) increased from 1751–54 to 1755–59 by about 35 % and decreased from 1761 to 1764 by about 32 %.

It is not only the events and the political discussions that are similar between Sweden and Britain. Also the intellectual and scientific level of knowledge was raised to a surprisingly high degree in both countries. In Sweden, this was particularly true in the case of P. N. Christiernin who published his main work in 1761, "*Lectures on the High Price of Foreign Exchange in Sweden*".[2] Even if he did not reach quite the width and depth of Ricardo and Thornton his piece is extremely clear and concise and closer in understanding to those two economists than to most others of this time.

Christiernin explained that the main reason for the increase in foreign exchange rates was the over-issue of banknotes. This led to higher total demand in the economy with rising demand also for imported goods and an increase in both prices and exchange rates. "But general high prices that affect all products, labor wages, house rents, real estate prices, and the price of foreign exchange, etc. cannot be caused by other than the increase in the money supply. All these phenomena result from an excess of money. A decline in the general purchasing power of money results."[3]

As a parenthesis in this context it should be mentioned, however, that

[1] Reproduced from Eagly (1971), p. 12.
[2] Translated in Eagly (1971).
[3] Eagly (1971), p. 65.

Christiernin had a carefully described theory about the effects of a drastic reduction of the supply of bank notes on unemployment, quite similar to Thornton's analysis, and he consistently warned the Cap party of the effects of their deflationary monetary policy.

"2. When the currency is appreciated in terms of specie (i.e., the price of specie is decreased in terms of bank notes), not all prices fall immediately. People continue for a long time to demand the old price for their products, despite the change in the metallic content of the monetary unit. There are instances of this in other countries and in Sweden in 1633 and in 1719.

3. It is easy for prices to adjust upward when the money supply increases, but go get prices to fall has always been more difficult. No one reduces the price of his commodities or his labor until the lack of sales necessitates him to do so. Because of this the workers must suffer want and the industriousness of wage earners must stop before the established market price can be reduced."[1]

In 1770 Christiernin became a full professor but he then left economics and went into philosophy, probably in despair over how impossible it was to persuade the politicians to listen to his advice.

IV. The Interwar Debate

Let us now sum up what we have found out about the theory of flexible exchange rates prior to and during the nineteenth century. If we then look at the height of the theoretical discussions and clear away all inferior material and more or less confused reasoning a picture seems to take form and crystallize into two fundamentally different views. *One view is the monetary approach to exchange rates.* According to this view the foreign exchange rates are determined only by the money supply (Ricardo) or mainly by the money supply (Christiernin, Thornton). In the event that two or more countries are on a paper standard it is instead the relative money supplies that will determine the exchange rates.

The other view is the balance of payments theory. It says that the foreign exchange rates are determined by changes in the balance of payments such as international loans, foreign remittances and shifts in exports and imports independently of the behavior of the money supply. This view was held by the Hat party in Sweden, by the Anti-Bullionists in Britain and it has returned to the forefront many more times in history.[2]

The blossoming debates and the elegant analyses in Sweden and Britain were set off by the startling events in their foreign exchanges. The quietness of the second half of the nineteenth century may then perhaps be explained analogously by the general stability of the gold standard which was successively adopted by more and more countries. There was one exception, how-

[1] Eagly (1971), p. 90.

[2] For some reason this view seems to be very popular among central bankers and other politicians responsible for the conomic situation.

ever, and that was a little book by Goschen (1863) in which he expertly combined theoretical insights with a great deal of practical knowledge. He developed in particular the role of interest rates for capital movements and exchange rates.

During the remainder of the gold standard period not much was said about flexible exchange rates, but in the whirlpool of events after the outbreak of the First World War the behavior of the exchange rates once again became the problem of the day. However, it seems to be the fate of our subject that important discoveries or parts of analysis are frequently forgotten. The survivor after a hundred years was not the monetary approach but the balance of payments theory. Einzig for example says "... the balance of payments theory was looked upon during the early war years as axiomatic by those trying to explain the abnormal war-time exchange movements".[1] Or in the more ironic words of Knut Wicksell: "It is well known that in Germany not only prominent bankers —I believe even the Chief Director of the Reichsbank—but also well-known political economists seriously maintained to the very last that Germany's soaring rate of exchange on neutral countries was not attributable to any actual deterioration of the currency, but wholly and solely to Germany's adverse trade balance during the war. Whether they would also apply this argument to the Austrian currency, which has now managed to fall to less than one-fifth of its nominal value and is at present excluded from our exchange market quotations, I am unable to say."[2]

It was Gustav Cassel who rediscovered Ricardo[3] and reformulated his theory under the name of the purchasing power parity theory, PPP as we will call it. One of the merits of Cassel's forceful attack was that he managed to sell this theory, at least for a while. His intensive writings, his clarity and his gathering of data made him rise like a star. His basic theory can be stated as follows: "Our willingness to pay a certain price for foreign money must ultimately and essentially be due to the fact that this money possesses purchasing power as against commodities and services in that foreign country. On the other hand, when we offer so and so much of our own money, we are actually offering a purchasing power as against commodities and services in our own country. Our valuation of a foreign currency in terms of our own, therefore, mainly depends on the relative purchasing power of the two currencies in their respective countries ... When two currencies have undergone inflation, the normal rate of exchange will be equal to the old rate multiplied by the quotient of the degree of inflation in the one country and in the other. There will naturally always be found deviations from this new normal rate, and during the transition period these deviations may be expected to be fairly wide. But the rate that

[1] Einzig (1970), p. 264.
[2] Wicksell (1958), p. 231.
[3] Evidently he never discovered Thorton; nor does he seem to be aware of his countryman Christiernin. An even earlier forerunner is the Salamanca School. Grice-Hutchinson (1952).

has been calculated by the above method must be regarded as the new parity between the currencies, the point of balance towards which, in spite of all temporary fluctuations, the exchange rates will always tend. This parity I call *purchasing power parity*."[1]

Now if we compare this with the view of the Bullionists it should be clear that the two statements amount to essentially the same thing, although more than 100 years later Cassel was able to formulate it more consciously and show that it was a more long-run relationship. He also had observations from some countries to support his views. It should be pointed out once again that we have here a combination of two propositions. The first is that the quantity of money determines prices in the two countries under consideration and the second states that the ratio of the price levels will determine the exchange rate between the two countries.[2] In more recent years it seems as if the PPP has often been thought of as only the second proposition, but it should be quite clear that Cassel included the quantity of money as a very important ingredient.

Cassel was careful to state the exceptions to the validity of his theory, such as tariffs and other impediments to free trade. He also admitted that such a thing as speculation could lead the exchange astray from the PPP for a while, but that this was a temporary phenomenon. He even used it himself as an explanation for the behavior of the German exchange rate in 1919.[3] In the *Economic Journal* in December, 1919, even the young Keynes seemed to accept this explanation wholeheartedly:

> "The actual statistical relation between volume of currency, prices, and rates of exchange is in so close a conformity with the predictions of theory, as to surprise even theorists, having regard to the many disturbing factors of the present time. The only really anomalous case—that of Germany—is dealt with by Professor Cassel in his article above."

In his article in 1917, F. W. Taussig tried to explain the effects of an international loan on real trade under a depreciated paper currency.[4] In his book ten years later he used this example as counter-evidence against the PPP. "The price of foreign exchange thus may change without any movement in the general range of prices in either country."[5]

Wicksell, in a comment to Taussig's article,[6] pointed out the importance of changes in total demand for this type of transfer process and the reduced requirement of relative price changes. Twelve years later this problem became

---

[1] Cassel (1922), pp. 138–140.
[2] For many purposes the *relative* version is more reasonable. It states the same thing in terms of changes from a base period.
[3] Cassel (1919).
[4] Taussig (1917).
[5] Taussig (1927), Chapter 26.
[6] Wicksell (1917–18).

the focus for the debate between Keynes (1929) and Ohlin (1929) on the German reparation payments, with Ohlin using Wicksell's argument.[1]

The Keynes–Ohlin exchange is an example of a problem that has existed since Hume, namely the nature of the adjustment process. In the work of Hume–Ricardo–Mill–Taussig, the relative price changes were stressed. The other view, represented by Wicksell and Ohlin, was that changes in excess demands would be enough, with negligible relative price adjustment. (For a good discussion of this problem and the views of many nineteenth century economists, see Frenkel (1976).)

As to the question of determinants of the exchange rates, Wicksell had the same view as his colleague in Stockholm. "... the really large fluctuations in rates of exchange can never be attributed to such causes as trade and credit, but always presuppose a positive deterioration—be it actual or merely anticipated—*in the value of the country's currency*".[2]

In 1923, Keynes was still very much in sympathy with the PPP-theory[3] but by 1930 his enthusiasm had almost disappeared.[4] The reason for this change seems to be the same as the rationale behind Viner's rather negative attitude.[5] It concerns the problem of how to treat non-traded goods and it is interesting to note that this problem was there all the time; Cassel was well aware of it, and it is still causing a lot of heated discussion today. We will have more to say about this later on.

Thus far the objective of this presentation has been to survey the literature until the beginning of World War II. The survey has not been aimed at completeness but at indicating the major steps in the development of the theory of flexible exchange rates and focusing attention on the crucial issues and major controversies.

The theoretical literature on flexible exchange rates after World War II has to a large extent followed a line starting before the War with Keynes (1923), Nurkse (1944), Kindleberger (1937) and Einzig (1937). The focus of this research is on the more short-run problems of forward markets, hedging, covering, arbitrage and speculation. Many advances have been made in the understanding of these phenomena,[6] but it is our view that this development has had the unlucky side effect of putting too much emphasis on speculation and the volatility of exchange rates. For analytical convenience these theories do not allow for any interaction with the real sector of the economy, but this has very often led to neglect of the more basic factors determining the exchange

[1] The whole debate is extensively discussed and placed in historical context by Iversen (1935).
[2] Wicksell (1918), p. 231.
[3] Keynes (1923), pp. 95–116.
[4] Keynes (1930), p. 74.
[5] Viner (1937), pp. 379–387.
[6] See for example Spraos (1953), Jasay (1958), Tsiang (1958), (1959–60), Hansen (1958–59), Grubel (1966), Kenen (1965), Basevi (1972), Poole (1967*b*), Stein (1962), Halm (1969), Lanyi (1969), Kemp (1972), Frenkel & Levich (1974), and Black (1973).

rates. It is probably also indirectly responsible for the widespread beliefs among politicians and many economists in the postwar period about the non-viability of flexible exchange rates.

However, it has been clearly pointed out by e.g. Sohmen that "Whichever form they take, the speculative components of all foreign-exchange transactions share one important characteristic: the (long or short) foreign-exchange position is eventually liquidated. This can formally be expressed by the condition that the algebraic sum of all speculative foreign-exchange transactions (following a convention of such as attaching a positive sign to sales, a negative one to purchases) will approach zero over a sufficiently long time interval".[1] Some forty years earlier Keynes himself wrote: "We may safely attribute most of the major fluctuations of the exchanges from month to month to the actual pressure of trade remittances, and not to speculation, ... General opinion greatly overestimates the influence of exchange speculators acting under the stimulus of merely political and sentimental considerations. Except for brief periods the influence of the speculator is washed out; and political events can only exert a lasting influence on the exchanges in so far as they modify the internal price level, the volume of trade, or the ability of a country to borrow on foreign markets."[2]

The introduction of expectations resulted in a long, drawn-out discussion about speculation and the stability of the exchange market. Friedman (1953) and Johnson (1967) were the chief defenders of the viability and stability of flexible exchange rates. Johnson makes the important point that the size of speculation sometimes observed in the postwar period is due to the "adjustable peg system" which makes speculation a no loser's game and, because of the size of actual exchange rate changes, also a "much to win" game. "It is obviously fallacious to assume that private speculators would speculate in the same way and on the same scale under the flexible rate system, which offers them no such easy mark to speculate against."[3]

Speculation builds on expectations and expectations are formed about market developments and economic policy. There does not seem to be any reason to expect destabilizing speculation for a stable and known policy. With an erratic policy, which has often been the case, or with a policy that tries to keep the futue course of policy secret, the risk of destabilizing speculation increases.

In order to be able to evaluate some of the critical problems we need a specified model. The next section is devoted to the construction of such a model.

---

[1] Sohmen (1969), p. 61.
[2] Keynes (1923), p. 112.
[3] Johnson (1969), p. 20.

V. Model[1]

We assume two countries, the domestic economy and the foreign economy. In the domestic economy there are only two assets to be held, money and claims to the return streams of real capital. The demand for assets is homogenous in wealth and the portfolio choice is therefore described by the definition of wealth and the money market equilibrium condition. The definition of wealth is

$$W = m + \frac{y^{DK}}{a}, \tag{1}$$

where m is real money balances, y^{DK} is the return stream to real capital accruing to domestic residents and r is the interest rate. Equilibrium in the money market is achieved when the supply of money is equal to demand,

$$m = \alpha(r)\,W. \tag{2}$$

The demand for money as a proportion of wealth depends negatively on the rate of interest.

In the production sector of the economy one output good is produced with a constant, fully employed labor force. It is also assumed that the capital stock is constant. The total income that is generated domestically will then be

$$F(N_0, K_0) = q_0 + y^K, \tag{3}$$

where q_0 is labor income and y^K is income to capital. The latter is interpreted as an "equalized" income stream.[2] The domestic disposable income is accordingly

$$y = q_0 + y^{DK} - t, \tag{4}$$

where t is taxes. Private expenditures are assumed to be

$$E = E(r, W, y). \tag{5}$$

The balance of trade is equal to exports minus imports

$$B = X - IM, \tag{6}$$

but it is also equal to domestic production minus absorption under the assumption that the government budget is balanced

$$B = q_0 + y^{DK} - E(r, W, y). \tag{7}$$

Saving is equal to

---

[1] This model is a simplified version of the model in Myhrman (1973) and (1975). It is obviously very much influenced by the work of Branson (1974), Dornbusch (1975) and Frenkel & Rodriguez (1975), See also Holmes (1972).

[2] See Hirshleifer (1970), p. 36.

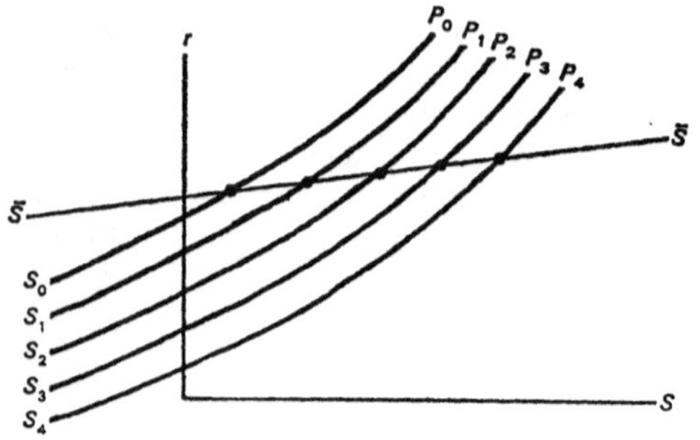

Fig. 1

$$S = q_0 + y^{DK} - E(r, W, y), \tag{8}$$

the current account is defined as

$$C = B + y^{DK} - y^K \tag{9}$$

and we therefore have that saving is equal to the current account balance.

Finally, we have the competitive arbitrage assumption about prices that

$$P = P^* e, \tag{10}$$

where e is the exchange rate. It is also assumed that there are no tariffs, transport costs or other impediments to trade.

Assuming the same type of structural equations to hold for the foreign economy, we can describe the conditions for instantaneous equilibrium in the world economy. These conditions consist of market clearing equations for the two money markets.

$$m = \alpha(r)\, W \tag{11}$$

$$m^* = \alpha^*(r)\, W^*. \tag{12}$$

The world output market clears under the following condition

$$S(r, W, y) + S^*(r, W^*, y^*) = 0.^1 \tag{13}$$

The general equilibrium in this model can be illustrated in the following diagrams, which are adapted from Meltzer (1951) and (1968), Dornbusch (1976) and Frenkel (1976).

In Fig. 1 every S–P curve shows the desired savings in the domestic economy as a function of the rate of interest, r, for a certain price level, P, and for given money stock and asset stock. For every r there is only one price level that gives portfolio equilibrium. If we connect all such points in Fig. 1 we get

[1] This form of the savings function is, in this context, equivalent to a "target-wealth" type of savings function.

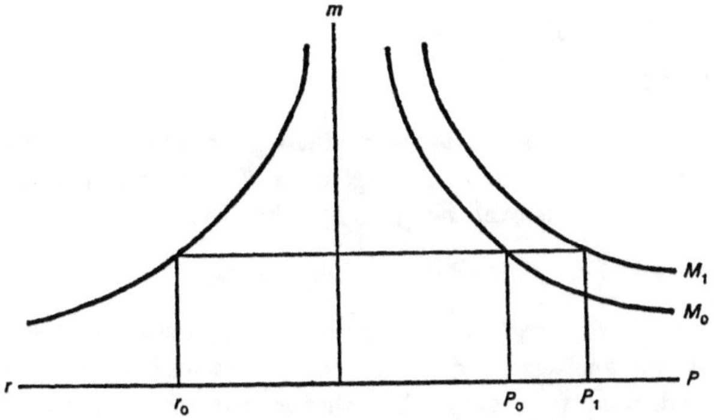

Fig. 2

the reduced form savings function $\bar{S}$–$\bar{S}$ indicating the desired savings at every interest rate with simultaneous portfolio equilibrium.

The left-hand side of Fig. 2 shows a liquidity preference function and the right-hand side shows how, for every level of the money supply M_0, M_1 and so on, there is only one price level that will give portfolio equilibrium for every interest rate, namely P_0, P_1 and so on.

If we do the same for the foreign economy an equivalent relationship can be derived for its savings behavior. This is drawn in Fig. 3 as a decreasing function of the rate of interest because it is a negative savings function. Determination of the real balances in the domestic and foreign economies is shown in the two accompanying side figures.

Formally, eqs. (11), (12) and (13) can be solved to give equilibrium values for P, e and r. Under certain assumptions[1] we can determine the effects of each of the predetermined entities in this short-run equilibrium. Writing the variables as reduced form functions we have

$$P = h^1(M, M^*, y^{DK}, y^{DK*}, q_0, q_0^*) \tag{14}$$

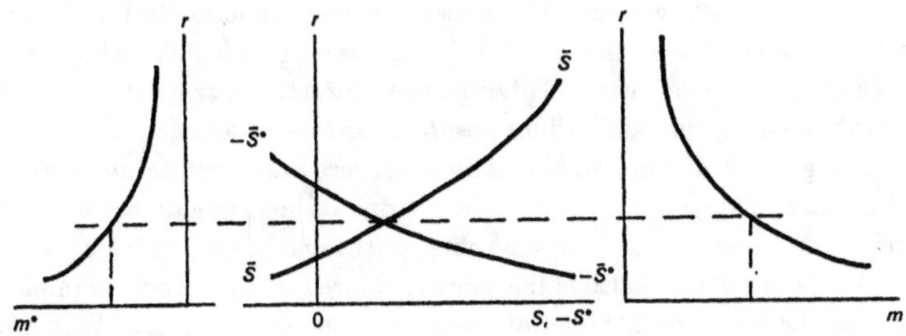

Fig. 3

1 That an equilibrium solution exists and is unique and that wealth effects are comparatively small.

$$e = h^2(M, M^*, y^{DK} \; y^{DK^*}, q_0 \; q_0^*) \tag{15}$$

$$r = h^3(M \; M^*, y^{DK}, y^{DK^*}, q_0, q_0^*). \tag{16}$$

We are now in a position to evaluate the conflicting views about the influence on and determination of flexible exchange rates. For this reason we concentrate on the solution for the exchange rate. We then have

$$e_M > 0, \quad e_{M^*} < 0, \quad e_{(y^{DK})} \gtrless 0, \quad e_{(y^{DK^*})} \gtrless 0, \quad e_{q_0} \gtrless 0, \quad e_{q_0^*} \gtrless 0.$$

The effect on the exchange rate, e, of an increase in domestic assets is uncertain because of two countervailing forces. One is that an increase in y^{DK} leads to an excess demand for money. The other is that an increase in y^{DK} lowers savings and increases expenditures. We assume that the latter dominates.

It was concluded earlier that the major competing views about the determinants of the exchange rate were the monetary explanation and the balance of payments theory. It is obvious from our results that the monetary explanation has a theoretical foundation, but does it go all the way? Let us look at the balance of payments theory. Its adherents used several arguments, but the essence was that autonomous changes in different items in the balance of payments explained the exchange rate. Examples used were foreign remittances, crop failures and so on. Let us take the case of a war subsidy to the foreign economy. In our model that is equivalent to a reduction in domestic claims and an increase in foreign claims. This will evidently affect the exchange rate. We therefore conclude that in the short run both schools could conclude they were right.

However, let us also study what happens in the long run. For the domestic economy the short run equilibrium determines a rate of saving which is normally different from zero. This will then determine the dynamics of the model. The rate of change in domestic assets is given by

$$y^{DK} = rS(r, W). \tag{17}$$

An increase in assets will shift the domestic savings function in Fig. 3 to the left and the same will be true for the foreign savings schedule. The desired rate of savings will be reduced and after further shifts the curves will eventually end up in their long-run equilibrium positions with zero savings.

In the long run stationary state equilibrium there is an equilibrium distribution of assets in the sense that everyone is happy to hold exactly the assets he has and neither more nor less at the ruling prices and yields, which of course also implies that actual wealth is the same as desired wealth. Another implication is that the real asset holdings are now endogenous. This means that if we derive the long-run reduced form equations for the prices and yields, they will be independent of real asset holdings. We then have, for the exchange rate,

$$e = \Phi(M, M^*, q_0, q_0^*). \tag{18}$$

If we further assume that the real output in both countries is constant (or growing at the same rates) we reach the conclusion that the exchange rate is determined by the domestic and foreign money supplies. This is probably what Ricardo had in mind, and it is also an expression of Cassel's purchasing power parity theory as it was first presented. We know, however, by the way this conclusion was arrived at, that there are some special assumptions behind it, which may or may not be important. Let us first take care of two objections that are easy to meet. We assumed in our model that there was no investment and a constant capital stock. Changing this assumption to allow for balanced growth of the economy does not alter anything except for a change in the variables from levels to growth rates. Second, we have constantly avoided incorporating any expectations into our model. This is clearly inappropriate if our purpose were to explain week-to-week or month-to-month behavior of the exchange rate where forward markets and speculation may have some importance, as Einzig (1970) always points out. But we consider these phenomena to be rather short-run in nature and they will always give way to the more basic determinants of the exchange rates as time goes on. It is our view that in many instances in economics, too much emphasis has been concentrated on short-run behavior, where the movements are to a large extent delayed adjustments and random variation, leading to assertions about the need for "disequilibrium models". It seems to us that such *day-to-day economics* has its place for some problems but that it should not be allowed to overshadow the more basic, underlying economic relationships that will be rule over a slightly longer time period.

Let us now return to our main theme. It is obvious that our reduced form equation (18) only says that *given a stable structure* the exchange rate will be determined by the domestic and foreign money supply (if output does not change). However, if we go behind the reduced form we find that there are three other possibilities. These consists of a possible shift in (*a*) liquidity preference, (*b*) savings behavior and (if we allow for investment), (*c*) investment demand (τ, τ^*). Or, in another reduced form which we write in growth rates

$$e = \Psi(M, M^*, S, S^*, \alpha, \alpha^*, \tau, \tau^*, q, q^*). \tag{19}$$

It thus seems as if the monetary approach has to give in to a more eclectic view of the determination of exchange rates, allow for several possible explanatory factors. However, there is good eclecticism and there is bad eclecticism. The latter usually contends that everything could be possible and ends up in a fruitless enumeration of possible causes and theories. This is completely contrary to what Karl Popper has called "Conjectures and Refutations" and we leave it to itself to discover new possibilities. The good type of eclecticism is represented by Assar Lindbeck[1] and holds that there does not necessarily

[1] See Claassen–Salin (1972).

have to be only one explanation for some observed phenomena, but a narrow range. We accept this view but we want to extend it to a more operational conjecture. Our theory is that all the variables in equation (19) may explain the exchange rate but that changes in the savings behavior, in liquidity preference and in investment demand are small and infrequent relative to changes in the growth rate of money. To distinguish it from the other theories we will call our theory *the monetary impulse theory.*[1] What this theory says is essentially that (*a*) under conditions of slow and stable monetary growth the exchange rates will be simultaneously determined by several economic relationships. The more stable these relationships are, the more the relative development of the money supply in two countries will determine their exchange rate. (*b*) The more the two money supplies fluctuate, the more they will denominate the exchange rates. (*c*) This holds true regardless of the reason for the change in the money supply; (*d*) it does not deny the potential influence of large shifts in the private sector's economic behavior but it assumes that these shifts have been relatively small and infrequent relative to the fluctuations in the money supply. Finally, (*e*) we do not expect a hard and fast relationship on a quarterly basis or even on a yearly basis, but over a slightly longer period of a couple of years, the relationship will be closer. Because of information costs and adjustment costs, economic agents can be expected to react and adjust first when the pressure has become strong enough to filter through and make readjustment worthwhile.

Two things remain to be discussed. The first is fiscal policy. It should in principle be included in equation (19) but when it is defined as fiscal measures with a constant growth rate of money it is likely to be small whenever the government sector is small. (It is a different matter that an underbalanced budget was often the way in which the money supply was increased.)

The second problem concerns the exchange rate, the price level index and the existence of non-traded goods. As we mentioned earlier this problem was brought up by the PPP-theory, it nagged Cassel all the time, it changed Keynes' opinion and it was a central issue in Viner's critique. It was never a problem in our model above because there was only one (composite) good in the economy. In the multi-goods case there would in principle be a problem because the exchange rate is then also dependent on the relative size of the non-traded goods sectors in the two countries. This adds another aspect to the model and to the conclusions. What was said earlier is not drastically changed, only slightly modified.[2]

[1] Thoughts along this line can be traced in writings by Christiernin, Thornton and Cassel. It disappeared with the "Keynesian Revolution" but has been brought up again by Karl Brunner and Allan Meltzer. See Brunner (1970).

[2] See the article by Rudiger Dornbusch in this volume for a development of this problem.

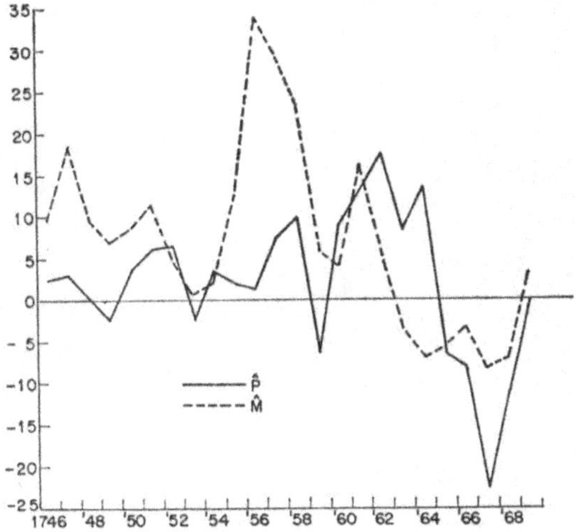

Fig. 4. Sweden 1746–1768. Money and prices.

VI. Empirical Evidence

In this section we attempt to review some of the available empirical evidence. It is tempting to go as far back in history as possible, but after some distance in time we loose every possibility of checking the content of the data. We have therefore chosen to start with Sweden in the eighteenth century because there are data available and because we know from other sources that they are of a fairly reliable quality. From 1746 to 1769, there are 24 yearly observations on the number of bank notes, price level, price of gold coins and the exchange rate on Hamburg, which did not have a paper standard at this time. There is not enough information available to permit a formal test of different theories but we have calculated the growth rates of the different variables. In Fig. 4 we have plotted the changes in the money supply and the price level together for the whole period. It is clear from a first inspection that there is no close covariation between the money supply and the price level on a year-to-year basis. However, it is also evident that, on the average, the changes in the money supply seem to drag the price level along with it. It is as if the money supply forces an unwilling and resistant price level to follow it with many excursions along the path. The period can be divided into two subperiods. The first is the acceleration period from 1755 to 1763. The second is a deceleration period from 1764 to 1769. The reverse causation problem is thereby avoided because the first period consisted of a deliberate policy of money supply increase as described in Section III and the second period witnessed a decisive reduction in the money supply. It is almost like a controlled experiment. For the period as a whole the average increase in the money supply was 7.2 %. If we

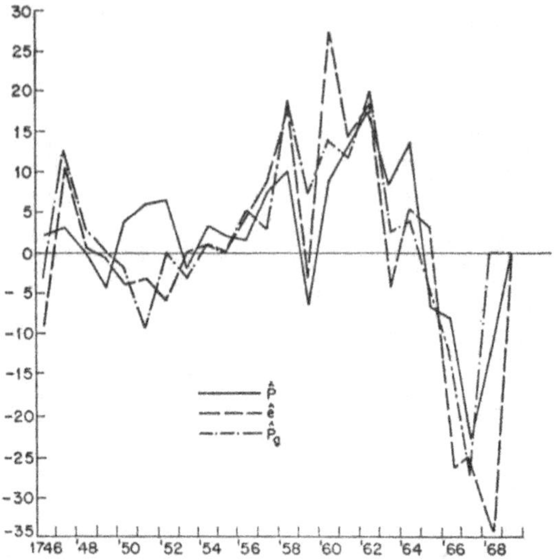

Fig. 5. Sweden 1746–1768. Prices, exchange rate and price of gold.

further take into account the estimated change in real output[1] of 4 per cent, we are not too far from using the monetary impulse theory as our explanation.

Figure 5 shows the changes in the price level, the price of gold coins and the exchange rate on Hamburg. The covariation over the whole period is close enough to have made Gustav Cassel quite satisfied with his PPP-theory.

As has been mentioned earlier, the drastic reduction in the growth rate of money and after a while even a negative growth rate produced considerable unemployment between 1764 and 1769. Just as predicted by Christiernin.

Next, let us take a look at Great Britain some fifty years later. Like Sweden it also had a period of paper standard with some inflation, although it should be pointed out that neither was a hyperinflation. Even in Britain the period consisted of an earlier subperiod with inflation and a later subperiod of deflation. Just as in Sweden, the whole period consists of 24 years. The relationship between money and prices is shown in Fig. 6. The pattern is similar to the Swedish pattern. Also here it is difficult to find any close relationship on a year-to-year basis but some covariation over a slightly longer horizon can be distinguished. The only difference is that the British variation is around a lower average, but the standard deviation is of about the same size in both cases. The British inflation averaged only 0.4 per cent over the period and the money supply growth 3.5 %. Assuming a real income growth of no less than 2 %, we would have an unexplained change in velocity of about the same size as in Sweden.

[1] See Eagly (1971), p. 12.

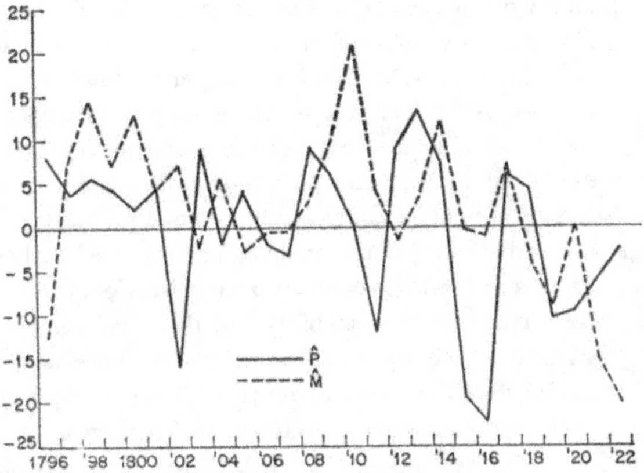

Fig. 6. England 1796–1822. Prices and money.

The relationship between the price level, the exchange rate and the price of silver is shown in Fig. 7. It is also similar to the Swedish case.

In general the British economy shows a less stable pattern than the Swedish economy in the earlier period. We must remember, however, that England was taking part in a major war and that on some occasion this led to real scarcities causing prices to change without a previous monetary impulse. At the same time the whole Continent was affected by the war and the exchange rate on Hamburg, $\hat{e}$ in the figure, varied in some instances because of financial disruptions on the Continent which did not originate in England. All this is in accordance with our theory but it means that a more careful study of the actual events would be necessary for this period in order to establish the year-to-year variations in prices and exchange rates.

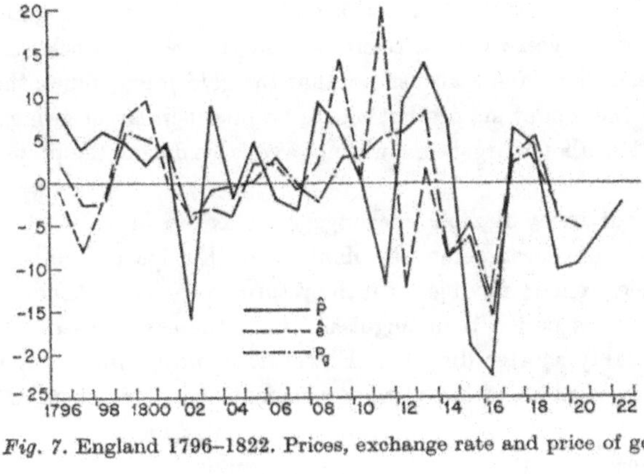

Fig. 7. England 1796–1822. Prices, exchange rate and price of gold.

Leland B. Yeager (1969) has written a thorough study describing the development in Austria and Russia in the second half of the 19th century. Austria was on a paper standard from 1879 to 1891. During this period there was a money supply growth of only about 2 % per year on the average and a variability between −3.9 and +6.7. Also, both prices and the exchange rate were rather stable but with a rising trend. The latter phenomenon is explained by the fact that England and the other gold standard countries had falling prices during this period. This also indicates that the exchange rate moved in line with the relative money supplies in the two countries over the period.

Yeager also made a careful study of the "stability" of the exchange rate and he found that the monthly variability was just about the same as for Canada after World War II. He says that one explanation for this could be a relatively well-developed market for forward transaction which then implies stabilizing speculation. While Austria thus had a "stable" period of flexible exchange rates, Russia had a period of much larger fluctuations. One problem in this case is the lack of reliable data. However, Yeager explains the larger fluctuations by two main factors. One is the relatively large amounts of government intervention in the foreign exchange market. The other is political instability in a wide sense, including corruption and similar things. All this seems to have increased speculation of a destabilizing nature.

An episode from the US in the 19th century may also illustrate a flexible exchange rate case. "During the American Civil War, when the West Coast kept the gold standard while the rest of the Union used paper greenbacks, the commodity price level in the East rose by roughly the same percentage as the greenback price of gold. The price level in the East roughly doubled from 1860 to 1864, while prices stayed about the same on the West Coast. A Federal employee earning 100 greenback dollars a month could buy roughly the same amount of goods, whether he spent his greenbacks in the East or exchanged them for 50 gold dollars and spent them in the West."[1]

Next there is Argentina from 1885 to 1900, and once more we recognize the pattern of some early years with accelerations in the money stock and then a period of deceleration. Fig. 8 also shows that the gold price follows the general movement of the money supply but moves around it in larger swings. (Additional information about Argentina was not available during the preparation of this paper.)

Another episode with freely flexible exchange rates began in 1919 when most wartime controls had been removed. Many West European countries then let their currencies remain flexible until the return to the gold standard which began in 1925. This period is distinguished from the earlier cases because it is of considerably shorter duration. However, monthly data is now available making a closer examination of the movements possible. There are

[1] Quoted from Yeager (1966), p. 177.

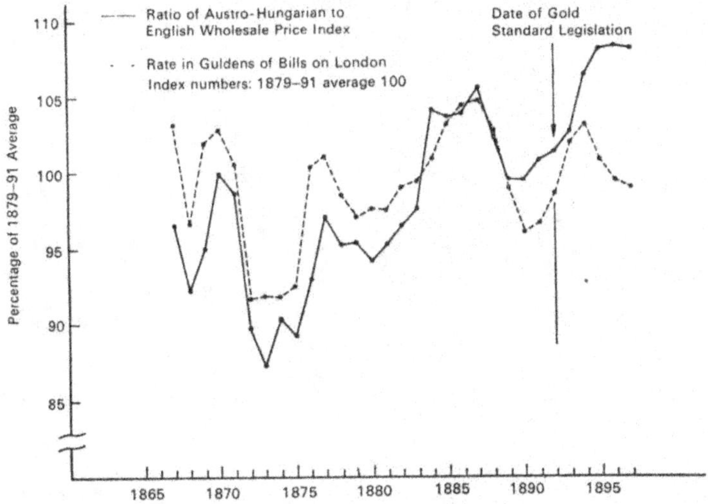

Fig. 8. Austro-Hungarian and English prices and exchange rate, 1867–97. Source: Jankovich's price index for Austria-Hungary, Sauerbeck's for England, and the annual-average exchange rate from Jankovich (1899), pp. 492, 568. Source: Yeager, 1969, p. 63.

also several studies of this period and we will use their interpretations to a large extent.

Let us first take a look at England in Fig. 9. The dominant impression is the striking similarity in the movements of the money supply, prices and exchange rates. There are two major deviations. The first is the fall in the exchange rate in late 1920 and early 1921. Both Tsiang (1959) and Aliber (1966) attribute this to the easing of US monetary policy and the subsequent reduction in bank loans and trade credits from US banks and exporters. The

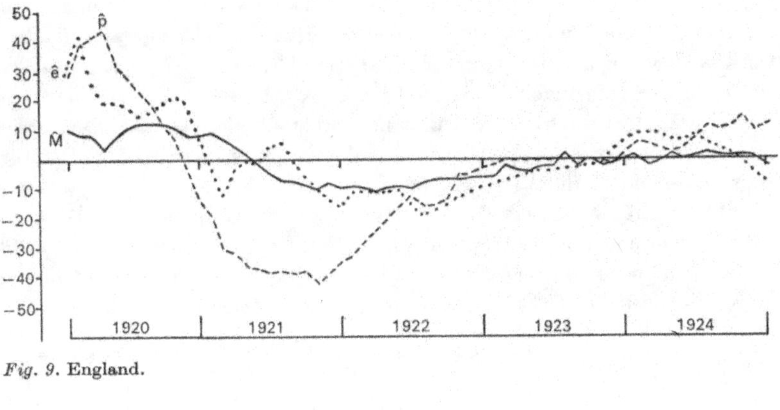

Fig. 9. England.

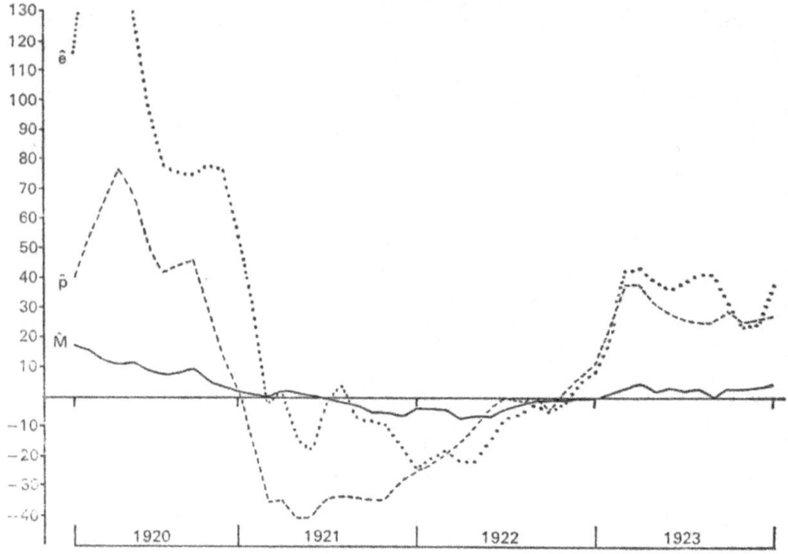

Fig. 10. France.

second deviation is the very obvious decline in prices in 1921 which was not accompanied by a movement in the money supply or the exchange rate to the same extent.[1]

In the case of France (see Fig. 10) the deviations of prices and the exchange rate from the money supply are much more pronounced. However, even for this relatively short period, prices and the exchange rate seem to follow the movements of the money supply on the average, but with a lot of short-run resistance. The general development was similar to the British experience until 1922, with a steady reduction in the rate of growth of the money supply and a fall in prices and the exchange rate. There was also a considerable increase in the rate of unemployment in both countries. However, the short-run fluctuations were wider and the purchasing power relationship between prices and the exchange rate much looser in France. After 1922 the development in France was very different from that in Britain. While money supply, prices and the exchange rate approached a stable situation in the latter country, they continued to fluctuate in France. According to Tsiang (1959) this was mainly due to two factors. First, political developments, such as the break with Britain and the disagreement about German war reparation payments, encouraged speculation. Second, a low interest policy facilitated speculative activities and made it easy to move from bonds to money.

[1] The price indices are for wholesale prices for both England and France, which explains some of the volatility.

Along with France, Norway also went into an inflationary period after 1929, but contrary to France it did not intervene in the foreign exchange market. After some speculative attacks on the Norwegian Crown, the monetary policy was strongly tightened, the price increases slowed down and speculation stopped. The Norwegian case is also an example of a flexible exchange rate regime where speculative activity did not dominate the development of the exchange rate.

Finally, in the postwar period there is the Canadian experience during the 1950's. This case is rather well-known and well documented. The common evaluation seems to be that the exchange rate was even more stable than expected.

VII. Conclusions

After periods of stability in the international payments system, people (and economists) immediately seem either to forget the experience of earlier periods with more turmoil in international events or to remember an incorrect picture about what really took place. For example, a very widespread opinion or belief prevailing in the postwar period seems to have been that the interwar period provided evidence of instability and destabilizing speculation under flexible exchange rates.

In this paper we have surveyed different periods and different countries with a flexible exchange rate regime and the various theories for the determinants of the exchange rate. We also developed a model to evaluate the different arguments. It was then found that in the long run the exchange rate was basically determined by changes in the relative money supply, relative productivity and some behavior relationships such as the savings function. The theory was further developed into the monetary impulse theory which says that the variability of the money supplies in different countries will be larger and more frequent than changes in the behavioral relationships and will therefore dominate the development of the exchange rate.

Empirical evidence was then presented for most of the historical episodes of flexible exchange rates and it was found that in almost all cases the data seem to be in conformity with the monetary impulse theory.

Furthermore, our own data and the opinion of most other economists writing about these periods, with the exception of Nurkse (1944), seem to agree about the conclusion that there is very little evidence of inherent instability and destabilizing speculation, except for Germany under hyperinflation and possibly Russia in the 19th century and France in the 1920's. In the latter two cases available information indicates that a lack of control of the money supply was probably the main reason behind this. But as Yeager (1958) expressed it: "Situations are nevertheless conceivable in which an exchange-rate movement could govern a country's general price level with the support of passively accommodating changes in the money supply. Such situations, if observed, would (aside from the matter of direction of causation) support, rather than refute the purchasing-power-parity relation between relative price levels and exchange rates and would further suggest that if the money supply *had* been autonomously controlled, the exchange rate could *not* have dominated the price level." This may lead us to formulate the following conclusion. Whenever the money supply is handled in an *unpredictable* way there is a risk that flexible exchange rates will imply considerable instability. Or, if we make a comparison with fixed exchange rates: *Flexible exchange rates require predictable money supply changes to work smoothly. Fixed exchange rates require predictable and consistent money supply changes among countries.*[1]

"Like other great generalizations in physics, the law of universal gravitation cannot be proved but is supported by a large and increasing body of evidence."[2] We may paraphrase this and conclude that like other generalizations in economics, the monetary impulse theory cannot be proved but is supported by a large and increasing body of evidence.[3]

References

Aliber, R.: Speculation in the foreign exchanges: The European experience, 1919–1926. *Yale Economic Essays*, 1962.

Angell, J.: *The theory of international prices*. Harvard University Press, 1926.

Balassa, B.: The purchasing-power parity doctrine: A reappraisal. *Journal of Political Economy*, December 1964.

Basevi, G.: A model for the analysis of official intervention in the foreign exchange markets. In A. Swoboda and M. Conolly (eds.), *International Economics: The Geneva Lectures*, London, 1972.

Black, S.: International money markets and flexible exchange rates. *Princeton Studies in International Finance*, No. 32, 1973.

Branson, W.: Stocks and flows in international monetary analysis. *International Aspects of Stabilization Policies*, Federal Reserve Bank of Boston, Conference Series No. 12, 1974.

Bresciano-Turroni, C.: *The economics of inflation*. London, 1937.

Brunner, K. & Meltzer, A.: The central bankers' paradigm: Some prospectives from the 19th century. January 1970 (mimeographed).

Brunner, K.: The 'monetarist revolution' in monetary theory. *Weltwirtschaftliches Archiv*, No. 1, 1970.

Brunner, K.: A Fisherian framework for the analysis of international monetary problems in *Inflation in the World Economy* (eds. Parkin & Zis), Manchester, 1976.

Cassel, G.: The depreciation of the German mark. *Economic Journal*, December 1919.

Cassel, G.: *Money and foreign exchange after 1914*. London, 1922.

Claassen, E. & Salin, P. (eds.): *Stabilization policies in interdependent economies*. Amsterdam, 1972.

Dornbusch, R.: Flexible exchange rates, capital mobility and macroeconomic equilibrium. Forthcoming in *Recent issues in international monetary economics* (ed. E. M. Claassen and P. Salin). 1976.

Eagly, R. V.: The Swedish and English bullionist controversies. From *Events*,

[1] Cf. Friedman (1953), Giersch (1973) and Johnson (1969).
[2] McCormick (1969), p. 125.
[3] It is worthwhile pointing out that this line of thought is in accordance with the early Swedish view as represented by Wicksell (1917–18) and Ohlin (1929), but not with the later Stockholm School where money was put more and more in the background.

ideology, and economic theory. Detroit, Michigan, 1968.

Eagly, R. V.: *The Swedish bullionist controversy*. Philadelphia, 1971.

Einzig, P.: *The theory of forward exchange*. London, 1937.

Einzig, P.: *A dynamic theory of forward exchange*. New York, 1968.

Einzig, P.: *The history of foreign exchange*. Macmillan, 1970.

Frenkel, J.: Adjustment mechanisms and the monetary approach to the balance of payments: A doctrinal perspective in *Recent Issues in International Monetary Economics* (ed. E. M. Claassen and P. Salin). 1976.

Frenkel, J. & Levich, R.: Covered interest arbitrage: Unexploited profits? *Journal of Political Economy*, April 1975.

Frenkel, J. & Rodriguez, C.: Portfolio equilibrium and the balance of payments: A monetary approach. *American Economic Review*, September 1975.

Friedman, M.: The case for flexible exchange rates, In *Essays in Positive Economics*. Chicago, 1953.

Giersch, H.: Some neglected aspects of inflation in the world economy. *Public Finance*, No. 2, 1973.

Goschen, G.: *The theory of the foreign exchanges*. London, 1863.

Grice-Hutchinson, M.: *The school of Salamanca*. London, 1952.

Grubel, H.: *Forward exchange, speculation, and the international flow of capital*. Stanford, California, 1966.

Halm, G.: Toward limited exchange-rate flexibility. *Essays in International Finance*, March, Princeton, 1969.

Hansen, B.: Interest policy and exchange policy. *Skandinaviska Banken Quarterly Review*, October 1958 and January 1959.

Hawtrey, R. G.: *The art of central banking*. London, 1933.

Hawtrey, R. G.: *A century of bank rate*. London, 1938.

Hicks, J.: *Critical essays in monetary economics*, London, 1967.

Hirshleifer, J.: *Investment, interest and capital*. Prentice Hall, 1970.

Hollander, J.: The development of the theory of money from Adam Smith to Ricardo. *Quarterly Journal of Economics*, 1910–11.

Holmes, J.: The existence of capital flows, fixed and flexible exchange rates and full employment. *Canadian Journal of Economics*, May 1972.

Iversen, C.: *Aspects of the theory of international capital movements*. Copenhagen, 1935.

Jasay, A.: Making currency reserves 'go round'. *Journal of Political Economy*, 1958.

Johnson, H.: The case for flexible exchange rates, 1969. *Federal Reserve Bank of St. Louis Review*, June 1969.

Johnson, H.: *Major issues in monetary economies*. Oxford Economic Papers, 1974.

Jonung, L.: Money and prices in Sweden 1732–1972 in *Inflation in the World Economy* (eds. Parkin & Zis', Manchester, 1976.

Jörberg, L.: *A history of prices in Sweden 1732–1914*, Vol. I and II. Lund, 1972.

Kemp, M.: Towards a reformulation of the short-run theory of foreign exchange. From *International economics and development: essays in honor of Raul Prebisch*. New York, 1972.

Kenen, P.: Trade, speculation, and the forward exchange rate. In *Trade, growth and the balance of payments*. North Holland, 1965.

Kindleberger, C. P.: *International short-term capital movements*. New York, 1937.

Keynes, J. M.: *A tract on monetary reform*. London, 1923.

Keynes, J. M.: The German transfer problem. *Economic Journal*, March 1929.

Keynes, J. M.: *A treatise on money*. I. Macmillan, 1930.

Lanyi, A.: The case for floating exchange rates reconsidered. *Essays in International Finance*, February, Princeton, 1969.

McCormick, W.: *Fundamentals of university physics*. Macmillan, 1969.

Metzler, L.: The process of international adjustment under conditions of full employment: A Keynesian view. In

Caves and Johnson (eds.), *Readings in International Economics*. 1968.

Myhrman, J.: A macroeconomic model with asset equilibrium for an open economy. Seminar Paper No. 28, Institute for International Economic Studies, University of Stockholm, 1973.

Myhrman, J.: Balance of payments adjustment and portfolio theory: a survey in *Recent Issues in International Monetary Economics* (ed. E. M. Claassen and P. Salin). 1976.

Myhrman, J.: Monetary and fiscal policy and stock-flow equilibrium in an open economy. 1975 (mimeographed).

Nurkse, R.: International Currency Experience. League of Nations, 1944.

Ohlin, B.: The reparation problem: A discussion. *Economic Journal*, June 1929.

Poole, W.: Speculative prices as random walks: an analysis of ten time series of flexible exchange rates. *Southern Economic Journal*, April 1967*a*.

Poole, W.: The stability of the Canadian flexible exchange rate, 1950–1962. *Canadian Journal of Economics*, 1967*b*.

Popper, K. R.: A pluralist approach to the philosophy of history. In *Roads to Freedom* (ed. Erich Streissler). London, 1969.

Ricardo, D.: *Economic essays by David Ricardo*. London, 1926.

Ricardo, D.: *Minor papers on the currency question 1809–1823* (ed. Jacob Hollander). Baltimore, 1932.

Samuelson, P.: An exact Hume–Ricardo–Marshall model of international trade. *Journal of International Economics*, No. 1, 1971.

Sohmen, E.: *Flexible exchange rates*. Chicago, 1969.

Spraos, J.: *The theory of forward exchange and recent practice*. Manchester School, 1953.

Spraos, J.: Speculation, arbitrage and sterling. *Economic Journal*, March 1959.

Stein, J.: The nature and efficiency of the foreign exchange market. *Essays in International Finance*, Princeton, October, 1962.

Taussig, F. W.: International trade under depreciated paper. A contribution to theory. *Quarterly Journal of Economics 31*, 1916–17.

Taussig, F. W.: *International trade*. Macmillan, 1927.

Thornton, H.: *An enquiry into the nature and effects of the paper credit of Great Britain*. New York, 1802.

Tsiang, S. C.: A theory of foreign exchange speculation under a floating exchange system. *Journal of Political Economy*, 1958.

Tsiang, S. C.: Fluctuating exchange rates in countries with relatively stable economies. *IMF Staff Papers*, April 1959.

Tsiang, S. C.: The theory of forward exchange and effects of government intervention on the forward exchange market. *IMF Staff Papers 7*, 1959–60.

Wicksell, K.: International freights and prices. *Quarterly Journal of Economics 32*, 1917–18.

Wicksell, K.: *Selected papers on economic theory*. Harvard University Press, 1958.

Viner, J.: *Studies in the theory of international trade*. New York and London, 937.

Yeager, L.: A rehabilitation of purchasing-power parity. *Journal of Political Economy*, 1958.

Yeager, L.: *International monetary relations*. New York, 1966.

Yeager, L.: Fluctuating exchange rates in the nineteenth century: the experiences of Austria and Russia. In R. A. Mundell and A. Swoboda (eds.), *Monetary problems of the international Economy*. Chicago, 1969.

Yntema, T. O.: *A mathematical reformulation of the general theory of international trade*. University of Chicago Press, 1932.

COMMENT ON J. MYHRMAN, "EXPERIENCES OF FLEXIBLE EXCHANGE RATES IN EARLIER PERIODS: THEORIES, EVIDENCE AND A NEW VIEW"

David Laidler

University of Western Ontario, London, Canada

Johan Myhrman's excellent paper leaves me with little to say. I learned a great deal from reading it and, moreover, enjoyed myself in the process. Though ostensibly mainly a survey paper, the way in which the history of economic ideas, contemporary economic theory, and historical evidence are brought together under the discipline of an explicitly stated methodology ensures that this essay significantly advances the branch of knowledge with which it deals.

The paper's first theme is that contemporary debates about domestic inflation and the behavior of exchange rates are in large measure repetitions of earlier disputes. As Myhrman so clearly shows, the twin questions, are domestic price level fluctuations and exchange rate fluctuations the result of instability in the behavior of the money supply or of instability on the real side of the economy—including the structure that underlies the demand side of the money market—have been with us for at least two hundred years. The paper's second theme involves sorting out the extent to which these issues involve, on the one hand, disagreement about the appropriate theoretical framework with which to model particular economic problems and, on the other hand, disagreement about the magnitudes and stability of particular parameters within a commonly accepted theoretical structure.

As Myhrman shows, these two issues are easy to confuse. It appears at first sight that those who put the emphasis on the role of real shocks to the system find support for their views in short run models that concentrate on the analysis of impact effects while those who stress the role of money base their propositions on steady state properties of long run models. The "Ricardian vice" is to ignore the short run, but there is an equally pernicious "Keynesian vice" of concentrating exclusively on the short run. Myhrman makes a compelling case that the post war literature on flexible exchange rates has all too often fallen into this latter trap. However, he is careful to note that the long run results that appear to give a predominant role to money in determining exchange rates do so only because of the assumption that the economy has a stable structure. Thus, even when derived from long run models, propositions about the determination of exchange rates that give a predominant role to the quantity of money, are essentially empirical in nature. Hence the need for the empirical evidence presented in the third substantive section of the paper.

I would raise only one warning about Myhrman's paper. The evidence he presents is certainly consistent with what he calls the "monetary impulse hypothesis". However, it would be open to a "real impulse" theorist to argue that (*a*) correlation is not evidence of causation, and that (*b*) the monetary changes that Myhrman observes are the consequence and not the cause of exchange rate and price level variations. In short he could apply a line of argument well known in monetary economics to a new problem. There is no quick answer to this attack. In my view the questions it raises can only be settled by detailed historical and institutional studies of particular episodes, studies that pay particular attention to the factors that actually were determining the behavior of the money supply at specific times and places. The model for such work is, of course, Friedman and Schwartz's monumental *Monetary History of the United States*[1] and I am not suggesting for a moment that Myhrman could possibly have extended his paper to encompass work of this nature on all the episodes he cites. However, it is important for the reader to remember that a thorough testing of the "monetary impulse" hypothesis does require that such work be done and its results integrated with those of the type presented here.

Finally, let me comment on one strand in the literature on flexible rates and monetary policy upon which Myhrman has not explicitly commented, namely that which is directly concerned with the constraints that exchange rate schemes of various sorts do or do not put upon the conduct of domestic monetary policy. The conscious use of monetary policy to achieve domestic ends has a history that goes back at least as far as John Law, and it has been recognized, at least since the Attwoods, that the maintenance of fixed exchange rates can inhibit its use to certain ends. The theme that the adoption of flexible exchange rates removes a constraint upon monetary policy is a long standing one in the literature, and has received its most compelling statement in recent years in Friedman's *Programme for Monetary Stability*.[2] There are venerable fallacies to be found in this stream of the literature, though *not* in Friedman's work, I hasten to add. Those who have advocated flexible exchange rates as a means to making monetary policy easier to deploy have all too often confused its undoubted capacity to generate short-term expansion and inflation with an ability that it does not possess, namely the power to promote long-term

[1] Milton Friedman and Anna Schwartz, *A Monetary History of the United States 1867–1960*, Princeton, N. J., Princeton University Press (or the NBER), 1963.
[2] Milton Friedman, *A Programm for Monetary Stability*, New York, Fordham University Press, 1959.

growth.[1] John Law made just this error and produced the Mississippi Bubble; less excusably the Heath government in Britain made the identical mistake in 1972, with results that are now apparent for all to see. Here is another theme then of vital contemporary interest and with considerable historical continuity: the interaction of views on the appropriate institutional setting for exchange rate determination and on what are the proper aims of domestic monetary policy. Of course Myhrman could not deal with these matters in the present paper, there would have been too much material. However, having enjoyed this paper so much, let me end by encouraging him to start work on a companion piece that does deal with these issues.

---

1 Friedman's presidential address to the American Economics Association was, of course, devoted to the issue of what goals monetary policy could and could not be expected to achieve. Cf. Milton Friedman, "The Role of Monetary Policy", *American Economic Review* 58 (1), March 1968, pp. 1–17.

A MONETARY APPROACH TO THE EXCHANGE RATE: DOCTRINAL ASPECTS AND EMPIRICAL EVIDENCE

*Jacob A. Frenkel**

University of Chicago, Chicago, Illinois, USA and Tel-Aviv University, Tel-Aviv, Israel

> "What, then, has determined and will determine the value of the Franc? First, the quantity, present and prospective, of the francs in circulation. Second, the amount of purchasing power which it suits the public to hold in that shape."
>
> *Keynes* (Introduction to French edition, 1924, xviii).

Abstract

This paper deals with the determinants of the exchange rate and develops a monetary view (or more generally, an asset view) of exchange rate determination. The first part traces some of the doctrinal origins of approaches to the analysis of equilibrium exchange rates. The second part examines some of the empirical hypotheses of the monetary approach as well as some features of the efficiency of the foreign exchange markets. Special emphasis is given to the role of expectations in exchange rate determination and a direct observable measure of expectations is proposed. The direct measure of expectations builds on the information that is contained in data from the forward market for foreign exchange. The empirical results are shown to be consistent with the hypotheses of the monetary approach.

Introduction

This paper deals with the determinants of the exchange rate. The approach that is taken reflects the current revival of a monetary view, or more generally an asset view, of the role of the rates of exchange.[1] Basically, the monetary approach to the exchange rate may be viewed as a dual relationship to the monetary approach to the balance of payments. These approaches emphasize the role of money and other assets in determining the balance of payments

* I am indebted to John Bilson for comments, suggestions and efficient research assistance. In revising the paper I have benefited from helpful assistance from R. W. Banz and useful suggestions by W. H. Branson, K. W. Clements, R. Dornbusch, S. Fischer, R. J. Gordon, H. G. Johnson, M. Parkin, D. Patinkin and L. G. Telser. Financial support was provided by a grant from the Ford Foundation.

[1] This view has been forcefully emphasized by Dornbusch (1975, 1976, 1976*a*). See, too, Frenkel and Rodriguez (1975), Johnson (1975), Kouri (1975) and Mussa (1974, 1976). For an early incorporation of monetary considerations in exchange rate determination see Mundell (1968, 1971).

when the exchange rate is pegged, and in determining the exchange rate when it is flexible.

Being a relative price of two assets (moneys), the equilibrium exchange rate is attained when the existing *stocks* of the two moneys are willingly held. It is reasonable, therefore, that a theory of the determination of the relative price of two moneys could be stated conveniently in terms of the supply of and the demand for these moneys.

The renewed emphasis on the role of the supply of and the demand for moneys and assets as stocks in contrast with the circular flow approach to the determination of the exchange rate (that gained popularity with the domination of the Keynesian revolution), revives the basic discussion of the Bullionist controversy culiminated in the early 1800's and led to the developments of the "Balance of Trade Theory" and the "Inflation Theory" of the determination of the exchange rate (Ricardo, 1811; Haberler, 1936; Viner, 1937). Reminiscence of that controversy can be traced to present times in the various discussions and interpretation of the purchasing power parity doctrine. It may be argued that the long experience with the gold standard and with the gold exchange standard may have led to the retrogression of the theory of flexible exchange rates (Wicksell, 1911, p. 231; Gregory, 1922, p. 80).[1]

The first part of the paper traces some of the doctrinal origins of approaches to exchange rate determination. Its purpose is to provide some perspective into the evolution of the theory.[2] The main emphasis of the paper lies in its second part where we examine some of the empirical hypotheses of the monetary approach. In that part we analyze the role of expectations, we describe a direct measure thereof, examine the efficiency of the foreign exchange market during the German hyperinflation, and provide some evidence which supports the asset view of exchange rate determination.

I. A Doctrinal Perspective to Exchange Rate Determination

I.1. *The Purchasing Power Parity Doctrine: The Nature of Equilibrium*

The purchasing power parity doctrine (in its absolute version) states that the equilibrium exchange rate equals the ratio of domestic to foreign prices. The relative version of the theory relates changes in the exchange rate to changes in price ratios. Many of the controversies around that doctrine relate to the

[1] It is of interest to note that the introduction of the "liquidity preference" schedule which emphasizes the role of asset markets and characterizes much of the Keynesian revolution in macroeconomic analysis of the closed economy, did not carry over to the popular versions of the Keynesian theories of the balance of payments. The Keynesian analysis of the balance of payments emphasizes the circular flow of income, the foreign trade multiplier and, in its popular version, ignores to a large extent the role of money and other assets. For a notable exception, see Metzler (1968).

[2] An analogous doctrinal perspective of the evolution of the monetary approach to the balance of payments under fixed exchange rate is contained in Frenkel & Johnson (1976) and Frenkel (1976). For a further analysis see Myhrman (1976).

question of choice of proper price indices to be used in computing the parity.[1] One extreme view argues that the proper price index should pertain to traded goods only (Angell, 1922; Bunting, 1939; Heckscher, 1930; Pigou, 1930; Viner, 1937), while according to the other extreme view the proper price index should cover the broadest range of commodities (Hawtrey, 1919, p. 109; Cassel, 1928, p. 33).[2]

Those who advocate the use of traded goods index emphasize the role of commodity arbitrage while those who advocate the broader price index emphasize the role of asset equilibrium as determining the rate of exchange. If the role of the exchange rate is to clear the money market by equating the purchasing power of the various currencies, then the relevant measure should be a consumer price index.[3] Proponents of this view reject the use of the wholesale price index since it gives an excessive weight to traded goods (Ellis, 1936, pp. 28–9; Haberler, 1945, p. 312 and 1961, pp. 49–50).

The two views differ fundamentally in the interpretation of the equilibrium exchange rate. The commodity arbitrage view goes even further in arguing that no aggregate price index is relevant and only individual commodity prices should be analyzed:

"Foreign exchange rates have nothing to do with the wholesale commodity price *level* as such but only with individual prices" (Ohlin, 1967, p. 290).

The equilibrium exchange rate reflects spatial arbitrage from which non-traded goods are excluded:

"Patently, I cannot import cheap Italian haircut nor can Niagra-Falls honeymoons be exported" (Samuelson, 1964, p. 148).

The asset view takes it for granted that the operation of commodity arbitrage equates the prices of traded goods and emphasizes that if the doctrine only applies to traded goods, then:

"the purchasing power parity doctrine presents but little interest ... (it) simply states that prices in terms of any given currency, of same commodity must be the same everywhere ... Whereas its essence is the statement that exchange rates are the index of the monetary conditions in the countries concerned" (Bresciani-Turroni, 1934, p. 121).

In fact since the exchange rate links the purchasing power values of moneys in terms of the broad definition of the price level, one may imagine a situation in which all traded goods possess the same price, when expressed in common currency, but the exchange rate is in disequilibrium:

---

[1] See Viner (1937) and Johnson (1968).

[2] It might be of interest to compare these discussions with those concerning the range of transactions and prices that is relevant for the quantity theory of money. The latter ranged from suggestions to include transactions in assets and prices of securities to suggestions to include only what is defined as national product.

[3] On the relevance of the consumer price index as a measure of the purchasing power of money see Marshall (1923, p. 30) and Keynes (1930, p. 54).

"The equilibrium to which the foreign exchange market tends is an equilibrium of the *price level* ... If the currency units of two countries be considered in terms of foreign trade products only, then the rate of exchange between the two currency units will approximate closely to the ratio of their purchasing power so calculated... But that is not the condition of equilibrium ... It is to the price level in general, of home trade products as well as foreign trade products, that the rate of exchange must adjust" (Hawtrey, 1919, p. 109).

To completely divorce the determination of exchange rates from considerations of commodity arbitrage, one could even go further in developing an argument for using price indices of non-traded goods only. Such an argument was advanced by Graham:

"Strictly interpreted then, prices of non-internationally traded commodities only should be included in the indices on which purchasing power pars are based" (Graham, 1930, p. 126, n. 44).

Further pursuit of that idea leads to the use of the price of the least traded commodity—the wage rate parity—advocated by Rueff in 1926 (reproduced in Rueff, 1967), and similar views can also be found in Hawtrey (1919, p. 123) and Cassel (1930, p. 144). The wage rate approach was extended to the concept of production cost parities advocated by Hansen (1944, p. 182), Houthakker (1962, pp. 293–4) and Friedman and Schwartz (1963, p. 62).

Whatever the price index used for computations of parities, the question remains of distinguishing between an equilibrium relationship and a causal relationship. Most authors recognized that prices and exchange rates are determined simultaneously. A minority, however, argued that there exists a causal relationship between prices and exchange rates. While Cassel (1921) claimed that the causality goes from prices to the exchange rate, Einzig (1935, p. 40) claimed the opposite.

I.2. *The Asset View*

Since in general both prices and exchange rates are endogenous variables that are determined simultaneously, discussions of the link between them provide little insights into the analysis of the determinants of the exchange rate. The original formulation of Cassel (1916) was stated in terms of the relative quantities of money. The formulation was then translated into a relationship between prices via an application of the quantity theory of money. Conceptually, however, it seems clear that the role of prices in Cassel's computation of the equilibrium exchange rate serves only to proxy the underlying monetary conditions. The determination of exchange rates does not seem to rely, directly or indirectly, on the operation of arbitrage in goods.

In retrospect it seems that the translation of the theory from a relationship between moneys into a relationship between prices—via the quantity theory of money—was counterproductive and led to a lack of emphasis on the fundamental determinants of the exchange rate and to an unnecessary amount of ambiguity and confusion. It is noteworthy that the originators of the theory (although not in its present name)—Wheatley (1803) and Ricardo —stressed the monetary nature of the issues involved as well as the irrelevance of commodity arbitrage as determining the equilibrium rate:

"In speaking of the exchange and the comparative value of money in different countries, we must not in the least refer to the value of money estimated in commodities in either country. The exchange is never ascertained by estimating the comparative value of money in corn, cloth or any commodity whatever but by estimating the value of the currency of one country, in the currency of another" (Ricardo, 1821, p. 128).

When considering moneys for the purpose of determining the exchange rate, the relevant concept is that of a stock rather than of a flow. These concepts were an integral part of monetary theory:

"We may consequently think of the supply (of currency) as we think of the supply of houses, as being a stock rather than the annual produce ... (and) of the demand for currency as being furnished by the ability and willingness of persons to *hold* currency" (Cannan, 1921, pp. 453–4).

Indeed, as Dornbusch (1976) puts it "The exchange rate is determined in the stock market". It is this conception of money as a stock that resulted in Keynes' perceptive statement that was quoted at the start of this paper. The asset view of exchange rate determination became the traditional view as witnessed by Joan Robinson:

"The traditional view that the exchange value of a country's currency in any given situation depends upon the amount of it in existence is thus seen to be justified, provided that sufficient allowance is made for changes in the internal demand for money" (Robinson, 1935–6, p. 229).

I.3. *The Role of Expectations*

A natural implication of the asset approach is the special role expectations play in determining the exchange rate. The demand for domestic and foreign moneys depends, like the demand for any other asset, on the expected rates of return. Thus it may be expected that current values of exchange rates incorporate the expectations of market participants concerning the future course of events. This notion can account therefore, for large changes in prices resulting from large changes in expectations. This was indeed the logical argument used by Mill (1864, p. 178) in accounting for the sharp change in the price of bills occuring with the news of Bonaparte's landing from Elba.

The specific role of expectations in determining the exchange rate has been also emphasized by Marshall (1888), Wicksell (1919, p. 236), Gregory (1922, p. 90) and Einzig (1935, p. 120). If the foreign exchange market is efficient —as many other asset markets appear to be—then current prices should reflect all available information. Therefore, an expectation of monetary expansion should be reflected in the current spot exchange rate since asset holders will incorporate the anticipated reduction in the real rate of return on the currency in their pricing of the existing stocks. This notion was clearly stated by Cassel:

"A continued inflation ... will naturally be discounted to a certain degree in the present rates of exchange" (Cassel, 1928, pp. 25–26).

Similarly:

"The international valuation of the currency will, then generally show a tendency to anticipate events, so to speak, and becomes more an expression of the internal value the currency is expected to possess in a few months, or pherhaps in a year's time" (Cassel, 1930, pp. 149–50).

The empirical analysis in Section II will be concerned with details of the role of expectations in determining the exchange rate.

Prior to concluding this section it should be emphasized that its purpose has *not* been to argue that "It's all in Marshall". On the contrary, a rereading of the writings of some of the eminent classical and neo-classical economists reveals the great need for supplementing their general conceptions with a detailed analysis of the transmission mechanisms. On the other hand, however, it is important to gain perspective and to recognize that some of the general conceptions and framework of analysis have already been developed by earlier generations of economists. It is appropriate, therefore, to view the recent revival of the monetary approach as a natural evolution rather than a revolutionary change in views.[1]

II. Empirical Evidence: A Reexamination of the German Hyperinflation

The foregoing discussion contained a doctrinal perspective to the assets approach to the determination of exchange rates. In this section we develop further some of the theoretical aspects and reexamine the determinants of the exchange rate during the German hyperinflation in light of these considerations. That episode is of special interest since it provides an opportunity to examine the assets approach to a situation in which it is clear that the source of disturbances is monetary. Furthermore, during the hyperinflation domestic

1 There are, of course, fundamental difficulties in defining the nature of the various junctions of intellectual understanding. As noted by H. G. Johnson: "the concept of revolution is difficult to transfer from its origins in politics to other fields of social science. Its essence is unexpected speed of change, and this requires a judgement of speed in the context of a longer perspective of historical change the choice of which is likely to be debatable in the extreme" (Johnson, 1971, p. 1).

A casual reading of many of the popular textbook versions of balance of payments theories suggests, however, that the conditions, outlined by Johnson, for a rapid propagation of a new theory may be satisfied: "the most helpful circumstances for a rapid propagation of a new and revolutionary theory is the existence of an established orthodoxy which is clearly inconsistent with the most salient facts of reality, and yet is sufficiently confident of its intellectual power to attempt to explain those facts, and in its efforts to do so exposes its incompetence in a ludicrous fashion" (Johnson, 1971, p. 3).

(German) influences on the exchange rate dominate those occurring in the rest of the world. It is therefore possible to examine the relationship between monetary variables and the exchange rate in isolation from other factors, at home and abroad, which in a more normal period would have to be considered.

II.1. *Money and the Exchange Rate*

Prior to a more elaborate analysis it may be instructive to examine the association between the German money stock and its relative price in terms of foreign exchange (i.e., the exchange rate). This association is shown in Figure 1 which describes the time series of the monthly logarithms of the German money supply and the mark/dollar exchange rate for the period February 1920–November 1923 (data sources are outlined in the Appendix). As evident from Fig. 1 the two time series are closely related. A high supply of German marks is associated with its depreciation in terms of foreign exchange.

This relationship can be examined further by estimating a polynomial distributed lag of the effects of the money supply on the exchange rate. The estimates reported in Table 1 pertain to (i) the effects of current and lagged values of the money supply on the current *level* of the exchange rate and (ii) the effects of current and lagged values of the *rates of change* of the money supply on the current *rate of* change of the exchange rate. The estimates of the distributed lags for the equation of the rates of change reveal that the current rate of change of the exchange rate depends only on the current rate of

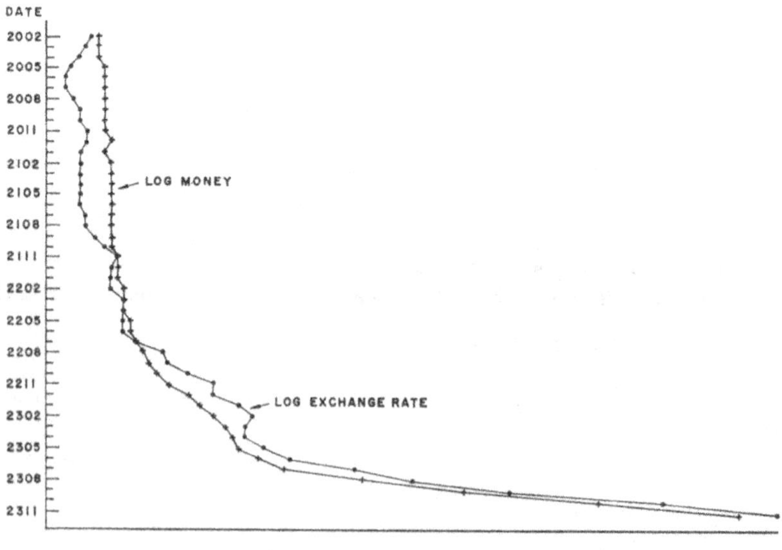

Fig. 1.

Table 1. *Money and the exchange rate: polynomial distributed lag model. Monthly data: February 1920 – November 1923*

	Lag structure						
	0	1	2	3	4	5	Sum
	1.032 (0.140)	−0.019 (0.099)	−0.248 (0.127)	−0.009 (0.082)	0.348 (0.107)	0.468 (0.125)	1.572 (0.177)
Dependent variable: Log Exch. $R^2 = 0.996$, s.e. $= 0.379$, D.W. $= 2.05$, $\varrho = 0.775$, $\sigma_u = 0.617$							
	0.975 (0.147)	0.114 (0.121)	−0.186 (0.130)	−0.136 (0.101)	0.052 (0.189)	0.168 (0.203)	0.987 (0.357)
Dependent variable: Δ Log Exch. $R^2 = 0.895$, s.e. $= 0.390$, D.W. $= 2.27$							

Note: In the polynomial distributed lag equation, a fourth degree polynomial with the sixth lag coefficient constrained to zero, was employed. The first equation relates the logarithm of the exchange rate to current and past levels of the logarithm of the money supply. The second equation relates the percentage rate of change of the exchange rate to current and past percentage rates of change of the money supply. ϱ is the final value of the first order autocorrelation coefficient. An iterative Cochran–Orcutt transformation was employed when first order serial correlation in the residuals of the regression equations was evident. σ_u given in the Table is the standard error of the regression equation when the autoregressive component of the error is included. All of the other statistics are for the transformed model. Standard errors are in parentheses below the coefficients.

monetary expansion. Furthermore, an acceleration of the rate of monetary expansion induces an equi-proportionate contemporaneous acceleration in the rate at which the currency depreciates. None of the lagged variables are statistically significant. The distributed lags on the level of the exchange rate also show a unit elastic contemporaneous effect. In this case, however, some lagged values exert a significant effect on the rate of exchange. The sum of the coefficients is 1.57, i.e., during that period the elasticity of the exchange rate with respect to the money stock exceeded unity.[1] The magnification effect of money on the exchange rate is consistent with the prediction of Dornbusch's model (1976*a*) as well as with the prediction of the rational expectations models of Black (1973) and Bilson (1975). If the money supply process is generated by an autoregressive scheme, expectations will multiply the influence of current changes in the money stock since these changes are transmitted into the future through the autoregressive scheme.[2]

[1] The first equation in Table 1 should be interpreted with some caution since the high first order autocorrelation coefficient may reflect a misspecification. Its purpose is to provide a preliminary description of the relationship between money and the exchange rate. A more detailed analysis follows.

[2] Previous empirical work emphasizing monetary considerations in the analysis of the German exchange rate during the hyperinflation include Graham (1930), Bresciani-Turroni (1937) and more recently, Tsiang (1959–60) and Hodgson (1972).

II.2. *The Building Blocks of the Monetary Approach*

The foregoing analysis indicated the close association between monetary developments and the exchange rate. In this section we outline the major building blocks of the monetary approach to the exchange rate. Since in what follows we apply the framework to examine data pertaining to the German hyperinflation, the following presentation is simplified considerably by ignoring developments in the rest of the world.

Consider first the demand for real cash balances m^d as a function of the expected rate of inflation π^*:

$$m^d \equiv g(\pi^*); \; \partial g/\partial\pi^* < 0 \tag{1}$$

The formulation in eq. (1) reflects the assumption that during the hyperinflation, changes in the demand for money were dominated by changes in inflationary expectations so that the effects of changes in output and the real rate of interest may be ignored.

The supply of real balances is M/P where M denotes the nominal money stock and P "the" price level (we bypass for the moment the question of what is the appropriate price level). Equating the supply of money with the demand enables us to express the price level as a function of the nominal money stock and inflationary expectations:

$$P = M/g(\pi^*); \quad \partial P/\partial M > 0, \quad \partial P/\partial\pi^* > 0. \tag{2}$$

The elasticity of the price with respect to π^* should approximate the (absolute value of the) interest elasticity of the demand for money, and in the absence of money illusion the elasticity of the price with respect to the money stock should be unity.

The second building block of the theory links the domestic price level with the foreign price level P^* through the purchasing power parity condition:

$$P = SP^* \tag{3}$$

If the purchasing power parity condition holds we can substitute eq. (3) into (2) to get a relationship between the exchange rate, the money stock, inflationary expectations and the foreign price level. Since during the German hyperinflation it is justifiable to assume that P^* is practically fixed (as compared with P), we can normalize units and define P^* as unity. Thus the exchange rate can be written as

$$S = M/g(\pi^*); \quad \partial S/\partial M > 0; \quad \partial S/\partial\pi^* > 0. \tag{4}$$

It is noteworthy that the implication that $\partial S/\partial\pi^* > 0$ is in conflict with some of the theories of exchange rate determination. It should be possible, therefore, to discriminate among alternative theories by examining the empirical relationship between anticipated inflation and the exchange rate. A popular ana-

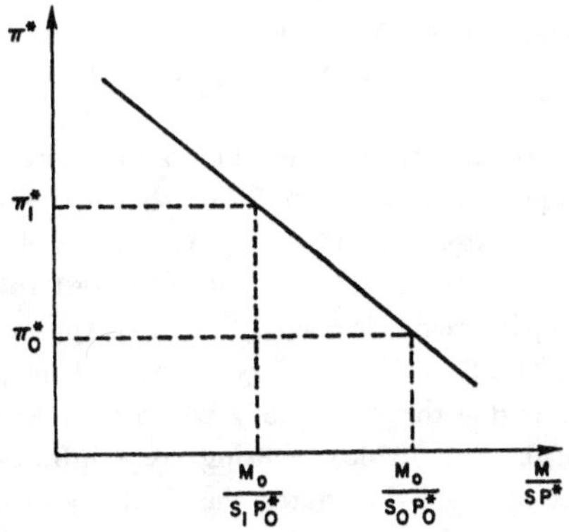

Fig. 2.

lysis of this relationship goes as follows: a higher anticipated inflation raises the nominal rate of interest which induces a surplus in the capital account by attracting foreign capital, and thereby induces a *lower* spot exchange rate (i.e., an appreciation of the domestic currency). A variant of this approach would argue that the higher rate of interest lowers spending, and thus induces a surplus in the balance of payments which leads to a lower spot exchange rate. A third variant would reach the same result by emphasizing the implications of the interest parity theory (which is discussed in the next Section). Accordingly, a higher rate of interest implies a higher forward permium on foreign exchange and if the rise in the forward exchange rate is insufficient to induce the required premium on foreign exchange, the spot exchange rate will have to fall (i.e., the domestic currency will have to appreciate). Whatever the route, the above analyses predict a *negative* relationship between the rate of interest and the spot exchange rate while equation (4) predicts a positive relationship.

The alternative theory presented here emphasizes the role of asset equilibrium in determining the exchange rate and its implications are illustrated in Fig. 2. A rise in anticipated inflation from π_0^* to π_1^* lowers the demand for real balances, and given the nominal money stock, asset equilibrium requires a higher price level. Since the domestic price level is tied to the foreign price via the purchasing power parity, and since the foreign price is assumed fixed, the higher price level can only be achieved through a *rise* in the spot exchange rate from S_0 to S_1 (i.e., a depreciation of the domestic currency).

The foregoing analysis did not specify the cause of the rise in the domestic rate of interest. It is necessary to emphasize that the exact analysis of the effects of a change in interest rates depends upon the source of the disturbance. The presumption, however, is that during the hyperinflation the source of disturbances was monetary. The higher interest rate may be thought of as resulting from a rise in the rate of monetary expansion which is immediately incorporated (via the Fisher effect) in inflationary expectations; to complete the experiment, it is possible to imagine (at least analytically) an acceleration in the monetary growth rate which does not instantaneously affect the monetary *stock*.

The result has an intuitive appeal in that easy money induces a depreciation of the currency. It emphasizes again the possible confusion that may arise from viewing the interest rate as an indicator of tight or easy monetary policy. The traditional expectation of a negative relationship between interest rates and the exhange rate may, however, be reconciled with the asset approach if it emphasizes the short run liquidity effect of monetary changes. Thus, in the short run, a higher interest rate is due to tight money which induces an appreciation of the currency (Dornbusch, 1976*a*). During hyperinflation, however, the expectations effect completely dominates the liquidity effect resulting therefore in a predicted *positive* relationship between the rate of interest and the price of foreign exchange.

The previous discussion emphasized the role of expectations about future events in determining the current value of the exchange rate. A major difficulty in incorporating the role of expectations in empirical work has been the lack of an observable variable measuring expectations. Thus, for example, in analyzing the demand for money during the hyperinflation, Cagan (1956) in his classic study constructed a time series of expected inflation using a specific transformation of the time series of the actual rates of inflation. The conceptual difficulty with such an approach stems from the fact that expectations are assumed to be based only on past experience and the choice of the specific transformation used to generate the series of expectations is to a large extent arbitrary. The third building block of the approach involves the choice of the measure of expectations that is appropriate for empirical implementation. In what follows we propose a direct measure of expectations which is then incorporated in the analysis of the determination of the exchange rate.

The fundamental relationship that is used in deriving the market measure of inflationary expectations relies on the interest parity theory. That theory maintains that in equilibrium the premium (or discount) on a forward contract for foreign exchange for a given maturity is (approximately) related to the interest rate differential according to:

$$\frac{F-S}{S}=i-i^{*} \tag{5}$$

where F and S are the forward and spot exchange rates (the domestic currency price of foreign exchange), respectively, i the domestic rate of interest and i^* the foreign rate of interest on comparable securities for the same maturity. Evidence available for various countries over various time periods suggest that this parity condition holds (Frenkel & Levich (1975*a*, 1975*b*); for an early analysis of the 1920's see Aliber (1962)). Although, due to lack of data, no comparable study has been done on the period of the German hyperinflation, it is assumed that the parity condition has been maintained. Furthermore, it is reasonable to assume that during the hyperinflation most of the variations in the difference between domestic and foreign anticipated rates of inflation were due to anticipated domestic (German) inflation. It follows, therefore, that the variations of the forward premium on foreign exchange $(F-S)/S$, may be viewed as a measure of the variations in the expected rate of inflation (as well as the expected rate of change of the exchange rate).

II.3. *The Efficiency of the Foreign Exchange Market*

Prior to incorporating the forward premium as a measure of expectations, it is pertinent to explore the efficiency of the foreign exchange market during the turbulent hyperinflation period. Evidence on the efficiency of that market will support the approach of using data from that market as the basis for inference on expectations.

If the foreign exchange market is efficient and if the exchange rate is determined in a similar fashion to other asset prices, we should expect the behavior in that market to display characteristics similar to those displayed in other stock markets. In particular, we should expect that current prices reflect all available information, and that the residuals from the estimated regression should be serially uncorrelated.

To examine the efficacy of the market we first regress the logarithm of the current spot exchange rate, $\log S_t$, on the logarithm of the one-month forward exchange rate prevailing at the previous month, $\log F_{t-1}$.

$$\log S_t = a + b \log F_{t-1} + u \tag{6}$$

The expectation is that the constant term does not differ significantly from zero, that the slope coefficient does not differ significantly from unity and that the error term is serially uncorrelated. Since data on the German Mark-Pound Sterling (DM/£) forward exchange rate are available only for the period February 1921 – August 1923, eq. (2) was estimated over those 31 months. The resulting ordinary-least-squares estimates are reported in eq. (6′) with standard errors in parentheses below the coefficients.

$$\log S_t = \underset{(0.24)}{-0.46} + \underset{(0.03)}{1.09} \log F_{t-1} \tag{6′}$$

$\bar{R}^2 = 0.98$, s.e. $= 0.45$; D.W. $= 1.90$

As can be seen, the constant term does not differ significantly from zero at the 95 percent confidence level (although it seems to be somewhat negative), the slope coefficient is somewhat above unity (at the 95 percent confidence level) and, most importantly, the Durbin-Watson statistics indicates that the residuals are not serially correlated. The fact that the slope coefficient is slightly

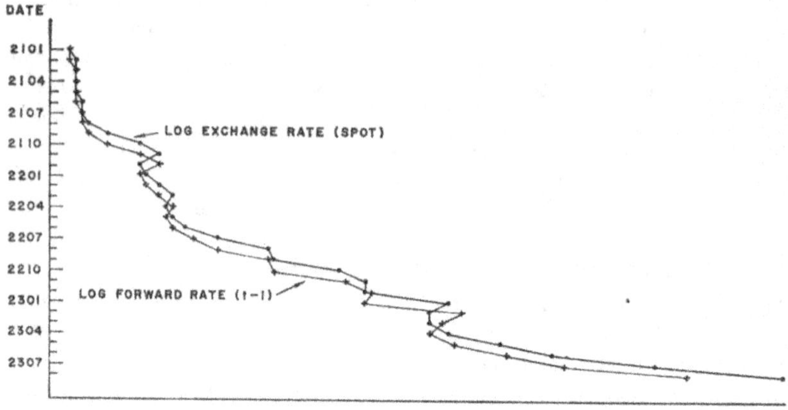

Fig. 3.

above unity may be explained in terms of transaction costs or in terms of the Keynesian concept of normal-backwardation (Keynes, 1930, vol. II, p. 143).[1]

Fig. 3 describes the monthly time series plot of the logarithms of the spot exchange rate and the forward rate prevailing in the previous month. The general pattern reveals that typically, when the spot exchange rate rises, the forward rate lies below it while when the spot exchange rate falls the forward rate exceeds it. This pattern is also suggested by the fact that the elasticity of the spot rate with respect to the previous month's forward rate is somewhat above unity.

To explore further the implications of the efficient market hypothesis we examine whether the forward exchange rate summarizes all relevant information. In an efficient market F_{t-1} summarizes all the information concerning the expected value of S_t that is available at period $t-1$. Specifically, one of the items of information available at $t-1$ is the stock of information available at $t-2$, and if the market is efficient, that information will be contained in F_{t-2}. If however F_{t-1} summarizes all available information including that contained in F_{t-2}, we should expect that adding F_{t-2} as an explanatory variable to the right-hand side of (6) will not affect the coefficient of determination and will have a coefficient that is not significantly different from zero. Eq. (6″) reports the results of that regression:

$$\log S_t = \underset{(0.26)}{-0.45} + \underset{(0.08)}{1.10} \log F_{t-1} - \underset{(0.08)}{0.006} \log F_{t-2} \qquad (6'')$$

$\bar{R}^2 = 0.98$, s.e. $= 0.46$; D.W. $= 1.91$

The results in (6″) support the efficient market hypothesis.

[1] The joint hypothesis that the constant term is zero *and* that the slope coefficient is unity is rejected at the 95 percent confidence level.

To examine further the stability of the regression coefficients during the various phases of the hyperinflation we divided the sample into two parts: "Moderate" hyperinflation and "severe" hyperinflation, where the latter characterized the last eight months of the sample period. A Chow test was performed on the estimates of equations (6′) and (6″) to test the equality of each and every coefficient of the two sub-period's regressions. This procedure showed that the hypothesis that the regression coefficients do not differ between the two sub-periods cannot be rejected at the 95 percent level.

The results reported in this section provide support to the notion that during the hyperinflation expectations may have behaved "rationally" in the Muth sense. In fact, it should not be surprising that even during the turbulent period of the hyperinflation the efficient market hypothesis cannot be rejected. It stands to reason that the larger variability of exchange rates increases the rate of return from and the amount of resources invested in accurate forecasting.[1]

II.4. *Prices, Money and Expectations*

In this section we examine the empirical content of the first building block of the monetary approach to the exchange rate by using the market measure of inflationary expectations in estimating eq. (2). Log-linearizing eq. (2) and adding an error term yields:

$$\log P = a + b_1 \log M + b_2 \log \pi^* + u \tag{2'}$$

One of the difficulties of using the double-log form is that during some months, early in the sample period, the forward premium on foreign exchange was negative (reaching −0.8 percent per month in early 1921) reflecting the initial expectation that the price rise has been temporary, that the process will reverse itself and prices will return to their previous levels. Since the logarithm of a negative quantity is not defined, the independent variable was transformed from π^* to $(k+\pi^*)$ which henceforth is referred to as π. Thus, the estimated equation was:

$$\log P = a' + b_1' \log M + b_2' \log \pi + u. \tag{2''}$$

A maximum likelihood estimation of the coefficients in (2″) along with the value of k resulted in a value of k ranging between 0.9 and 1.1 percent per month.[2] For ease of exposition, in what follows we set the value of k at 1 percent per month, and thus the coefficient $b_2 = b_2'\pi^*/(1+\pi^*)$.

[1] For an application of the "rational" expectations hypothesis to the German hyperinflation see Sargent & Wallace (1973).

[2] While the anticipated difference between the domestic and the foreign rates of inflation that is proxied by the forward premium π^* may be negative, the nominal rate of interest may not. In principle, a relevant variable in the demand for money is "the" nominal rate of interest which from (5) is equal to $\pi^* + i^*$. Our estimate of k, therefore, is not unreasonable in proxying "the" foreign nominal rate of interest. Since the purpose of this section is to indicate, in somewhat general terms, the implication of the first building block rather than to provide a precise estimate of the parameters of the demand for money, the procedure that was followed seems justifiable. In a separate paper we apply the market measure of expectations to a more detailed reexamination of the functional form and the estimates of the demand for money during the German hyperinflation (Frenkel, 1975).

Table 2. *Prices, money and expectations. Monthly data: February 1921 – August 1923*

Estimated equation: Log $P = a + b_1 \log M + b_2 \log \pi + u$

Dependent variable	Constant	log M	log π	s.e.	R^2	D.W.	ϱ	σ_u
LWPI	−5.983 (0.611)	1.021 (0.041)	0.497 (0.061)	0.193	0.996	1.88	0.525	0.227
LWIG	−5.423 (0.779)	0.997 (0.041)	0.293 (0.053)	0.144	0.998	1.95	0.909	0.366
LWHG	−4.923 (0.925)	0.983 (0.051)	0.374 (0.069)	0.187	0.996	1.79	0.889	0.429
LCOL	−7.215 (0.450)	1.073 (0.029)	0.236 (0.044)	0.125	0.998	2.13	0.729	.0182
LWAG	−10.027 (0.749)	1.103 (0.051)	0.194 (0.074)	0.254	0.992	2.06	0.373	0.274

Note: LWPI = log wholesale price index, LWIG = log imported-goods price index, LWHG = log home-goods price index, LCOL = log cost of living index, LWAG = log wage index. Standard errors are in parentheses below each coefficient. ϱ is the final value of the auto-correlation coefficient. An iterative Cochran-Orcutt transformation was employed to account for first order serial correlation in the residuals. s.e. is the standard error of the equation and σ_u is the standard error of the regression when the autoregressive component of the error is included.

It may be recalled that in postulating eq. (2) we bypassed the question of the appropriate price deflator. To a large extent that question is empirical and depends on the theory that underlies the derivation of the demand for money. The presumption, however, is that if the aggregate demand for money is dominated by household behavior, then the relevant price index should be the consumer price index (the cost of living). Table 2 reports the results of estimating eq. (2″) using alternative price deflators. Judged by the goodness of fit it seems that the cost of living index is the most appropriate deflator although, strictly speaking, such a comparison is insufficient since the various equations in Table 2 differ in the dependent variable.

Judged as a whole it seems that the results in Table 2 are consistent with the first building block of the monetary approach to the exchange rate. In all cases the elasticity of the price level with respect to the money stock is close to unity and the elasticity with respect to π is positive as predicted from the consideration of the demand for money.

II.5. *The Purchasing Power Parity*

The second building block of the theory of exchange rate determination is the purchasing power parity. The high statistical correlation between prices and the exchange rate typically observed during periods of monetary disturbances led to the development of the purchasing power parity doctrine. Figs. 4, 5

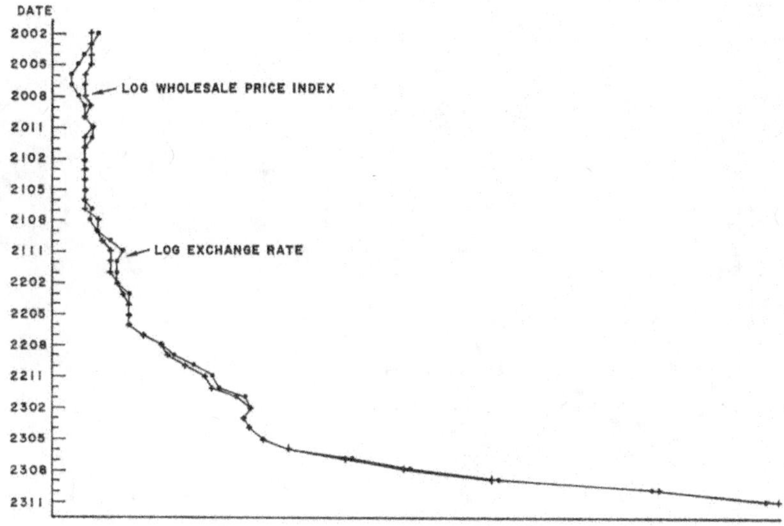
DATE
2002
2005
2008
2011
2102
2105
2108
2111
2202
2205
2208
2211
2302
2305
2308
2311
LOG WHOLESALE PRICE INDEX
LOG EXCHANGE RATE

Fig. 4.

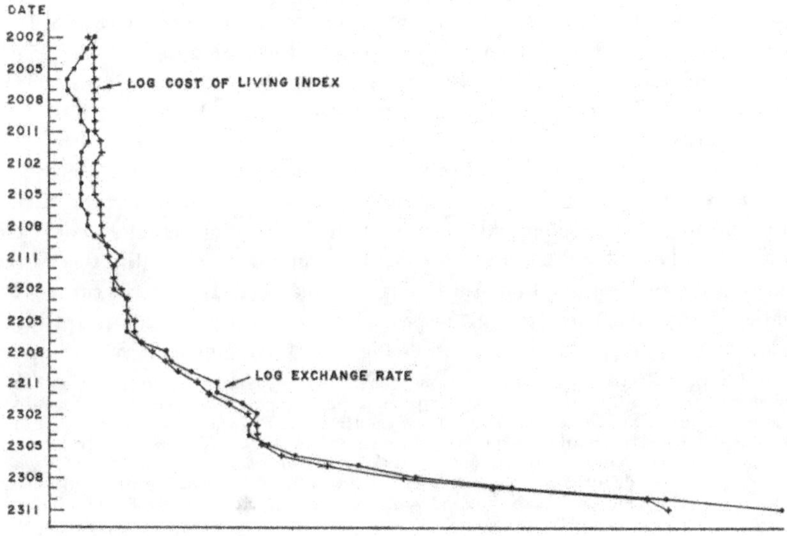
DATE
2002
2005
2008
2011
2102
2105
2108
2111
2202
2205
2208
2211
2302
2305
2308
2311
LOG COST OF LIVING INDEX
LOG EXCHANGE RATE

Fig. 5.

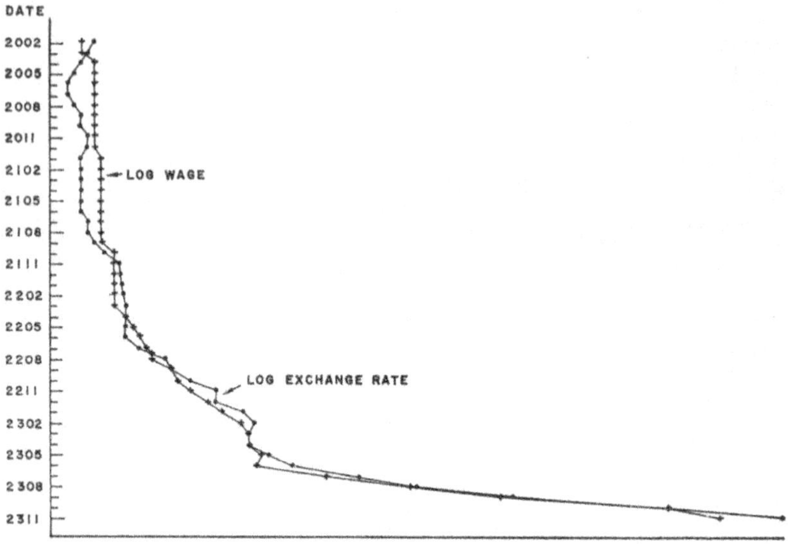

Fig. 6.

and 6 show the relationships between (DM/$) exchange rate and the whole-sale price index, the cost of living index and the wage rate index, and Figs. 7–8 show the relationships between the percentage change of the exchange rate and prices. These relationships correspond to the various price indices advocated for the computation of purchasing power parities.[1] In view of the observed high correlation among prices and the exchange rate, even the skeptics agreed that the doctrine may possess an element of truth when applied to monetary disturbances (e.g., Keynes (1930, p. 91), Haberler (1936, pp. 37–8), Samuelson (1948, p. 397)).

Table 3 reports the results of estimates of the purchasing power parity for the alternative price indices. The estimated equations are derived from equation (3) by log-linearizing and assuming that during that period P^* could be viewed as being fixed. As can be seen this building block of the theory of exchange rate determination also stands up rather well. In all cases the elasticities of the exchange rate with respect to the various price indices are very close to unity. It also seems that while the cost of living index may be the ap-

[1] In addition to pure monetary disturbances some sharp turning points in the path of the exchange rate (and its rate of change) can be attributed to political events which created facts and affected expectations. The following outlines some of the critical events that are reflected in the sharp turning points (based on Tinbergen (1934)). August 29, 1921: Murder of Erzberger; October 20, 1921: League of Nations decision concerning partition of Upper Silesia—renewed disturbances. On that date there was the Wiesbaden agreement between Rathenau and Loucheur concerning deliveries in Rind. April 16, 1922: Rapallo Treaty with Russia. June 24, 1922: Murder of Rathenau leading to a heavy depreciation of the mark. January 11, 1923: Ruhr territory occupied by French. End of February 1923: Beginning action to support the mark. April 18, 1923: Collapse of supporting measures.

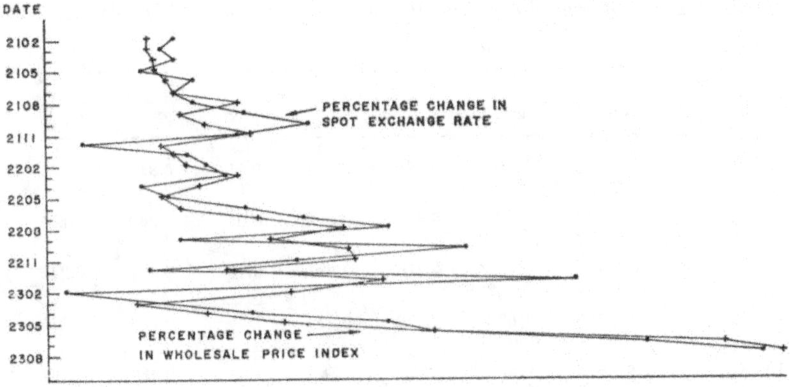

Fig. 7.

propriate deflator in estimating money demand functions, the wholesale price index performs best in the purchasing power parity equations.[1]

There remains, however, a question of interpretation. Does the doctrine specify an equilibrium relationship between prices and exchange rates or does it, in addition, specify casual relationships and channels of transmission. While the high correlation between the various price indices and the exchange rate is of some interest in describing an equilibrium relationship or in manifesting the operation of arbitrage in goods (depending on the price index used), they are of little help in *explaining* and analyzing the *determinants* of the exchange rate.

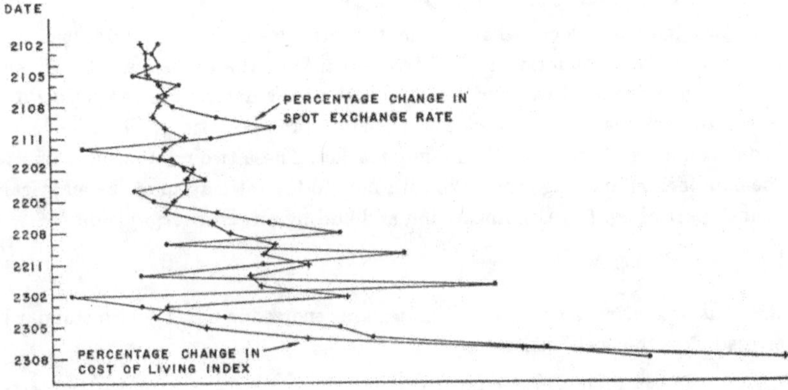

Fig. 8.

[1] It is of interest to note that during the recent float (1973–74) the percentage deviation of the wholesale price index from purchasing power parity exceeded that of the consumer price index (Aliber (1976)).

Table 3. *Exchange rate and prices. Monthly data: February 1921 – August 1923*

Estimated equation: $\log S = a + b \log P + u$

Independent variable	Constant	$\log P$	s.e.	R^2	D.W.	ϱ	σ_u
LWPI	0.146 (0.114)	1.006 (0.010)	0.124	0.998	2.01	0.356	0.135
LWIG	−0.219 (0.177)	1.058 (0.017)	0.208	0.996	2.01	0.269	0.216
LWHG	−0.383 (0.244)	1.031 (0.022)	0.215	0.995	2.09	0.471	0.241
LCOL	0.115 (0.311)	1.076 (0.030)	0.273	0.993	1.97	0.499	0.325
LWAG	4.415 (0.788)	0.887 (0.070)	0.350	0.988	1.94	0.889	0.767
LWAG 2SLS	2.682 (0.310)	1.074 (0.038)	0.360	0.987	1.66	0.471	0.414

Note: LWPI = log wholesale price index, LWIG = log imported-goods price index, LWHG = log home-goods price index, LCOL = log cost of living index, LWAG = log wage index. Standard errors are in parentheses below each coefficient. ϱ is the final value of the autocorrelation coefficient. An iterative Cochran-Orcutt transformation was employed to account for first order serial correlation in the residuals. s.e. is the standard error of the equation and σ_u is the standard error of the regression when the autoregressive component of the error is included. To allow for a possible simultaneous equation bias due to the endogeneity of the various prices the above equations were also estimated using a two-stage least squares procedure with the percentage change in the money supply and the money-bond ratio as instruments. None of the coefficients was significantly affected except for the equation using LWAG as the independent variable. The 2SLS estimates are reported in the last line of the Table.

II.6. *The Determinants of the Exchange Rate*

The two building blocks analyzed in the previous sections provide the ingredients to the estimation of the determinants of the exchange rate. Given the foreign price level the purchasing power parity determines the ratio P/S. Given the nominal money stock and the state of expectations, the price level is determined so as to clear the money market. These two relationships imply the equilibrium exchange rate. We turn now to the estimation of the emprical counterpart of eq. (4). Log-linearizing and adding an error term yields

$$\log S = a' + b_1' \log M + b_2' \log \pi + u \tag{4'}$$

where as before, $\pi \equiv 1 + \pi^*$. The estimates are reported in eq. (4″) with standard errors below the coefficients:

$$\log S = \underset{(0.731)}{-5.135} + \underset{(0.050)}{0.975} \log M + \underset{(0.073)}{0.591} \log \pi \tag{4''}$$

$R^2 = 0.994$; s.e. $= 0.241$; D.W. $= 1.91$.

As is evident these results are fully consistent with the prior expectations.

The elasticity of the exchange rate with respect to the money stock does not differ significantly from unity (at the 95 percent confidence level) while the elasticity of the spot exchange rate with respect to the forward premium is positive. The order of magnitude of the latter elasticity is similar (in absolute value) to the interest elasticity of the demand for money.[1] In comparison with the polynomial distributed lag of Table 1 it is seen that the standard error of equation (4″) is significantly smaller. It is also noteworthy that the lower elasticity of the exchange rate with respect to the money stock is consistent with the intuitive explanation provided to the high elasticity of Table 1. There it was argued that the magnification effect was due to the role of expectations. Indeed as is shown in eq. (4″) when expectations are included as a separate variable, the homogeneity postulate reemerges, the magnification effect of the money stock disappears and thus indicating that the equations in Table 1 might have been misspecified.

II.7. *Conclusions, Limitations and Extensions*

The foregoing analysis examined the empirical relationships among money, prices, expectations and the exchange rate during the German hyperinflation. Concentrating on that period provided the opportunity to isolate empirically some of the key relationships relevant to exchange rate determination. In particular, special attention has been given to simultaneous roles played by expectations and by monetary policy in determining the exchange rate. The empirical results are consistent with the monetary (or the asset) approach to the exchange rate.

It should be emphasized that the monetary approach to the exchange rate *does not* claim that the exchange rate is determined only in the money (or the asset) market and that only stock considerations matter while flow relationships do not. Clearly, the exchange rate (like any other price) is determined in general equilibrium by the interaction of flow and stock conditions. In this respect the asset market equilibrium relationship that is used in the analysis may be viewed as a reduced form relationship that is chosen as a convenient framework.

Concentration on the period of the hyperinflation has, however, some shortcomings. First it does not provide any insight into the exchange rate effects of real disturbances like structural changes (see for example Ballasa (1964); Hekman (1975)). Second, and probably more important, the rapid developments occuring during the hyperinflation prevented a detailed analysis of

---

[1] Recall that due to the transformation on the independent variable the (average) interest elasticity of the exchange rate b_2 is $b_2'\pi^*/(1+\pi^*)$ where π^* is the average forward premium. Over the sample period the average π^* was about 6.2 percent per month, yielding therefore an estimate of about 1/2 as the interest elasticity. This estimate of the elasticity is consistent with the estimates in Frenkel (1975) as well as with the predictions of the various models of the transactions demand for cash.

Table 4. *Correlation matrix: prices, exchange rate and money. Monthly data February 1920 – November 1923*

	LWPI	LWIG	LWHG	LCOL	LWAG	LEXC	LMON
LWPI	1.000	0.9986	0.9985	0.9959	0.9969	0.9992	0.9933
LWIG		1.000	0.9956	0.9934	0.9947	0.9968	0.9942
LWHG			1.000	0.9945	0.9949	0.9987	0.9892
LCOL				1.000	0.9984	0.9956	0.9875
LWAG					1.000	0.9960	0.9927
LEXC						1.000	0.9850
LMON							1.000

Note: LWPI = log wholesale price index, LWIG = log import-goods price index, LWHG = log home-goods price index, LCOL = log cost of living index, LWAG = log wage index, LEXC = log exchange rate index, LMON = log money supply index.

the channels of transmission of disturbances among the various sectors in the economy. For example, it might be useful to examine the exact pattern and chronological order by which monetary disturbances get transmitted into changes in the various price indices. The monthly data used in the present paper do not permit such a detailed analysis since most of the dynamics of adjustment occur within the month. The extent of this phenomenon is reflected in Table 4—a correlation matrix of the various variables for the monthly data over the entire period (February 1920 – November 1923). To gain insight into the more refined details of the adjustment process, it may be necessary to analyze the period using weekly data. A preliminary examination of the weekly data suggests that the various prices do differ in the details of their time paths but at this stage no conclusive evidence can yet be offered.[1]

Although the monthly data do not reveal the details of the adjustment process, they do reveal some systematic relationships among the coefficients of variation of the (logarithms of the) variables as reported in Table 5. As is seen in Table 5, the coefficient of variation of the money stock is about 0.15 while the coefficients of variation corresponding to the various price indices are about twice as large—about 0.30. In this respect all price indices (wholesale, imported-goods, home-goods and cost of living) display a common behavior. A third group of variables includes the various exchange rates (spot and forward) *and* the wage rate. All of these variables display a similar coefficient of variation—about 0.40. The interesting phenomena are that the extent of variations in the various exchange rates (and in the wage rate) exceeds the extent of variations in the various prices which in turn exceeds the variation in the money stock. Furthermore, in view of the wage rate approach to the exchange rate (some of the doctrinal origins of which were mentioned in Section I), the association among variations in the wage rate and the various

[1] An inspection of Figs. 7–8 reveals that changes in the cost of living index lag behind changes in the wholesale price index which are closely related to changes in the exchange rate.

Table 5. *Summary statistics: prices, exchange rate and money. Monthly data February 1921 – August 1923*

Variable	Mean	Variance	Standard deviation	Coef. of variation
LMON	15.3567	5.0948	2.2571	0.1469
LWPI	10.0477	9.5613	3.0921	0.3077
LWIG	9.8978	8.6178	2.9356	0.2965
LWHG	10.3210	9.1950	3.0323	0.2938
LCOL	9.4337	7.9337	2.8166	0.2985
LWAG	7.0522	7.6616	2.7679	0.3924
LEXC	8.6235	10.3370	3.2151	0.3728
LSPO	8.6235	10.3370	3.2151	0.3728
LFOR	8.6853	11.0123	3.3184	0.3820

Note: LMON = log money supply index, LWPI = log wholesale price index, LWIG = log import-goods price index, LWHG = log home-goods price index, LCOL = log cost of living index, LWAG = log wage index, LEXC = log (DM/$) spot exchange rate index, LSPO = log (DM/£) spot exchange rate index, LFOR = log (DM/£) one month forward exchange rate index.

exchange rates deserves a special notice. While a detailed analysis of the implications of Table 5 is beyond the scope of the present paper, it is of interest to note the association among the exchange rates and the price of labor services—the commodity which may be most naturally classified as a non-traded good.

Appendix: Data Sources

Data on the DM/$ exchange rate (spot) are taken from Graham (1930) and from *International Abstract of Economic Statistics 1919–30*. London: International Conference of Economic Services, London, 1934.

The one-month forward exchange rate (DM/£) as well as the (DM/£) spot rates are from Einzig (1937). The primary source for this data is the weekly circular published by the Anglo-Portuguese Colonial and Overseas Bank, Ltd. (originally the London branch of the Banco Nacional Ultramarino of Lisbon). The rates quoted are those of the Saturday of each week, but in cases where the market was closed, the latest quotation available prior to that Saturday is used.

Data on money supply are from Graham and *Historical Statistics* as well as some interpolations. Prices and wages are from *Historical Statistics* and some interpolations and primary sources.

Outstanding Treasury-Bills are from Graham.

References

Aliber, R. Z.: Speculation in the foreign exchanges: The European experience, 1919–1926. *Yale Economic Essays*, Spring 1962.

Aliber, R. Z.: The firm under fixed and flexible exchange rates. *Scandinavian Journal of Economics 78*, No. 2, pp. 309–322, 1976.

Angell, J. W.: International trade under inconvertible paper. *Quarterly Journal of Economics 36*, 309–412, 1922.

Balassa, B.: The purchasing power parity doctrine: a reappraisal. *Journal of Political Economy 72*, No. 6, 584–96, 1964.

Bilson, J. F.: Rational expectations and flexible exchange rates. Unpublished manuscript, University of Chicago, 1975.

Black, S. W.: International money markets and flexible exchange rates. *Princeton Studies in International Finance*, No. 32. Princeton University, 1973.

Besciani-Turroni, C.: The purchasing power parity doctrine. *Egypte Contemporaire*, 1934. Reprinted in his *Saggi Di Economia*, 1961, Milano, pp. 91–122.

Bresciani-Turroni, C.: *The Economics of Inflation*. Allen & Unwin, London, 1937.

Bunting, F. H.: Purchasing power parity theory reexamined. *Southern Economic Journal 5*, No. 3, 282–301, 1939.

Cagan, P.: The monetary dynamics of hyperinflation. In M. Friedman (ed.), *Studies in the Quantity Theory of Money*. University of Chicago Press, Chicago, 1956.

Cannan, E.: The application of the theoretical apparatus of supply and demand to units of currency. *Economic Journal 31*, No. 124, 453–61, 1921.

Cassel, G.: The present situation of the foreign exchanges. *Economic Journal 26*, 62–65, 1916.

Cassel, G.: "Comment", *Economic Journal 30*, No. 117, 44–45, 1920.

Cassel, G.: *The World's Monetary Problems*. Constable and Co., London, 1921.

Cassel, G.: *Post-War Monetary Stabilization*. Columbia University Press, New York, 1928.

Cassel, G.: *Money and Foreign Exchange after 1919*. Macmillan, London, 1930.

Dornbusch, R.: "Discussion". *American Economic Review Papers and Proceedings*, 147–151, 1975.

Dornbusch, R.: The theory of flexible exchange rate regimes and macroeconomic policy. *Scandinavian Journal of Economics 78*, No. 2, pp. 255–275, 1976.

Dornbusch, R.: Capital mobility, flexible exchange rates and macroeconomic equilibrium. In E. Claassen and P. Salin (eds.), *Recent Issues in International Monetary Economics*. North-Holland, 1976.

Einzig, P.: *World Finance, 1914–1935*. Macmillan & Co., New York, 1935.

Einzig, P.: *The Theory of Forward Exchange*. Macmillan, London, 1937.

Ellis, H. S.: The equilibrium rate of exchange. In *Explorations in Economics. Notes and Essays contributed in honor of F. W. Taussig*. McGraw-Hill, New York, 1936.

Frenkel, J. A.: Adjustment mechanisms and the monetary approach to the balance of payments. In E. Claassen and P. Salin (eds.), *Recent Issues in International Monetary Economics*. North-Holland, 1976.

Frenkel, J. A.: The forward exchange rate, expectations and the demand for money during the German hyperinflation. Unpublished manuscript, University of Chicago, 1975.

Frenkel, J. A. & Johnson, H. G.: The monetary approach to the balance of payments: essential concepts and historical origins. In J. A. Frenkel and H. G. Johnson (eds.), *The Monetary Approach to the Balance of Payments*. Allen & Unwin, London and University of Toronto Press, Toronto, 1976.

Frenkel, J. A. & Levich, R. M.: Covered interest arbitrage: unexploited profits? *Journal of Political Economy 83*, No. 2, 325–338, 1975*a*.

Frenkel, J. A. & Levich, R. M.: Transactions cost and the efficiency of international capital markets. Presented at the Conference on The Monetary Mechanism in Open Economies, Helsinki, Finland, August, 1975*b*.

Frenkel, J. A. & Rodriguez, C. A.: Portfolio equilibrium and the balance of payments: A monetary approach. *American Economic Review 65*, No. 4, 674–88, 1975.

Friedman, M. & Schwartz, A.: *A Monetary History of the United States, 1867–1960*. Princeton University Press, Princeton, 1963.

Goschen, G. J.: *The Theory of the Foreign Exchanges*. 1st ed. London, 1861; 2nd ed. London, 1863; 4th ed. reprinted, 1932.

Graham, F.: *Exchange Prices and Production in Hyper-Inflation: Germany, 1920–23*. Princeton University Press, Princeton, N.J., 1930.

Gregory, T. E.: *Foreign Exchange before, during and after the War*. Oxford University Press, London, 1922.

Haberler, G.: *The Theory of International Trade*. William Hodge and Co., London, 1936.

Haberler, G.: The choice of exchange rates after the war. *American Economic Review 35*, No. 3, 308–318, 1945.

Haberler, G.: *A survey of international trade theory*. Special Papers in International Economics 1 (July 1961). International Finance Section, Princeton University.

Hansen, A. H.: A brief note on fundamental disequilibrium. *Review of Economics and Statistics 26*, No. 4, 182–84, 1944.

Hawtrey, R. G.: *Currency and Credit*. Longmans, Green and Co., 1st ed. 1919, 4th ed. 1950, London.

Hekman, C. R.: Structural change and the exchange rate: an empirical test. Unpublished manuscript, University of Chicago, 1975.

Heckscher, E. F., et al.: *Sweden, Norway, Denmark and Iceland in the World War*. New Hawen, 1930.

Hodgson, J. S.: An analysis of floating exchange rates: The dollar sterling rate, 1919–1925. *Southern Economic Journal 39*, No. 2, 249–257, 1972.

Houthakker, H. S.: Exchange rate adjustment. *Factors Affecting the U.S. Balance of Payments*. Joint Economic Committee, 87th Congress, 2nd Session, December 14, 1962, pp. 289–304.

Johnson, H. G.: The Keynesian revolution and the monetarist counterrevolution. *American Economic Review 61*, No. 2, 1–14, 1971. Reprinted in Ch. 7 in H. G. Johnson, *Economics and Society*. University of Chicago Press, Chicago, 1975.

Johnson, H. G.: Theory of international trade. In *International Encyclopedia of the Social Sciences*. The Macmillan Company and Free Press, 1968.

Johnson, H. G.: World inflation and the international monetary system. *The Three Banks Review*, No. 107, 3–22, 1975.

Keynes, J. M.: A tract on monetary reform. 1st ed. 1923, French Edition, 1924; vol. IV in *The Collected Writings of J. M. Keynes*. Macmillan, London, 1971.

Keynes, J. M.: *A Treatise on Money*. Vol. I. Macmillan, London, 1930.

Kouri, P. J. K.: Exchange rate expectations, and the short run and the long run effects of fiscal and monetary policies under flexible exchange rates. Presented at the Conference on The Monetary Mechanism in Open Economies, Helsinki, Finland, August 1975.

Lursen, K. & Pedersen, J.: *The German Inflation 1918–1923*. North-Holland, Amsterdam, 1964.

Marshall, A.: *Memorandum to the Effects which Differences between the Currencies of Different Nations have on International Trade*, 1888.

Marshall, A.: *Money, Credit and Commerce*. London, 1923.

Metzler, L. A.: The process of international adjustment under conditions of full employment: a Keynesian view. In R. E. Caves and H. G. Johnson (eds.), *Readings in International Economics*, pp. 465–86. Irwin, Homewood, Ill., 1968.

Mill, J. S. *Principles of Political Economy*. 5th ed. Parker & Co., London, 1862.

Mundell, R. A.: *Monetary Theory*. Pacific Palisades, Goodyear, 1971.

Mundell, R. A.: *International Economics*. Macmillan, New York, 1968.

Mussa, M. L.: A monetary approach to balance of payments analysis. *Journal of Money, Credit and Banking 6*, No. 3, 333–351, 1974.

Mussa, M. L.: The exchange rate, the balance of payments and monetary and fiscal policy under a regime of controlled floating. *Scandinavian Journal of Economics 78*, No. 2, pp. 229–248, 1976.

Myhrman, J.: Experiences of flexible exchange rates in earlier periods: theories, evidence and a new view. *Scandinavian Journal of Economics 78*, No. 2, pp. 169–196, 1976.

Ohlin, B.: *Interregional and International Trade.* Revised ed., Harvard University Press, Cambridge, Mass., 1967; 1st ed. 1933.

Pigou, A. C.: Some problems of foreign exchanges. *Economic Journal 30*, No. 120, 460–472, 1920.

Ricardo, D.: The high price of bullion. London, 1811. In *Economic Essays by David Ricardo.* Edited by E. C. Conner. Kelley, New York, 1970.

Ricardo, D.: *Reply to Mr. Bosaquet's practical observations on the report of the Bullion Committee.* London, 1811. In *Economic Essays by David Ricardo.* Edited by E. C. Connor. Kelley, New York, 1970.

Ricardo, D.: *Principles of Political Economy and Taxation.* London, 1821. Edited by E. C. Connor. G. Bell and Sons, 1911.

Ringer, F. K. (ed.): *The German Inflation of 1923.* Oxford Press, New York, 1969.

Robinson, J.: Banking policy and the exchanges. *Review of Economic Studies 3*, 226–29, 1935–36.

Rueff, J.: *Balance of Payments.* Macmillan, New York, 1967.

Rueff, J.: *Les fondements philosophiques des systèmes economiques.* Payol, 1967.

Samuelson, P. A.: Disparity in postwar exchange rates. In S. Harris (ed.), *Foreign Economic Policy for the United States*, pp. 397–412. Harvard University Press, Cambridge, 1948.

Samuelson, P. A.: Theoretical notes on trade problems. *Review of Economics and Statistics 46*, No. 2, 145–154, 1964.

Sargent, T. J. & Wallace, N.: Rational expectations and the dynamics of hyperinflation. *International Economic Review 14*, No. 2, 328–50, 1973.

Taussig, F. W.: *International Trade.* New York, 1927.

Tinbergen, J. (ed.): *International Abstract of Economic Statistics 1919–30.* International Conference of Economic Services, London, 1934.

Tsiang, S. C.: Fluctuating exchange rates in countries with relatively stable economies *IMF Staff Papers 7*, 244–273, 1959–60.

Viner, J.: *Studies in the Theory of International Trade.* Harper and Bros., New York, 1937.

Wheatley, J.: *Remarks on Currency and Commerce.* Burton, London, 1803.

Wicksell, K.: The riddle of foreign exchanges. 1919. In his *Selected Papers on Economic Theory.* Kelley, New York, 1969.

COMMENT ON J. A. FRENKEL, "A MONETARY APPROACH TO THE EXCHANGE RATE: DOCTRINAL ASPECTS AND EMPIRICAL EVIDENCE"

Giorgio Basevi

University of Bologna, Italy

1. As many papers in this conference, Frenkel's deals with the determinants of the exchange rate and uses the analytical framework provided by the monetarist approach to the balance of payments. The paper is divided in two main sections. In the first one Frenkel shows, with appropriate quotations, that the new monetarist approach has deep roots in economic doctrine. In the second part, Frenkel aims at an empirical verification of the monetarist approach, and in order to do so he chooses a period in which we may say without doubt that monetary disturbances dominated over real, and domestic over foreign ones. His case is the German hyperinflation during the years 1920–23.

In a first rough examination of that episode he finds a high statistical correlation between both (*a*) the level of the exchange rate and the level of the money stock, and (*b*) the rates of change in these variables. It is interesting to note that, in this first statistical analysis, the elasticity of the exchange rate with respect to the supply of money is larger than unity, a result which is consistent with the magnification effect of expectations in Dornbusch's model.

Frenkel turns then to the explicit consideration of expectations, and here he obtains very good results. With some manipulation of the demand-equal-supply-of-money condition, Frenkel derives equation (4′), which should be estimated in order to test whether indeed the money stock and the expected rate of inflation determine the spot rate of exchange. He then obtains an estimating equation (4″) with all the "a priori" expected coefficients and high statistical significance. It is worth noting, in particular, that the elasticity of the spot rate with respect to money stock has now dropped below unity, since the magnification effect of expectations has been absorbed by their explicit introduction into the equation.

2. I come now to my own view of these matters. Some of my comments are limited to Frenkel's paper; others start from it and try to cover the broader ground that has been explored in other contributions to this conference.

Frenkel starts by identifying, in a sort of dual relationship, the monetarist approach to the balance of payments with the asset approach to exchange rate determination. This is a very useful framework to start with, if by modern monetary approach to the balance of payments we mean that which was inaugurated by Harry Johnson's celebrated article "Towards a general theory of the balance of payments". In that article Johnson emphasized, among other things, how a non-zero balance of payments amounts to a change in one component of the balance sheet of the central bank, thus implying changes in other components as well. This asset-and-liabilities, or portfolio approach was further developed by Oates, McKinnon, Branson and others, by introducing, in addition to the balance sheet of the banking sector, an explicit analysis of the relationship between the balance of payments and the balance sheets of the Government and of the non-banking private sectors. Thus, not only monetary assets, but also private and Government bonds, were explicitly included into the analysis. On the other hand, Frenkel's asset approach is a great simplification on the assets framework proposed by McKinnon and his followers. It is the monetarists' contention that, by concentrating on money market equilibrium much is gained and little is lost in terms of understanding the determinants of exchange rate or of balance of payments equilibrium. I disagree on this point.

A theory of the determinants of the exchange rate that says that the exchange rate depends on the stock supply and demand for money, is to me no theory of the exchange rate at all. It is simply another application of the tools of elementary price theory—demand and supply—, although I admit that the emphasis on stock- rather than flow-demand and supply was perhaps necessary (but Frenkel shows that the stock view was already clear to Ricardo). In order to appreciate with an example why this seems to me a non-theory, let me quote from M. Mussa's contribution to this conference. Talking about the surplus of oil producing countries he says (p. 100): "It is because the Saudis decided to spend a significant portion of their increased income on the accumulation of official foreign exchange assets that they ran a large official settlements surplus."

To consider this a theory, I would like an analysis of what determines the demand and supply of money. As for demand, of course, we do not lack a theory. With respect to supply, on the other hand, I think that by not continuing along the track that McKinnon and others have traced, the monetarists have put themselves in the position of not being willing to answer the question that Max Corden has raised in this conference (why does the Central Bank overexpand its money supply?), other than by saying: we should stop somewhere in the analysis, and the Central Bank seems a convenient point to stop.

However, the portfolio approach reminded us that the supply of money is one of the two ways the Government has to finance its deficit, the other being the issuing of bonds. Thus the McKinnon version of the assets approach opened new horizons in looking at the balance of payments and the exchange rate, that are not brought within the viewpoint of the narrow monetarist approach. In the portfolio analysis the current account imbalance becomes the reflection of the Government budgetary imbalance when the private sector is satisfied with its own holdings of financial assets; and the inability of the Government to sell bonds to foreigners without an excessive fall in their prices and/or depreciation of the currency, gets reflected in an overall balance of payments deficit.

To be honest to Frenkel, he is worried about causality, but he does not go beyond money supply. From figure 1, he infers that the high supply of marks was associated with depreciation in terms of foreign exchange. Under hyper-inflation, there is of course no doubt about that; but I asked him how he explained that in figure 1 the exchange rate leads the money supply in the early stages of their increase. He replied that it was all due to expectations: people expected the money supply to increase in Germany. I asked why, and he replied that it was because they did not believe that the Government could finance in any other way the deficit required by the reparations payments. Now, I don't know whether this account is right, but at least Frenkel's answer shows how he has to rely on a more complete assets model, and to introduce the Government budget constraint, in order to account for the expansion in money supply and the consequent depreciation of the currency.

The title of this conference is "Flexible exchange rates and stabilization policy". It seems to me that many contributors have either ignored the second part of the title (Stabilization policy), or interpreted it to mean: stabilization of the exchange rates. Someone explicitly said here that in order to stabilize exchange rates we have to harmonize monetary policies. Which, again, is perfectly right, but does not tell us much that is interesting. The problem is stabilization of income and employment along a reasonable growth path, and the question then is: are uncoordinated monetary policies, and hence erratic exchange rates, helping in solving this problem? Now, I think we have heard little on this problem here, and the reasons are, in my view, at least two.

First, as already explained, by concentrating on money demand and supply, we are bound to abandon a policy-oriented approach, which, on the other hand, naturally follows from a more general portfolio approach. Secondly, and more fundamentally, by concentrating on large monetary aggregates, and in particular on the general price level, and how it is influenced by exchange rates or vice versa, we have lost sight of the fact that Ricardo—as carefully Frenkel reminds us—indicated that the exchange rate was just a way to adjust money wages to the real wages implied by labour productivity, and thus transform absolute advantage or disadvantage into comparative advantage. Here again, McKinnon seems to indicate the right track in his most recent paper, presented in Helsinki this month, from which I quote (McKinnon, p. 3, p. 25): "... with the capital stock fixed in the short run so that output from newly employed labor is subject to diminishing returns, output can only increase if fiscal policy succeeds in raising the domestic price level relative to money wages. To be effective when money wages are rigid, therefore, fiscal policy must somehow induce a devaluation. (...) Because of the limited influence of fiscal policy on macro-economic activity in an open economy, a given (or increased) level of money wages that substantially depresses output and employment can only be offset by discretionary monetary policy: either by increasing the money supply directly in a floating exchange-rate regime or indirectly by engineering a discrete devaluation through a change in the official parity."

Let me conclude by pulling these various strings together. Monetary policy is but a particular form of Government's budgetary policy, and in many countries it is subsidiary to the need for the Government to finance its deficit. If this cannot be done by issuing bonds, and if the private sector is in portfolio equilibrium, the pressure falls on foreign exchange reserves or on the exchange rate. Thus, the Government deficit eventually determines the current account.

In a paper presented at the Congress of the Econometric Society last week, Jim Ball has used the London Business School econometric model to test the British version of the McKinnon policy prescription, which goes under the name of "new Cambridge school". This school suggests that fiscal policy should be directed towards the balance of payments, with the exchange rate used to determine the level of domestic activity by export-led growth. Ball's model, when appropriately shocked and simulated, shows that for the U.K. such an approach is not feasible: the Government budget does indeed determine the current account, but "the output effects of the exchange rate change is transitory, since the competitive advantage is subsequently wiped out by the adjustment of money wages to traded goods prices, restoring production costs to previous levels" (Ball et al., p. 39). Thus, while monetary policy, by affecting the exchange rate, aims at controlling the relationship between real wages and profits, it does not succeed in doing so in the long run, and only creates inflation and depreciation in attempting to do it. Rather than having a disguised incomes policy under the appearances of a monetary policy, it may therefore be better to aim at an explicit incomes policy. The role of an incomes policy, in this context anyway, is not to act directly on the general price level, but rather to allow the exchange rate to perform its stabilizing function by keeping down real wages and therefore assuring a level of profits consistent with full employment and growth of the economy.

Bibliographical References

BALL, R. J., BURNS, T. & LAURY, J. S. E.: The role of exchange rate changes in balance of payments adjustment—The United Kingdom case. Econometric Forecasting Unit, D.P. no. 32, July 1975, London Graduate School of Business Studies.

MCKINNON, R. I.: The limited role of fiscal policy in an open economy. Mimeographed, 1975.

THE EXCHANGE RATE, THE BALANCE OF PAYMENTS AND MONETARY AND FISCAL POLICY UNDER A REGIME OF CONTROLLED FLOATING

Michael Mussa

University of Rochester, Rochester, New York, USA

Abstract

This paper considers the extension of the fundamental principles of the monetary approach to balance of payments analysis to a regime of floating exchange rates, with active intervention by the authorities to control rate movements. It makes four main points. First, the exchange rate is the relative price of different national monies, rather than national outputs, and is determined primarily by the demands and supplies of stocks of different national monies. Second, exchange rates are strongly influenced by asset holder's expectations of future exchange rates and these expectations are influenced by beliefs concerning the future course of monetary policy. Third, "real" factors, as well as monetary factors, are important in determining the behavior of exchange rates. Fourth, the problems of policy conflict which exist under a system of fixed rates are reduced, but not eliminated, under a regime of controlled floating. A brief appendix develops some of the implications of "rational expectations" for the theory of exchange rates.

Introduction

The current system of controlled floating differs significantly from the exchange rate system which existed prior to 1971 and from textbook descriptions of freely flexible rates. Governments no longer seek to maintain fixed parities; neither do they forego direct intervention in the foreign exchange markets. Nevertheless, it is the central contention of this paper that the basic theoretical framework of the monetary approach to the balance of payments, developed for a fixed rate system, remains applicable. This approach emphasizes that both the balance of payments (meaning the official settlements balance) and the exchange rate are essentially monetary phenomena.[1] The proximate determinants of exchange rates and balances of payments are the demands for and the supplies of various national monies. When the demand for a particular

[1] A number of recent contributions to the monetary approach to balance of payments analysis are contained in Frenkel & Johnson (1975). See, also, Dornbusch (1973), Kemp (1975), and Mussa (1974).

money rises relative to the supply of that money, either the domestic credit component of the money supply must be expanded, or the exchange rate must appreciate, or the official settlements balance must go into surplus, or some combination of the three.

This paper will elaborate on the monetary approach to exchange rate and balance of payments theory and will discuss the applicability of this theory to recent experience. To focus on broader issues, while avoiding excessive concern with formal details, the discussion will proceed at a general level. In addition to summarizing the monetary approach, this paper will make four basic points. First, in accord with the general principles of the monetary approach, exchange rates are best thought of as relative prices of different national monies, rather than as relative prices of different national outputs. Exchange rates are determined primarily by the conditions for equilibrium between the demands for the *stocks* of various national monies and the stocks of these monies available to be held. Second, like all prices determined in asset markets, exchange rates are strongly influenced by asset holders' expectations of the future behavior of asset prices. Since national monetary authorities can exert substantial control over the supplies of national monies, expectations concerning the behavior of these authorities are of critical importance for the behavior of exchange rates. Third, while the exchange rate and the official settlements balance are monetary phenomena, they are not exclusively monetary phenomena. Changes in exchange rates are frequently induced by "real" factors, operating through monetary channels; and, changes in exchange rates usually have real effects which are of legitimate concern to government policy. Fourth, the problems of policy conflict which exist under a system of fixed rates are potentially reduced, but not eliminated, under a regime of controlled floating. The relaxation of the commitment to fixed parities allows greater independence in use of monetary and fiscal policies by introducing an additional policy instrument, the exchange rate, but undesired real effects of exchange rate changes limit the usefulness of this additional instrument.

I. A Monetary Approach to Exchange Rate Theory

The monetary approach to balance of payments analysis is built on the assumption that the demand for money is a stable function of a limited number of arguments, at least over periods of a year or two. This money demand function constrains the equilibrium size of the money supply. Under a system of fixed rates, where governments are committed to buy or sell foreign exchange to maintain the par value of their national money, the foreign source component of the money supply is endogenous. If there is a change in one of the arguments of the money demand function which leads to an increase in money demand, and if the domestic source component of the money supply is not increased, the monetary approach predicts that the country will experience a balance payments surplus. Eventually, to prevent the exchange rate from appreciating, the monetary authority will be compelled to purchase foreign exchange and, thereby, to increase the foreign source component of the money supply. On the other hand, if the monetary authority were to increase the domestic source component of the money supply, without any change in the arguments in the money demand function, the result would be an excess of money supply over money demand. Eventually, this would lead to downward pressure on the exchange rate, forcing the monetary authority to contract the foreign source component of the money supply by the amount of the increase in the domestic source component. The process whereby the initial disturbance is transmitted to the balance of payments and the speed with which adjustment occurs will depend on particular circumstances and institutional arrangements. The ultimate result is determined by the condition for equilibrium between money demand and money supply.

This simple theory of the balance of payments under fixed rates is easily converted into a theory of the exchange rate under freely flexible rates. Under freely flexible rates, the foreign source component of the money supply is fixed. Hence, if there is a change in one of the arguments of the money demand function or in the domestic credit component of the money supply, equilibrium cannot be achieved by induced adjustment of the foreign source component of the money supply. Instead, the exchange rate adjusts. These adjustments affect the variables which enter into the money demand function: prices, incomes, expected returns from holding domestic rather than foreign money, etc. Ultimately, the exchange rate must change sufficiently so that money demand is brought into equilibrium with money supply.

The monetary theory of the exchange rate and the balance of payments under a regime of controlled floating is a combination of these two simple theories. Under this regime, monetary authorities actively intervene in the foreign exchange market to control fluctuations in exchange rates, but do not seek to maintain fixed rates. A change in the demand for money relative to the supply available from domestic credit sources puts pressure on the exchange rate. The monetary authorities must decide the extent to which this pressure will be relieved by allowing the exchange rate to change and the extent to which it will be absorbed through variations in foreign exchange reserves. The extent of the initial monetary disequilibrium determines the total adjustment which is required. The authorities must decide on the division of this adjustment between exchange rate changes and foreign exchange reserve changes.

This monetary theory of the exchange rate and the balance of payments is useful in interpreting some of our experience in recent years. First, consider the substantial appreciation of the Swiss franc relative to other European currencies which occurred in 1974. Was this due to an increase in the competitiveness of Swiss industry or to an increase in the demand for Swiss watches and Swiss ski resorts? Clearly not. The explanation is that there was a substantial increase in the demand to hold Swiss money, at the old exchange rates, and that this increase in demand was not met by an increase in the supply of Swiss money, thus requiring an appreciation of the Swiss franc.

Second, consider the relative performance of the German mark and theBritish pound during 1974. Both countries are large importers of oil, and both suffered from the large increase in the price of oil. Nevertheless, the mark was strong while the pound was weak. The monetary explanation of this result is to be found in the monetary policies of Germany and England. The Bundesbank pursued a very tight policy with respect to domestic credit expansion, while the Bank of England pursued a much easier policy.

Third, consider the balance of payments of Saudi Arabia. The increase in the price of oil has meant a large increase in the real income of Saudi Arabia. This increase in income made possible the large balance of payments surplus of Saudi Arabia. But, the surplus also reflected a choice concerning how to spend the increase in income. If the income had all been spent on foreign goods or on shares in foreign companies, Saudi Arabia would not have experienced an official settlements surplus. It is because the Saudis decided to spend a significant portion of their increased income on the accumulation of official foreign exchange assets that they ran a large official settlements surplus.

Finally, consider the appreciation of the U.S. dollar relative to other currencies during the early summer of 1975. The explanation of this event from a monetary perspective, is to be found in the simultaneous tightening of U.S. monetary policy and the loosening of monetary policies in most other countries. In late June and early July, the U.S. Federal Reserve provided convincing evidence of its desire to keep the rate of monetary expansion below 7½% per year by clamping down on a previous surge in the money supply and increasing short term interest rates. At virtually the same moment Chancellor Schmidt announced that Germany would pursue a strong reflationary policy, and the governments of France and Japan announced similar policies. The combined effect of these policy changes on asset holders' expectations of future exchange rates was sufficient to induce an approximately 10% appreciation of the dollar.

II. The Exchange Rate as the Relative Price of Two Monies

In this brief sketch of the monetary approach, no mention has been made of the traditional elements of exchange rate theory: the demand for foreign exchange and the supply of foreign exchange and the price of elasticities of import demands and export supplies. In the traditional theory, the demand for foreign exchange is determined by the amount which domestic residents spend on imports, measured as a *flow* of foreign money, and the supply of foreign exchange is determined by the amount which foreign residents spend on domestic exports, measured as a *flow* of foreign money. Under fixed rates, the excess of the demand for foreign exchange over the supply of foreign exchange is equal to the balance of payments deficit. A devaluation, it is argued, increases the price of imports in terms of domestic money and reduces the price exports in terms of foreign money. Provided that the Robinson–Metzler–Bickerdike condition on the elasticities of demands for imports and supplies of exports is satisfied, a devaluation improves the balance of payments. Under flexible exchange rates, the balance of payments is zero, and the exchange rate is determined by the condition that the demand for foreign exchange must equal the supply of foreign exchange. The Robinson–Metzler–Bickerdike condition becomes the condition for the stability of the exchange rate.[1]

From the perspective of the monetary approach, however, all of this discussion of elasticities is fundamentally irrelevant since the traditional theory on which it is based contains two serious conceptual errors. First, it views the exchange rate as the relative price of national outputs, rather than as the relative price of national monies. Second, it assumes that the exchange rate is determined by the conditions for equilibrium in the markets for flows of funds, rather than by the conditions for equilibrium in the markets for stocks of assets.

The identification of the exchange rate with the relative price of national outputs is implicit in the assertion that the balance of payments effects of a change in the exchange rate arise because exchange rate changes induce changes in the relative prices of domestic and foreign goods. The fallacy in this view is most easily seen when two countries produce the same goods. Commodity trade still occurs since the pattern of commodity production need not match the pattern of commodity consumption in each country. The law of one price, however, requires that the same good have the same price in both countries, adjusted for the exchange rate, and taking account of transport costs, tariffs, etc. In such a situation, a devaluation by the home country will increase the domestic money price of every good relative to the foreign money price of that good by exactly the amount of the devaluation. But, there is no strong reason to believe that this change in nominal prices should be associated with any particular change in relative commodity prices.

This argument does not deny that there are circumstances in which exchange rate changes do have significant effects on relative commodity prices or that relative price changes affect the balance of payments. But such effects must come through the impact of these relative price changes on the demand for money. Specifically, if a devaluation reduces the relative price of domestic

---

1 There are a variety of approaches which yield restrictions on price elasticities as the condition for a successful devaluation; see, for instance, Pearce (1970, ch. 4), and Caves & Jones (1973, ch. 4 and 5).

output in terms of foreign output and, thereby, induces an expansion of domestic output and contraction of foreign output, the demand for domestic money should rise and the demand for foreign money should fall. This change in money demands will induce a flow of foreign exchange reserves from the foreign country to the home country. On the other hand, if the demand for money in the home country and the demand for money in the foreign country were unaffected by a devaluation, and if the domestic credit components of the money supplies were held constant, there could be no permanent balance of payments effect from an exchange rate change. A devaluation might lead to a temporary change in relative commodity prices which might induce a temporary flow of foreign exchange. But, this flow would produce an excess of the supply of money over the demand for money in one country and a corresponding deficiency in the other country. Eventually, the restoration of monetary equilibrium would require that any initial foreign exchange flow in one direction be matched by a later foreign exchange flow in the opposite direction.

The second fallacy in the traditional approach is the concentration on the markets for flows of funds and the neglect of the markets for stocks of assets. In the traditional approach, under a system of fixed rates, a "fundamental disequilibrium", created by incorrect relative commodity prices, generates a permanent divergence between the flow demand for and the flow supply of foreign exchange. Since the effects of asset flows on asset stocks are usually not considered in the traditional approach, these deficits and surpluses presumably continue, without repercussions or self-limiting adjustments, until some country exhausts its reserves. In contrast, in the monetary approach, the critical equilibrium condition is the requirement that the demand for the *stock* of each national money must equal the *stock* of that money available to be held. Flows of funds occur in order to correct existing monetary disequilibria or to prevent new disequilibria from emerging. But, the demands and supplies of flows of funds are a reflection of the requirements for asset market equilibrium, rather than the basic determinant of equilibrium.

The distinction between the monetary approach, with its emphasis on stocks, and the traditional approach, with its emphasis on flows comes out most forcefully in analyzing disturbances in the flow markets. Consider an increase in foreign aid payments from one country, the home country, to another, the foreign country. (For simplicity, assume a two country world.) The traditional conclusion is that such an increase in foreign aid will create a permanent balance of payments deficit for the home country and a permanent balance of payments surplus for the foreign country. The home country will either have to devalue or pursue policies which improve the competitiveness of its export and import competing industries. The monetary approach takes quite a different view. The increase in the flow of foreign aid will reduce income in the home country and increase income in the foreign country. This will have a once and for all effect on the demand for the stock of money in the two countries which, in the absence of changes in domestic credit, will require a small temporary flow of reserves to restore monetary equilibrium. After this equilibrium is achieved, the official settlements balance of both countries will be zero. The home country will experience a balance of trade surplus and the foreign country will experience a balance of trade deficit. In the balance of payments accounts, the trade surpluses and deficits will be balanced by the payments and receipts of foreign aid.

The traditional approach which emphasizes flows of funds derives much of its appeal from technical details of the operation of foreign exchange rate markets. Traders in foreign exchange markets may take open positions, on a very short term basis, in order to smooth out very short-run fluctuations in exchange rates. Aside from this very short-run smoothing, however, traders seek to set rates which will balance the inflow and outflow of each national currency. Foreign exchange traders operate in much the same way as specialists on the stock exchange. They make the market. They seek to set a price which will balance purchases and sales.

The perspective of the foreign exchange trader, or the stock market specialist, however, is not the relevant perspective from which to analyze the determination of asset prices. Stock prices can change rapidly, even though the flow through the market is very small. Conversely, the volume of trade can be large and stock prices may remain essentially unchanged. The condition which determines the value of a particular company is that the outstanding shares of that company be willingly held. If sentiment concerning the future profitability of the company changes suddenly, the values of its shares will change suddenly. The volume of trade in the company's shares reflects primarily the divergence of views among asset holders: if sentiment is unanimous, prices will change with little or no trade. If sentiments differ, the volume of trade will be large.

The same principles apply to the foreign exchange markets. If money holders decide that the Deutsche mark is undervalued relative to the U.S. dollar, the mark will appreciate relative to the dollar. The flow through the mark–dollar exchange market may be very small. The circumstance in which the flow through the market becomes large is when opinions regarding the appropriate exchange rate differ. The most spectacular instances occur during exchange crises when official authorities hold one view regarding the appropriate exchange rate and everyone else holds a different view, as, for instance, the day on which the Bundesbank purchased two billion U.S. dollars.

It should be emphasized that the asset market view of the determination of exchange rates does not require that all money holders be prepared to shift their holdings from one money to another on short notice. As in any asset market, all that is required is that there be a sufficient number of active participants to make the market work. As a practical matter, these active participants are most likely to be professional traders, banks, and multinational corporations who, in the regular course of business, are used to holding on to a variety of different national monies. These particular money holders are likely to be the most sensitive to exchange rate changes and the most agressive in shifting their holdings when such changes are anticipated.

III. Expectations and Exchange Rates

The identification of the exchange rate as the relative price of national monies and the emphasis on asset market equilibrium permits the monetary approach to explain one of the major anomalies of the post 1971 period: the large, short-term fluctuations of exchange rates between the currencies of the major developed countries. These movements cannot be explained by changes in the relative prices of different national outputs. However, it has been observed for many years that prices determined in organized asset markets, such as an index of stock prices, can move up and down by significant amounts over short intervals of time. The monetary approach holds that the relative prices of national monies are determined by forces which are similar to those which operate in any asset market and, hence, that substantial short-term fluctuations in exchange rates are to be expected if the forces which lie behind exchange market equilibrium are themselves subject to substantial short term fluctuations.

The factor which is usually held to be responsible for fluctuations in asset prices is changes in the expectations of asset holders concerning the returns (including capital gains) which are likely to accrue to particular assets. Expectations are also of critical importance in determining exchange rates. If everyone expects a particular currency to appreciate, the increase in the demand to hold that currency will force its appreciation, unless the monetary authorities permit its quantity to expand sufficiently to absorb the increase in demand. The problem is to identify the things which influence expectations concerning the returns to holding particular currencies and to explain why expectations have tended to fluctuate.

If the monetary approach is correct, then *one* of the critical determinants of the equilibrium value of any national money is the supply of that money available to be held. Hence, one of the critical variables influencing asset holders expectations of future exchange rates is their prediction of the future supplies of various national monies. (This issue is analyzed more thoroughly in the appendix.) Expectations about money demand are also important, as in the case of the Swiss franc. Further, fiscal policy is likely to influence the exchange rate and, hence, expectations about the exchange rate, since budget deficits are frequently financed, at least in part, by the central bank.

The role of expectations in influencing exchange rates during the last four years has a counterpart during the earlier fixed exchange rate period. Normally, during this period, the official commitments to the maintenance of fixed parities led to the expectation that these parities would be maintained. Occasionally, however, people would come to believe that a change in the official parity was imminent, resulting in an exchange rate crisis in which huge flows of reserves would be drained from a country which was expected to devalue or would inundate a country which was expected to revalue. In the traditional approach to balance of payments theory, such "speculative flows of short-term capital" are usually treated as a special phenomenon, outside the scope of the theory. In the monetary approach, the explanation of these flows is an integral part of the theory. If asset holders expect that a currency will be devalued, the demand for that money clearly falls.

IV. Real Causes and Effects

So far, this paper has emphasized money demand and money supply as the proximate determinants of exchange rates and the balances of payments. "Real" variables are also important. The most important real variable affecting the exchange rate and the balance of payments of developed countries is the level of real income. As pointed out by Mundell, countries which enjoy rapid growth of real income will also experience rapid growth in the demand for money. Unless the domestic credit component of the money supply expands more rapidly than the demand for money, high growth countries should experience balance of payments surpluses and/or appreciating exchange rates. Fluctuations of real income around its normal trend also affect the exchange rate and the balance of payments since they affect the demand for money. Further, real disturbances affect the balance of payments and the exchange rate through the induced response of the policy authorities to such disturbances. If output and employment decline, governments are likely to pursue expansionary monetary and fiscal policies. Such policies have monetary consequences in the form of balance of payments deficits and/or depreciating exchange rates.

An important real variable affecting the balance of payments of many developing countries is the price of their primary exports. This has been illustrated dramatically for the oil exporting countries. It is also apparent in the experience of countries where export earnings are heavily dependent on a single commodity. It should be emphasized, however, that while changes in primary export prices are appropriately regarded as real disturbances, such disturbances must operate through monetary channels in order to affect the exchange rate or the official settlements balance. The tendency to run balance of payments surpluses when export prices are high and balance of payments deficits when export prices are low implies that real domestic consumption does not fluctuate by the full amount of fluctuations in export earnings. This dampening effect may not be deliberate. It may simply reflect the extent to which the government calls upon the central bank to finance its own deficit. When government receipts from royalties and taxes on exports are high, the central bank does not have to print much money. When government tax and royalty receipts decline, the central bank must finance the deficit by expanding the domestic credit component of the money supply.

Whatever may be the cause of changes in exchange rates, real or monetary, such changes usually have important real effects. These real effects are apparent in the recent experience of the United States and various Western European countries. The depreciation of the dollar relative to most other currencies has improved the competitive position of U.S. export industries and worsened the competitive position of European export industries. This is apparent in the experience of the steel industry in the United States which has continued to enjoy relative prosperity, despite the current recession. Further, while the auto industry all over the world has been depressed, Volkswagen has been particularly hard hit. One of the reasons appears to be that Volkswagen exports a large fraction of its output to the United States. The large appreciation of the mark relative to the dollar (up to June of 1974) has increased the price of Volkswagens relative to American cars and has reduced the size and profitability of Volkswagen's exports.

The explanation of these real effects of exchange rate changes has to do with the role which money plays in the economy. Domestic money is the unit of account for domestic contracts. For this reason, an important part of an exporter's costs are likely to be fixed, at least in the short run, in terms of domestic money. If the exchange rate of domestic money in terms of foreign money appreciates, the exporter must either increase his prices in terms of foreign money or see his profit margin eroded by a decline in his selling price relative to his production costs. Firms that produce highly standardized goods have little choice but to adjust their prices in terms of foreign money to those that prevail in world markets (unless they have a significant share of the market). Firms which produce more differentiated products have some latitude in increasing their prices in terms of foreign money, at the expense of some decline in sales.[1]

V. Policy Conflict and Policy Coordination

From the perspective of policy makers, the most important real effects of exchange rate changes are their effects on employment, output, and the price level. If prices of domestic outputs and domestic wages tend to be fixed, in the short run, in terms of domestic money, then the expansion of the nominal

[1] Previous discussions of the monetary approach have frequently dealt with the "small country case" in which the prices of traded goods in terms of foreign money are assumed to be given by conditions in world markets. This assumption is primarily a matter of convenience. There is no difficulty in incorporating differentiated national outputs or large countries into the general framework of the monetary approach.

demand for domestic goods which is induced by a decline in their relative price in world markets expands domestic output and employment. The price level is influenced directly by the impact of exchange rate changes on the prices of standardized internationally traded commodities. Beyond this direct influence, a depreciation contributes to inflation (and an appreciation contributes to deflation) through the gradual adjustment of the prices of non-traded goods and non-standardized traded goods to the new prices of standardized traded goods and through the adjustments of wages to the unexpected changes in real incomes.[1]

The fact that exchange rate changes have real effects makes such changes a concern of government policy. It also implies that governments can use exchange rates as instruments of government policy. This possibility has been recognized for some time. During the thirties, a number of governments devalued in the hope that this would stimulate domestic output and employment. Policy conflicts arose because everyone wanted to devalue relative to everyone else. This problem of policy conflict, however, is not an inevitable consequence of a system of controlled floating. Indeed, a system of controlled floating offers greater possibilities for avoiding policy conflict than a system of fixed rates. Under fixed rates, conflict is likely to arise whenever one government wants to expand and another government wants to contract. These different policies will put a strain on the balance of payments, with the country which is pursuing expansionary monetary and fiscal policies losing reserves to the country pursuing contractionary policies and with these reserve flows interfering with the policies of both countries. Under flexible rates, this source of conflict can be eliminated by permitting the currency of the expansionary country to depreciate relative to the currency of the contractionary country. Policy conflict is likely to arise when two countries want to expand output and employment or reduce inflation simultaneously, and when each wants to use their mutual exchange rate in pursuing its objective.

The potential for policy conflict gives rise to the need for policy coordination. What the monetary approach contributes to the discussion of policy coordination is a clearer understanding of the policies which must be coordinated. Specifically, to avoid the problem of competitive depreciation which plagued the thirties, it is usually suggested that governments agree not to intervene against their own currencies in the foreign exchange markets. The monetary approach suggests that this rule is fundamentally inadequate. What matters is the supply of money, not whether this money is created by buying domestic or foreign assets. A government can cause its currency to depreciate almost as well by having its central bank buy domestic bonds as by having it buy foreign currency. Thus, policy coordination requires essentially the coordination

[1] Recent events in England and Israel indicate that workers have caught on the fact that a devaluation is likely to reduce the real value of any given nominal wage. Workers appear to be quite prompt in demanding nominal wage increases to compensate for the effects of devaluation.

of monetary policies. Fiscal policies also matter to the extent that such policies are financed by money creation or have an impact on money demand.

Finally, it is worthwhile discussing the insulation from foreign disturbances and independence of domestic monetary policy which a system of flexible rates is supposed to provide. The argument that flexible exchange rates insulate an economy from foreign disturbances is usually presented in a model in which national outputs are distinct and capital is immobile. In such a situation, the only link between the domestic economy and the rest of the world is through the relative price of domestic and foreign goods. Under flexible rates the exchange rate adjusts this relative price so as to keep foreign demand for domestic goods constant, thereby, insulating the domestic economy.

Formally, this argument is correct.[1] As a practical matter, it may be essentially descriptive of the relationships between the United States and China. But, the argument does not apply to relationships between the United States and Canada. If the United States experiences a deep recession, so will Canada, regardless of whether the Canadian dollar floats relative to the U.S. dollar. The reason is that goods markets and capital markets in the United States and Canada are all highly integrated. The automobile industry in the two countries is really a single industry. If the demand for autos falls in the U.S., the output of autos in both countries will fall. The same holds true for many other industries. Further, the integration of the capital markets provides an important channel for the transmission of disturbances. If aggregate demand in the U.S. falls, the U.S. demand for Canadian goods will fall, tending to produce a trade balance deficit for Canada. This deficit, however, need not force a depreciation of the Canadian dollar and a corresponding cheapening of Canadian goods which restores U.S. demand for these goods. Rather, the trade imbalance can be financed by capital inflow into Canada, with the result that part of the reduction in U.S. aggregate demand is transmitted to Canada.

The failure of flexible exchange rates to insulate an economy from foreign disturbances implies that flexible exchange rates do not permit total independence of national stabilization policies. Flexible exchange rates do, however, permit different long-term rates of inflation. The explanation of why flexible rates permit different long-term rates of inflation returns us to the basic theme of this paper: the exchange rate as a monetary phenomenon. It is now a well established principle of monetary analysis that fluctuations in the money supply have real effects on employment and output only if these fluctuations are not anticipated.[2] The same is true for exchange rates. If one country's money depreciates continually relative to another country's money, these changes in the exchange rate will come to be anticipated. Once they are anticipated, they will cease to have any real effects.

[1] Actually, this argument neglects the Laursen–Metzler effect of a change in the terms of trade on desired saving, and, hence, on aggregate demand.

[2] In connection with this issue, see especially the work of Lucas (1972 and 1973), Sargent (1973), and Sargent & Wallace (1975).

Appendix

Rational Expectations, Monetary Policy, and the Exchange Rate

The purpose of this appendix is to develop a simple model which illustrates a number of conclusions concerning the interaction between monetary policy, exchange rates and exchange rate expectations. The model is built on the assumption that the exchange rate is fundamentally an asset price which is proximately determined by the relationship between the willingness to hold domestic money and the stock of domestic money available to be held. Expectations of future exchange rates affect the willingness to hold domestic money. These expectations are assumed to be "rational" in the sense that they reflect asset holders' knowledge of the structure of the economy, in particular, the structure of the stochastic processes generating money demand and money supply.[1]

I. *The Model*

Suppose that the stock of domestic money which domestic and foreign residents are willing to hold is given by

$$m(t) = \lambda \cdot e(t) - \eta \cdot \pi(t) + \zeta(t), \quad \lambda \text{ and } \eta > 0; \tag{1}$$

where $m(t)$ is the logarithm of the stock of domestic money at time t; $e(t)$ is the logarithm of the exchange rate (defined as the price of a unit of foreign money in terms of domestic money); $\pi(t)$ is the expected rate of change in the exchange rate,

$$\pi(t) \equiv E_t(e(t+1) - e(t)) \tag{2}$$

where $E_t(\ )$ indicates the expectation at time t, based on the information available to asset holders at that time; and $\zeta(t)$ summarizes all of the influences on the willingness to hold domestic money other than $e(t)$ and $\pi(t)$. The right hand side of (1) should be thought of as the final reduced form of a general equilibrium model with the usual structure of goods and asset market equilibria.[2] The prices, quantities and rates of return on all goods and assets (except m, e and π) have been solved out of the system, and the influence of all of these variables on the willingness to hold domestic money is subsumed

[1] For the application of the concept of "rational" expectations to exchange rate theory, see Black (1972) and (1973). Also see Kouri (1975). For a general survey of the literature on rational expectations in macroeconomic models see Shiller (1975) or Sargent (1973).

[2] The general procedure for deriving such a final reduced form relationship is indicated in Mussa (1975*b*). A variety of models could be used as the basis for the relationship given in (1), for instance, those of Dornbusch (1976), and Kouri (1975). The simplest model would be one in which there is a single traded good with a domestic price equal to the exchange rate times the foreign price level and where the real demand for money depends on the expected rate of inflation (which is identical to the expected rate of depreciation). This is essentially the model analyzed by Sargent & Wallace (1973) and Mussa (1975*a*) for the closed economy. The model could be made more realistic by the methods suggested by Dornbusch.

in the variable $\zeta(t)$ and in the values of the elasticities, λ and η. In particular $\zeta(t)$ incorporates the effects of disturbances in the foreign money supply, foreign prices, and foreign interest rates on the willingness to hold domestic money.

The assumption that λ and η are positive is plausible for virtually any basic model of exchange rate determination. An increase in the exchange rate increases the domestic price of internationally traded commodities and may also increase domestic output and income, all of which suggests an increase in the desire to hold domestic money. An increase in the exchange rate reduces the ratio of the value of domestic money to foreign money and to all assets denominated in foreign money (or in real terms) and should, from a portfolio balance perspective, increase the nominal demand for domestic money. An increase in the expected rate of depreciation (an increase in π) decreases the attractiveness of domestic money relative to foreign money and relative to assets denominated in foreign money. An increase in π also suggests an increase in the expected rate of inflation which should reduce the demand for money.

Substituting (2) into (1) and solving for $e(t)$ yields

$$e(t) = \left(\frac{1}{\lambda+\eta}\right) \cdot [m(t) - \zeta(t) + \eta \cdot E_t(e(t+1))] \tag{3}$$

To complete the determination of $e(t)$, it is necessary to know the current expectation of $e(t+1)$. We impose the assumption that expectations are formed "rationally". Specifically, asset holders are assumed to know (or act as if they know) equation (3) and apply it to next period's exchange rate; thus

$$E_t(e(t+1)) = \frac{1}{\lambda+\eta} \cdot E_t[m(t+1) - \zeta(t+1) + \eta \cdot E_{t+1}(e(t+2))] \tag{4}$$

Using the fact that $E_t(E_{t+1}(e(t+2))) = E_t(e(t+2))$ and applying the same procedure iteratively to $E_t(e(t+2))$, $E_t(e(t+3))$, etc., it follows that[1]

$$\begin{aligned} E_t(e(t+1)) &= \left(\frac{1}{\lambda+\eta}\right) \cdot \left\{E_t\left[m(t+j) - \zeta(t+1) + \frac{\eta}{\lambda+\eta}(E_t(m(t+2)) \right.\right. \\ &\qquad \left.\left. - \zeta(t+2) + \ldots)\right]\right\} \\ &= \left(\frac{1}{\lambda+\eta}\right) \sum_{j=1}^{\infty} E_t[m(t+j) - \zeta(t+j)] \cdot \left(\frac{\eta}{\lambda+\eta}\right)^{j-1}. \end{aligned} \tag{5}$$

II. *Two Examples*

It is reasonable to assume that people have relatively little information about events far in the future, except possibly in the form of predictions of long-run

[1] The form of (5) is almost identical to that given by Sargent & Wallace (1973). See, also, Mussa (1975*a*).

average levels or rates of growth. This assumption eliminates all but a finite number of terms from (5). In this section, we consider two examples which focus on short-run deviations of $m(t)-\zeta(t)$ around long-run levels or rates of growth. For simplicity we assume that $\zeta(t)=k$, a constant.

Example 1: A fixed mean with autocorrelated disturbances. Suppose that $m(t)$ is determined by

$$m(t)=\bar{m}+u(t), \quad u(t)=\varrho\cdot u(t-1)+\varepsilon(t) \tag{6}$$

where $\bar{m}$ is the mean level of the money supply, $u(t)$ is an autocorrelated disturbance with correlation coefficient, ϱ, $0\leqslant\varrho\leqslant1$, and $\varepsilon(t)$ is a serially uncorrelated, normally distributed random variable with zero mean and variance σ_ε^2. Assuming that asset holders know the properties of the stochastic process generating the money supply, including the mean, $\bar{m}$, and also know $m(t)$ and hence $u(t)=m(t)-\bar{m}$, it follows that

$$E_t(m(t+j))=\bar{m}+\varrho^j\cdot u(t) \tag{7}$$

Substitution of this result into (5) yields

$$E_t(e(t+1))=\bar{e}+\left(\frac{\varrho}{\lambda+\eta(1-\varrho)}\right)\cdot u(t), \tag{8}$$

which together with (3) implies

$$e(t)=\bar{e}+\left(\frac{1}{\lambda+\eta(1-\varrho)}\right)\cdot u(t) \tag{9}$$

where $\bar{e}\equiv(1/\lambda)(\bar{m}-k)$ is the long-run expected level of e, the value of e which is consistent with $m=\bar{m}$. From (2), (8) and (9), it follows that

$$\pi(t)\equiv E_t(e(t+1))-e(t)=(1-\varrho)\cdot(\bar{e}-e(t)). \tag{10}$$

The intuitive explanation of this result is the following. When ϱ is small money holders expect the exchange rate to converge rapidly to $\bar{e}$. A temporary increase in the money supply will cause $e(t)$ to rise; domestic money depreciates relative to foreign money. However, money holders expect a rapid reappreciation. This expectation induces them to hold larger domestic money balances which, in turn, limits the current depreciation. In contrast, if ϱ is large, money holders will not expect a rapid return to $\bar{e}$. The current exchange rate will have to move further in order to equilibrate the current demand and supply of domestic money. In the limit, when $\varrho=1$, any current disturbance to the money supply is expected to persist forever. In fact, m is a random walk, and this makes e a random walk. Any current disturbance to the money supply affects the current and all expected future exchange rates by the same amount. Since money holders do not expect the exchange rate to regress to any normal level, the current exchange rate must absorb the full effect of any change in the current money supply.

Example 2: A random walk on levels and rates of growth. The second example assumes that the rate of growth as well as the level of the money supply is randomly determined. Specifically,

$$m(t) = m(t-1) + \alpha(t) + \varepsilon(t) \tag{11}$$

where $\varepsilon(t)$ has the same properties as in the first example and $\alpha(t)$ is a random walk,

$$\alpha(t) = \alpha(t-1) + \delta(t) \tag{12}$$

where $\delta(t)$ is a serially uncorrelated, normally distributed random disturbance with zero mean, variance σ_δ^2, and independent of the ε's. $\alpha(t)$ should be interpreted as the (expected) long-term rate of growth of the money supply which changes randomly over time. In additíon to the randomness in the long-term rate of growth, there are also disturbances to the level of the money supply, the ε's.

Assuming that money holders know the properties of the stochastic process generating the money supply, it follows that

$$E_t(m(t+j)) = m(t) + j \cdot \hat{\alpha}(t) \tag{13}$$

where $\hat{\alpha}(t) \equiv E_t(\alpha(t))$ is not necessarily equal to $\alpha(t)$. Whether this equality holds depends on the information available to money holders at time t. Substituting (13) into (5) yields

$$E_t(e(t+j)) = \frac{1}{\lambda} \cdot \left[m(t) - k + \left(\frac{\lambda + \eta}{\lambda} \right) \cdot \hat{\alpha}(t) \right] \tag{14}$$

which together with (3) implies

$$e(t) = \frac{1}{\lambda} \left[m(t) - k + \left(\frac{\eta}{\lambda} \right) \cdot \hat{\alpha}(t) \right] \tag{17}$$

If money holders always know the current values of α and ε as well as the current value of m, it follows that $\hat{\alpha}(t) \equiv E_t(\alpha(t)) = \alpha(t)$ and $\hat{\varepsilon}(t) \equiv E_t(\varepsilon(t)) = \varepsilon(t)$. The effect on the exchange rate of an unexpected increase in the money supply depends on the source of this increase. The expected increase in the money supply from period $t-1$ was $\alpha(t-1) = E_{t-1}(m(t) - m(t-1))$. If m increases by more than this amount because of a positive value of $\varepsilon(t)$, money holders will know that is only a disturbance to the level of the money supply. The current value of e will rise by a factor $1/\lambda$ times $\varepsilon(t)$. The expected value of $e(t+1)$ will rise by the same amount. However, if the expected increase in $m(t)$ is known to arise from a positive value of $\delta(t)$, money holders know that this portends larger increases in the money supply in every future period.

The current value of e will rise by a factor of $(1/\lambda)(1+(\eta/\lambda))$ times $\delta(t)$. This is a greater increase than for the positive $\varepsilon(t)$. Further, the expected value of $e(t+1)$ rises by even more than $e(t)$ because the increase in the expected long-term rate of growth of the money supply leads people to expect more rapid depreciation of domestic money.

On the other hand, suppose that money holders only observe the time path of m and must infer from this information the values of α and ε. It can be shown (see, for instance, Mussa (1975*a*)) that under rational expectations

$$\hat{\alpha}(t) = \hat{\alpha}(t-1) + a\cdot(m(t) - m(t-1) - \hat{\alpha}(t-1)). \tag{18}$$

The magnitude $m(t) - m(t-1) - \hat{\alpha}(t-1)$ is the difference between the observed change in m, $m(t) - m(t-1)$, and its a priori expected value $\hat{\alpha}(t-1)$. A fraction, a, of this difference is added to last period's $\hat{\alpha}$ in order to obtain the current $\hat{\alpha}$. The fraction, a, is determined by the relative likelihood that a deviation of $m(t) - m(t-1)$ from its a priori expected value is caused by an unexpected change in α rather than by a random disturbance to the level of m; specifically,

$$a = \frac{\theta^2 + \sigma_\delta^2}{\theta^2 + \sigma_\delta^2 + \sigma_\varepsilon^2} \tag{19}$$

where

$$\theta^2 = \tfrac{1}{2}\cdot[-\sigma_\delta^2 + \sqrt{\sigma_\delta^4 + 4\cdot\sigma_\delta^2\cdot\sigma_\varepsilon^2}].$$

In the present case, an increase in the long-term rate of growth of m (a positive $\delta(t)$) has the same effect as an increase in the level of m (a positive $\varepsilon(t)$). The reason is that money holders cannot, at time t, distinguish between a positive $\varepsilon(t)$ and a positive $\delta(t)$. The current value of e rises by a factor of $(1/\lambda)[1 + a\cdot(\lambda + \eta/\lambda)]$ times either $\varepsilon(t)$ or $\delta(t)$. It should be emphasized, however, that the errors which are made under incomplete information are neither permanent nor irrational. The errors are not permanent because in periods $t+1$, $t+2$, etc., additional information will be received concerning the true value of α; if there has been a change in α, money holders will ultimately discover it. Further, any errors which are made are not irrational because "rationality" is defined with respect to an information set. People form the best expectations they can, given the limitation on their information.

III. *Some Implications*

These examples illustrate a number of important conclusions. First, the way in which exchange rate expectations are formed should depend on the underlying economic structure, including the stochastic structure of disturbances to the demand and supply of money. In the first example, if $\varrho < 1$, expectations are "regressive" in the sense that a current depreciation of the exchange rate leads to the expectation that the exchange rate will re-appreciate to its average level. On the other hand, if $\varrho = 1$, any change in $e(t)$ is believed to be permanent and is reflected in an equal change in $E_t(e(t+1))$. These considerations may have practical relevance. The exchange rate between the Canadian and U.S. dollars has been within 10% of parity for more than 100 years. This may explain the apparent regressivity of exchange rate expectations concerning the Canadian dollar.

Second, since the way in which expectations are formed is likely to depend on the characteristics of monetary and fiscal policy, it is incorrect to assume that the expectations mechanism will long remain unchanged in the face of a significant change in the basic characteristics of policy. This important point has been made in a much broader context by Lucas (1970). In the context of example 1, exchange rate expectations are highly regressive when ϱ is close to zero. However, if policy is changed to make $\varrho=1$, expectations will lose their regressivity as soon as the change in policy is discovered. If policy is changed to that of example 2, the change in the mechanism of expectation formation will be even more dramatic. At a practical level, if Canada began to pursue a highly inflationary policy, relative to the United States, which drove the exchange rate outside of its usual bounds, it probably would not be very long before the normal regressivity of expectations was eliminated.

Third, the exchange rate which prevails at any instant, and the expectations which are held at that instant concerning future exchange rates, depend on the information available to asset holders at that instant. This principle was illustrated in the second example in the comparison between behaviour with full information and behaviour with limited information. As a practical matter, of course, information is always limited in the sense that we never know the future course of all variables relevant to our current decisions. After the fact, it will appear that errors have been made. However, after the fact is not the appropriate perspective from which to judge the "rationality" of exchange rate expectations or the "efficiency" of the exchange markets. Large up and down movements of exchange rates appear irrational and inefficient, after the fact, but do not provide evidence of a capacity to make better predictions or more profitable transactions, before the fact.

Fourth, the two examples suggest caution in making general assumptions concerning the response of forward rates to variations in spot rates. For simplicity, identify the forward rate with the expected future spot rate. In the first example we have the following results. If $\varrho=0$, the forward rate is constant and changes in the spot rate have no effect on the forward rate. If ϱ is between 0 and 1, the forward rate moves in the same direction as the spot rate, but not by as much. If $\varrho=1$, the spot and forward rates move together. In the second example, with full information, the spot and forward rates move together for changes in the level of m, and the forward rate moves more than the spot rate for changes in the rate of growth of m. With incomplete information, the forward rate always responds more strongly than the spot rate to an unexpected change in m.

Fifth, exchange rate fluctuations may be more extensive than fluctuations in the money supply or in money demand. From equation (3) it is apparent that if $\lambda + \eta < 1$, fluctuations in either $m(t)$ or $\zeta(t)$ will have a magnified effect on $e(t)$. Further, if, as in example 2, disturbances to $m(t)$ lead to the conviction that the rate of growth as well as the level of the money supply have changed, the exchange rate will respond immediately to both the disturbance in $m(t)$ and to the anticipated change in the rate of depreciation.

Sixth, in both examples, the process generating disturbances in the money supply was an arbitrarily prescribed stochastic process, a stochastic black box. In fact, there is likely to be a good deal of economic structure which lies behind the nature of disturbances to the money supply, including the structure of the banking system, the aggressivity of "stabilization" policy, and the extent to which the government resorts to the printing press as a means of financing its deficits. However, so long as the internal workings of the black box continue to generate the same sort of stochastic outcomes, it is not necessary for asset holders to understand these workings in order to form their exchange rate expectations. The internal structure becomes important when something inside the box changes. For instance, in the context of example 1, suppose that the "structure" is changed by a shift from $\varrho = 0$ to $\varrho = 1$. If asset holders understand the implications of this change in structure, exchange rate expectations will shift immediately from being regressive to a random walk. If asset holders do not understand the structure, it will probably take some time for them to realize that regressive expectations are no longer appropriate.

Finally, the two examples have strong implications concerning the concept of "stabilizing expectations". Exchange rate expectations are frequently said to be "stabilizing" if they are regressive; that is, if current depreciation (or appreciation) is limited by the expectation that the exchange rate will later re-appreciate (or re-depreciate). In example 1, with $\varrho < 1$, exchange rate expectations are regressive. They are regressive because the underlying behaviour of the money supply makes regressive expectations appropriate. However, in example 1, with $\varrho = 1$, and in example 2, exchange rate expectations are not regressive. These expectations are, nevertheless, "stabilizing" in the fundamental sense that they are the best possible predictions of future exchange rates, given the nature of monetary policy and the information available to asset holders.

References

Black, S.: The use of rational expectations in models of speculation. *Review of Economics and Statistics*, May 1972.

Black, S.: *International Money Markets and Flexible Exchange Rates.* Princeton Studies in International Finance, No. 32, 1973.

Caves, R. E. & Jones, R. W.: *World Trade and Payments.* Little Brown, Boston, 1973.

Dornbusch, R.: Money, devaluation, and non-traded goods. *American Economic Review 63*, No. 5, 1973.

Dornbusch, R.: The Theory of Flexible Exchange Rates and Macroeconomic Policy. *Scandinavian Journal of Economics 78*, No. 2, pp. 255–275, 1976.

Frenkel, J. & Johnson, H. G.: *The Monetary Approach to the Balance of Payments.* George Allen and Unwin, 1975 forthcoming.

Kemp, D. S.: A monetary view of the balance of payments. Federal Reserve Bank of St. Louis *Review* 57, No. 4, April 1975.

Kouri, P.: Exchange rate expectations, and the short run and the long run effects of fiscal and monetary policies under flexible exchange rates. Presented at the Conference on the Monetary Mechanism in Open Economies, Helsinki, August 1975.

Lucas, R. E.: Econometric testing of the natural rate hypothesis. In O. Eckstein (ed.), *The Econometrics of Price Determination.* Board of Governors of the Federal Reserve System, Washington, D.C., 1970.

Lucas, R. E.: Expectations and the neutrality of money. *Journal of Economic Theory 4*, No. 2, April 1972.

Lucas, R. E.: Some international evidence on output-inflation trade-offs. *American Economic Review 63*, No. 3, June 1973.

Mundell, R. A.: *International Economics.* Macmillan, New York, 1968.

Mussa, M. L.: A monetary approach to balance of payments analysis. *Journal of Money, Credit and Banking 6*, No. 3, August 1974.

Mussa, M. L.: Adaptive and regressive expectations in a rational model of the inflationary process. *Journal of Monetary Economics 1*, No. 4, October 1975*a*.

Mussa, M. L.: Equities, interest, and the stability of the inflationary process. *Journal of Money, Credit and Banking,* November 1975*b*.

Pearce, I. F.: *International Trade.* Norton, New York, 1970.

Sargent, T. J.: Rational expectations, the real rate of interest, and the natural rate of unemployment. *Brookings Papers on Economics Acitivity*, 1973.

Sargent, T. J. & Wallace, N.: Rational expectations and the dynamics of hyperinflation. *International Economic Review*, June 1973.

Sargent, T. J. & Wallace, N.: Rational expectations, the optimal monetary instrument and the optimal money supply rule. *Journal of Political Economy 83*, No. 2, April 1975.

Shiller, R.: Rational expectations, and the dynamic structure of macroeconomic models. Paper presented at the Conference on the Monetary Mechanism in Open Economies, Helsinki, August 1975.

COMMENT ON M. MUSSA, "THE EXCHANGE RATE, THE BALANCE OF PAYMENTS AND MONETARY AND FISCAL POLICY UNDER A REGIME OF CONTROLLED FLOATING"

Michael Parkin

University of Western Ontario, London, Canada

"[The] central contention of ... [Mussa's] ... paper [is] that the basic theoretical framework of the monetary approach to the balance of payments remains applicable" (see above, page 97) to the world of controlled floating which has existed since 1971. The paper itself is informal and the discussion general but, there is also a more formal appendix. This comment summarizes and evaluates both the paper and the appendix.

Four basic points are made and they are worth summarizing at the outset. First, an exchange rate is a relative price of two national monies and is determined by the conditions for *stock* equilibrium in the markets for national monies and not in *flow* markets for goods. Secondly, one of the factors which influences the demand for money and, therefore, the exchange rate, is the expected future exchange rate. That expectation is formed rationally and depends, therefore, on expected future monetary policy. Thirdly, the exchange rate is not purely a monetary phenomenon. Real factors which affect the demand for money also affect the exchange rate. Fourthly, the problem of policy conflict which exists under fixed rates is modified rather than eliminated by floating rates.

The basic monetary approach is sketched out in part I of the paper. That approach centres on the equations:

$$M^s = R + C \tag{1}$$

$$M^d = L(\ )EP_w \tag{2}$$

$$M^s = M^d \tag{3}$$

where

R = foreign exchange reserves

C = domestic credit

$L(\ )$ = demand for real balances

P_w = world price level
E = exchange rate (units of domestic currency per unit of foreign currency)
M = nominal money balances (superscripts d and s denote demand and supply).

Eq. (1) is a definition of the relationship between the supply of money, foreign exchange reserves and domestic credit which arises from a consolidation of the balance sheets of the central bank and the commercial banks. Eq. (2) is a demand for money function which incorporates degree one homogeneity in the price level and assumes purchasing power parity (i.e., the domestic price level is the product of the exchange rate (E) and the world price level (P_w)). Eq. (3) is the stock equilibrium condition. Combining (1), (2) and (3)

$$R + C = L(\ )EP_w \tag{4}$$

Under *fixed* exchange rates, E is fixed and a rise in the value of $L(\ )$ (arising from a rise in real income or a fall in the nominal interest rate), a rise in P_w or a fall in C will lead to an overall balance of payments surplus—i.e., a rise in R. Under floating exchange rates, R is fixed and the above changes lead to an appreciation of the currency, i.e., to a fall in E. Under a regime of controlled floating, the central bank chooses a combination of E and R constrained by (4).

One of the arguments of $L(\ )$ is the domestic nominal rate of interest which, in turn, is influenced by the expected rate of change of the exchange rate. This means that in order to determine the exchange rate (under a regime of free floating or controlled floating) it is necessary to analyze the determinants of exchange rate expectations. The hypothesis advanced by Mussa is that those expectations are "rational" and are based on expectations of future changes—the demand for and supply of money. This is formalized in the Appendix. Here, money market equilibrium is given by:

$$m(t) = \lambda e(t) - \eta\pi(t) + \zeta(t), \quad \lambda, \eta > 0 \tag{5}$$

where a lower case letter denotes a natural logarithm,

$$\pi(t) \equiv E_t[e(t+1) - e(t)] \tag{6}$$

where $E_t[\ ]$ denotes an expectation formed on the basis of the information available at t and where $\zeta(t)$ absorbs all the other influences on the demand for nominal balances. Using (6), eq. (5) can be 'solved' for the exchange rate at t as:

$$e(t) = \frac{1}{\lambda + \eta}(m(t) - \zeta(t) + \eta\, E_t[e(t+1)]) \tag{7}$$

Rational expectations imply that

$$E_t e(t+i) = \frac{1}{\lambda+\eta} E_t[m(t+i) - \zeta(t+i) + \eta E_t[e(t+i+1)]] \tag{8}$$

for all $i \geq 1$.

Using (8), iteratively for all $i \geq 1$ with (7) implies that

$$e(t) = \frac{1}{\lambda+\eta}\left(m(t) - \zeta(t) + \eta \sum_{i=1}^{\infty} E_t[m(t+i) - \zeta(t+i)]\left(\frac{\eta}{\lambda+\eta}\right)^{i-1}\right) \tag{9}$$

Eq. (9) states that the exchange rate at t will depend on the money supply at t ($m(t)$), the values taken on by all the factors which affect the demand for money at t, ($\zeta(t)$), and the expectation conditional on the information available at t (E_t) of the future values of m and ζ for all future time. To make (9) operational it is necessary to make some stronger statements about expections of future m and ζ. Two examples are worked out by Mussa: one with a fixed mean for m and autocorrelated disturbances and one with a random walk on both the level and growth rate of m. In both examples, $E_t[\xi(t+i)] = k$ for all $i \geq 1$ where k = constant. The first example is sufficient to illustrate the general point which Mussa wants to make. In that case,

$$m(t) = \bar{m} + u(t),\ u(t) = \varrho u(t-1) + \varepsilon(t) \tag{10}$$

with $0 \leq \varrho \leq 1$ and $\varepsilon(t)$ is an i.i.d., normal disturbance. The expectation of $m(t+i)$ is given by:

$$E[m(t+i)] = \bar{m} + \varrho^i u(t) \tag{11}$$

Using this with (9) together with the long-run expected value of e,

$$\bar{e} = \frac{1}{\lambda}(\bar{m} - k) \tag{12}$$

yields

$$e(t) = \bar{e} + \frac{1}{\lambda + \eta(1-\varrho)} u(t) \tag{13}$$

Three important implications of (13) are worth spelling out. First, the "noisier" is m (i.e., the bigger is the variance of ε (or u)), the "noisier" is the behavior of the exchange rate. Secondly, the bigger is ϱ, i.e., the stronger the autocorrelation, the bigger the effects of random disturbances on e. Thirdly, if $\varrho = 1$, the exchange rate follows a random walk. However, there is nothing unstable about e in this case. It is simply doing what it has to do given the behavior of the money supply. All this can be put more directly by saying that the more ill behaved is the money supply, the more ill behaved will it be expected to be and the more variable will be the exchange rate.

Although the above discussion has focussed on the effects of the money supply on the exchange rate, it is clear that the behavior of ζ (treated as constant) is also crucial. This subsumes such real factors as real income fluctuations and such other nominal magnitudes as the world price level and inflation rate which, in turn, will be influenced by monetary policy in the rest of the world.

Let me now turn to an evaluation of Mussa's argument and analysis. First, it is impossible to dispute Mussa's central proposition that exchange rates are, by definition, relative prices of national monies. However, it does not follow from that proposition that "[t]he proximate determinants of exchange rates ... are the demand for and supplies of various national monies" (above, page 97). Rather, that is an implication of the fact that there are well organized markets in exchanging national monies and facilities for the rapid exchange and collation of information on excess demand and supplies. Because of this, it seems reasonable to suppose that the foreign exchange market achieves a close approximation to a tâtonnement process in which there is rapid convergence to a market clearing price.

There is an interesting parallel between what might be called the modern quantity theory of money explanation of the proximate determinants of the exchange rate and the older quantity theory of money explanation of the proximate determinants of the price level in a single money closed economy.

In the quantity theory tradition, most convincingly presented by Irving Fisher (1911, ch. IV), the price level (and therefore the *value* of money) was regarded as being proximately determined by stock equilibrium in the money market. Any discrepancy between the rate of change of prices arising from this money market equilibrating process and the expected rate of price change would lead to adjustments in real output as producers responded to misread information about relative prices. Thus, the line of causation in the quantity theory of Fisher went from money to prices (i.e., money proximately determined the price level) and from prices relative to expected prices to real output and employment.

The modern post-Keynesian view of the role of stock equilibrium in the money market reverses the two links in the Fisher causation story. The *proximate* determinants of the price level are now seen as the price expectations and assessments of excess demands by price setting firms (and households) in individual markets for goods and services (and factors of production). Given a price level thus determined, stock equilibrium in the money market arises from interest rate and real output adjustments. In other words, it is interest rates and real aggregate demand which are proximately determined by the equality of the supply of and demand for money.

Is Mussa returning (in an open economy context) to the earlier Fisher view of the world in making the exchange rate adjust to clear the money market or is his analysis firmly in the post-Keynesian tradition? Clearly the latter, for the exchange rate, or rather the exchange rate together with its expected future value represent the opportunity cost of holding money and not the value of money. Thus, in placing the adjustment of an open economy's money market on the exchange rate is equivalent to placing the adjustment in a closed economy on the level of interest rates.

Although we gain important insights by recognizing that exchange rates are determined by supplies of and demands for national monies, it may, nevertheless, take us nowhere in terms of a practical analysis of exchange rate determination. Let us now consider the operational usefulness of this view. The usefulness of the monetary approach depends essentially on two related matters. First, the approach requires that there exists a demand for money which is a stable function of a small number of variables. Secondly, the arguments of the demand for money function must themselves be easily predicted and, more importantly, independent of the size of or rate of change of the supply of money. Are these conditions met? The answer clearly depends on the length of time aggregate that we are considering. For very short time aggregates—hours perhaps to a few weeks—we know little about the stability of the demand for money. It seems at least likely that there may be a good deal of noise in the relationship. This seems especially likely in view of the fact that money is held mainly as a "buffer stock" to meet expenditures, the magnitudes and timing of which are uncertain. Thus, over very short intervals, it may be important, from an operational point of view, to analyze a potentially large number of factors which cause shifts in the demand for money function. It may well be that *flows* especially in international trade are crucial factors in causing such temporary shifts. Hence, there is no unambiguous presumption that flow considerations are unimportant.

Over somewhat longer periods - quarterly to annual intervals - we know a great deal about demand for money functions. They do appear to be stable functions of three key arguments, the price level (with degree one homogeneity), real income and an opportunity cost variable (see Laidler, 1969, for a review of the evidence). In the floating rate economy, the expected change in the exchange rate will clearly be a key element in the latter. Thus, over periods longer than a quarter, it seems safe to predict that, *given the levels of real income and prices*, the exchange rate will be a function of the money supply (and the expected future money supply). However, the second requirement of the monetary approach now begins to look implausible. Can we treat real income and the price level as being independent of the money supply and the exchange rate over periods of such length? Clearly not. It becomes necessary therefore to develop models which explain the determination of income and prices *simultaneously* with the exchange rate. The monetary approach survives as part of that process but only as one part of it. Dornbusch (1976) has already analyzed the simultaneous determination of prices and the exchange rate for a given (full employment) level of output. The development of a simple model of the simultaneous determination of all three variables—the exchange rate, the price level, and real output—remains one of the most important, outstanding tasks in monetary economics.

References

Dornbusch, R.: The theory of flexible exchange rate regimes and macroeconomic policy. *Scandinavian Journal of Economics 78*, No. 2, pp. 255–275, 1976.

Fisher, I.: *The Purchasing Power of Money.* Macmillan, New York, 1911. (Latest edition A. M. Kelly, New York, 1963.)

Laidler, D. E. W.: *The Demand for Money: Theories and Evidence.* International Textbook Company, Scranton, Pa., 1969.

THE THEORY OF FLEXIBLE EXCHANGE RATE REGIMES AND MACROECONOMIC POLICY*

Rudiger Dornbusch

Massachusetts Institute of Technology, Cambridge, Mass., USA

Abstract

This paper develops three perspectives on the determination of exchange rates and their interaction with macroeconomic equilibrium and aggregate policies. A long-run view characterizes exchange rate determination in terms of monetary and real factors where the real aspects include an explicit consideration of relative price structures. A short-run or "liquidity" view of the exchange rate emphasizes the role of asset market equilibrium and expectations. A policy view, finally, analyses the effectiveness of aggregate policies and points out that in the short-run nominal disturbances will tend to be transmitted internationally. The paper concludes with an analysis of dual exchange rate systems as a stabilizing policy in the presence of speculative disturbances.

This paper is concerned with some issues in the theory of flexible exchange rates. Specifically, we study the determinants of the exchange rate, both in the short and long run, the role of capital mobility and speculation in that context, and the scope for the international transmission of disturbances. In discussing the transmission of disturbances particular emphasis is given to the idea that in the short run monetary and price disturbances are not offset by matching exchange rate changes and, for that reason, are spread internationally.

The issues raised in this paper have been, to a large extent, discussed in the literature. We note here, in particular, Mundell (1964, 1968) and Fleming (1962) in their discussion of stabilization policy under flexible exchange rates as well as the subsequent work by Argy & Porter (1972) that formalizes the role of expectations in this context. Work by Black (1973, 1975) has emphasized the role of asset markets in exchange rate determination and a paper by Niehans (1975) has explored the interaction of exchange rate expectations and relative price responses to question the effectiveness of monetary policy under flexible rates.

The present paper adds to that strand of literature in that it distinguishes shortrun effects of policies, sustained in part by price rigidities and expecta-

* I wish to acknowledge helpful comments on an earlier draft from Stanley Black, Stanley Fischer, Jacob Frenkel and Dwight Jaffee. Financial support was provided by a grant from the Ford Foundation.

tional errors, from the longer run effects where relative prices and homogeneity are given emphasis. The aggregation departs from the standard Keynesian model of complete specialization and two traded goods in distinguishing traded goods as a composite commodity and nontraded goods. Such an aggregation is preferred since it breaks the identification of the exchange rate with the terms of trade, introduces scope for a monetary interpretation of the exchange rate and leaves room at the same time for intersectoral considerations.

In Section I we lay out a general equilibrium framework for the discussion of exchange rates from a long-run perspective. The critical assumptions of that theory are purchasing power parity for traded goods and monetary equilibrium. In Section II the assumption of purchasing power parity is relaxed to yield a short-run or "money-market" theory of the exchange rate. In Section III we return to purchasing power parity and investigate the role of speculation in affecting the scope for the international transmission of monetary disturbances and for the operation of monetary and fiscal policy. In Section IV the discussion is extended to a dual exchange rate system.

I. A General View of Exchange Rate Determinants

In this section we outline a fairly general and eclectic view of the determinants of exchange rates. Such a view links monetary and real variables as jointly influencing the equilibrium level of the exchange rate. The view is appropriate to full equilibrium or the 'long run' and is a benchmark from which to judge departures and alternatives.

A critical ingredient of this approach is purchasing power parity, in the narrow sense of goods arbitrage for internationally traded goods, so that the exchange rate equates the prices of traded goods in alternative currencies:[1]

$$P_T = eP_T^* \tag{1}$$

where P_T and P_T^* represent the domestic and foreign currency prices of traded goods and where e is the domestic currency price of foreign exchange.[2]

The prices of traded goods can be related to the price levels, P and P^*, respectively. The appropriate relationship is given by the equilibrium *relative* price of traded goods in terms of the price levels, θ and θ^*:

$$P_T = \theta P;\ P_T^* = \theta^* P^* \tag{2}$$

The determinants of the equilibrium relative price structure, denoted here by θ and θ^*, will be discussed below.[3] For the present it suffices to note that

[1] We abstract here from tariffs and transport costs that introduce obvious modifications in (1).
[2] All starred variables refer to the foreign country.
[3] See pp. 264–265 below.

an increase in the equilibrium price of traded goods by x percent raises their relative price θ by $(1-\gamma)x$ percent where γ and $(1-\gamma)$, respectively, denote the shares of traded goods and nontraded goods in the price index.

Using (2) in eq. (1), we can express the exchange rate in terms of price levels and relative prices:

$$e = (P/P^*)(\theta/\theta^*). \tag{3}$$

The next step is to link up the discussion with the monetary sector. This is achieved by multiplying and dividing (3) by the domestic and foreign nominal quantity of money, M and M^*.[1] Furthermore, imposing the conditions of monetary equilibrium:

$$M/P = L(\ );\ M^*/P^* = L^*(\ ), \tag{4}$$

where L and L^* represent the domestic and foreign demand for real balances, we arrive at (5):[2]

$$e = (M/M^*)(L^*/L)(\theta/\theta^*). \tag{5}$$

Eq. (5) collects the principal determinants of exchange rates. These are, respectively, the nominal quantities of monies, the real money demands, and the relative price structure. It can be viewed as an *equilibrium* exchange rate since in its derivation we have used the conditions of goods arbitrage, money market equilibrium and, implicitly in using (2), home goods market equilibrium. The usefulness of (5) is enhanced by considering the logarithmic differential denoting a percentage change by a "^":

$$\hat{e} = (\hat{M} - \hat{M}^*) + (\hat{L}^* - \hat{L}) + (\hat{\theta} - \hat{\theta}^*). \tag{6}$$

The first term in (6) captures the effects of monetary changes on the exchange rate. Other things equal, the country with the higher monetary growth will have a depreciating exchange rate. This particular term captures the effect of differences in long-run inflation rates between countries and their reflection in exchange rates.

The effect of changes in real money demand is captured in the second term in (6). The country that experiences a (relative) increase in real money demand will have an appreciation in the exchange rate. Among the factors that exert an influence on real money demand, we note here, in particular, interest rates, expected inflation, and real income growth. The real money demand term in (6) constitutes one of the links between the exchange rate, the monetary sector and the real sector. This term helps explain how changes in productivity, for example, get reflected in exchange rate changes.

---

[1] The choice of monetary aggregate in (4) is presumably that for which real money demand is most stable. Furthermore, we do not require that in (4) the same monetary aggregate for both countries be used.

[2] For a similar equation that concentrates on traded goods, see Collery (1971).

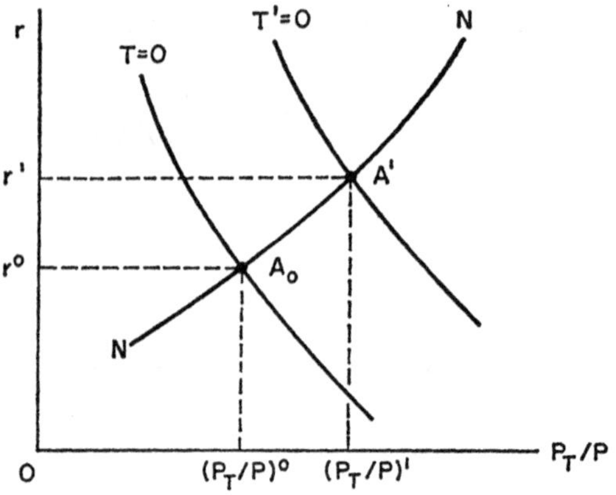

Fig. 1.

The last term in (6) collects the effect of changes in the relative price structure on the exchange rate. This term arises entirely from real considerations and, in fact, has been identified in some literature as the "real exchange rate".[1] Given the nominal quantity of money and the demand for real balances, and therefore the price level, an increase in the equilibrium relative price of traded goods will be reflected in a depreciation in the exchange rate. Changes in absorption, shifts in demand, or biased output growth, *given* a monetary policy that sustains the price level, will therefore directly affect the exchange rate.

An example will show how eq. (6) can be applied. Assume that in the home country we have an increase in spending that falls entirely on traded goods, while abroad everything remains unchanged. Assume further that because of the absence of capital mobility the exchange rate adjusts to maintain trade balance equilibrium. In Fig. 1 we show the equilibrium in the home goods market along the NN schedule. At higher interest rates, and hence lower real spending, we require a higher relative price of traded goods to clear the home goods market. An increase in interest rates has an expenditure reducing effect that has to be offset by the expenditure and production switching effects of a relative price change. Along the $T=0$ schedule, we have trade balance equilibrium. At lower interest rates and hence higher aggregate real spending, we require a higher relative price of traded goods to maintain trade balance. The initial equilibrium is at point A_0.

An increase in spending that falls on traded goods creates at the initial equilibrium an excess demand for traded goods and therefore requires higher

[1] See, for example, Corden (1971, Chapter 5) and Dornbusch (1974*b*). Much of the partial equilibrium literature concerned with real trade questions uses implicitly (3) together with the assumption that monetary or fiscal policies maintain constant the level of prices, P and P^*. Under these assumptions the exchange rate can be identified with the relative price structure.

interest rates and/or a higher relative price of traded goods to maintain trade balance. The $T=0$ schedule accordingly shifts to $T'=0$, and our new equilibrium is at point A' with an increase in both interest rates and the relative price of traded goods. The higher interest rate is required to restore balance between income and spending. At that higher interest rate, spending on home goods has declined and we accordingly require a reduction in their relative price.

Consider next the implications of this disturbance for the exchange rate. The higher equilibrium interest rate lowers the demand for real balances and therefore contributes, via an increase in the price level, to a depreciation of the exchange rate. This effect is further enhanced by the required increase in the relative price of traded goods so that the net result is an unambiguous depreciation of the exchange rate.[1]

The example features several aspects of the exchange rate determination that are worth spelling out in more detail. First, and perhaps foremost, the exchange rate is determined in a general equilibrium framework by the interaction of all markets (and countries). A particularly important feature is that the equilibrium obtains in *both* the flow and stock markets so that the exchange rate is in no manner determined by the current flow demands and supplies of foreign exchange.[2]

Next we give emphasis to the role of *monetary* considerations in the context of exchange rate determinations. As has been emphasized by J. Robinson (1935), the exchange rate is proximately determined by the balance between money supply and real money demand. The fact that the approach taken here is "monetary" in no manner precludes the role of "real" factors since these must be expected to enter as determinants of the demand for real balances and thus exert an effect on the exchange rate. Mussa (1974) has emphasized this point for the analysis of the balance of payments and has noted the obvious extension to a flexible rate regime.

Since the exchange rate is determined as part of the general, real and monetary equilibrium of the system, there is no relevant sense in which one would want to assert that the exchange rate is an exclusively monetary phenomenon. Indeed, the equilibrium exchange rate can change without any accompanying change in the money supply, or the real money demand. Such would, for example, be the case if there were a change in the composition of production

[1] If the increased spending had fallen entirely on home goods, the required relative price adjustment would have been a fall in the relative price of traded goods and therefore ambiguity in the net effect of the disturbance on the exchange rate.

[2] There is a peculiar tradition in the discussion of the markets for both bonds and foreign exchange, and unlike in the discussion of equity prices, that associates price formation with the rate at which funds flow, rather than with the conditions required for the existing stocks to be held. The "tradeable funds" approach in the foreign exchange market has a "loanable funds" equivalent in the bond market. This issue is not new. See, for example, Pollak (1944) and Laursen (1955). The latter raises the issue quite explicitly and opts for a stock approach. See, also, Dornbusch (1974*a*, 1975), Johnson (1975), and, in particular, Black (1973).

between home goods and traded goods. Having noted the role of real considerations in this context, it is important, however, to recognize that organizing thought about the exchange rate around the monetary sector is likely to be a direct and informative approach. To appreciate this point, consider the alternative of a "wage approach".

A wage approach can be formulated by using in (3) the definition of real wages, $w = W/P$ and $w^* = W^*/P^*$, to obtain an equation similar to (6):

$$\hat{e} = (\hat{W} - \hat{W}^*) + (\hat{w}^* - \hat{w}) + (\hat{\theta} - \hat{\theta}^*). \qquad (6)'$$

Provided the general equilibrium structure is used to fill in the details of (6)′, we arrive at the same answer as we would obtain from (6). The choice then must lie in an assumption about the stability of the relevant behavioral equations and, perhaps, an assumption about the dominant source of disturbances.

A third feature of this approach is the *long-run* or *equilibrium* nature of exchange rate determination. This view is implicit in the fact that we allow all markets to clear and that we explicitly impose the condition of monetary stock equilibrium, goods market equilibrium and purchasing power parity for traded goods. Either of these conditions may not hold in the short run, and, therefore, exchange rates can depart from the prediction in (6)′.

For short-run purposes, we will assume that the exchange rate is altogether dominated by the asset markets and more specifically by capital mobility and money market equilibrium. Arbitrage of traded goods prices and goods market equilibrium is attained only over time.[1] Within such a perspective, we could assume that the price level and real income, at a point in time, are given and that the interest rate is determined by the quantity of money along with elements that shift the demand for real balances. Interest arbitrage for given expected future spot rates, determined by speculators, will then set the spot rates. Such a view is explored in the next section.

II. Short-Run Determination of Exchange Rates

In the short run, the scope for goods arbitrage may be limited, and accordingly purchasing power parity as in (1) may only obtain for a limited set of commodities. Under these conditions, it is useful to abstract altogether from the detail of goods markets and rather view exchange rates as being determined entirely in the asset market. Such a view will assume capital mobility and indeed assign a critical role to it. Exchange rates in this perspective are determined by interest arbitrage together with speculation about future spot rates. To provide an example of this approach, we consider the effects of an increase in the nominal quantity of money in a "small country".

[1] Magee (1974) has presented information on the adjustment time for purchasing power parity, or arbitrage, to be achieved. The evidence suggests a significant lag and a substantial dispersion across commodities.

Given real income and other determinants of the demand for real balances, the equilibrium interest rate, at which the existing quantity of money is willingly held, will be a function of the real quantity of money:[1]

$$r = r(M/P, \ldots). \tag{7}$$

Interest arbitrage, assuming that on a covered basis domestic and foreign assets are perfect substitutes, requires that the domestic interest rate, less the forward premium on foreign exchange, λ, be equal to the foreign interest rate, r^*:[2]

$$r - \lambda = r^*, \tag{8}$$

where the forward premium is defined as the percentage excess of the forward rate, $\bar{e}$, over the current spot rate:

$$\lambda \equiv (\bar{e} - e)/e.$$

Substituting (7) and λ in (8) we have a relationship between the real money supply, the spot rate and the forward rate:

$$r(M/P, \ldots) = r^* + \bar{e}/e - 1 \tag{8$'$}$$

Differentiating (8)′ and denoting the interest responsiveness of money demand by σ we obtain:[3]

$$\hat{e} = \hat{\bar{e}} + (1/\sigma)\hat{M} \tag{9}$$

where by assumption the foreign interest rate and the price level are held constant. Eq. (9) suggests that a change in the forward rate induces an equiproportionate change in the spot rate, while an increase in the money supply causes a depreciation in the spot rate that is inversely porportional to the interest responsiveness of money demand. Since the interest responsiveness of money demand is of the order of $\sigma = 0.5$, a monetary expansion will be matched by significantly more than proportionate depreciation.

So far we have assumed that the forward rate is exogenous. The next step is therefore to link the forward rate to the analysis. For the point to be made it is sufficient to assume that the forward rate is set by speculators in a perfectly elastic manner at the level of the expected future spot rate and that

---

[1] Eq. (7) is obtained by solving the money market equilibrium condition, $M/P = L(r, \ldots)$.

[2] For recent evidence on covered interest arbitrage, see Frenkel & Levich (1975).

[3] From the conditions of money market equilibrium $M/P = L(r, \ldots)$, we have: $dr = \hat{M}(M/P)/L_r \equiv -(1/\sigma)\hat{M}$. The interest responsiveness of money demand, that is, the semilogarithmic derivative $\sigma \equiv -L_r/L$, is for the short run significantly less than unity. Econometric models such as the MPS model estimate a short run elasticity of $-rL_r/L = 0.05$, so that with an interest rate of $r = 0.1$ we obtain a value $\sigma = 0.5$.

expectations about the latter are formed in an adaptive manner. With these assumptions we have:

$$\bar{e} = \pi e + (1-\pi)e_{-1}; \quad 0 < \pi < 1 \tag{10}$$

The impact effect of a change in the spot rate is therefore to raise the forward rate but proportionately less, so the price of foreign exchange is at a forward discount. Substituting from (10), the expression $\hat{\bar{e}} = \pi\hat{e}$ in (9) yields the total impact effect of a monetary expansion on the spot rate:

$$\hat{e} = \frac{1}{(1-\pi)\sigma}\hat{M} \tag{9$'$}$$

We note that the adaptive expectations serve to increase the impact effect of money on the exchange rate. In fact, the more closely the forward rate is determined by the current spot rate, the closer π is to unity, the larger the exchange rate fluctuations induced by a variation in money.

In interpreting the effect of a monetary expansion on the exchange rate, three considerations stand out: First domestic and foreign assets are assumed perfect substitutes on a covered basis as is reflected in (8). This implies that, independently of any particular assumptions about expectations, a reduction in domestic interest rates has to be matched by a forward discount on foreign exchange in order to equalize the net yields on domestic and foreign assets. The next two considerations are dependent on the particular expectations assumption in (10) and concern, respectively, the direction and magnitude of the change in the spot rate. A reduced domestic interest rate, for asset market equilibrium, has to be matched by an expected appreciation of the exchange rate. The expectations mechanism in (10) implies that a depreciation in the spot rate will give rise to such an expectation, since the elasticity of expectations, π, is less than unity. With an elasticity of expectations less than unity, a depreciation of the spot rate is accompanied by a less than proportionate depreciation of the expected future spot rate, or an anticipated appreciation. Finally, the magnitude of the depreciation in the spot rate that is required depends on both the interest response of money demand, σ, and the elasticity of expectations, π. The smaller the interest responsiveness of money demand, the larger the interest rate change that is brought about by a monetary expansion and therefore, the larger the expected appreciation that has to be brought about by a depreciation in the spot rate. Furthermore, a given depreciation of the spot rate will give rise to an expected appreciation of the future spot rate that is smaller, the larger the elasticity of expectations. Accordingly, large exchange rate changes will arise in circumstances where interest response of money demand is small and the elasticity of expectations is large.

The short run determination of exchange rates is entirely dominated by the conditions of equilibrium in the asset markets and expectations. The *liquidity* effect of money on the interest rate has a counterpart in the immediate depreciation of the spot rate that has to be sufficient to cause the existing stock of domestic assets to be held. It is in this sense that in the short run the exchange rate is determined in the asset markets.

Over time the exchange rate is determined by the interaction between goods markets and asset markets. This is so because the price level will rise to match the expansion in the nominal quantity of money until, in the long run, the monetary expansion is exactly matched by a price increase so that real balances and interest rates are unchanged and the spot and forward rate depreciate in the same proportion as the increase in the nominal quantity of money. The exact dynamics of that adjustment process will depend on the speed with which prices respond as compared to expectations. The response of prices will be due, in part, to the traditional effect of a reduced interest rate on aggregate spending. There will be in the present framework an additional channel that serves to speed up the responsiveness of prices to a monetary expansion. The impact effect of a monetary expansion on the spot rate, as of a given price level, will cause a departure from goods arbitrage. Domestic goods will become relatively cheap as compared to foreign goods and therefore induce a substitution of world demand toward domestic goods. This additional channel implies that even if domestic aggregate spending were unresponsive to the interest rate, or slow to adjust, there remains a subsidiary channel, the arbitrage effect, that serves to drive up domestic prices and causes the real effects of a monetary expansion to be transitory.

III. Speculation, Macroeconomic Policies and the Transmission of Disturbances

In the present section we go beyond the impact effect of disturbances and consider the behavior over time of the economy in response to policy-induced or speculative disturbances. In particular, we want to show that speculation that is not guided by "rational expectations" allows monetary changes to be transmitted internationally even under circumstances where prices are fully flexible. For the purposes of the present section, we continue to assume that the home country is small and therefore faces given world prices of traded goods and a given world rate of interest. We furthermore assume that goods arbitrage is continuously maintained. In addition to internationally traded commodities, the home country produces and consumes nontraded goods. Price and factor cost flexibility ensure that markets clear all the time and full employment is maintained.

The analysis focuses on the equilibrium conditions in the markets for home goods and in the asset market. Consider first the home goods market. The excess demand for home goods will depend on the relative price of traded goods in terms of the price level, P_T/P, the interest rate that determines absorption for a given level of real income, and the level of government spending on nontraded goods, g:

$$N(P_T/P, r, g) = 0; \quad N_{P_T/P} > 0, N_r < 0, N_g = 1 \tag{11}$$

An increase in the relative price of traded goods creates an excess demand as consumers substitute toward home goods, while productive resources move into the traded goods sector, thus reducing the supply of home goods. An increase in the interest rate reduces absorption, part of which falls on home goods and to that extent creates an excess supply. Finally, an increase in government spending directly adds to home goods demand. We can solve the equilibrium condition in (11) for the equilibrium relative price of traded goods in terms of the interest rate and government spending:

$$P_T/P = \theta(r; g); \quad \theta_r > 0, \theta_g < 0. \tag{11}$$

Eq. (11)′ is plotted in Fig. 1 as the NN schedule.[1]

Consider next the condition of equilibrium in the money market. With a demand for real balances that depends on interest rates and real income, we can solve the money market equilibrium condition for the equilibrium interest rate as a function of the real money supply and real income.

$$r = r(M/P; y); \quad r_{M/P} < 0, r_y > 0. \tag{12}$$

Next we substitute the equilibrium interest rate in (11), and noting that purchasing power parity obtains with a given price of foreign goods, $P_T = eP_T^*$, we can write the home goods market equilibrium condition as:

$$\tilde{N}(eP_T^*/P, r(M/P), g) = 0 \tag{13}$$

where $\tilde{N}$ denotes the reduced form that embodies the condition of money market equilibrium and where the constant level of real income is suppressed as an argument.

In Fig. 2 we show the home goods market equilibrium schedule $\tilde{N}\tilde{N}$. The schedule is positively sloped and flatter than a ray through the origin. The reason is as follows. At a higher price level, we have lower real balances, higher interest rates, and therefore reduced real spending. Part of the reduction in real spending falls on home goods and creates an excess supply that has to be eliminated by a decline in their *relative* price, that is, by an increase in the exchange rate or the price of traded goods relative to the price level.[2] The

[1] The trade balance is given by $T = T(P_T/P, r)$ where the relative price term again reflects substitution between home goods and traded goods and the interest rate term reflects absorption or the level of spending. Accordingly, an increase in the relative price of traded goods worsens the trade balance, while an increase in the interest rate improves the trade balance.

[2] For a given foreign currency price of traded goods, the ratio e/P represents the domestic relative price of traded goods in terms of the price level.

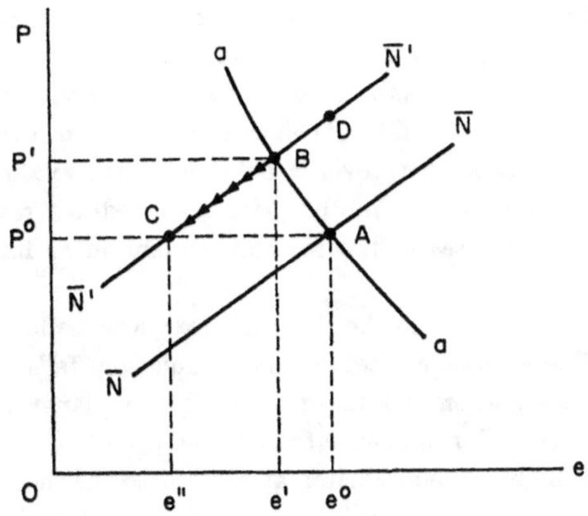

Fig. 2.

$\bar{N}\bar{N}$ schedule is drawn for a given nominal quantity of money and a given foreign currency price of traded goods.

We again assume that covered interest arbitrage ensures that interest rates are linked internationally so that (8) continues to hold. The forward rate is set by speculators, according to the adaptive expectations scheme in (10). Substituting the expression for the forward rate in (8), and using the equilibrium interest rate in (12), we obtain the condition for money market equilibrium together with covered interest arbitrage:

$$r(M/P)-(1-\pi)(e_{-1}/e-1)=r^*, \tag{14}$$

A critical property of the speculative behavior is that an increase in the spot rate creates a forward discount, since it will cause the forward rate to rise less than proportionately. To maintain interest parity, a forward discount on foreign exchange has to be accompanied by a reduction in domestic relative to foreign interest rates. Given the nominal quantity of money, such a decline in interest rates would arise if the domestic price level declined. The asset market equilibrium schedule *aa* in Fig. 2 reflects eq. (14) for a given foreign interest rate, a given nominal quantity of money, and a given past spot rate e_{-1}. The initial equilibrium obtains at point *A* with all markets clearing and the forward rate at par so that no revision of expectations is required.

Consider next the effect of an increase in the foreign price level. We note from (14) that there is no direct effect on the asset market and therefore the *aa* schedule remains unaffected. Consider next the home goods market. At an unchanged exchange rate, the increase in the foreign price level raises the domestic currency price of traded goods and hence their relative price, so that an excess demand for home goods would arise. To eliminate the excess demand, the exchange rate would have to appreciate to fully offset the foreign price increase. This is represented in Fig. 2 by a leftward shift of the $\bar{N}\bar{N}$ schedule to $\bar{N}'\bar{N}'$ in the proportion of the foreign price increase.

The short-run effect of the price increase is to move the economy to point B with an appreciation in the exchange rate that falls short of the foreign price increase and an increase in the domestic price level. Furthermore, the *relative* price of traded goods rises, and the increase in the price level reduces real balances and therefore raises interest rates with a matching premium on forward exchange.

Quite obviously, the foreign price change in the short run exerts real effects in the home country. The flexible exchange rate, in this formulation, fails to isolate the home country from foreign nominal disturbances. The explanation for this nonneutrality lies in the behavior of speculators.

The adjustment process from the initial equilibrium at point *A* to the short-run position of equilibrium can be viewed in the following manner: The increase in the foreign currency price of traded goods, at the initial exchange rate, raises the domestic currency price of traded goods, the price level and therefore the rate of interest. Such a position is shown at point *D* where the home goods market clears and the price level has risen, although proportionately less than the price of traded goods. At that point covered, interest arbitrage is not satisfied, since the increased interest rate is not compensated by an offsetting forward premium on foreign exchange. Therefore, an *incipient* capital inflow develops that causes the spot rate to appreciate until the appropriate premium has been generated. This is the move from point *D* to the short run equilibrium at point *B*.[1]

In the short run the failure of exchange rates to fully offset the foreign price increase implies that the domestic nominal and real equilibrium is affected by a foreign nominal disturbance. The domestic price level rises as do interest rates. Domestic absorption declines and real spending on home goods falls so that a deflationary effect is exerted on that sector. The reduction in absorption and the induced increase in the relative price of traded goods imply an expansion in the production of traded goods and a trade balance surplus. The trade surplus in turn is financed by a capital outflow.

The equilibrium at point *B* is only transitory, since it is sustained by expectational errors. Speculators underpredict the actual appreciation of the exchange rate and therefore will revise their forecast. That revision causes at each current rate the premium to decline and therefore to create a covered differential in favor of the home country that leads to continued appreciation of the exchange rate. That process moves the economy from point *B* to *C* over time. The process will continue until the exchange rate has sufficiently appreci-

---

[1] The effect of a foreign price increase on the exchange rate at point *B* is given by $\hat{e} = [-\delta/(\delta + \sigma(1-\pi))]\hat{P}^*_T$ where δ is the elasticity of the price level with respect to the price of traded goods along the $\bar{N}\bar{N}$ schedule. Unless $\pi = 1$, the exchange rate change does not fully offset the increase in foreign prices. See Appendix I.

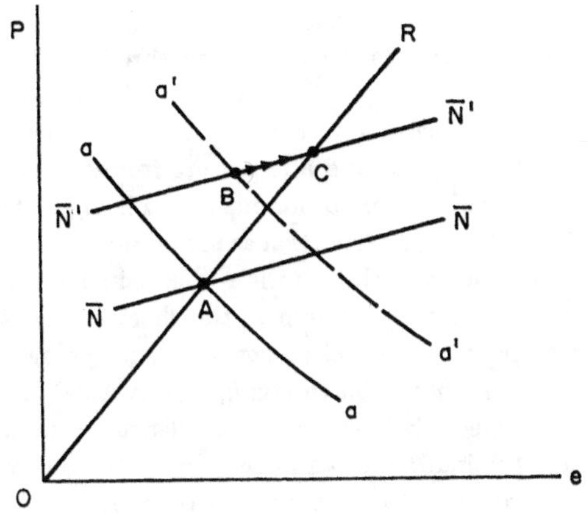

Fig. 3.

ated to fully offset the increase in foreign prices. This is true at point C, where the domestic price level and hence interest rates have returned to their initial level.[1]

The lack of homogeneity that the system exhibits in the short run applies similarly to an increase in the domestic money stock. In the short run, price flexibility notwithstanding, the price level and the exchange rate increase proportionately less than the money supply, and accordingly, the interest rate decreases while the forward rate goes to a discount. The change in the spot rate induced by a monetary expansion in the short run is given by:

$$\hat{e} = \frac{\delta}{\delta + \sigma(1-\pi)} \hat{M}, \quad 0 < \delta < 1 \tag{15}$$

where δ is the elasticity of the price level with respect to the price of traded goods along the $\bar{N}\bar{N}$ schedule. We note that in the present context, and unlike in Section II, the exchange rate changes proportionately less than the nominal quantity of money. This is entirely due to the adjustment in prices that is permitted here and that serves to lower the increase in real balances associated with a given increase in the nominal quantity of money.

Over time, as expectations are revised, the system will converge to neutrality in the sense that the monetary change leaves all real variables unchanged. The short run real effects of a monetary change are again due to expectational errors, or more precisely, to the fact that speculators use irrelevant information and therefore affect the real equilibrium. If instead the equilibrium exchange rate in (5) were used as a basis of prediction, the system would be homogeneous, even in the short run.

[1] The dynamics and stability of the adjustment process are studied in Appendix I.

The adjustment process to a monetary disturbance is illustrated in Fig. 3. Initial equilibrium obtains at point A, with a relative price structure indicated by the slope of the ray OR. The increase in the nominal quantity of money at the initial equilibrium exchange rate and prices lowers interest rates and therefore creates an excess demand for home goods and a departure from covered interest arbitrage. For home goods equilibrium to obtain, the exchange rate and prices would have to increase in the same proportion as the nominal quantity of money. This is indicated by an upward shift of the $\bar{N}\bar{N}$ schedule in the proportion $AC/OA = \hat{M}$. The asset market equilibrium in the short run does not possess homogeneity properties, since the elasticity of exchange rate expectations is less than unity, which is equivalent to saying that expectations are sticky. Accordingly, the *aa* schedule shifts upward in a smaller proportion. Short run equilibrium will obtain at point B with an increase in the exchange rate and prices that are porportionately smaller than the increase in money. In that short-run equilibrium, the relative price of home goods will be higher compared to A, which is a reflection of the fact that in the short run the interest rate declines and absorption expands. The adjustment of expectations over time will shift the $a'a'$ schedule up and to the right until the long run real equilibrium is restored at point C, where expectational errors have subsided and prices and exchange rates fully reflect the monetary change.

In discussing stabilization policy under flexible exchange rates, Mundell (1964, 1968) notes that with perfect capital mobility monetary policy exerts strong effects on nominal income, while fiscal policy has no effect. The reason is that, in the absence of forward market considerations, the given interest rate in the world determines the domestic interest rate and hence velocity. Given velocity, fiscal policy has no effect on nominal income, while monetary policy becomes most powerful. The present framework, following Mundell (1964) and Wonnacott (1972), notes that the short-run changes in forward premia allow interest rate and hence velocity changes that tend to dampen the effect of monetary policy. In the short run, monetary policy causes a depreciation of the exchange rate accompanied by a premium on forward exchange and a decline in interest rates. The decline in interest rates lowers velocity and therefore dampens in the short run the nominal income expansion. Over time the revision of expectations eliminates the premium and therefore restores interest rates and velocity to their initial level and thus causes monetary changes to be reflected in equiproportionate changes in nominal income.

In concluding this section we return to the transmission of foreign price disturbances and ask what policies the government could pursue to offset the transmission process. Here the choice has to be made between price level stability, or stability of the real equilibrium, that is, of interest rates, absorption and relative prices. If the preference is for stability of the real equilibrium, then the government should peg the interest rate, or the exchange rate, and therefore increase the domestic nominal quantity of money in the same proportion as the foreign price increase. If such a policy is followed, domestic prices move along with foreign prices at constant exchange rates and without any real effects. The alternative of a constant domestic price level will require a reduction in the nominal quantity of money in the short run and will involve larger relative price fluctuations. Noting that a constant price level policy will require in the adjustment process, first a decline in the nominal price of home goods, and increase in the nominal price of traded goods with a subsequent reversal, any downward rigidity of prices will make such a policy costly. The same argument applies to the automatic adjustment process associated with a constant nominal quantity of money. These remarks accordingly provide a support for a policy of pegging interest rates and exchange rates in the case of foreign nominal disturbances.

IV. Speculative Disturbances and Dual Exchange Rates

In the present section, we will investigate the effects of exogenous speculative disturbances and proceed from there to a discussion of a dual exchange rate system that has been advocated as a remedy against the influence of speculation on the real sector.

To allow for an exogenous change in the expected future spot rate, we modify (10) to:

$$\bar{e} = \pi e + (1-\pi)e_{-1} - eu, \tag{16}$$

where u denotes a current shift term in expectations. Specifically, an increase in u implies that given the current and past spot rate, we have an expected appreciation in the exchange rate and therefore a forward discount. Using the present form of the forward rate in the asset market equilibrium condition yields:

$$r(M/P) - (1-\pi)(e_{-1}/e - 1) + u = r^*. \tag{17}$$

Consider now the implication of an anticipated appreciation of the exchange rate. In Fig. 4 we have the initial full equilibrium at point A. An increase in the expected future spot rate will shift the asset market equilibrium schedule down and to the left to $a'a'$. At the initial equilibrium interest rate and prices, the anticipated appreciation creates a covered differential in favor of the home country and therefore causes an incipient capital inflow that appreciates the exchange rate.

Short-run equilibrium obtains at point B. The anticipated increase in the future spot rate is reflected in an appreciation in the current spot rate, a discount on forward exchange, and a decline in the domestic interest rate. More importantly, the decline in traded goods prices that is implied by the

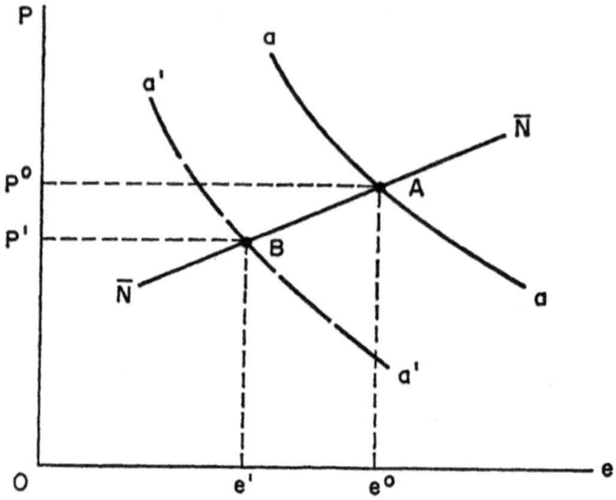

Fig. 4.

appreciation and the decline in the relative price of traded goods imply a deflationary influence in that sector. Traded goods prices decline relative to costs, and for that reason, the speculative attack imposes a real cost on the traded goods sector. This is very much the problem currently experienced by strong currency countries and, in particular, Switzerland.[1]

The short-run equilibrium at B is sustained by expectations that will prove erroneous and, to that extent, will over time give rise to revision of expectations and a return to the initial equilibrium. More likely, however, the sectoral problems caused by the speculative pressure on the exchange rate will give rise to some form of intervention. There would seem to be a case for dual exchange rates that isolate the current account transactions from speculative attacks; alternatively, and this has been a solution favored by the Swiss, to join a strong currency area and thereby share the burden of a speculative attack.

A dual or two-tier exchange market can be readily introduced in the preceding analysis. Under such a regime, we distinguish the official rate, $\tilde{e}$, applicable to current account transactions, from the free rate that applies to capital account transactions.[2] In the following, we will assume that interest earnings can be converted at the free rate, e. The latter assumption implies that the analysis underlying the asset market equilibrium schedule *aa* in Fig. 5 remains unchanged. Equilibrium in the asset market continues to require that covered interest arbitrage obtains where the forward rate continues to be

[1] Under the heading, "Are the Swiss Enjoying Their Strong Currency? No. Not in the Least", the *Wall Street Journal* of February 27, 1975 notes: "And what is it like to be the cynosure of international money markets? It is, the Swiss will tell you, increasingly uncomfortable, if not miserable."

[2] For a discussion of dual exchange rate systems, see Fleming (1971), Swoboda (1974), and Sheen (1974).

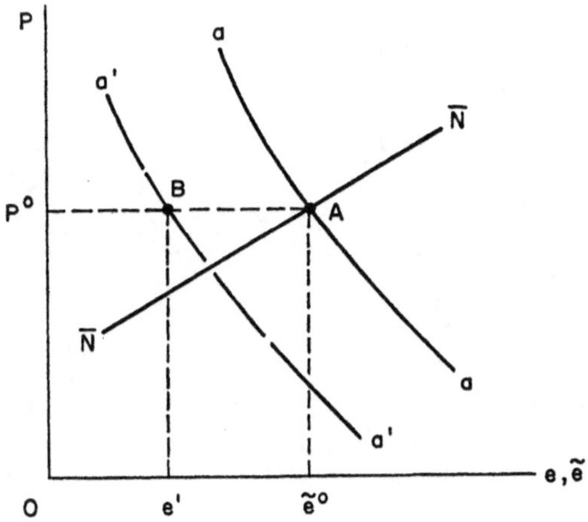

Fig. 5.

formed by an adaptive expectations mechanism.[1] The home goods market equilibrium schedule $\bar{N}\bar{N}$ is drawn as a function of the official rate $\tilde{e}$. Initial equilibrium obtains at point A, where the official rate, $\tilde{e}^0$, happens to coincide with the free rate.

To illustrate the working of the system, now consider again in Fig. 5 the problem of a speculative attack in the form of an increase in the expected future spot rate. The incipient capital flow will immediately bid up the free rate to e', where the spot rate has appreciated sufficiently to offset the expected appreciation. There is no effect at all on the equilibrium price level, relative prices, or interest rate because the relevant rate for the determination of relative prices is the fixed official rate $\tilde{e}^0$. Under these circumstances, the economy is entirely shielded from the effects of speculation on the real sector. How does the system differ from a unified free rate? Under the latter, the appreciation of the exchange rate would have put downward pressure on traded goods prices and the price level, while here the international price connection via the official rate remains undisturbed.

How does a dual exchange rate system affect the scope of domestic policies? Consider an increase in government spending or a cut in taxes that gives rise to an expansion in aggregate real spending. In Fig. 6, we show that, as a consequence of higher real spending, we have an excess demand for home goods and therefore the market equilibrium schedule shifts up to $\bar{N}'\bar{N}'$. With

[1] What determines the level of the free rate in the long run? The present model is not equipped to answer that question because the adaptive expectations mechanism implies that in the long run the forward rate is equal to the spot rate. In the absence of a difference between spot and forward rates, interest rates will be equated at any level of the free rate. The free rate has no effect on the real system and therefore, in the present model, is indeterminate in the long run.

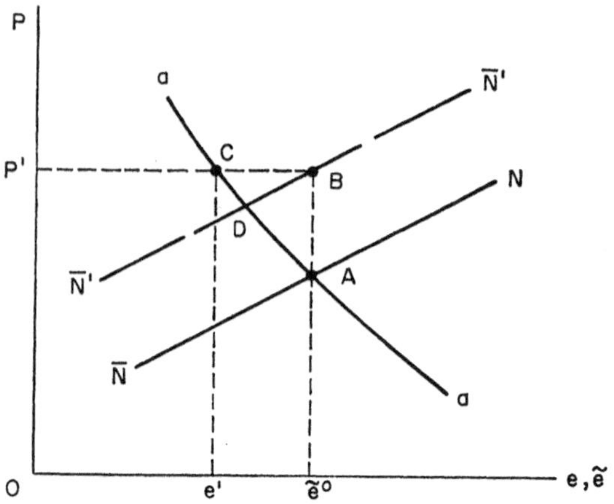

Fig. 6.

the official rate fixed at $\tilde{e}^0$, the increased spending causes an increase in the domestic price level and in the relative price of home goods, to P'. The increased price level, in turn, implies higher interest rates. To maintain asset market equilibrium in the face of higher domestic interest rates, we experience an appreciation in the spot free rate to e'. At that rate, the spot rate has sufficiently fallen relative to the forward rate to generate a premium that offsets the higher domestic interest rate.

The equilibrium at point B implies that fiscal policy under a dual exchange rate system exerts a stronger effect on interest rates and the price level and that the same increase in spending gives rise to a smaller increase in the relative price of home goods. The latter point can be appreciated by noting that under a unified free rate we would be at point D. The explanation is simply that under a dual system we have larger increases in interest rates and therefore more of a dampening of the increased spending and for that reason require only smaller *relative* price changes. The counterpart of the smaller relative price changes is, however, a larger change in nominal income. To the extent that sectoral considerations are relevant, and they most assuredly are, the question of relative prices and intersectoral resource allocation is important. From that perspective, the dual rate system is more nearly neutral than a system with a free unified rate.

Concluding Remarks

This paper has developed models of the determination of exchange rates and of the operation of a flexible exchange rate system. Among the conclusions, two deserve emphasis here. First, that the exchange rate, as a first approximation, is determined in the asset markets. This implies that expectations and changes in expectations as much as changes in money supplies dominate the course of the exchange rate in the short run.

The second conclusion that we wish to retain here concerns the lack of homogeneity that a flexible rate system is likely to exhibit in the short run. With prices sticky, or exchange rate expectations sticky, monetary changes as much as foreign price disturbances will be transmitted internationally and thus destroy the argument that a flexible rate system provides isolation from and for monetary disorder.

Appendix I

In this appendix we will derive some of the results presented in Section III and discuss the stability of the adjustment process. We start with the equation for the $\tilde{N}\tilde{N}$ schedule that embodies equilibrium in the home goods market, given monetary equilibrium:

$$\tilde{N}(eP_T^*/P, r(M/P), g) = 0. \tag{1}$$

We can solve that equation for the equilibrium price level, $\overline{P}$, as a function of the money supply, traded goods prices in terms of foreign currency and the exchange rate:

$$P = \overline{P}(eP_T^*, M, g). \tag{2}$$

Nothing that the excess demand in (1) is homogeneous of degree zero in all prices and the quantity of money it follows that the equilibrium price level in (2) is homogeneous of degree one in the quantity of money and the domestic currency price of traded goods. Accordingly, we can write the logarithmic differential of (2) as follows:

$$\hat{P} = \delta(\hat{e} + \hat{P}_T^*) + (1-\delta)\hat{M}; \quad 0 < \delta < 1 \tag{3}$$

where government spending is held constant.

Taking similarly the differential of the asset market equilibrium condition:

$$r(M/P) = r^* + (1-\pi)(e_{-1}/e - 1) \tag{4}$$

we obtain:

$$\hat{M} - \hat{P} = -\sigma(1-\pi)(\hat{e}_{-1} - \hat{e}) \tag{5}$$

where the foreign interest rate is held constant. Combining (3) and (5) yields an expression for the change in the spot rate as a function of the disturbances:

$$\hat{e} = \frac{\delta}{\delta + \sigma(1-\pi)}(\hat{M} - \hat{P}_T^*) + \frac{\sigma(1-\pi)}{\delta + \sigma(1-\pi)}\hat{e}_{-1} \tag{6}$$

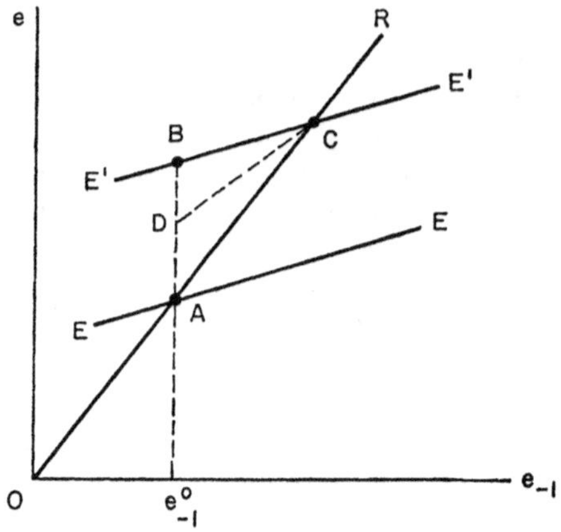

Fig. 7.

In the short run $\hat{e}_{-1}=0$ and the first term in (6) indicates the impact effect of a monetary or foreign price disturbance. In the long run, $\hat{e}=\hat{e}_{-1}$, and therefore nominal disturbances are reflected in corresponding exchange rate changes.

Consider next the stability question.[1] Substituting the equilibrium price level, $P(\ )$ in (4) yields a final reduced form equation that relates the current spot rate to the past spot rate for given money and foreign prices:

$$r(M/\overline{P}(eP^*_T, M, g))-(1-\pi)(e_{-1}/e-1)=r^* \tag{7}$$

Eq. (7) is a difference equation in the exchange rate. To determine stability we differentiate (7) and evaluate at equilibrium the derivative to obtain:

$$de/de_{-1}=\frac{\sigma(1-\pi)}{\delta+\sigma(1-\pi)}<1 \tag{8}$$

which ensures stability.

In Fig. 7 we show eq. (7) for an initial nominal quantity of money as the upward sloping line *EE* with a slope less than unity. An increase in the nominal quantity of money shifts the schedule upward in the same proportion to *E'E'*. From the initial equilibrium at *A*, the spot rate immediately jumps to point *B* and then moves along *E'E'* until the new equilibrium at point *C* is reached. We have inserted, too, in Fig. 7 the path of the forward rate *ADC*. The forward rate by (10) will always lie between the current and past spot rate and therefore consistently underpredicts the actual exchange rate. This departure from rational expectations forms the basis of the transitory real effects of a monetary disturbance.

[1] There is a growing body of partial equilibrium models exhibiting instability in the foreign exchange market because of a failure to link that sector with the asset markets. See, for example, Allen & Miller (1974) and Britton (1970). Minford (1974) in a very interesting formulation shows that instability can be attributed to a failure to consider the monetary effects of exchange rate changes.

References

Allen, W. & Miller, M.: The stability of the floating exchange rate. Unpublished manuscript, Bank of England, 1974.

Argy, V. & Porter, M.: The forward exchange market and the effects of domestic and external disturbances under alternative exchange rate systems. *I.M.F. Staff Papers 19*, No. 3, 1972.

Black, S.: *International Money Markets and Flexible Exchange Rates*. Princeton Studies in International Finance, No. 32. Princeton University, 1973.

Black, S.: Exchange rate policies for less developed countries in a world of floating rates. Unpublished manuscript, Vanderbilt University, 1975.

Britton, A. J. C.: The dynamic stability of the foreign exchange market. *Economic Journal 80*, 91–96, 1970.

Collery, A.: *International Adjustment, Open Economies and the Quantity Theory of Money*. Princeton Studies in International Finance, No. 28, Prinetocn University Press, 1971.

Corden, M.: *The Theory of Protection*. Clarendon Press, Oxford, 1971.

Dornbusch, R. (1974*a*): Capital mobility, flexible exchange rates and macroeconomic equilibrium. Forthcoming in *Recent Developments in International Monetary Economics* (ed. E. Claassen and P. Salin), North-Holland, 1976.

Dornbusch, R.: Tariffs and nontraded goods. *Journal of International Economics 4*, 177–185, 1974*b*.

Dornbusch, R.: A portfolio balance model of the open economy. *Journal of Monetary Economics 1*, 3–19, 1975.

Fleming, J. M.: Domestic financial policies under fixed and floating exchange rates. *I.M.F. Staff Papers 9*, 369–379, 1962.

Fleming, J. M.: *Essays in International Economics*. Allen and Unwin, 1971.

Frenkel, J. & Levich, R.: Transactions costs and the efficiency of international capital markets. Unpublished manuscript, University of Chicago, 1975.

Johnson, H. G.: World inflation and the international monetary system. Unpublished manuscript, University of Chicago, 1975.

Laursen, S.: The market for foreign exchange. *Economia Internazionale 8*, 762–783, 1955.

Magee, S.: U.S. import prices in the currency contract period. *Brookings Papers on Economic Activity 1*, 117–164, 1974.

Minford, P.: Structural and monetary theories of the balance of payments. Unpublished manuscript, University of Manchester, 1974.

Mundell, R. A.: Exchange rate margins and economic policy. In Murphy, C. (ed.), *Money in the International Order*. Southern Methodist University Press, 1964.

Mundell, R. A.: *International Economics*. MacMillan, 1968.

Mussa, M.: A monetary approach to balance of payments analysis. *Journal of Money, Credit and Banking* (3), 333–351, 1976.

Niehans, J.: Some doubts about the efficacy of monetary policy under flexible exchange rates. *Journal of International Economics 5*, 275–281, 1975.

Polak, J. J.: European exchange depreciation in the early twenties. *Econometrica 12*, 151–162, 1964.

Robinson, J.: Banking policy and the exchanges. *Review of Economic Studies 3*, 226–229, 1936.

Swoboda, A. K.: The dual exchange rate system and monetary independence. In Aliber, R. Z. (ed.), *National Monetary Policies and the International Financial System*. University of Chicago Press, 1974.

Sheen, J.: Dual exchange rates and the asset markets. Unpublished manuscript, International Monetary Project, London School of Economics, 1974.

Wonnacott, P.: The floating canadian dollar. American Enterprise Institute, Foreign Affairs Study 5, 1972.

COMMENT ON R. DORNBUSCH, "THE THEORY OF FLEXIBLE EXCHANGE RATE REGIMES AND MACROECONOMIC POLICY"

Stanley Fischer

Massachusetts Institute of Technology, Cambridge, Mass., USA

The paper by Rudiger Dornbusch first sets out a theory of the long run determination of the exchange rate and then discusses a number of issues connected with the operation of flexible exchange rate regimes over a shorter period characterized by expectational errors. Since the paper is admirably lucid, there is little for the discussant to do beyond expressing minor reservations at certain points and emphasizing some aspects of the analysis.

I shall comment in turn on the three major parts of the paper, consisting respectively of Section I on the long run determinants of the exchange rate, Sections II and III on the role of capital mobility in determining the exchange rate in the shorter run, and Section IV on the dual exchange rate system.

I. The Long-Run Framework

The long run analysis starts from purchasing power parity for traded goods and then uses the aggregation for each country of traded and non-traded goods respectively to express the exchange rate as in (3):

$$e = (P/P^*)(\theta/\theta^*) \tag{3}$$

where P is the general price level, θ is the price of traded goods relative to P, and asterisks denote the foreign country.

At this stage there is a question about the usefulness of the framework for long run analysis since the aggregation into traded goods assumes fixed terms of trade for each country. To the extent that there are changes in the terms of trade over long periods, the analysis is incapable of analyzing their impact on the exchange rate without further disaggregation to treat imports and exports separately. Now, of course, one can argue that "long run" means "steady state" so that changes in the terms of trade are excluded by assumption but in steady state the relative prices of traded goods are also constant and then the analysis could as well use simple purchasing power parity without starting from traded goods in particular. Thus one should note that the particular aggregation of this paper is probably not well suited for analysis of economic developments that result in terms of trade changes.

From (3) the paper proceeds to substitute for P and P^* the ratios of the stock of nominal balances to the real demand for money in each country, leading to

$$e = (M/M^*)(L^*/L)(\theta/\theta^*) \tag{5}$$

where M is the money stock and $L(\ )$ the demand for real balances function.

Now why substitute $M/L(\ )$ for P? After all, since $L(\ )$ is a function of endogenous variables such as the interest rate, income and perhaps wealth, all that is achieved is the substitution of a function of a number of endogenous variables ($L(\ )$) for a single endogenous variable (P). Presumably the particular substitution reflects an empirical judgement that the value of $L(\ )$ varies little over time relative to movements in M. This empirical judgement is no doubt valid for inflation rates in excess of 5–10% over long periods.

Second, at the analytic level, why use $M/L(\ )$ rather than, for example, $B/J(\ )$ where B is the domestic stock of outside nominal bonds and $J(\ )$ the excess demand function of the private sector for such bonds? The primary reason must be convenience. The particular form (5) cannot by itself be used to examine the effects of anything other than changes in the money stock on the exchange rate (since it is reasonable to assume money is neutral in the long run and thus that a change in M leaves $L(\ )$ unaffected in the long run). It is noteworthy that when the apparatus is put to work to analyze the effects of a change in domestic spending patterns on the exchange rate, a macro-economic model has to be appended to (5) to undertake the analysis. It so happens in that case that the full macro-economic model shows that θ rises and $L(\ )$ falls as a result of the spending pattern change, so that the exchange rate unambiguously falls. However, one could also analyze changes that cause θ and $L(\ )$ to move in the same direction; then it might be convenient to use $B/J(\ )$ (defined in the first sentence of this paragraph) in place of $M/L(\ )$ in (5).

In brief, although the paper argues that "organizing thought about the exchange rate around the monetary sector is likely to be a direct and informative approach", that point remains to be substantiated except for periods of fairly substantial inflation.

II. The Exchange Rate in the Short Run and the Transmission of Monetary Disturbances

Sections II and III are of interest because they concentrate on the short run and discuss the real effects of monetary changes for a small country with a flexible exchange rate that faces a given world interest rate. In Section II the price level is taken as given while in Section III the price level is assumed to adjust to maintain full employment. The reason that changes in the money stock have real effects is that expectations are not rational.

How can a small country affect its domestic interest rate if there are no restrictions on capital flows and the world interest rate is given? The simple explanation is contained in equation (8)′: any action that affects the forward premium must also affect the domestic interest rate. Now if a change in the domestic money stock does not lead to an equiproportionate change in the forward rate and the spot exchange rate, it will lead to a change in the domestic interest rate that will have real effects.

A change in the domestic money stock can have such real effects either if expectations are not formed rationally, as in Section III of the paper, or if domestic prices do not adjust instantly, as in Section II of the paper. Note particularly that rational expectations by themselves do not preclude real consequences of changes in the money stock if prices do not adjust freely.

The paper notes that the real consequences of domestic nominal disturbances also imply that foreign nominal disturbances have real consequences for the domestic economy. To avoid such real consequences it is suggested that the domestic money stock should be increased in proportion to the foreign price increase. As usual, one should note that the identification of reasons for foreign price changes is not straightforward and that a policy that is appropriate for a foreign nominal disturbance will not provide an optimal response to a foreign real disturbance.

Despite this obvious *caveat*, the analysis of Sections II and III is of importance in that it studies exchange rate determination over the short period that is relevant to countercyclical policy. This short period, replete with inflexible prices and perhaps expectations that are not rational, is inevitably an analytically less pleasing environment than the long run of Section I, but it is the environment in which policy is formulated. Further developments of the analysis should be awaited with interest.

III. The Dual Exchange Rate System

The analysis of the dual exchange rate system is remarkably sanguine. In such a system, an official rate is applicable to current account transactions while capital account transactions take place at a freely determined rate that generally differs from the official rate.

It is shown first that with unified rates, exogenous speculative disturbances have real effects on the domestic economy. It is next demonstrated that in the dual rate system such speculative attacks affect only the free rate.

It would accordingly appear that dual rate systems are desirable. There are, however, some arguments on the other side. First, money is fungible. And second, the dual rate system isolates the economy from world capital markets. To the extent that the monetary authority permits access to the world capital market at the official rate for approved purposes, it comes close to operating a fixed or managed floating exchange rate system—and the problem with that system is precisely in trying to decide when the exchange rate should be moved. In other words, the problem is to recognize a disequilibrating capital flow.

THE EXCHANGE RATE AND THE BALANCE OF PAYMENTS IN THE SHORT RUN AND IN THE LONG RUN: A MONETARY APPROACH*

Pentti J. K. Kouri

Stanford University, Stanford, California, USA and Institute for International Economic Studies, Stockholm, Sweden

Abstract

This paper analyzes, by way of a dynamic model, the role of momentary asset equilibrium and expectations in the determination of the exchange rate in the short run, and the role of the process of asset accumulation in the determination of the time path from momentary to long-run equilibrium.

I. Introduction

A simple dynamic model of the determination of the exchange rate in the short run and in the long run is developed in this paper. The model is an extension, to the regime of flexible exchange rates, of the monetary approach to balance of payments and devaluation.[1] It goes beyond the recent studies by Dornbusch (1976), Genberg & Kierzkowksi (1975) and others by analyzing explicitly the dynamic interaction between the exchange rate, exchange rate expectations and the balance of payments under the regime of a freely floating exchange rate, and under alternative assumptions about the formation of expectations using an approach similar to Black's (1973).

The essence of the monetary, or asset market, approach to exchange rates adopted in this paper is that the exchange rate, as a relative price of monies, is viewed as one of the prices that equilibrates the international markets for

* When this paper was written, the author was at the Massachusetts Institute of Technology, on leave from the Research Department of the International Monetary Fund. The views expressed in the paper are those of the author and not necessarily those of the IMF. I wish to thank Stanley Black, Rudiger Dornbusch, Stanley Fischer, Assar Lindbeck, Ronald McKinnon and members of Jouko Paunio's money workshop at Helsinki University for helpful comments on an earlier draft.

[1] Some of the most relevant references are Johnson (1958, 1973, 1975), Mundell (1968, 1971), Dornbusch (1973, 1974), Frenkel (1971), Frenkel and Rodriguez (1975), Kemp (1968), Krueger (1974), Negishi (1968), Mussa (1974), Pearce (1961), Polak (1958), Prais (1960), and Samuelson (1971). Some of these references are collected in Frenkel & Johnson (1976). This paper also draws on the portfolio balance models of McKinnon & Oates (1966), and McKinnon (1969). More recent contributions in this strand of literature include Branson (1974), Brunner & Meltzer (1974), and Myhrman (1975).

various financial assets. Therefore, the behavior of the supplies of various monies and other financial assets, as well as the behavior of the demands for these assets, have to be examined in order to explain the behavior of exchange rates. This is in contrast to the traditional approach to flexible exchange rates which focuses on the behavior of imports and exports and of capital flows between countries. The distinction is similar to that between the liquidity preference theory of interest on the one hand, and the flow of loanable funds theory on the other.

It should be emphasized that the choice between the stock approach and the flow approach is to some extent an empirical matter. In the stock approach it is assumed that financial markets equilibrate very fast. Transactions costs are so small that it may be assumed that financial assets are always held in desired proportions. For example, if a market participant has too many sterling assets in his portfolio, he can exchange these assets for dollar assets in a very short time. For a large segment of the international short-term money market, this is probably a reasonable simplifying assumption. Revisions of existing portfolios are much larger in size than marginal additions to asset demands from new savings.

In contrast, it is assumed in the flow approach that transaction costs prohibit instantaneous adjustments of portfolios. Financial markets are equilibrated only "in the margin". Thus the exchange rate is determined to equilibrate the flow supply of (demand for) foreign exchange from a current account surplus (deficit) with the net desired additions (subtractions) of foreign assets by holders of financial assets. In this sense, the choice between the two approaches is an empirical question.

However, it is often assumed in the literature that portfolio equilibrium is obtained instantaneously and yet the exchange rate is viewed as a price that equilibrates the balance-of-payments flows. This is shown to involve two logical problems. First, in general, the balance of payments flow account is no more than an *ex-post identity* which in no sense can be interpreted as an *ex-ante equilibrium condition*. This is because the assumption of continuous portfolio equilibrium implies that market demand equations cannot be defined in terms of changes in desired asset holdings. It is shown that the expected, or planned, change in the stock of foreign assets equals the realized *ex-post* change only if expectations are correct. In the case of perfect foresight, the balance-of-payments flow account is shown to define a second-order differential equation in the exchange rate, which must be satisfied along a perfect foresight adjustment path. However, there is an infinite number (in fact, a continuum) of such exchange rate paths, so that the balance-of-payments flow account is not sufficient to determine the behavior of the exchange rate.

In order to accentuate the analysis of these issues, a number of simplifying assumptions are made in this paper. First, it is assumed that the economy is small and produces only internationally traded goods. Second, prices and wages are assumed to be flexible, so that the labor force is always fully employed. Third, the structure of financial markets is very rudimentary. The only two assets are domestic paper currency and foreign money. There is no accumulation of real capital, nor any equity claims on real capital. Simple as the model is, it can still be used to analyze a number of interesting problems.

One of these is a reformulation of the problem concerning the stability of the exchange rate. Since the exchange rate is viewed as a relative price of two financial assets, the critical determinants of stability are linked to asset substitution effects and the nature of expectations formation, rather than relative price elasticities of exports and imports.

In this connection the assumption of perfect foresight or rational expectations, which is often made in the analysis of foreign exchange markets, is shown to imply a basic indeterminacy of the exchange rate, familiar from similar problems in other areas of economics. From any initial exchange rate there is a path along which markets are in equilibrium and expectations are continuously fullfilled. Only one of these paths is such that the rate of change in the exchange rate will approach a constant (if the rate of monetary expansion is constant). In order for this path to be chosen, it has to be assumed that speculators have *long-run foresight* and rule out the possibilities of both hyperinflation and hyperdeflation.

Another problem investigated in this paper is the nature of the adjustment path, and the link between the short-run momentary equilibrium and the long-run stationary state. There is a gap in the literature between the portfolio balance, stationary state models, and the short-run models which take the asset supplies and expectations as given. In general, the short-run impact of policies can be quite different from the long-run impact, depending on the nature of the expectations. It is shown that this dilemma can be resolved by assuming long-run foresight. In that case, the long-run impact on the *exchange rate and asset supplies* correctly predicts the short-run impact on the *exchange rate and the balance of payments*.

The plan of this paper is as follows. The concept of a momentary equilibrium is developed in Section II. This is followed by an analysis of the short-run effects of various shifts on the current account and the exchange rate with given exchange rate expectations. This section also contains a comparison between the stock model of the exchange rate and the flow model. Section III analyzes the long-run effects of the same shifts on the stationary state in which the current account is in balance, asset supplies constant, and exchange rate expectations correct. Section IV analyzes the problem of the dynamic stability of the exchange rate and the balance of payments under alternative assumptions about the formation of expectations. Dynamic stability is defined as the convergence of the sequence of momentary equilibria to the stationary state. Section V analyzes the dynamic response of the exchange rate and the balance of payments to various shocks, thereby connecting the short-run analysis in

Section II with the stationary state analysis in Section III. We conclude by discussing the limitations and required extensions of the simple model developed in this paper, as well as the implications of the new approach that go beyond this or other models.

II. Momentary Equilibrium

In this section we develop the concept of a momentary equilibrium and analyze the short-run effects of various shocks on the exchange rate and on the balance of payments. To simplify the analysis, we assume that the economy produces only traded goods the relative price of which is fixed in the world market. We also assume that the world price level is constant and equal to one so that the domestic price level and the rate of exchange amount to the same thing. Labor is the only factor of production and it is fully employed. Domestic output (Y) is therefore constant. Domestic absorption is equal to the sum of private consumption (C) and government expenditure (G). Private consumption is a function of real disposable labor income ($Y-T$) and the stock of real financial wealth (A) in accordance with Modigliani's life cycle model of consumption.[1] The excess of domestic output over domestic absorption equals the trade account surplus:[2]

$$B = Y - C(Y-T, A) - G. \tag{1}$$

The stock of financial wealth consists of domestic money (M) and foreign assets (F):

$$A = \frac{M}{P} + F. \tag{2}$$

The demand for real balances is a function of the expected rate of inflation (exchange rate depreciation), π, the level of real income and the stock of

---

[1] Dornbusch (1973) uses an alternative formulation. In his model money is the only store of value. He assumes that the flow of *saving* is a function of the discrepancy between the long-run demand for real balances and the current stock of real balances. This approach is identical to ours with a fixed exchange rate but has different implications if the price level is changing. It implies that investors stabilize saving and let capital gains and losses be reflected on consumption. This is both implausible and at variance with empirical evidence.

[2] The equality of the excess of domestic absorption over domestic output and the current account deficit is the essence of the absorption approach to the balance of payments. See Alexander (1952) and Johnson (1958) for a discussion of this approach. Dornbusch (1973) and Mussa (1974) emphasize the similarity between the monetary approach and the absorption approach in the process of adjustment. The link between the two approaches disappears, however, once there are other assets. The excess of income over absorption represents a change in wealth, and not necessarily a change in the holdings of money balances.

wealth. Since we assume that foreigners do not hold domestic paper currency, in equilibrium the domestic demand for money equals the supply of money:

$$\frac{M^d}{P} = L(\pi, Y, A) = \frac{M}{P}. \tag{3}$$

The other equilibrium condition is that the demand for foreign assets equals the stock of foreign assets:

$$F^d = F(\pi, Y, A) = F. \tag{4}$$

Because of the wealth constraint only one of equations (3) and (4) is independent. Substituting the definition of real wealth in equation (3) we obtain the equilibrium condition for the asset markets:

$$L\left(\pi, Y, \frac{M}{P} + F\right) = \frac{M}{P}. \tag{5}$$

Given the expected rate of depreciation (π), the stock of foreign assets (F) and the nominal supply of money (M), *this condition of equilibrium in the asset markets determines the exchange rate.* Equally well, we could say that the exchange rate is determined to *equilibrate the demand for foreign assets with the existing stock of foreign assets.*[1]

Equations (5) and (3) can be solved for the reduced form real balance and wealth equations:

$$\bar{M} = \frac{M}{P} = H(\underset{(-)}{\pi}, \underset{(+)}{Y}, \underset{(+)}{F}) \tag{6.1}$$

$$A = A(\underset{(-)}{\pi}, \underset{(+)}{Y}, \underset{(+)}{F}). \tag{6.2}$$

An increase in the expected rate of depreciation reduces the stock of real balances and hence the real value of financial wealth by causing the exchange rate to depreciate.

In order to complete the model we need to introduce the government budget equation and the behavior of the money supply. For convenience, we assume that the Central Bank acquires all government debt and does not intervene continuously in the foreign exchange market. Therefore, the nominal budget deficit is equal to the change in the supply of money. The government can independently determine only three of the variables under its control: real tax

[1] This strong separation is obtained only because we assume a small open economy producing only traded goods. In a two country model or in a model with non-traded goods, the asset market equilibrium and the commodity market equilibrium are determined simultaneously. Thus it would be incorrect to say that the exchange rate is determined only in the asset markets, since it depends on the relative prices of commodities which are determined simultaneously with the exchange rate. But even in the more general case, it is incorrect to say that the exchange rate is determined to equilibrate the balance of payments flows.

revenue (T), real expenditure (G), and the change in the money stock ($\dot{M}/P$). We assume that it fixes the rate of change in the nominal money stock (m) and the real tax revenue, and adjusts real expenditure accordingly. This gives us the government expenditure function:

$$G = T + m\frac{M}{P}. \tag{7}$$

An increase in the price level reduces the real value of new debt issue and hence government expenditure. Substituting equation (7) into equation (1), along with the definition of real wealth, we obtain ***the capital flow or current account equation***:

$$\dot{F} = B = Y - C\left(Y - T, \frac{M}{P} + F\right) - T - m\frac{M}{P} = B(\underset{(+)}{Y}, \underset{(-)}{T}, \underset{(-)}{F}, \underset{(+)}{\pi}, \underset{(-)}{M}). \tag{8}$$

We assume that the rate of interest on foreign assets is equal to zero.

The last expression is the reduced form current account (capital flow) equation, obtained by substituting the reduced form real balance equation for M/P. An increase in real income increases the current account surplus as long as the marginal propensity to consume out of income—after allowing for the effect of income on the real value of financial wealth—is less than one. We assume this to be the case. A tax financed increase in government expenditure reduces the current account surplus, as long as the private propensity to consume is less than one. An increase in the stock of foreign assets increases consumption and hence reduces the current account surplus. An increase in the expected rate of depreciation reduces the real value of financial wealth and hence improves the current account. An increase in the rate of growth of the money stock increases government expenditure and hence reduces the current account surplus.

Equations (5) and (8) constitute the temporary equilibrium model. Equations (6.1) and (6.2) and the right-hand side of equation (8) define the endogeneous variables as functions of the current stocks of assets and expectations regarding the future.

(a) The Flow Model of the Foreign Exchange Market

The point of departure in the literature on the foreign exchange market is usually the *ex-post* balance-of-payments identity:[1]

$$\text{current account} + \text{capital account} = B - \dot{F} = 0. \tag{9}$$

The problem inherent in this approach is that, in general, this accounting identity has no meaning as an *ex-ante* equilibrium condition. The reason is that

[1] A classic reference on the traditional theory of the foreign exchange market is Robinson (1949). For representative modern discussions, see Kindleberger (1973, Chapter 17), Sohmen (1969, especially Chapter 1), and Stern (1973, Chapter 2).

when using the assumption of a continuous portfolio equilibrium, the "flow demand equations" for individual assets cannot be defined. At each instant, investors choose the composition of their wealth and the rate of consumption. The change in the real value of wealth is then equal to the sum of new savings ($S = Y - T - C = (\dot{M}/P) + \dot{F}$ in the model) and the change in the valuation of existing assets ($-(M/P)(/\dot{P}/P)$ in the model). The latter is not known to the investors in advance unless they have perfect foresight. Therefore, they cannot determine *ex ante* the change in the real value of wealth, or in the various components of wealth.

The *planned* change in the stock of foreign assets (*ex-ante* capital flow equation) could be defined as:

$$\dot{F}^d = F_\pi \dot{\pi} + F_A \dot{A}^e = F_\pi \dot{\pi} + F_A S - F_A \frac{M}{P} \pi. \tag{10}$$

The first term ($F_\pi \dot{\pi}$) represents the *stock shift* induced by the change in the expected return on domestic assets. The second term ($F_A \dot{A}^e$) is the *flow component* of capital movements representing the proportion of expected new savings allocated to foreign assets.[1] Intuitively, equation (4) tells how much the investors expect their foreign asset position to change *ex-ante* in the next instant. The realized change in the stock of foreign assets is:

$$\dot{F} = F_\pi \dot{\pi} + F_A \dot{A} = F_\pi \dot{\pi} + F_A S - F_A \frac{M}{P} \frac{\dot{P}}{P}. \tag{11}$$

The difference between the planned (*ex-ante*) change in the stock of foreign assets on the one hand and the realized (*ex-post*) change on the other is then:

$$\dot{F}^d - \dot{F} = F_A \frac{M}{P} \left(\frac{\dot{P}}{P} - \pi \right). \tag{12}$$

The two are equal only if expectations are always correct.[2]

Even if there is perfect foresight so that $\dot{F}$ and $\dot{F}^d$ are equal, there is no way in which the balance-of-payments identity can be interpreted as an equilibrium condition which determines, *ceteris paribus*, the exchange rate. To see this, observe that the current account can be written as:

[1] In discussing the extension of the portfolio model of an open economy to the regimes of flexible exchange rates, Branson (1974) in essence substitutes $\dot{F}^d$ in the balance-of-payments identity and allows "... the foreign exchange market to determine the exchange rate so that the balance of payments ... is equal to zero" (Branson, *op. cit.*, p. 47). He recognizes the problems inherent in this approach but leaves them unresolved. Mundell's famous article on flexible exchange rates (1968, Ch. 18) avoids the stock-flow problem by assuming "perfect capital mobility" in which case any surplus of deficit in the current account is always financed by capital inflow or outflow at a fixed interest rate.

[2] For an excellent discussion of the distinction between stock and flow models in monetary analysis, see Foley (1975). He shows in a more general model that the assumption of stock equilibrium and the assumption of perfect foresight imply flow equilibrium, and that the assumption of simultaneous stock and flow equilibrium implies perfect foresight.

$$B = Y - C - G = S - m\frac{M}{P}, \tag{13}$$

where the government's budget constraint has been used. Substituting this and $\dot{F}^d$ from equation (10) into the balance-of-payments equations (9), and using the fact that F_π equals $-L_\pi$, and F_A equals $1 - L_A$ because of the balance sheet constraint, we can rewrite the balance-of-payments equation as:[1]

$$L_\pi \dot{\pi} + L_A \dot{A} = \left(\dot{M} - \frac{\dot{P}}{P}\right)\frac{M}{P} = \left(\frac{\dot{M}}{P}\right). \tag{14}$$

But this is nothing more than the stock equilibrium condition (5) differentiated with respect to time. With perfect foresight, $\dot{\pi}$ is equal to $\ddot{P}/P$ so that equation (14) defines a second-order differential equation that any equilibrium path of the exchange rate must satisfy. The problem is that there are an infinite number, in fact, a continuum of such paths so that the balance-of-payments "equilibrium condition" is not sufficient to determine the behavior of the exchange rate (see section IV (*b*) below).

The flow model of the foreign exchange market can be reformulated in a logically correct way by dropping the assumption of instantaneous portfolio equilibrium and instead specifying functions for the desired changes in the stocks of foreign assets and real money balances. A rigorous formulation of such a model involves a number of difficult problems which are, however, beyond the scope of this paper.[2]

(*b*) *Determination of the Exchange Rate and the Balance of Payments in the Short Run*

The short-run determination of the exchange rate and the current account is illustrated by Fig. 1. The *MM* curve implies equilibrium in the asset markets. The *DD* curve (defined by equation (10)) gives domestic absorption as a function of the exchange rate. If the initial stock of foreign assets held by the private sector is F_0, the momentary equilibrium value of the exchange rate is P_0. At that exchange rate, domestic absorption equals $P_0 B_0$, which is less than domestic output, so that the current account is in surplus. Therefore, the economy will not stay in this momentary equilibrium position; with static expectations the economy moves to the right along the *MM* schedule. As a result, the exchange rate appreciates, which, along with the increasing stock

[1] From equation (10),

$$\dot{F}^d = F_\pi \dot{\pi} + F_A S - F_A \frac{M}{P}\pi = F_\pi \dot{\pi} + F_A S - F_A \frac{M}{P}\frac{\dot{P}}{P},$$

because of the assumption of perfect foresight. Setting $\dot{F}^d$ equal to B, we obtain equation (14).

[2] For a good discussion of these problems, see Foley (1975).

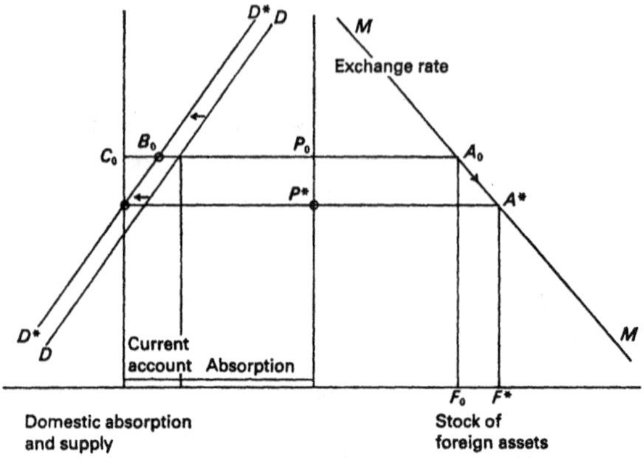

Fig. 1. The short-run determination of the exchange rate and the current account.

of foreign assets, increases domestic absorption until *stationary state equilibrium* is reached with zero current account balance and a constant stock of wealth. A stationary state is obtained in the diagram when the stock of foreign assets equals F^*, the exchange rate is P^* and the D^*D^* schedule intersects the supply curve at that exchange rate. (We assume here for expositional convenience that the nominal money stock is constant.)

Figure 2 illustrates the response of the momentary equilibrium exchange rate and the current account to the following two types of shifts. (i) an increase in the expected rate of depreciation (a stock shift). This causes an increase in the "desire to lend abroad" (cf. Robinson (1949), Section II), without directly affecting domestic absorption. The MM curve shifts to the right

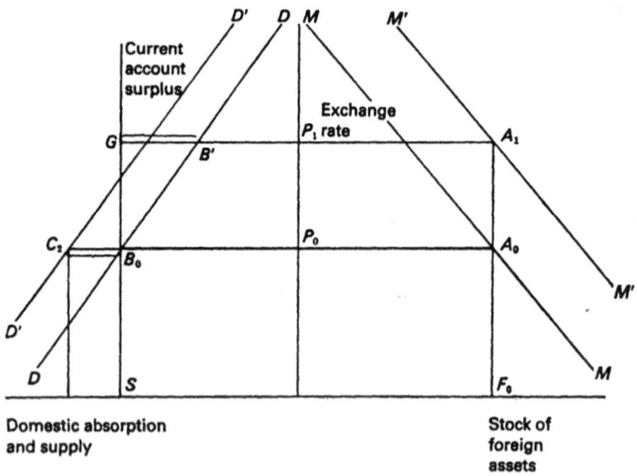

Fig. 2. The short run effects of stock and flow shifts.

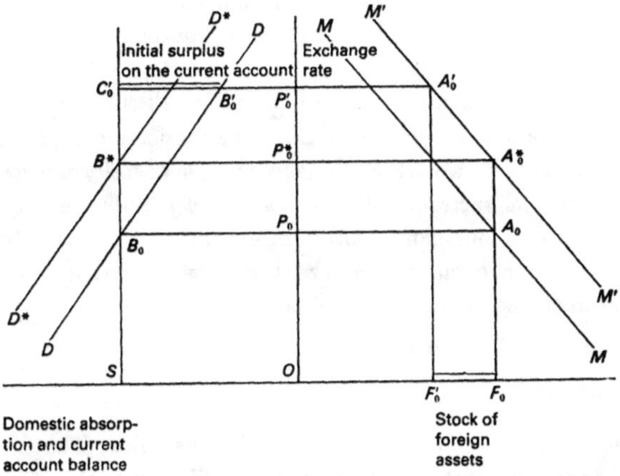

Fig. 3. **Short run effects of central bank intervention in the foreign exchange market.**

causing the exchange rate to depreciate. The depreciation causes the current account to move to a surplus (C_1B_1 in the figure). This surplus gradually increases the stock of foreign assets which tends to appreciate the exchange rate and cause the current account surplus to diminish. The complete dynamic analysis of this adjustment process with explicit treatment of expectations will be taken up in Section V below and analysis of the ultimate stationary state effects in Section III. (ii) A tax financed increase in government expenditure (*a flow shift*, cf. Robinson (1949), Section III) shifts the DD schedule to the left but, *ceteris paribus*, leaves the MM schedule unchanged. Therefore, the exchange rate remains unchanged and the current account moves to a deficit. The current account deficit reduces the stock of foreign assets, which causes the exchange rate to depreciate. Both of these effects reduce private absorption and gradually bring the economy to stationary equilibrium with a zero current account.

Thus, with stationary expectations, a *shift in absorption that does not affect asset demands has no effect on the exchange rate in the short run*. We shall see later on that if expectations are rational, the anticipated future effects on the exchange rate induced by the current account deficits will be reflected on the current exchange rate (see Section V below).

Fig. 3 illustrates the short-run effects of Central Bank intervention in the foreign exchange market. The economy starts from a position of full equilibrium at A_0 with stock of foreign assets F_0 and exchange rate P_0. The Central Bank suddenly purchases $F_0'F_0$ of foreign exchange from the private sector with domestic money. The private sector's initial foreign asset position reduces to F_0' and the MM curve shifts upwards to $M'M'$. The exchange rate jumps to P_0'. The sharp reduction in real financial wealth causes the current account to become a surplus ($B_0'C_0'$ in the figure). The surplus begins to move the economy back to a new stationary state equilibrium position. It is shown in the next section that in the new long run equilibrium position the private sector's stock of foreign assets is the same as it was initially. All that happens is that the exchange rate depreciates by exactly the same proportion that the money supply is initially increased. Note that *the exchange rate initially depreciates more than in proportion to the increase in the supply of money.* Subsequently, the rate appreciates down to its long-run equilibrium level. One may view the impact effect of foreign exchange market intervention as a capital levy on money balances—much in the same way as devaluation.[1]

III. The Stationary State

In this section we investigate the long-run effects of various shifts. The dynamic adjustment path from the short-run momentary equilibrium to the long-run stationary state is analyzed in Section V. In the stationary state, the stock of real wealth and its composition are constant, all nominal variables grow at the same rate and the expected rate of inflation equals the actual rate of inflation and hence the rate of change in the money stock.[2]

The constancy of real wealth requires that the current account is equal to zero:

$$C(Y-T, \bar{M}+F)+T+\pi\bar{M} = Y \text{ (cf. equation 8).} \tag{15}$$

Equation (15) defines the locus of $\bar{M}$ and F, implying balance of payments equilibrium. It is illustrated by the FF schedule in Fig. 4. The schedule is downward sloping—for the trade account to remain in zero balance when the stock of foreign assets increases, the stock of real balances must fall to prevent an increase in absorption.

The second stationary state equilibrium condition requires that the stock of wealth is held in desired proportions:

$$L(\pi, Y, \bar{M}+F) = \bar{M} \text{ (cf. equation 5).} \tag{16}$$

The description of the stationary state is complete once we observe that the expected rate of inflation (π) equals the actual rate of inflation ($\dot{P}/P$), which in turn equals the rate of growth in the money stock (m):

$$\pi = \frac{\dot{P}}{P} = m. \tag{17}$$

---

[1] Cf. Dornbusch (1973).

[2] The stationary state model is similar to that of McKinnon & Oates (1966), except that we assume fixed output and variable price level (exchange rate) whereas they assume a fixed price level and variable output even in the long run.

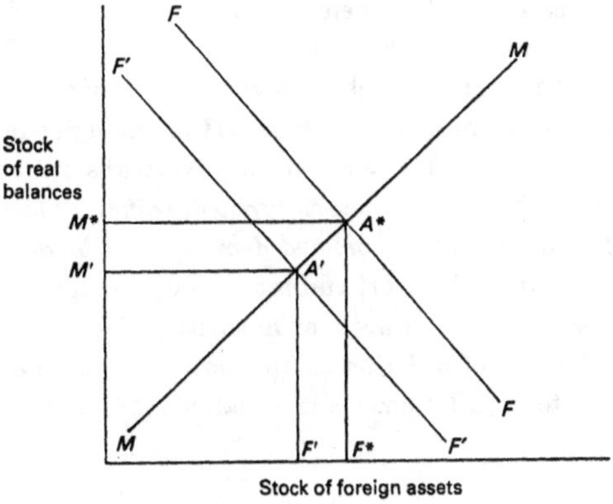

Fig. 4. The stationary state.

The locus of the stocks of foreign assets and real balances that are consistent with portfolio equilibrium is illustrated by the *MM* schedule in Fig. 4 (cf. Fig. 1). It is upward sloping because an increase in the stock of foreign assets increases the demand for real balances. The intersection of the *FF* and *MM* schedules at point A^* determines the long-run stationary state stock of foreign assets (F^*) and real balances ($\bar{M}^*$). It is assumed throughout this paper that there exists a unique stationary state for all rates of inflation greater than some negative $\bar{\pi}$. The long-run exchange rate *path* (obviously, we cannot talk about a long-run exchange rate if that rate is steadily depreciating) is defined by:

$$\ln P(t) = \ln M_0 + mt - \ln \bar{M}^*. \qquad (18)$$

There is thus a one-to-one correspondence between the long-run exchange rate path and the stock of real balances. The lower the stock of real balances, the "higher" the exchange rate path. Subsequently, when we refer to a long-run depreciation of the exchange rate, we mean an upward shift in the exchange rate path.

It follows immediately from equations (16) and (17) that a once-and-for-all intervention in the foreign exchange market has no long-run real effects—all that happens is that the exchange rate increases proportionately. This implies that a purchase of X units of foreign exchange by the Central Bank will be followed by a period of current account surpluses which add up to exactly X units of foreign exchange.

Fiscal policy can affect the long-run equilibrium position in two ways, i.e. by changing the tax revenue and by changing the rate of growth of public debt, and hence the rate of inflation. These two methods constitute two alternative forms of taxation. The first is a lump sum tax on income, the second a capital levy on cash balances. They have quite different long-run effects because the inflation tax changes the desired portfolio composition.

The long-run effect of an increase in government expenditure financed by higher taxes can be established unambiguously with reference to Fig. 4. The FF schedule shifts down to $F'F'$; at a given stock of foreign assets there is an increase in absorption. In order for the balance of payments to remain in equilibrium, the stock of real balances must fall and reduce private absorption. Therefore, *a tax financed increase in government expenditure will reduce the long-run stock of foreign assets held by the private sector, and depreciate the long-run exchange rate.* This means that between the short-run momentary equilibrium and the long-run stationary state, the current account must be in deficit.

The effect of an increase in the rate of inflation on the stationary state depends on the magnitude of the rate of inflation. From equations (16) and (18) we obtain:

$$\hat{M} = \frac{C_A L_\pi - L_A \bar{M}}{\Delta} \hat{\pi} \tag{19}$$

$$\hat{F} = \frac{L_A \bar{M} - (C_A + \pi) L_\pi - \pi \bar{M}}{\Delta} \hat{\pi} \tag{20}$$

$$\hat{A} = \frac{-\pi L_\pi - \bar{M}}{\Delta} \hat{\pi}, \tag{21}$$

where $\Delta = C_A + \pi L_A$. The effect of a higher rate of inflation on the stationary state stock of real balances is unambiguously negative. Therefore, we may write the stationary state demand for money function in the form $M/P = L^*(\pi, Y)$, with L_π negative.[1] The effect on the stock of foreign assets and the stock of real wealth is ambiguous. If L_π is well-behaved, the stock of wealth at first reduces with the rate of inflation reaching the minimum when the rate of inflation equals the inverse of the inflation elasticity of money demand, and thereafter increasing with the rate of inflation. The stock of real private financial wealth is minimized when the government revenue from the inflation tax is maximized.[2] As the rate of inflation approaches infinity, the stationary state stock of wealth approaches what it would be if the rate of inflation were zero. This is because, in both cases, the average real rate of interest is the same, namely zero.[3] An increase in the rate of inflation at first reduces the stock of foreign assets but after a while the substitution effect begins to dominate and the stock of privately held foreign assets begins to increase. It is clear from equation (17) that this occurs before the revenue maximizing rate of inflation is reached.

---

[1] This is the Archibald–Lipsey long-run demand for money function. See Archibald & Lipsey (1958). See also McKinnon (1969) for a discussion as to why the stock of wealth does not appear in the long-run asset demand equations.

[2] See the recent treatment of the optimal inflation tax by Phelps (1973).

[3] With zero rate of inflation, equation (12) is of the form $C(Y-T, A) + T = Y$. With an infinite rate of inflation, $\pi\bar{M}$ becomes zero (under appropriate conditions for the inflation elasticity of money demand) so that equation (12) is of the same form: $C(Y-T, A) + T = Y$.

An increase in the rate of inflation may thus be accompanied either by a period of current account deficits (when the rate of inflation is low) or a period of current account surpluses (when the rate of inflation is high). The dynamic response pattern depends critically on how expectations are formed (see Section V).

IV. The Dynamic Stability of the Ajustment Process

In this section we investigate the dynamic stability of the balance of payments adjustment process under flexible exchange rates. Dynamic stability in this context refers to the convergence of the sequence of momentary equilibria to the stationary state. We shall examine three mechanisms of expectations formation:

(*a*) *static expectations:* $\pi = m$
(*b*) *myopic perfect foresight:* $\pi = \dot{P}/P = m - \dot{x}$
(*c*) *adaptive expectations:* $\dot{\pi} = \beta(\dot{P}/P - \pi) = \beta(m - \dot{x} - \pi)$,

where X is equal to the logarithm of the stock of real balances ($\ln \bar{M}$). The adjustment process is defined by one of the above expectations equations and the following two equations:

$$\dot{F} = k(\pi, F) \quad \text{(cf. equation 8)} \tag{22}$$

$$X = h(\pi, F) \quad \text{(cf. equation 6.1).} \tag{23}$$

(*a*) *Static Expectations*

With static expectations, π is constant and equation (22) becomes an ordinary differential equation in F. Because k_F is negative and we assume a unique stationary state, the adjustment process is globally stable. In Fig. 4, the economy moves along the asset market equilibrium line (MM). Along the static expectations path the exchange rate changes continuously in a way that implies profit opportunities for speculators, so that it is hardly an adequate representation of the adjustment process.

(*b*) *Myopic Perfect Foresight*

The strong stability result obtained in the case of static expectations suggests that the question of dynamic stability hinges on the nature of expectations formation. It is shown in this section that perfect foresight renders the exchange rate *indeterminate*; from any initial exchange rate there is an exchange rate and foreign asset path such that expectations are continuously fulfilled and all markets are in equilibrium. This problem of indeterminacy has been raised in a different context by Black (1974). It is also well known in the

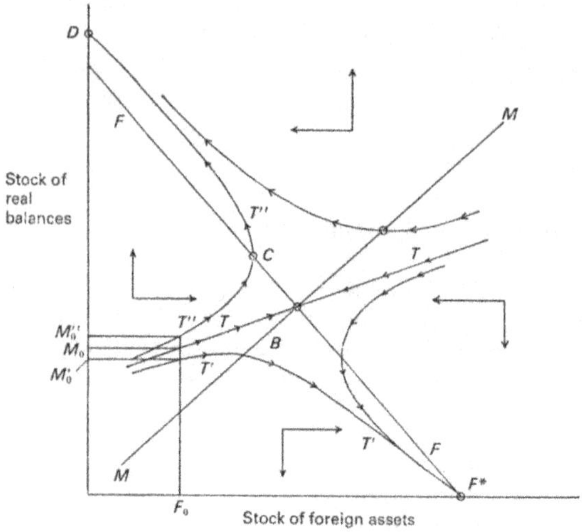

Fig. 5. The adjustment process with perfect foresight.

models of money and growth and in growth models with many capital goods.[1] There is only one path along which the economy converges to the stationary state—provided that it gets on that path in the first place.

The fact that the stationary state is a saddle point can be established by considering the dynamic system consisting of equations (22) and (23) with $m - \dot{x}$ substituted for π. It is straightforward to show that the characteristic roots of the resulting dynamic system, linearized around the stationary state, are real and of opposite sign, which is a sufficient condition for the stationary state to be a saddle point locally.[2]

The dynamic behavior of the stock of real balances and the stock of foreign assets with perfect foresight is illustrated in Figure 5. The *MM* curve implies that the stock of real balances is constant (whence the rate of depreciation of the exchange rate equals the rate of growth of the nominal money stock). The *FF* schedule implies that the current account is zero and hence the stock of foreign assets is constant. The assumption of a unique stationary state implies that the *FF* curve cannot be steeper than the *MM* curve although it can be

---

[1] For a discussion of this problem in models of money and growth see Hahn (1969) and references contained therein. See also the recent paper by Brock (1975). Brock resolves the problem of indeterminacy by assuming an economy of identical, infinitely lived intertemporal optimizers. The transversality condition enables him to eliminate the deviant paths. It is not clear, however, what market forces enforce the transversability condition. Other useful references are Burmeister & Dobell (1970), Chapter 6, and Stein (1970), especially Chapter I, Section E.

[2] The details of the mathematical derivations are omitted since they are straightforward.

locally upward sloping.[1] The assumption of the existence of a stationary state for positive rates of inflation also implies that the stock of foreign assets never exceeds the stationary state level of wealth with zero rate of inflation. This is why the FF curve cuts the X-axis at a finite stock of foreign assets F^*.

The arrows in Fig. 5 indicate the direction of movement. Suppose that the initial stock of foreign assets is F_0. The initial exchange rate should be set in such a way that the initial stock of real balances is equal to M_0 in order for the economy to converge to the stationary state along the TT trajectory. If the exchange rate is initially undervalued, the stock of real balances is too low—M_0' in the figure—the exchange rate appreciates initially as people build up their domestic money balances faster than they accumulate foreign assets in order to restore portfolio equilibrium. After a while, the stock of real balances reaches a point where it stops increasing (point B in the figure). At this point, the exchange rate begins to depreciate. The speculators catch on immediately and start the flight out of domestic money. Hyperinflation ensues and foreign money renders domestic money valueless. The opposite outcome occurs if the currency is initially overvalued so that the initial stock of real balances is too high. Both the stock of real balances and the stock of foreign assets will increase at first, but after a while (point C in the figure) the substitution effect begins to dominate and the domestic residents start reducing their foreign assets because of the high yield on domestic assets. It is implausible that the boom in the foreign exchange market could continue much beyond point D in the figure when domestic residents no longer have any foreign assets. At that point the appreciation suddenly stops, the market collapses and speculators incur a large capital loss. If speculators have *long-run perfect foresight* they will anticipate this outcome and will prevent the hyperdeflation from ever getting started.

It is less clear how hyperinflation might be ruled out since there does not appear to be any good reason why domestic currency could not be replaced by foreign money even in domestic transactions. Of course, society as a group loses from this because it has to give up real resources (cut down on consumption) in order to accumulate foreign money. There is no self-evident competitive market mechanism which rules out society making itself worse off by destroying the value of its money through speculation. In addition to merely ruling out such a possibility because it seems unreasonable (Sargent & Wallace, 1974), or because it has never happened without excessive monetary expansion, it could be argued that a minimum stock of real balances is always needed to carry out some transactions—for instance, payments of taxes. If this is the case, *long-run perfect foresight* rules out hyperinflation as well. There remains the troublesome question of how the speculators should compute the initial exchange rate which will take the economy to the stationary state. We shall

---

[1] See Samuelson & Liviatan (1969) for a detailed analysis of the properties of saddlepoints in optimal growth models. The problems of local instability and multiple equilibria can also arise in our model but we assume them away.

not attempt to tackle this question; instead, we use the assumption of long-run perfect foresight (rational expectations) as a convenient tool for dynamic analysis.

Fig. 5 shows the important property of the rational expectations adjustment path, that is *the stock of foreign assets and the stock of real balances always move monotonically and in the same direction.* This result will prove very helpful in the next section.

(c) *Adaptive Expectations*

With adaptive expectations the dynamic evolution of the economy is defined by equations (22) and (23) and the adaptive expectations equation (c). It is straightforward to show that a sufficient condition for the local stability of this system is that the product of the absolute value of the inflation elasticity of the demand for real balances (h_π) and the speed of revision of expectations (β) is less than one:

$$h_\pi \beta < 1. \tag{24}$$

If the system is stable, the convergence to equilibrium is nonoscillating. This stability condition is the same as the condition of stability in Cagan's model of hyperinflation except that here, h_π is a reduced form elasticity, unlike in his model. Our model of the inflationary process differs from Cagan's analysis among other things because equilibrium can be restored not only through price changes but also through changes in the stock of the money substitute.

V. Dynamic Response of the Exchange Rate and the Balance of Payments to Various Shocks

In this section we analyze the dynamic response of the exchange rate and the balance of payments to the various shocks considered in Sections II and III from the short-run and long-run perspective. Our strategy is to use the phase-diagram introduced in the previous section and infer from that what the response of the exchange rate and the current account will be. The response of the exchange rate can be established easily from the response of the stock of real balances and the response of the current account from the direction of change in the stock of foreign assets. We shall examine separately each of the three shocks considered above and in each case compare the response pattern under the three different hypotheses about expectations formation.

(a) *The Dynamic Effects of a Once-and-for-all Intervention in the Foreign Exchange Market*

In Fig. 6 the economy is initially in a stationary state with stock F^* of foreign assets and M^* of real money balances. The MM and FF curves have the same

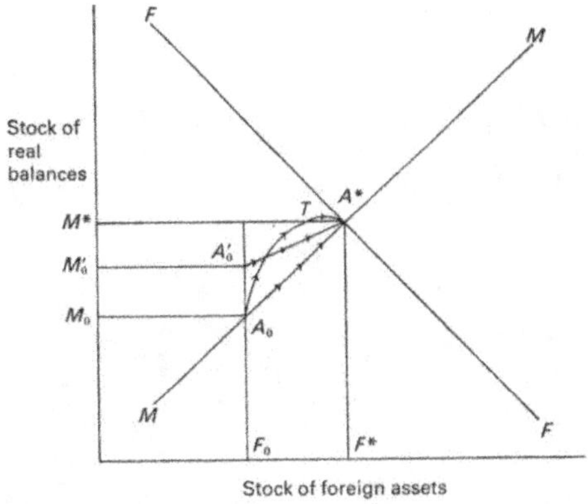

Fig. 6. The dynamic effects of a once-and-for-all intervention in the foreign exchange market.

interpretation as before. The Central Bank purchases F_0F^* of foreign assets. This leaves both the MM and the FF schedules unchanged. With static expectations, the economy stays on the MM schedule so that the stock of real balances declines to M_0. Thereafter, the economy moves back to the same stationary state with the exchange rate *appreciating* and the current account *in surplus*. The static expectations path implies an appreciating exchange rate which the speculators persistently ignore. With foresight, this is not possible whence the initial decline in the stock of real balances is less (implying that the initial devaluation is also less). Thereafter, the behavior of the economy is similar to that under static expectations. This case illustrates that speculators with long-run foresight cushion the exchange rate against discrete and *non-repeated* changes in the money stock. A possible response pattern of the economy under adaptive expectations is illustrated by the A_0TA^* trajectory. The initial point is the same as with static expectations. As the exchange rate subsequently appreciates, the speculators revise their expectations upwards. Hence, the stock of real balances must always be above what it is under static expectations (thus the exchange rate is below what it is along the static expectations path). Speculators may cause the stock of real balances to go above the stationary state value which means that the exchange rate will, after a period of appreciation, start to depreciate. However, the current account cannot move into a deficit (this is implied by the stability condition).

To summarize, in all cases the exchange rate initially depreciates more than in proportion to the change in the money stock. Thereafter, the exchange rate appreciates and the current account is in surplus until the economy has reached a new equilibrium position with a higher exchange rate but the same values for the real variables.

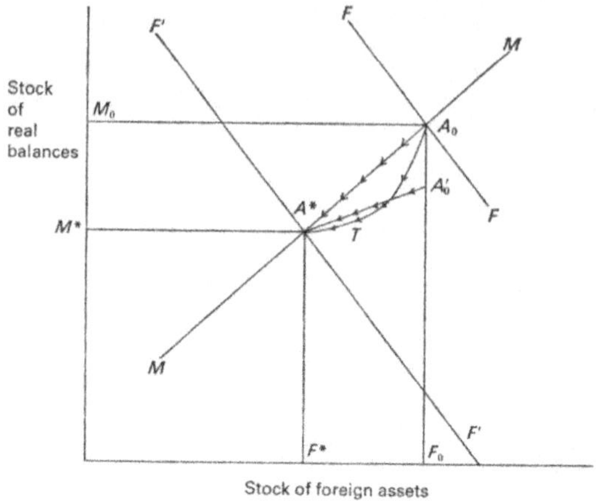

Fig. 7. The dynamic effects of an increase in tax financed government expenditure.

(b) *The Dynamic Effects of a Tax Financed Increase in Government Expenditure*

An increase in government expenditure financed by taxes will shift the FF schedule down and leave the MM schedule unchanged (see Fig. 7). Before the shift, the economy is at point A with stock F_0 of foreign assets and M_0 of real balances. In the new equilibrium position both F^* and M^* are less, respectively. With static and adaptive expectations, the stock of real balances and hence the exchange rate remain initially unchanged. The only impact effect of the shift is that the current account moves to a deficit (cf. Section II*b*). Over time this causes the exchange rate to depreciate. Rational speculators foresee this possibility and cause the exchange rate to depreciate *immediately*, thereby bringing about a larger current account surplus than with static and adaptive expectations. Thereafter, the rational expectations path is similar to the static expectations path. Both of them differ from the adaptive expectations path which may cause the exchange rate to overshoot, as is illustrated by the ATA^* trajectory.

Three points that emerge from this analysis merit re-emphasis:

(i) In all cases, the long-run effect on the stock of foreign assets correctly predicts the short-run effects on the current account.

(ii) If long-run foresight is assumed, the long-run effect on the exchange rate correctly predicts the short-run effect on the exchange rate.

(iii) The ensuing current account deficit is temporary and in no case reverses itself.

It is also of interest to note that the short-run change in the current account has informative value for speculators in terms of the future course of the exchange rate.

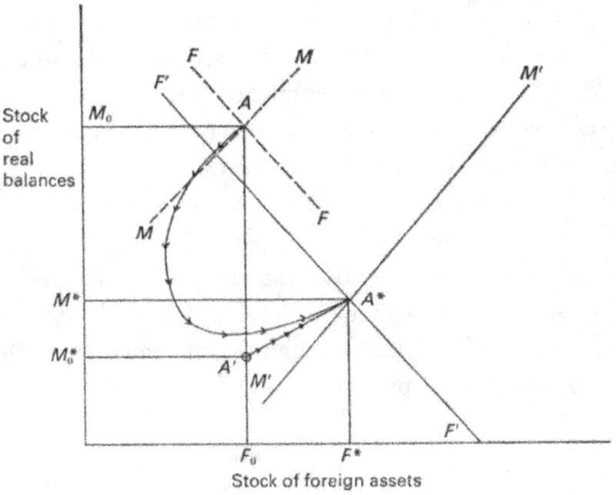

Fig. 8. The dynamic response to an increase in the rate of monetary expansion.

(c) *The Effects of an Increase in the Rate of Monetary Expansion*

With an increase in the rate of monetary expansion, two long-run outcomes are possible. The stock of real balances will unambiguously decline but the stock of foreign assets may either increase or decrease depending on the strength of the substitution effect (which itself depends on the magnitude of the rate of inflation). Fig. 8 illustrates the first case. The economy is initially at point A. The new equilibrium position is A^*, with stock F^* of foreign assets and M^* of real balances. The response to this change is radically different under adaptive and rational expectations. It is meaningless to assume static expectations in this case. With rational expectations, *there is an immediate, discrete devaluation of the exchange rate, after which the exchange rate appreciates relative to its new trend. The sharp depreciation causes the current account to move to a surplus* despite the increase in government expenditure. After the initial adjustment, the stock of real balances and the stock of foreign assets increase *pari passu* to the new equilibrium position. Note that *the short-run impact is correctly predicted by the long-run stationary state impact.*

With adaptive expectations there is no change in the initial exchange rate whence the increased government absorption causes the current account to move to a deficit. For a while, the stock of real balances and the stock of foreign assets decrease *pari passu,* but once speculators catch on, the substitution effect begins to dominate, capital begins to flow out and the current account moves to a surplus. The surpluses add up to the sum of the previous deficits and the long-run increase in the stock of foreign assets because of the lower rate of return on domestic assets.

The case where the stock of both real balances and foreign assets decline in the long run can be analyzed with reference to Fig. 7 since in both cases the new equilibrium position is to the southwest of the initial point. With rational expectations, there is an instant depreciation of the exchange rate attendant upon the (known) increase in the rate of monetary expansion. However, the depreciation is not sufficient to cause the current account to move to a surplus. The *exchange rate will continue to depreciate faster than the new growth rate of the money stock* and the stock of real balances and of foreign assets decline *pari passu*. Note that in the previous case the rate of depreciation was less than the rate of monetary expansion.

With adaptive expectations the path may look like trajectory A_0TA^* in Fig. 7. Initially, there is no change in the exchange rate. The current account deficits cause the rate to depreciate. Speculators catch on and may cause the rate to overshoot its long-run equilibrium path.

VI. Concluding Remarks

This section contains a summary of the main principles of the monetary approach to flexible exchange rates developed in this paper. The various implications of this approach that go beyond the particular model examined above are also discussed.

(i) In the long run there is symmetry between the regime of fixed and flexible exchange rates. Under fixed exchange rates, the exchange rate is exogeneous and the supply of money endogeneous. Under flexible exchange rates, the supply of money is exogeneous and the exchange rate endogeneous. A devaluation under fixed exchange rates increases the supply of money proportionately in the long run; under flexible exchange rates, an increase in the money stock increases the exchange rate proportionately in the long run. An important long-run difference between the two regimes is that under flexible rates the *rate of inflation* can be varied independently of the rest of the world. Changes in the rate of inflation can be interpreted as changes in the tax on domestic money and they will have systematic effects on the long-run stock of wealth and its composition. Other instruments of fiscal policy can be used in both regimes to alter the stationary state. Because fiscal policy and other real variables have an effect on the long-run demand for money, it is not correct to say that the exchange rate can be explained by monetary factors alone, even in the long run.

(ii) The adjustment process is quite different under the two regimes. In both systems, the *stock of wealth* adjusts to its long run desired level through deficits and surpluses *in the current account*. Under fixed exchange rates portfolio equilibrium between domestic money and foreign assets *at a given level of wealth* is obtained through *instantaneous* capital inflows and outflows because the Central Bank supplies foreign assets at a fixed price. Under flexible exchange rates instantaneous portfolio equilibrium is obtained through changes in the *valuation* of assets—that is, through changes in the exchange rate.

Whereas a desire to hold a larger proportion of foreign assets results in an *immediate* adjustment of private portfolios and has no long-run consequences under fixed exchange rates, such a shift under flexible exchange rates will give rise to a gradual adjustment process and will have long-run consequences. The exchange rate will depreciate initially and the current account will move to a surplus. This surplus increases the *actual stock* of foreign assets. In general, the exchange rate in the new equilibrium position will not be the same as before the portfolio shift because the long-run stock of wealth will be different.

(iii) The dynamic behavior of the exchange rate and of the balance of payments depends critically on the nature of expectations formation. Traditional theory has neglected the relevant problem of instability under flexible exchange rates, i.e. the problem of instability of *relative asset prices*, by focusing on balance of payments flows. The crude purchasing power parity theory of exchange rates has also bypassed the problem of possible instability by ignoring the fact that different monies, and assets denominated in different currencies, are substitutes. The requirement of no expected profits does not rule out dynamic instability.[1] In fact, in the case of perfect foresight the *exchange rate is indeterminate*—for any initial exchange rate, there is a path along which all markets clear and expectations are continuously fulfilled. Only one of these paths converges to the stationary state. Since hyperdeflation, or inflation seldom, if ever, develops by force of speculative behavior alone, there must be reasons why the deviant paths cannot be sustained. Some reasons for this are given in the paper.

(iv) This paper does not assign any role to relative price effects in the adjustment process, as emphasized by the traditional analysis of foreign exchange market stability. A necessary condition for stability in our model is that an increase in the stock of foreign assets reduces the current account surplus. With non-traded goods and low price elasticities, this may not happen, in which case the foreign exchange market would be dynamically unstable.

(v) If long-run perfect foresight is assumed, the short-run effects and the dynamic path of various disturbances can be inferred from the long-run effects of these disturbances. This result greatly enhances the usefulness of the portfolio balance models of open economies.

(vi) The view of the exchange rate as a relative asset price suggests that in a world where the underlying determinants—monetary and real—of the exchange rate change continuously and in a stochastic fashion, there is no reason to expect the exchange rate to be stable. In fact, the behavior of the exchange rate is likely to resemble the behavior of asset prices in other speculative markets, such as the stock market.

---

[1] However, if speculators have long-run foresight and rule out explosive price paths, speculation will cushion the exchange rate against reversible shocks, as has been correctly argued by Friedman (1953). However, *permanent* changes in the long-run determinants of the exchange rate will, even with—and in the case of "flow shifts", especially with—rational expectations, have an accentuated effect on the spot exchange rate.

(vii) The analysis in this paper suggests a framework for analyzing the effects of monetary policy under flexible rates which departs significantly from the traditional analysis. The immediate effect of a change in monetary policy is to change the relative price of assets—such as the exchange rate—and the rates of interest. These changes have effects on aggregate demand, prices and output through various channels: (*a*) by changing the real value of wealth and its distribution across countries, (*b*) by changing the rates of interest and thereby affecting the rate of investment, and (*c*) by changing relative commodity prices and real wages. The link between monetary policy and the inflow or outflow of capital goes through the effect of monetary policy on aggregate demand and output and thereby on the current account, which determines the capital account. The direct and immediate link between monetary policy and the capital account in traditional analysis has resulted in the false presumption that monetary policy acts quickly under flexible rates because it has an *immediate* effect on the current account and hence on aggregate demand. The correct reasoning, of course, is that monetary policy has an immediate effect on the current account *if* it has an immediate effect on aggregate demand.

(viii) Finally, the model developed in this paper can be extended in a straightforward manner to allow for rigid wages and unemployment, for changes in relative prices and for accumulation of real capital. The extension of the model to two or more countries would emphasize the fact that what ultimately connects the exchange rate and the current account is the transfer of wealth implied by current account deficits and surpluses and that asset preferences are likely to be different in different countries.

Bibliography

Alexander, S.: The effects of devaluation on the trade balance. *International Monetary Fund Staff Papers*, II, No. 2, 263–78, 1952.

Archibald, C. & Lipsey, R.: Monetary theory and value theory: A critique of Lange and Patinkin. *Review of Economic Studies 26*, 1–22. 1958.

Black, F.: The uniqueness of the price level in monetary growth models with perfect foresight. *Journal of Economic Theory 7*, No. 1, 53–66, 1974.

Black, S. W.: *International money market and flexible exchange rates*. Princeton Studies in International Finance, No. 72. International Finance Section, Princeton 1967.

Branson, W.: Stocks and flows in international monetary analysis. In Ando, Herring, and Marston (eds.), *International Aspects of Stabilization Policies*, Federal Reserve Bank of Boston, Boston. Conference Series, No. 12, 27–50, 1974.

Brock, W.: Money and growth: The case of long run perfect foresight. *International Economic Review 15*, No. 3, 1974.

Brunner, K. & Meltzer, A.: Monetary and fiscal policy in open economies with fixed exchange rates (unpublished manuscript). 1974.

Burmeister, E. & Dobell, A. R.: *Mathematical theories of economic growth*. MacMillan, New York, 1970.

Cagan, P.: The monetary dynamics of hyperinflation. In M. Friedman (ed.), *Studies in the Quantity Theory of Money*, Chapter II, pp. 25–117. The University of Chicago Press, Chicago, 1952.

Dornbusch, R.: Currency depreciation, hoarding, and relative prices. *Journal of Political Economy 81*, No. 4, 893–915, 1973.

Dornbusch, R.: Devaluation, money, and nontraded goods. *American Economic Review 62*, No. 5, 871–880, 1973.

Dornbusch, R.: Capital mobility, flexible exchange rates and macro economic equilibrium. In E. Claassen and P. Salin (eds.), *Recent Developments in International Monetary Economics*, North Holland, Amsterdam, 1976.

Foley, D.: On two specifications of asset equilibrium in macroeconomic models. *Journal of Political Economy 83*, No. 2, 303–324, 1975.

Frenkel, J.: A theory of money, trade and the balance of payments in a model of accumulation. *Journal of International Economics I*, No. 2, 159–187, 1971.

Frenkel, J. and Johnson, H. G.: *The monetary approach to the balance of payments.* Allen and Unwin, London, 1975.

Frenkel, J. & Rodriguez, C.: Portfolio equilibrium and the balance of payments: A monetary approach. *American Economic Review 65*, No. 4, 674–688, 1975.

Friedman, M.: The case for flexible exchange rates. In *Essays in positive economics.* University of Chicago Press, Chicago 1953.

Genberg, H. & Kierzkowski, H.: Short run, long run, and dynamics of adjustment under flexible exchange rates (unpublished manuscript). The Graduate Institute of International Studies, Genevà, 1975.

Hahn, F. H.: The balance of payments in a monetary economy. *Review of Economic Studies 26* (2), No. 70, 110–125, 1959.

Hahn, F. H.: On money and growth. *Journal of money, credit and banking I*, 172–188, 1969.

Johnson, H. G.: Towards a general theory of the balance of payments. In *International Trade and Economic Growth.* Cambridge University Press, Cambridge, 1958.

Johnson, H. G.: The monetary approach to the balance of payments. In A. Swoboda and M. Connolly (eds.), *International Trade and Money*. The University of Toronto Press, Buffalo, 1972.

Johnson, H. G.: The monetary approach to the balance of payments. *The Manchester School*, No. 3, 220–274, 1975.

Kemp, M.: *The pure theory of international trade and investment.* Prentice-Hall, Englewood Cliffs, N.J., 1969.

Kindleberger, C. P.: *International economics*, 5th ed. Richard D. Irwin, Homewood, Illinois, 1973.

Komiya, R.: Monetary assumptions, currency depreciation and the balance of trade. *The Economic Studies Quarterly 17*, No. 2, 9–23, 1966.

Krueger, A.: The role of home goods and money in exchange rate adjustments. In W. Sellekaerts (ed.), *International trade and finance: Essays in honor of Jan Tinbergen*, Chapter 7, pp. 141–161. International Arts and Sciences, 1974.

Liviatan, N. & Samuelson, P. A.: Notes on turnpikes: stable and unstable. *Journal of Economic Theory 2*, No. 4, 454–475, 1969.

McKinnon, R.: Portfolio balance and international adjustment. In R. Mundell and A. Swoboda (eds.), *Monetary problems of the international economy*. Chapter 4. Chicago University Press, 1969.

McKinnon, R. & Oates, W. E.: *The implications of international economic integration for monetary, fiscal, and exchange rate policy*. Princeton Studies in International Finance, No. 16. Princeton University, International Finance Section, Princeton, 1967.

Mundell, R. A.: *International economics.* MacMillan, New York, 1968.

Mundell, R. A.: *Monetary theory*. Goodyear, Pacific Palisades, Calif., 1971.

Mussa, M.: A monetary approach to balance of payments analysis. *Journal of Money, Credit, and Banking 6*, No. 3, 333–352, 1974.

Myhrman, J.: Monetary and fiscal policy and stock-flow equilibrium in an open economy. Unpublished manuscript, 1975.

Negishi, Takashi: Approaches to the analysis of devaluation. *International Economic Review 6*, No. 2, 218–227, 1968.

Pearce, I. F.: The problem of the balance of payments. *International Economic Review II*, No. 1, 1–28, 1961.

Phelps, E. S.: Inflation in the theory of public finance. *Swedish Journal of Economics 75*, 67–82, 1973.

Polak, J.: Monetary analysis of income formation and payments problems. *International Monetary Fund Staff Papers 6*, 1–50, 1958.

Prais, S. J.: Some mathematical notes on the quantity theory of money in an open economy. *International monetary fund staff papers 8*, No. 2, 212–226, 1961.

Robinson, J.: The foreign exchanges. In H. S. Ellis and L. A. Meltzer (eds.), *International trade*, Chapter 4, pp. 83–103. Blakiston Company, Philadelphia and Toronto, 1947.

Samuelson, P. A.: An exact Hume–Ricardo–Marshall model of international trade. *Journal of International Economics*, I, No. 1, 1–18, 1971. Reprinted in: R. C. Merton (ed.), *The Collected Scientific Papers of P. A. Samuelson*, III, Chapter 162, 356–374. M.I.T. Press, Cambridge, Mass., 1972.

Sargant, T. & Wallace, N.: The stability of models of money and growth with perfect foresight. *Econometrica 41*, No. 6, 1043–1048, 1973.

Sidrauski, M.: Rational choice and patterns of growth in a monetary economy. *American Economic Review 58*, 534–544, 1968.

Sohmen, E.: *Flexible exchange rates*, Revised edition. University of Chicago Press, Chicago, 1969.

Stein, J.: *Money and capacity growth.* Columbia University Press, New York, 1971.

Stern, R. M.: *The balance of payments.* Aldine Publishing Co., Chicago, 1973.

COMMENT ON P. J. K. KOURI, "THE EXCHANGE RATE AND THE BALANCE OF PAYMENTS IN THE SHORT RUN AND IN THE LONG RUN: A MONETARY APPROACH"

Alexander K. Swoboda

Graduate Institute of International Studies, Geneva, Switzerland

The requirements of asset-market equilibrium play a crucial role in determining the exchange rate. Changes in relative asset supplies and in the terms at which the public is willing to hold them—and these terms depend crucially on expectations—are therefore to be focused on in any analysis of exchange-rate variations in both the short and long run.

Pentti Kouri provides us with one of the several variations on this, one of the main themes to emerge from the conference. The product is differentiated by the choice of assumptions and the elements in the adjustment process that are given particular emphasis. As in Dornbusch, the choice between domestic and foreign assets is given pre-eminence, though without explicit treatment of the forward market and interest parity; unlike Dornbusch, an explicit formulation of the wealth accumulation process is provided, a feature shared with the model proposed by Genberg and Kierzkowski.[1] That model, unlike Kouri's, also offers an analysis of the implications of various disturbances for employment and relative prices in the traded and non-traded goods sectors; however, it does not investigate alternative formulations of expectations formation, an issue to which Kouri devotes much attention, like Mussa who, in addition, stresses the role of the time-path of disturbances and whether the latter are themselves "expected", a question of utmost importance to the proper design of macroeconomic policy.

What emerges from Kouri's focus is an excellent paper that outlines the role of asset equilibrium and expectations formation in the determination of the exchange rate in the short run and the role of the asset-accumulation process (through current-account surpluses) in defining the path from momentary to long-run equilibrium. The conclusions that emerge are "standard" ones from the point of view of the "new theory" presented at this conference—however iconoclastic they may be from that of the conventional widsom ("the flow model") which Kouri takes to task, sometimes a bit too harshly in my view. This is true in particular with respect to the prospects of short-run over-shoot-

[1] See Genberg, H. and Kierzkowski, H.: Short run, Long Run, and Dynamics of Adjustment under Flexible Exchange Rates. GIIS-Ford Foundation Discussion paper No. 5 (Graduate Institute of International Studies, June 1975).

ing of the exchange rate and the role of expectations formation therein. A full evaluation of Kouri's contribution is impossible in the limited space allotted for comments; that space can perhaps best be used by concentrating on "what makes Kouri's model tick", and then proceeding to a few remarks on the gains achieved and the costs incurred by adopting Kouri's specific approach.

The crucial assumptions made by Kouri are that the economy is small, that it produces only one composite, traded commodity for which perfect arbitrage (the law of one price)—and hence purchasing-power-parity—holds, that output is exogenous and fixed, and that there are only two assets—domestic and foreign money.[1] These assumptions, together with fairly standard behavior postulates—though not necessarily unobjectionable ones (particularly with respect to the treatment of consumption)—enable Kouri to define momentary and stationary state equilibrium in a particularly simple way. Two equations, (5) and (8), representing, respectively, portfolio equilibrium and zero world excess demand for the given national output of the composite good suffice to define momentary equilibrium—and also stationary state equilibrium, with the added proviso that the balance of trade be equal to zero. Under the assumption that the system is stable, and neglecting the process of adjustment, Kouri's comparative statics results follow in straightforward manner.

Consider, for instance, the conclusions that "the response of the exchange rate can be established easily from the response of the stock of real balances and the response of the current account from the direction of change in the stock of foreign assets" (p. 164). The first of these conclusions derives directly from purchasing-power-parity: since $\bar{M}=M/P$, and $P=e$, $e=M/\bar{M}$; M is a pre-determined variable and hence we know e if we know $\bar{M}$. The second conclusion derives directly from the assumption that the foreign asset bears no interest which enables Kouri to ignore the service account in the balance of payments. The simplicity this lends to Kouri's results can be illustrated with respect to one of the three disturbances he considers, a once-and-for-all purchase by the authorities of foreign money held by residents with newly issued domestic money. In the short run real money balances must fall to maintain portfolio equilibrium since all variables in (5), save the price level, are given at the initial instant of time and the stock of foreign assets has fallen. Turning to the long run, consider the requirement for trade equilibrium as expressed in equation (15). Y, T, and π $(=m)$ have not changed hence the same combinations of $\bar{M}$ and F as before will lead to trade balance. Together with the requirements of portfolio balance, this immediately implies that the final stocks of real balances and foreign assets must be equal to the initial ones. From this we can conclude at once that the domestic currency will depreciate in the long run (nominal balances have risen but real balances are restored to their initial

[1] A number of other assumptions, though crucial for specific conclusions, are less generally important, for instance, the postulated behavior of the authorities. The latter may play an important role in creating a minor indeterminacy in Kouri's results concerning the effects of an increase in the rate of monetary expansion.

level), that it will depreciate by even more, i.e., overshoot, in the short run (since real money balances initially fall), and that the trade balance must be in surplus during the adjustment period (since foreign assets are accumulated back to their original level).

Note that the simplicity of this result would most likely be lost were foreign assets to bear interest. For, in that case, the central bank would have acquired an income stream, the disposal of which should explicitely be taken into account together with the private wealth effects engendered by the operation. Furthermore, the change in the service account that would result would make it impossible to predict the balance of trade in as straightforward a manner as Kouri does. Nor would stability analysis be as simple; a potential for instability may well be introduced into the model. These are not entirely moot considerations when one reflects on the importance of foreign investment income for a country like Switzerland, to take but one example.

Let me hasten to add that the foregoing remarks are not intended as a criticism of simplicity. On the contrary, especially since it allows Kouri to proceed in clear fashion to an analysis of the role of alternative expectations formulations for stability and the process of adjustment. The discussion of stability seems to me somewhat unsatisfactory for two reasons. First, it would have been useful if the formal analysis had been provided, even if only in summary form and in an appendix. Second, the rather lengthy discussion of indeterminacy under myopic perfect foresight is somewhat redundant since this indeterminacy is well-known and shared by all similarly formulated infinite time-horizon models. As no new solution is provided one might as well jump immediately with Sargent and Wallace to long-run perfect foresight, a step that Kouri eventually takes, in order to concentrate on the interesting implications of the nature of expectations for the path of adjustment under that assumption.

Kouri's analysis of adjustment produces quite sensible and heuristically appealing results. The driving forces of the adjustment process are the speed at which assets are accumulated and the manner in which expectations are formed and revised.[1] As we would have expected, static expectations lead to overshooting and a simple path back to equilibrium; the other two expectations formulations also lead to overshooting but rational expectations, as we should rationally expect, lead to a dampening of the initial overshooting, adaptive expectations to a spreading out of this dampening over the adjustment period. Kouri's results are both encouraging and somewhat unsatisfying. They are encouraging in that they conform to intuition and provide a rationale for the overshooting of variables such as the exchange rate, a feature that

[1] Of course, alternative assumptions about both expectations and asset adjustment could have been adopted; for instance, portfolio equilibrium may not be instantaneous. Though these alternatives are quite relevant for some purposes and may be preferable when tackling empirical work, Kouri's choice seems quite appropriate to his mainly heuristic purposes.

many analysts have come to believe characterizes adjustment under floating rates in the light of recent experience. They are somewhat unsatisfying for two reasons. First, the behaviour of the exchange rate and other crucial variables is quite similar in terms of direction of change over the adjustment period, whichever of the expectations hypotheses is used. As a consequence, it would be quite difficult to discriminate among these hypotheses at an empirical level. Second, and this is a problem that arises with many current contributions (as Mussa notes), Kouri's formulation does not enable one to distinguish between the impact of disturbances that are foreseen in advance and those that are not. Nothing happens until, say, the money supply doubles, even if people knew a year ago that it would double today. This omission is important from the point of view of interpretation of historical events and from that of advice as to proper policy behavior under floating rates.

Where policy recommendations are concerned, the lesson from this conference is important but needs to be supplemented. The one recommendation is "don't make waves" (or you will overshoot and cycle)—eminently sensible advice, especially for a large country with a cosmopolitan conscience, but insufficient advice for a small country on whose shores the waves land. The implications of the "new view" for the proper use of policy tools in the face of various types of disturbances (domestic and foreign, real and monetary, etc.) need to be drawn out, in a manner that would relate them to classics in the field, be it the Mundellian assignment problem or optimum currency area question or Phillips' framework for the analysis of stabilization policy. In that task, it might well be that Dornbusch's emphasis on relating the new view to the standard framework (through capital mobility, interest arbitrage and a separate analysis of movements in the spot and forward rate), Mussa's insistence on the importance of the time path and character (anticipated or not, permanent or transitory) of disturbances, Genberg and Kierzkowski's focus on the impact of exchange-rate changes on relative prices and employment, offer better points of departure for analysis than Kouri's approach.

The latter, however, has great heuristic value. It reveals quite clearly the essential features of the new view and the pitfalls, actual and potential, of the more traditional "flow approach".[1] In this respect, Kouri's contribution helps lay the logical foundations of the analytical framework within which the policy questions referred to above can meaningfully be asked.

---

[1] I have been bothered, for some time, by the traditional approach for one quite general reason which leads to the new view by a slightly different route. The traditional approach focuses on the excess flow demand for "foreign exchange" without specifying carefully what foreign exchange is. One would say, for instance, that there are more dollars demanded than offered against pounds in "the foreign-exchange market". What meaning can reasonably be attached to such a statement other than that, given the level of the exchange rate and all other relevant variables, there is an excess demand for dollar-denominated cash and an excess supply of pound-denominated cash—whether "in" the foreign-exchange market or in any other market. If so, we are really talking about excess demand or supply of money and, presumably, portfolio equilibrium conditions and relative asset supplies should play a crucial role in determining the exchange rate—among other variables.

THE FIRM UNDER PEGGED AND FLOATING EXCHANGE RATES

Robert Z. Aliber

University of Chicago, Chicago, Illinois, USA

Abstract

This article seeks to answer the question about the impact of floating exchange rates on international trade and investment by comparing the costs and risks encountered by traders under floating rates with those under pegged rates. Data indicate that transactions costs are five to ten times higher under floating rates, with the larger increases associated with the more volatile currencies. Exchange risk is measured under the two exchange rate systems by comparing the mean forecast errors between the forward rate and the spot rate at the maturity of the forward contracts and the standard deviations of these forecast errors; both mean and standard deviation have increased by a factor of five to ten. Finally price risk, which involves variations in the domestic price of tradeables as a result of changes in exchange rates, is shown to be substantially higher under the floating rate system.

I. Introduction

The trade-off in the comparison of floating exchange rate systems and pegged exchange rate systems involves the costs and the benefits of segmenting the goods markets and the money markets internationally. Floating exchange rates segment both national money markets and national goods markets. Segmenting the money markets may enable individual countries to realize higher levels of employment because they are better able to pursue independent monetary policies, while segmenting goods markets means resource allocation is somewhat less efficient. The argument that floating rates are preferable rests on the presumption that the benefits from segmenting national money markets in terms of additional freedom to determine interest rates, price levels, and employment dominate the welfare loss from segmenting goods markets (Sohmen, 1969).

In a world of certainty, the two exchange rate systems are effectively the same, with the trivial difference of transactions costs (Aliber, 1972). In an uncertain world, the comparison involves the impact of uncertainty on the segmentation of the two markets.

I am grateful to Rolf Banz, John Bilson, Steve Hyde, and Richard Karplus for useful comments and assistance with the data.

The trade-off between the exchange rate systems is sometimes stated as to whether private parties or governments are better able to bear uncertainty about exchange rate changes. This statement, however, is incomplete, since it confuses two issues—one is whether government agencies or private parties are more effective in reducing exchange rate uncertainty; the second is whether the costs of segmenting the goods markets are larger or smaller than the benefits of segmenting the money markets.

The period since early 1973 provides an opportunity to examine the arguments about floating exchange rate systems and the impacts on international trade and investment. One assertion in the case for floating rates is that trade and investment would not be deterred by exchange rate uncertainty because traders and investors could hedge their commitments through forward market transactions (Friedman, 1953; Giersch, 1970). A claim sometimes heard since floating began is that international trade and investment have not been adversely affected, since recorded exports have increased. If these statements are correct, then the benefits attributed to floating rates of greater national monetary independence may have been achieved without the costs associated with goods markets segmentation.

Exchange rate movements in the last two years have been volatile, especially between the dollar and the currencies in Europe. The movements in trade-weighted or effective exchange rates for individual countries have been substantially smaller, both among the dollar area countries and among the countries participating in the joint float. While the use of trade-weighted exchange rates indicates how the total trade of individual countries has been affected by the exchange rate system, it by-passes the issue of how trade and investment are affected between two currency areas linked by a floating exchange rate.

On an *a priori* basis, it seems likely that international trade and investment would be adversely affected by the move from pegged rates to floating rates. Two arguments are relevant; one is straightforward, the other less direct. Under the pegged rate system, central banks subsidize purchases and sales of foreign exchange and hence international transactions; they "make a market" in foreign exchange at a lesser spread or markup than profit-oriented, competitive commercial bankers would (Lanyi, 1969). Increased uncertainty about exchange rates is likely to lead to a reduction in international transactions relative to domestic transactions, and so production is less specialized internationally; the analogy is an increase in a tax, however modest, on international transactions in goods and securities.

The less direct, more powerful argument is that similar financial assets denominated in various currencies are less perfect substitutes for each other under floating than under a pegged rate system. The increased uncertainty about future exchange rates that makes it possible to have greater monetary independence increases the costs and uncertainties of international transactions relative to domestic transactions, and hence segments national goods markets. The exercise of monetary independence in the form of changes in monetary policy may lead to sharp movements in exchange rates.

That the costs of segmentation goods markets are larger under floating rates than under alternative exchange rate systems is only one component in the arguments about the merits of pegged and of floating exchange rates. Its significance relative to the costs of the segmentation of money markets is an empirical issue, and beyond the scope of this paper. However, the choice between the two exchange rate systems is not made after a precise cost–benefit analysis of segmentation of these two markets. Instead, once the monetary environment—the desired rates of price level change in major countries—is given, there may be little freedom to choose the exchange rate system (Aliber, 1975). Once monetary authorities in the several countries determine the rates of growth of their money supplies, the investors determine the terms on which national monies exchange.

Floating rates have been inevitable over the last several years, given the world-wide inflation, and the efforts of Germany, Japan, Canada, and other countries to pursue price level targets different from that in the United States. If national price level targets are similar, then the equilibrium exchange rate is not likely to change significantly, and either pegged or floating rates is feasible, which is suggested by the Canadian experience of the 1950's (Helliwell, 1974); the economic significance of the difference between the two systems may then be trivial. If price level targets are dissimilar, pegged rates are not feasible, and currencies must necessarily float, which is the lesson both of the 1920's and the 1970's. With prices rising more rapidly in one country than in its trading partners, anticipated future exchange rates are likely to change sharply, and it seems heroic to believe exchange rates could be satisfactorily pegged. If pegged rates are not feasible, the question becomes how best to reduce the costs of goods market segmentation resulting from divergent monetary policies. The policy issue is the appropriate set of arrangements toward the exchange market given the divergence in national price level movements; the authorities may completely refrain from exchange market intervention, or lean against the wind, or continuously intervene, as in a crawling peg.[1]

Thus the traditional arguments about the relative merits of pegged rates and floating rates usually are inadequately specified, in that pegged rates are not an effective substitute for floating rates if national price level targets differ significantly, or the system is subject to severe shock. If price level targets are similar, pegged rates are feasible; whether pegged rates are then preferable is an empirical issue.

[1] A floating rate system provides a more effective transition as the equilibrium rate changes than pegged rates do; under the Bretton Woods system established parities have been retained long after they have become obsolete. These delays are somewhat purposeful, for they enable private market participants to avoid exchange losses, at the expense of the central banks.

The next section of the paper provides a brief analysis of the several risks encountered by the firm in the international market. Then the transactions costs under floating rates are compared with those under pegged rates. Exchange risk and price risk under both pegged and floating rates are discussed in turn. Finally the firm's ability to offset exchange risk and price risk is considered.

II. Risks and International Transactions

Three related decisions faced by the firm should be distinguished. The firm must decide whether to take on commercial or trade commitments which will oblige it to buy or sell foreign exchange at some future date. Second, it must decide when it should undertake these trade commitments. Third, given its commitments to pay or receive foreign currencies, the firm must decide when to exchange exposure. The first question involves the package of costs and risks on international transactions, the second involves price risk, and the third, involves exchange risk.

The firm deals in two markets, the goods market and the foreign exchange market.[1] Transactions in the goods market obligate one of the parties to the international transaction to under-take a transaction in the foreign exchange market; this transaction alters the firm's inventory of real or non-monetary assets, so that its net worth may be affected by changes in the domestic prices of these goods as a result of changes in exchange rates. Hence the firm is subject to price risk—the risk of a change in its net worth from an unanticipated change in the exchange rate.

The goods market transaction automatically alters the currency mix of the firm's financial assets and liabilities, and so the net worth of the firm may be affected by subsequent changes in the exchange rate; consequently the firm is subject to an exchange risk from unanticipated changes in the exchange rate. At some stage the firm may alter the currency mix of its balance sheet by a foreign exchange transaction to neutralize its exchange exposure; this foreign exchange transaction occurs on the settlement date which may coincide with or precede or lag the commitment date.

The timing of the two decisions is shown in Diagram 1. The goods market

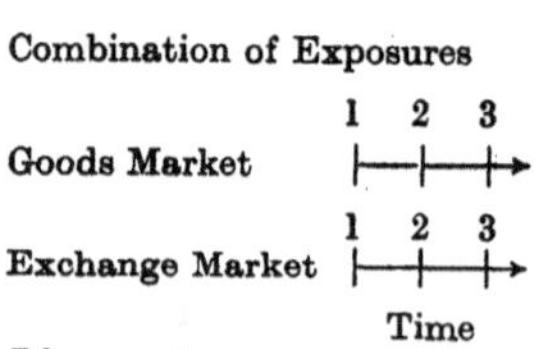

Diagram 1

[1] The discussion could be readily extended to international investment. Firms engaged in direct foreign investment or in portfolio investment are subject to exchange risk but not price risk.

transaction occurs on the commitment date; the exchange market transaction occurs on the settlement date. The goods market transaction and the foreign exchange transaction may occur at 1, 2, or 3. If the commitment date and settlement dates are matched, the firm avoids exposure to exchange risk; the firm remains exposed to price risk as long as it owns the tradeable good. If the commitment date is 2, the firm might buy the foreign currency at 1 and remain exposed to exchange risk during the 1 to 2 interval. Alternatively, if the settlement date is 3, the firm is exposed to exchange risk during the 2 to 3 interval.

III. Uncertainty and Transactions Costs

Firms are price-takers in the foreign exchange market. One party to nearly every international transaction must incur a foreign exchange commitment; subsequently a foreign exchange transaction must be made to settle this commitment.

Most foreign exchange transactions are undertaken with commercial banks. These banks play two roles in the foreign exchange market. They are brokers and intermediate between buyers and sellers of various national currencies and profit from the mark-up or bid-ask spread; and they are dealers for their own account and take a long or a short position in foreign currencies to profit from anticipated movements in exchange rates.[1] In both broker and dealer roles, the bank holds an inventory of foreign currencies; the spot inventory—but not necessarily the forward inventory—ties up some of the bank's capital. The larger the inventory, the better able the bank is to meet its customers demands. The bank is subject to risk in that the domestic value of the inventory varies with changes in the exchange rate; the risk is larger, the more volatile the exchange rate movement. There seems no reason to believe that the likelihood of losses from unanticipated changes in exchange rates has increased relative to the likelihood of gains.

The banks must be paid to cover their costs and to reimburse their risks; their income arises from the bid–ask spread and from changes in the domestic value of their inventory. The banks operate in a highly competitive market, especially in interbank transactions; the spreads between their buying and selling rates reflect market forces. In some countries exchange rates quoted to bank customers, especially the smaller ones, may be set on cost-plus basis in conformance with a cartel-like agreement; for example, the interbank closing rate of one day becomes the "cost" for calculating customers' buying and selling rates on the next day (Isobe, 1966; Aliber, 1969).

Each activity—the brokerage function and the dealer function—may be viewed as separate from the point of view of calculation of costs and return within the bank. Differences in the rates of return on these two activities are

[1] Banks deal at "inside rates", they buy and sell foreign exchange at rates more attractive than those available to their customers.

Table 1. *Summary statistics on transactions costs*

FL = Frenkel & Levich (pegged period represented by 1962–1967, floating period 1973–1974). RIM = R. McKinnon (pegged period represented by 1962–1967, floating period by January 31, 1974).

	Percentage cost			
	Spot		Forward	
Currency pair	Pegged	Floating	Pegged	Floating
US $, C $				
FL	.058	.810	.073	.440
RIM	.025*	.030	.045*	.050
US $, £				
FL	.058	.810	.058	.440
RIM	.021*	.071	.042*	.142
US $, DM				
RIM	.016	.280	.040	.420

consistent with a competitive solution in that the dealer activity is substantially riskier than the broker activity—no bank has failed because profits on its dealer activities were too low. Whether the dealer activity subsidizes the broker activity must remain conjectural—although it is plausible that the profits from the dealer activity subsidized the broker activity during the pegged rate period. On an *a priori* basis it seems unlikely that a similar transfer exists during the floating rate period.

The firm must pay the banks for acting as brokers between buyers and sellers. Different but complementary approaches have been taken to the measurement of transaction costs. One approach examines the bid–ask spread in the interbank market (Aliber, 1975; Fielke, 1974; McKinnon, 1974); these spreads are larger by a factor of five or ten, for both spot and forward transactions under the floating rate period. The second approach to measurement of transactions costs (Frenkel & Levich, 1975; 1975*b*) examines the deviations of predicted values of exchange rates from observed values using triangular arbitrage; most of the deviations are assumed to fall within a band which measures the total cost of transactions. Investors assure that deviations from triangular arbitrage cannot exceed the cost of transactions; thus the deviations are confined to a narrow band whose width measures these costs. Hence the indirect approach includes costs which are internal to the firm as well as those encountered in the market. The Frenkel–Levich study shows an increase in transactions costs by a factor in the range of 5 to 10 (see Table 1).

Both the direct and indirect approaches show sharp increases in transactions costs in percentage terms. The bid–ask spreads are relevant for money market segmentation and shifts of funds by banks from one center to another, while the broader concept of transactions costs is relevant for goods market segmentation. The paradox is that the move to floating rates appears to increase goods market segmentation substantially more than money market segmentation, in that the increase in indirect costs is greater. Nevertheless, the transactions costs are small in absolute terms, although the percentage increase seems substantially larger than might have been predicted. The sign of the argument for the impact of this cost increase on the level of international trade is unambiguous; the magnitude of the impact remains to be determined.

IV. Uncertainty and Exchange Risk

The firm which enters into an agreement to pay or receive foreign exchange becomes exposed to the risk of a change in its net worth from a change in the exchange rate. The firm may reduce, hedge or increase its exposure by a spot or a forward transaction on the commitment date or before or after this date.

If the firm hedges its exposure, its income will not be directly affected by changes in the exchange rate. The "cost" of altering exposure is the change in the return from maintaining an exposed position; this cost is the change in the exchange rate between the commitment date and the settlement date, plus any change in its interest income over the same period from the change in the currency mix of its portfolio. Maintaining a non-exposed position is the exchange market equivalent of holding a riskless asset in the domestic securities market. In contrast, an exposed position is risky, since future exchange rates are uncertain. The cost is an estimate; on or about the commitment date the firm must take a view on future exchange rates and decide whether the anticipated change in the exchange rate has been fully discounted in the forward exchange rate or the interest agio. In a certain world, the forward rate and the interest agio would accurately predict the future spot exchange rate; the anticipated change in the spot rate would be fully discounted. In an uncertain world, the anticipated spot exchange rate may not be realized and so the firm which remains exposed is subject to the risk of unanticipated changes in exchange rates. Hence the firm which contemplates hedging its exposure must compare the no-risk alternative of matching settlement and commitment dates with the risky alternative of maintaining an exposed position.

While the individual firm can hedge its foreign exchange exposure, someone must be paid to carry the risk. The "buyer" of the exposure demands a price to reimburse his costs and compensate for the risks. Some firms are on both sides of the market, and so if a firm which sells a currency forward incurs a cost in hedging its exposed position, the firm which buys this currency forward is sometimes said to earn the counterpart profit. One conclusion—an incorrect one—is that trade is unaffected.[1]

[1] Thus the argument seems to come full circle—nearly. Ten years ago it was frequently stated that the cost of altering exposure was the forward discount or premium, or the difference between current forward exchange rate and current spot exchange rate. Later

The difference between the anticipated spot rate inferred from the forward rate and the observed spot rate at the maturity of the forward contract is a payment to a firm which maintains an exposed position; it cannot be earned by a firm which has fully hedged its exposure. The recipient of this payment may be an investor seeking to profit from anticipated changes in exchange rates or it may be a trading firm, which has decided that the return from maintaining an exposed position is worthwhile in terms of the risk. This return is a payment for risk-bearing earned in a competitive market. This income does not reduce the cost of the firm's international transactions.

Estimates of the anticipated future spot rates can be obtained from the forward rates. The difference between these anticipated rates and the observed rates can be considered "forecast errors": forecast errors in the pegged rate period can be compared with those in the floating rate period. The risks in making the forecasts under the alternative exchange rate systems can be inferred from the standard deviations of the difference between the predicted exchange rates and the observed rates.

The several measures of exchange risk during both pegged and floating periods are shown in Table 2; the estimates were computed on the assumption that the forward exchange rate is an unbiased predictor of the spot rate on the maturity of the forward contract. The data are weekly observations; the observations for the floating period are from March 1973 to November 1974 while the pegged period of comparable length begins in December 1967 and ends in July 1969. The absolute mean deviations are shown, and except for Canada and France, are as much as ten times higher in the floating rate period than in pegged rates period for one month forward contracts. The very high forecast error for the French franc in the pegged period reflects the fears of devaluation associated with events of May 1968, which led to a devaluation of the franc in September 1969. The absolute deviations are higher in the floating rate period than under pegged rates for the entire maturity structure. The longer the maturity of the forward contracts, the smaller the increase in the mean absolute deviation of the floating rate period relative to the pegged rate period.

The standard deviation of the mean forecast error is generally from 5 to 10 times larger in the floating rate period than in the pegged rate period, although the increase appears smaller for the longer forward maturities. The increase in the standard deviation is larger, the more volatile the movements in the spot exchange rates; the increase in the standard deviations is larger for currencies in the joint float than for the Canadian dollar or for sterling.

Exchange risk is substantially higher under floating rates than under

---

it was sometimes asserted that the only cost was the transaction costs, since the forward premium or discount was a payment from one group of traders to another and hence a washout (Machlup, 1970). Now the statement is that the cost is the difference between current forward rate and future spot rate, and the payment is not a washout.

Table 2. *Measures of exchange risk, forecast errors—mean absolutes and standard deviation* (%)

Relative to US Dollar. P = weekly observations December 1,1967 to July 18, 1969; F = weekly observations March 2, 1973 to November 1, 1974. *M* represents the mean absolute deviation, while S.D. represents the standard deviation of the mean

		1 mo. forcast		3 mo. forcast		6 mo. forcast		1 y. forcast	
		M	S.D.	*M*	S.D.	*M*	S.D.	*M*	S.D.
Canada	P	0.235	0.301	0.533	0.509	0.905	0.870	1.937	0.933
	F	0.557	0.696	1.196	1.491	1.701	1.953	1.830	0.808
U.K.	P	0.414	0.403	0.757	0.550	1.445	0.875	4.383	2.244
	F	1.776	2.244	4.093	4.851	4.980	6.352	2.688	2.109
Belgium	P	0.215	0.242	0.493	0.423	1.023	0.647	2.296	0.722
	F	3.076	3.792	5.966	7.691	7.670	9.161	5.253	4.217
France	P	6.640	0.839	1.341	1.445	2.082	2.192	2.928	4.787
	F	2.890	3.774	5.481	7.295	9.514	10.696	11.719	4.020
Germany	P	0.481	0.477	0.858	0.684	1.483	0.514	2.968	0.662
	F	3.440	4.343	7.671	9.210	8.048	9.993	10.922	8.697
Italy	P	0.192	0.242	0.325	0.336	0.627	0.499	0.994	0.801
	F	2.227	2.883	3.993	5.271	4.898	5.449	10.922	2.976
Neth.	P	0.251	0.237	0.629	0.436	0.877	0.487	1.802	0.590
	F	3.213	3.887	5.545	7.152	6.788	7.942	4.229	4.964
Switz.	P	0.298	0.321	0.460	0.337	0.789	0.480	2.079	0.795
	F	2.991	3.799	5.721	7.024	7.124	8.957	3.917	4.880

Source: Weekly Review: International Money Markets and Foreign Exchange Rates.

pegged rates. Firms which hedge their foreign exchange exposure incur a much higher cost, those that do not hedge incur much greater uncertainty. The greater the uncertainty, the greater the disincentive to trade and investment. While the firm may bear these costs in the short run, it seems plausible that in the long run they are shifted forward to consumers or backward to suppliers. Exchange risk operates like both bid–ask spread and the implicit transactions costs in increasing segmentation of both money markets and goods markets; the orders of magnitude are similar.

V. Uncertainty and Price Risk

Price risk in the international economy involves unanticipated changes in the domestic value of tradables owned by the firm because of changes in exchange rates. Even if there is a comprehensive set of forward markets, so that the firm can readily avoid its exposure to exchange risk, the firm remains subject to price risk. Price risk occurs continuously in the domestic economy; in a one-currency world, the exchange rate and the distinction between foreign prices and domestic prices drop out, and the firm's net worth may change because of changes in the value of its inventory.[1]

If all changes in exchange rates reflect changes in price differentials, the distinction between international price risk and domestic price risk disappears; because Purchasing Power Parity holds in the long run, the distinction is important only in the short run. The international price risk reflects deviations from Purchasing Power Parity as a result of exogenous changes in exchange rates—changes which do not result from changes in relative price levels. Price risk can be measured on the assumption that autonomous changes in price levels in each country lead to contemporaneous and proportional changes in exchange rates. This approach to measurement of the price risk relies on the assumption that deviations from Purchasing Power Parity may occur in the short run as a result of changes in exchange rates. Hence there is an assymetry in that changes in relative prices are assumed to lead to contemporaneous changes in exchange rates, but changes in the exchange rate do not lead to equivalent changes in relative price levels. Since exogenous changes in exchange rates tend to induce accomodating price level changes, this approach may underestimate the price risk.

The estimates of price risk are shown in Table 3. The standard-deviation and range of the deviations for four periods of six months of observations for eight countries are shown; the periods are the last six months of each year. The deviations are calculated using both wholesale price indexes and consumer price indexes.

The first two observation periods occur in the pegged period; the latter two, in the floating period. However, the Canadian dollar was floating in the second half of 1970. Moreover, the mark was revalued in the second half of 1969, while the French franc was devalued, which may explain the sharp decline in the standard deviations and the range for both currencies from 1969II to 1970II.

The standard deviation and the ranges of the deviations are significantly larger in the floating rate period than in the pegged rate period for all countries by factors in the range of five to ten or more. The values for the currencies which have moved volatilely in the exchange market are substantially higher than those, such as the Canadian dollar, sterling, and the lira, which have moved less sharply. Price risk is positively related to the variance of the exchange rate. Moreover, for most but not all countries, the values using consumer prices are higher in the pegged period, which is consistent with the view that the source of disturbance is domestic inflation. On an *a priori* basis, it would seem that the deviations using the wholesale index would be smaller, since there are more internationally traded goods in the wholesale index.

[1] While the discussion is in terms of changes in net worth arising from changes in the value of the inventory, the case can be generalized to changes in the value of the firm resulting from changes in its competitive position as the relationship between domestic costs and world prices change.

Table 3. *Price risk—percentage deviation from purchasing power parity with United States*

1969II, 1970II, refer to the last six months of each calendar year

	WPI		CPI		WPI		CPI	
Period	S.D.	Range	S.D.	Range	S.D.	Range	S.D.	Range
	Great Britain				*Canada*			
1969II	0.32	0.78	0.66	1.89	0.52	1.40	0.35	0.94
1970II	0.45	1.17	0.44	1.30	0.42	1.11	0.65	1.68
1973II	3.59	10.18	2.32	6.29	1.33	3.79	0.45	1.18
1974II	2.85	7.07	2.73	8.15	1.98	3.54	0.48	1.30
	Belgium				*France*			
1969II	0.41	1.12	0.51	1.52	3.79	9.57	4.75	11.85
1970II	1.02	3.09	0.30	0.78	0.52	1.47	0.18	0.48
1973II	5.67	14.44	3.91	9.38	5.16	13.47	3.55	8.34
1974II	3.63	8.74	2.27	5.83	3.13	8.80	2.55	7.45
	Germany				*Italy*			
1969II	2.95	7.68	2.85	7.41	0.48	1.19	0.34	0.91
1970II	0.48	1.20	0.23	0.61	0.88	2.73	0.39	1.06
1973II	6.12	9.35	3.74	8.50	3.06	8.09	2.55	7.34
1974II	3.87	9.17	3.01	7.94	2.41	6.63	1.42	3.81
	Netherlands				*Switzerland*			
1969II	0.79	2.36	0.79	1.73	0.36	1.00	0.47	1.31
1970II	1.21	3.38	0.37	0.84	0.69	1.89	0.70	1.97
1973II	5.41	14.66	5.08	15.08	5.64	16.18	3.46	7.28
1974II	3.38	8.23	2.33	6.23	3.98	9.46	2.87	7.56

Source: International Financial Statistics.

In the long run, the deviations using the wholesale price, should not differ from that using the consumer prices. That the deviations using the wholesale prices are larger in the floating rate period reflects two factors—one is changes in the direction of the exchange rate movement and the second is the larger weight of tradables in the wholesale index.[1]

Price risk tends to segment the goods markets, in that the increased uncertainty of international transactions may induce some firms to reduce the volume of their international transactions relative to their domestic transactions.[2] There appears no ready way to measure the significance of this impact.

[1] I am indebted to James Hodder for this explanation.

[2] To the extent the goods involved are primary products traded on various commodity futures exchanges, it may be possible to hedge the price risk, but at a cost.

VI. Uncertainty, Exchange Risk, and Price Risk

The firm which is subject to exchange risk may be able to neutralize its exposure by holding or acquiring an inventory of tradables, while the firm which is subject to price risk may be able to neutralize its exposure by holding a short position in the foreign currency. Assume a firm commits itself to buy 100 000 units of imports at a set price in the foreign currency; immediately the firm has a long position in the tradable and a short position in the foreign currency. If the foreign currency appreciates, the reduction in the firm's net worth because of the increase in the domestic currency equivalent of its short position in the foreign currency is offset by the increase in the domestic currency value of its inventory. If Purchasing Power Parity holds, the firm's net worth remains unchanged. If there are deviations from Purchasing Power Parity, but in a known and systematic way, the size of the exposed foreign exchange position can be varied so that the exposures in goods and in money are fully offsetting. The firm might acquire a foreign exchange exposure as a low cost way to offset the price risk.

One qualification is that the firm must be able to predict the relationship between the changes in the exchange rate and changes in the local currency value of the inventory. The nature of the price risk is that the relationship is unsystematic, except that the sign of the argument is known. Perhaps the firm will be able to reduce its uncertainty, but it nevertheless remains uncertain about the size of the foreign exchange exposure necessary to offset a given inventory of tradables.

The second qualification is institutional, and involves the firm's perception of its exposure on inventory and on financial assets. For better or worse, many firms rely on accounting conventions for their estimation of their exposure. These conventions frequently are asymmetric in their treatment toward the net position of the firm in foreign currency and in tradables, in that they recognize exchange risk and fail to recognize price risk (Aliber & Stickney, 1975). Perhaps in the future, the firm may recognize that it is less extensively exposed than its accounting system suggests. Until that recognition becomes widespread, exposure is likely to be misestimated.[1]

VII. Conclusion

The shift from pegged rates to floating rates increases segmentation of both money markets and goods markets along national boundaries. If the segmentation of money markets increases much more than that of goods markets, then floating rates should facilitate domestic monetary independence at minimal

[1] Firms which produce in tradables and sell on a cost-plus basis (thus varying output) would be expected to price in their domestic currency. The currencies in which sales are priced and the currencies in which transactions are denominated need not be the same (Grassman, 1973).

cost in terms of less efficient resource allocation on a global basis. In contrast, to the extent that the floating rates lead to much more extensive segmentation of goods markets than of money markets, the gains in income from the higher level of employment might be smaller than the loss in income from reduction in trade and investment.

The choice between pegged and floating rates seems unlikely to be made on the basis of a cost–benefit analysis of the trade-offs involved in the segmentation of the two markets. If national price level movements are sufficiently similar so that currencies can be readily pegged, causal empiricism suggests that currencies will be pegged. In contrast, if national price level targets are not sufficiently similar, currencies will float. The monetary environment dictates the exchange rate system, and the institutional arrangements conform.

The move to floating rates in 1973 occurred as major countries began to differ on their price level targets. Floating rates led to increased segmentation of goods markets in various ways—transactions costs increased, as did both exchange risk and price risk, in comparison with pegged rates, by a factor of five to ten. The costs of segmentation of goods market might be better attributed to a less stable monetary environment than to the floating rate system.

The volatile movements in exchange rates over the last two years have resulted from changes in monetary policies or interest rate policies, primarily in the United States and Germany. If these efforts are taken as given, the policy problem is whether the costs of goods market segmentation can be reduced by exchange market intervention policies.

References

Aliber, R. Z.: *The International Market for Foreign Exchange*. Praeger, New York, 1969.

Aliber, R. Z.: Uncertainty, currency areas, and the exchange rate system. *Economica*, November 1972.

Aliber, R. Z.: Monetary interdependence under fixed and floating exchange rates. Presented at the Helsinki Conference on the Monetary Mechanism in Open Economies, August 1975.

Aliber, R. Z. & Stickney, C.: Measures of foreign exchange exposure: the long and short of it. *Accounting Review*, January 1975.

Fielke, N. S.: Exchange rate flexibility and the efficiency of foreign exchange markets. Federal Reserve Board, Discussion Paper 44, April 1974.

Frenkel, J. A. & Levich, R. M.: Covered interest arbitrage: unexploited profit opportunities. *Journal of Political Economy*, April 1975.

Frenkel, J. A. & Levich, R. M.: Transactions costs and the efficiency of international capital markets. Presented at the Helsinki Conference on the Monetary Mechanism in Open Economies, August 1975.

Friedman, M.: The case for flexible exchange rates. In *Essays in Monetary Economics*. Chicago, 1953.

Giersch, H.: Entrepreneurial risk under flexible exchange rates. In *Approaches to Greater Flexibility of Exchange Rates* (ed. George N. Halm). Princeton, 1970.

Grassman, S.: *Exchange Reserves and the Financial Structure of Foreign Trade*. Lexington Books, 1973.

Harris Trust and Savings Bank: *Weekly*

Review: International Money Markets and Foreign Exchange Rates, 1957–1975.

Helliwell, J. & Maxwell, T.: Monetary interdependence of Canada and the United States under alternative exchange rate systems. In *National Monetary Policies and the International Financial System* (ed. R. Z. Aliber). Chicago, 1974.

International Financial Statistics, International Monetary Fund, Washington, 1975.

Isobe, A.: The Japanese foreign exchange market. *Staff Papers*, July 1966.

Lanyi, A.: The case for floating exchange rates reconsidered. *Essays in International Finance 72*, Princeton, 1969.

Machlup, F.: The forward-exchange market: misunderstandings between practitioners and economists. In *Approaches toward Greater Flexibility of Exchange Rates* (ed. George N. Halm). Princeton, 1970.

McKinnon, R. I.: Floating Exchange Rates 1973–74: The Emperor's New Clothes. Mimeo, November 1974.

Reichers, E. A. & Cleveland, H. van B.: Flexible exchange rates and forward markers. In *Approaches toward Greater Flexibility of Exchange Rates* (ed. George N. Halm). Princeton, 1970.

Sohmen, E.: *Flexible Exchange Rates.* Chicago, 1969, revised edition.

COMMENT ON R.Z. ALIBER, "THE FIRM UNDER PEGGED AND FLOATING EXCHANGE RATES"

Dwight M. Jaffee

Princeton University, Princeton, N. J., USA and Institute for International Economic Studies, Stockholm, Sweden

In the introduction of his paper, Robert Aliber argues an *a priori* case that flexible exchange rate systems inhibit international trade. The body of the paper is then an attempt through theoretical constructions and empirical evidence to make this *a priori* case more precise in terms of the mechanisms that are at work. My main disappointment with the paper is that it failed to convince me beyond the intuitive notion that fluctuations in exchange rates do inhibit trade. To be clear, Aliber's analysis does faithfully present much of what we know about the effect of risk on international trade, so that my unhappiness is as much with the general state of our knowledge as with the particulars of the paper.

The analytic device of the paper, and I think a very useful one, is to separate *exchange risk* and *price risk*. *Exchange* risk is the risk faced by a trading firm when it has an open position in foreign currency. *Price risk* is the risk due to an open position in an inventory of traded goods. Aliber discusses each type of risk separately, and then combines them, and I will follow this format. Before proceeding, however, it should be stressed that the issue here is *not* a comparison of fixed and flexible exchange rate regimes. It is clear that trade inhibiting mechanisms can arise also under fixed exchange rate systems in the form of tariffs and capital restrictions. Moreover, fixed exchange rates simply may not be feasible when national monetary authorities follow widely disparate policies. Thus, the focus is solely on trade under flexible exchange rates.

Exchange Risk

The intuitive case that the risk of open positions in foreign currency inhibits trade must confront the equally intuitive case that hedging possibilities exist for the trading firm. Aliber notes two hedging possibilities: forward markets and the coordination of commitment and settlement dates. In fact, these possibilities are one and the same in the sense that forward markets are redundant and the same hedging results can always be obtained by an appropriate set of transactions in the spot exchange and credit markets (differential transactions costs aside). For convenience we focus on the forward market since the market price is then explicit.

I want to advance the proposition that *under balanced trade* forward markets provide a free hedging device for firms to avoid exchange risk. Aliber, in contrast, appears to argue (see especially footnote 1, page 183) that there is a cost measured by the difference between the expected future spot exchange rate and the forward rate. Now there is no doubt that such a *forward bias* can exist when there is uncertainty over national inflation rates. But the forward bias is not a net cost for the set of hedging traders. When a bias exists, there is simply a transfer from traders on one side of the forward market to traders on the other side of the market. Moreover, it is not at all clear that an empirically important bias does occur, and the measures shown in Table 2 of Aliber's paper have no bearing on the question of bias. His calculations show only that *forecast errors* are made (and increasingly so under flexible exchange rates)—not that there is a distinctive bias in the forecasts. Indeed, if there is a bias one would expect it to be more prominent under fixed exchange rates, since if a currency is under speculative attack, the market expectations would be masked in Aliber's calculations by the government intervention.

I look at the problem of exchange risk in a different fashion. If firms have no fixed costs, then forward markets provide a costless hedge under balanced trade. Realistically, however, firms do have fixed costs and it is fruitful to consider a firm deciding whether to make a fixed capital investment in a trading opportunity. Assume the horizon of the project is 10 years and consider the risk exposure at 3 points—1 year, 5 years, and 10 years. The one-year risk exposure can be hedged since active forward markets exist for this maturity. The ten-year risk equally clearly cannot be hedged—useful forward markets do not exist at this maturity. But over a ten-year horizon, it is unlikely that firms would feel any *differential* risk exposure from a flexible versus fixed rate system—over a ten-year period the two systems are unlikely to diverge. Moreover, exchange risk is likely to be swamped by other risk factors 10 years hence, and the profits at that point are highly discounted. So risk exposure at the ten-year point is not a special problem of flexible exchange rates.

The argument must thus turn to risk exposure at some intermediate point like a 5-year horizon. One consideration seems at the center of the issue. If intermediate maturity exchange risk is really a problem for firms, then one might expect appropriate markets to develop. One needs only an intermediary (broker) to bring together the risk averse traders on the two sides of the markets. Absence of such markets would then suggest absence of a problem.

So, I am lead to believe that exchange risk cannot be a detriment to trade unless trade is unbalanced. And in this sense I can share Aliber's *a priori* view that exchange risk might exist. But I fear we have managed only to define the problem, not to answer it.

Attention should also be paid to Aliber's section on the costs (for example bid-ask spreads) of foreign exchange transactions. He cites the evidence of McKinnon, and of Frenkel and Levich, to the effect that transactions costs have risen dramatically under recent flexible exchange rate experience. I think we can believe these numbers, but what do they suggest? Aliber's conclusion is disappointing: "The sign of the argument for the impact of this cost increase on the level of international trade is unambiguous; the magnitude of the impact remains to be determined".

Price Risk

Aliber's discussion of the risk of positions in inventories to exchange rate revaluations points to a frequently overlooked problem. It should be stressed, however, that all inventories of traded goods are not exposed to price risk. To the extent that inventories represent goods in process or in transportation pipelines, and given goods that are perishable on delivery, the effect of an exchange rate fluctuation will have its primary impact on the spot price in the market in which the good is traded only after inventories have cleared the pipeline. Price risk, in other words, can apply only to those inventories held by the firm as a dealer's stock to meet fluctuations in demand.

Aliber correctly notes that, in a purchasing power parity (PPP) world, price risk does not apply. Indeed in a PPP world exchange risk also does not apply. A formal argument to prove this would require more space than is available. The intuition, however, is as follows. Ultimately the only real risks concern fluctuations in real values. For traders, such risks can arise either from independent fluctuations in exchange rates or from independent fluctuations in the price levels in either of the two trading countries. However, under purchasing power parity, fluctuations in each exchange rates and fluctuations in relative price levels have a correlation of -1. Thus, this is the one case in which two risks can and are perfectly offsetting.

It is in this setting, of course, that Aliber's evidence on deviations from purchasing power parity is interesting, and I think worthy of serious consideration. However, it should be noted that deviations from PPP are a necessary, not sufficient, condition for price risk (or exchange risk). Also, in this context, Aliber's contention (p. 186) that PPP will rule in the long run is interesting. I think this is wrong, and it is certainly inconsistent with the existence of exchange risk and price risk in the long run. Perfect PPP requires perfect goods market arbitrage. But exchange risk and price risk rule out perfect goods market arbitrage, and therefore they rule out PPP. Of course, this does not deny that PPP may be a good approximation in that if a country's price level increases 1 000 %, its exchange rate is unlikely to deviate significantly from a 1 000 % depreciation. But for a trader, even small deviations around the PPP line could inhibit trade.

Conclusion

Aliber's final section then combines exchange risk and price risk. He argues that exchange risk and price risk can be offsetting, and indeed fully offsetting in special cases. For example, a normal position for a trader might be a long position in the foreign good and a short position in the foreign currency: the effects of an exchange rate fluctuation could then be balanced. The upshot, of course, is that exchange risk and price risk together may be unimportant.

So putting the pieces together, it is hard to find anything very concrete on which to build a case for trading risk under flexible exchange rates. Aliber has an interesting point, however, in suggesting that a firm's *perception* of trading risk, not the actual fact, will determine its behavior. Of course, ultimately perceptions should converge to the facts—or vice versa. That is, perceptions could be self-fulfilling in that firms do not carry out perfect arbitrage, therefore the exchange rate has a range of indeterminacy, and thus firms confirm the possibility of non-PPP exchange rate fluctuations. In this manner, moreover, a fixed rate system, in which there is no room for exchange rate fluctuations, has an advantage.

EXCHANGE-RATE FLEXIBILITY AND RESERVE USE*

John Williamson

University of Warwick, Coventry, England

Abstract

This paper examines whether, as has usually been assumed, there is a trade-off between the degree of flexibility in exchange rates and the extent of reserve use. The first section of the paper constructs a measure of reserve use in order to examine changes in the extent of reserve use since the advent of generalized floating. It is found that reserve use initially tended to increase following the move to floating, and that, despite some subsequent decline, it has remained substantial. The second section constructs and partially solves a formal model designed to illuminate the determinants of reserve use. It is shown that there need not necessarily be a trade-off between exchange-rate flexibility and the extent of reserve use.

1. Introduction

Prior to the advent of generalized floating in March, 1973, it was taken for granted that one of the (minor) attractions of floating exchange rates would be the resulting economy in the use of, and therefore the need for, official reserves.[1] It is of course tautologically true that the use of official reserves would be eliminated under a system of freely floating exchange rates, but the floating that has been practiced for the past two years, and that seems likely to be practiced for the indefinite future, has been managed rather than free floating. The first part of this paper is therefore addressed to the factual question as to whether reserve use has declined since the move from a par value system to a system of managed floating. The second part of the paper constructs a model designed to illuminate the determinants of reserve use. The model as constructed in this paper is not fully developed, and even the model as presented is by no means fully solved. It should therefore be regarded as

* The author is indebted to Denise R. R. Williamson for help in the preparation of this paper; to Esther Suss for statistical advice, and Nur Calika for computational assistance, on a previous draft which has been utilized here; and to Andrew Crockett and Duncan Ripley for useful comments on that earlier draft. The author alone is responsible for the interpretation of the facts and any errors.

[1] See, for example, IMF (1973) p. 44; Grubel (1969) Chapter 2; Williamson (1973) p. 694; Makin (1974).

providing a preliminary exploration of the impact of the exchange-rate regime and of intervention policy on reserve use, rather than as claiming to offer a definitive solution.

2. Reserve Use under Floating

Reserves are used either for intervention to support the domestic currency in the foreign exchange market, or for direct payment to foreign monetary authorities. Because reserve statistics are in general published only monthly, it is not feasible to base a measure of reserve use on the gross total of support intervention plus direct payments: it is necessary to work in terms of reserve changes over some period of time. The obvious approach is to base one's measure of reserve use on reserve changes over the shortest possible time period (i.e. one month), since this maximizes the number of observations and it can be shown that, if payments imbalances are drawn from a normal distribution with unchanging parameters, the standard deviation of reserve changes over longer periods will vary proportionately with the standard deviation over shorter periods.[1] However, since exchange rate changes can be expected to alter the parameters of the distribution from which payments imbalances are drawn, it is both prudent and appropriate to examine the size of reserve changes over longer periods as well.

There is a second way in which a useful measure of reserve use should diverge from the literal definition of reserve use. This consists in including reserve *increases*, as well as decreases, in the measure. The rationale for this is that in the long run it makes little difference whether reserve use is measured by the sum of absolute reserve changes or by the sum of reserve decreases, since the two will diverge only to the extent that there is secular growth in the level of reserves, but that during any short time period a misleading impression of a decreased *ex ante* propensity to use reserves would be created by a measure directed solely at reserve decreases whenever the balance of payments happened to move into surplus and thereby obviated the need for reserve use *ex post*. Since the time periods used in this paper are relatively short, the chosen measures of reserve use relate to the absolute value of reserve changes.

The two measures of reserve use chosen are the average absolute (*a*) monthly, and (*b*) annual, change in published reserves during the period in question. These measures are subject to two criticisms: that they will be influenced by changes in the valuation of reserve assets as well as by the intervention or direct transactions with other monetary authorities, and that published reserve statistics are sometimes a misleading guide to true reserve changes.

In recent years the value of international transactions has grown particularly rapidly. Consequently it would be possible for the measure of reserve

[1] Williamson (1975), p. 8.

Table 1. *Comparative reserve use under pegged and floating exchange rates*
Data from *International Financial Statistics* and *Direction of Trade.*

Country	Date of floating	Average monthly reserve use[a] Pegged rate period (1)	Floating to March 1974 (2)	Floating since March 1974 (3)	Average annual reserve use[b] Pegged rate period (4)	Floating Floating period (5)
Canada	May 1970	0.53	0.48	0.14	3.6	2.6
U.K.	June 1972	0.39	0.67	0.32	2.8	1.3
Switzerland	Jan. 1973	4.92	5.14	4.76	9.7	9.9
Japan	Feb. 1973	1.65	1.93	0.47	8.5	13.2
Italy	Feb. 1973	0.58	1.34	1.56	3.7	3.8
Portugal	March 1973	2.88	1.44	1.02	21.1	2.8
Iceland	June 1973	0.93	2.52	1.35	6.8	5.7
Malaysia	June 1973	1.99	1.59	0.55	9.7	6.4
Singapore	June 1973	1.21	0.46	n.a.	10.1	3.8

[a] Unit of measurement is a monthly reserve change, divided by an annual rate of trade flow, both measured in dollars, multiplied by 100.
[b] Unit of measurement is an annual reserve change, divided by an annual rate of trade flow, both measured in dollars, multiplied by 100.

use to register an increase, despite a decreased propensity to use reserves, if it were not normalized by a factor allowing for the value of international transactions. In practice this means deflating by the value of merchandise trade. Reserve changes, which were measured in dollars since the bulk of the reserve stock is dollar-denominated, were therefore deflated by the average dollar value of exports and imports.

There were nine countries that had independently floated their currencies for a sufficiently long period to generate enough data to permit a useful comparison of their reserve use under a par value system with that under floating when the calculations shown in columns (1) and (2) of Table 1 were made (Spring 1974). Column (1) shows the average absolute trade-deflated monthly change in reserves during a period immediately prior to the adoption of floating of equal length to the period used in column (2).[1] Column (2) shows the same measure of reserve use for the period from each country's adoption of floating up to March 1974, at which time increased oil payments might have been expected to inject a major additional cause of reserve volatility into the

[1] The reference period for the United Kingdom was taken as October 1969 – July 1971, so as to avoid the period of ambiguous floating between August 1971 and the Smithsonian Agreement. That for Italy was also pushed back a month to avoid the period of a floating capital rate. (The periods for each country were therefore as follows: Canada, June 1966 – April 1970 and May 1970 – March 1974; U.K., Nov. 1969 – July 1971 and July 1972 – March 1974; Switzerland, Nov. 1971 – Dec. 1972 and Jan. 1973 – Feb. 1974; Japan, Dec. 1971 – Jan 1973 and Feb. 1973 – March 1974; Italy, Dec. 1971 – Dec. 1972 and Feb. 1973 – Feb. 1974; Portugal, Feb. 1972 – Feb. 1973 and March 1973 – March 1974; Iceland, Malaysia and Singapore, Aug. 1972 – May 1973 and June 1973 – March 1974.)

system.[1] The trade deflator for a particular month was a weighted average of the trade levels of two adjacent years, with the weight for the later year increasing as the year progressed; 1974 trade levels were estimated by extrapolation.

Column (3) shows an updating of this calculation to utilize the most recent available data (March 1974–February 1975).[2] The trade deflator used in this case was the average value of exports and imports for 1974.

Columns (4) and (5) show similar measures of reserve use taken over annual periods before and after the adoption of floating.[3]

The comparison between columns (1) and (2) suggests the paradoxical conclusion that reserve use actually increased following the adoption of floating.[4] Comparison of columns (2) and (3) suggests the equally paradoxical conclusion that reserve use tended to fall in the period following the dramatic increase in oil payments. A comparison between columns (1) and (3), and also between (4) and (5), suggests that there has been some tendency for reserve use to decline since the adoption of floating, as has traditionally been expected. The decline has not, however, been either large or dependable. Whatever else is ambiguous, it is transparently clear that abandonment of the obligation to defend a par value did not result in anything approaching a cessation of reserve use. It is therefore of interest to consider within the framework of a formal model those factors that determine the extent of reserve use.

3. A Model of the Determinants of Reserve Use

The extent of reserve use depends, obviously enough, upon both the structure of payments flows and the intervention policy adopted by the authorities.

Payments flows depend upon both the level of, and the expected change in, the exchange rate. They are also, of course, influenced by a wide variety of other factors, most of which can for present purposes be regarded as random shocks. The exception is adjustment policy. Insofar as a particular outcome in the exchange market provokes the authorities into modifying their policies in ways which will influence the balance of payments, these reactions ought to be incorporated into the model. These possible reactions will, however, be ignored,

[1] The initial month of floating was excluded for the UK, since this included important reserve losses evidently carried over from the fixed rate period.

[2] Jan. 1975 for Portugal and Malaysia. The figure for Singapore was not calculated due to lack of data.

[3] The periods used for each country were as follows: Canada, March 1966 – March 1970 and June 1970 – June 1974; UK, June 1969 – June 1971 and Sep. 1972 – Sep. 1974; Switzerland, Japan and Italy, June 1969 – June 1970 and Dec. 1971 – Dec. 1972 and Feb. 1973 – Feb. 1975; Portugal, Iceland, Malaysia and Singapore, Dec. 1971 – Dec. 1972 and June 1973 – June 1974. Trade deflators were the average value of exports and imports in the year in which the reserve change mainly occurred, or, for June/June changes, the average value over the two years in question.

[4] This is consistent with the estimate that total intervention in the period March 1973–March 1974 probably surpassed the level attained during any similar period under pegged rates. See Debs (1974) p. 87.

on the grounds that within reasonably wide limits a country with a floating exchange rate can in fact allow the exchange rate to take the strain and avoid other methods of payments adjustment. In particular, it is assumed that reserve changes resulting from intervention are completely sterilized, and thus do not alter payments flows in the future.

Given the absence of deliberate adjustment policies, the current account of the balance of payments (c_t) is a function of present and past values of the exchange rate (r), and of stochastic shocks. The simplest linear model may be represented as

$$c_t = \alpha_1 - \alpha_2 r_t + u_t, \quad \alpha_1, \alpha_2 > 0, u_t \text{ is } N(0, \sigma_c^2). \tag{1}$$

If one wishes to allow for *J*-curve effects, this needs to be expanded to:

$$c_t = \alpha_1 + \alpha_3 r_t - \alpha_4 r_{t-1} + u_t, \quad \alpha_i > 0, (\alpha_3 - \alpha_4) < 0, \quad u_t \text{ is } N(0, \sigma_c^2). \tag{2}$$

There seems no compelling reason for regarding expected future values of the exchange rate as important influences on the current-account position; the timing of purchases and payments may indeed be influenced by expected exchange-rate changes, but these are properly considered as capital-account entries.

In striking contrast, there are rather few reasons for expecting the capital account to depend on the *level* of the exchange rate, but compelling reasons for expecting it to depend on the expected change in the rate. The expected future change in the exchange rate is, after all, one component of the expected yield, which is generally taken to be the prime influence on portfolio decisions. A change in the *level* of the rate may influence the expected profitability of direct investment, and, by changing the wealth of investors, it may also cause a measure of portfolio adjustment.[1] But these effects are probably second-order and may therefore reasonably be ignored in constructing a simple model. The capital account (k_t) may then, following standard assumptions, be postulated to be a constant fraction of the difference between the desired and actual stock of net foreign investment in the country:

$$k_t = a_1(K_t^* - K_t).$$

Since the desired stock of net foreign investment is a positive function of the expected rate of appreciation of the exchange rate,

$$K_t^* = a_2 + a_3[E(r_{t+1}) - r_t], \tag{3a}$$

one has

$$k_t = a_1[a_2 + a_3 E(r_{t+1}) - a_3 r_t - K_t]. \tag{3b}$$

[1] Girton & Henderson (1972) Part V.

After simplifying and adding an error term, one has the basic capital account equation that will be used in this paper,

$$k_t = \alpha_5 + \alpha_6 E(r_{t+1}) - \alpha_6 r_t - \alpha_7 K_t + v_t,\ \alpha_i > 0,\ v_t \text{ is } N(0, \sigma_k^2). \tag{3}$$

It should also be noted that

$$K_{t+1} = K_t + k_t. \tag{4}$$

The equilibrium properties of the non-stochastic model may be established without completing the model by adding a mechanism to determine expectations and an intervention policy. Equilibrium requires that $E(r_{t+1}) = r_t = r_{t+1} = \bar{r}$. In terms of the model composed of eqs. (1) and (3), the equilibrium exchange rate $\bar{r}$ is $(\alpha_1 + \alpha_5 - \alpha_7 K_t)/\alpha_2$. In terms of the model given by (2) and (3), it is $(\alpha_1 + \alpha_5 - \alpha_7 K_t)/(\alpha_4 - \alpha_3)$. By (3a), maintenance of an expected and actual equilibrium exchange rate implies that $K_t^* = a_2$, which, by (3b) and (4), implies that $k_t \to 0$ over time. In full equilibrium, therefore, both the current and capital accounts are balanced individually, and $K_t = \alpha_5/\alpha_7$. It follows that $\bar{r} = \alpha_1/\alpha_2$ or $\alpha_1/(\alpha_4 - \alpha_3)$; the equilibrium exchange rate depends solely on the parameters of the current account.

These conclusions depend, of course, on the assumption that all the parameters of (1)–(3) are constant. This is clearly very restrictive. If, for example, the country's policies are such as to give it a lower inflation rate than its competitors then α_1 will be increasing over time. Equilibrium would in this case be characterised by a continual, anticipated, appreciation of the exchange rate. An alternative possibility is that portfolio growth is occurring, which would be represented by a continual increase in α_5. This would result in a positive (negative) equilibrium value of K_t for a capital-importing (exporting) country, with a higher (lower) value of the exchange rate as a consequence. The remainder of this paper will, however, consider only the case in which the parameters are unchanging.

The third element of the model consists of an assumption about the determination of expectations. Three "pure" assumptions suggest themselves:

$$E(r_{t+1}) = r_t \quad \text{static expectations} \tag{5}$$

$$E(r_{t+1}) = r^* \quad \text{regressive expectations} \tag{6}$$

$$E(r_{t+1}) = \mu r_t + (1-\mu) E(r_t) \quad \text{adaptive expectations.} \tag{7}$$

The first assumption, that the market never expects the exchange rate to change, is not very appealing. The second assumption, that the market forms an estimate r^* of the equilibrium rate $\bar{r}$ and anticipates a rebound to that level, would seem to be implicit in many of the more enthusiastic endorsements of freely floating exchange rates. The third assumption, that a movement in the market rate creates expectations of a further movement in the same direction, would seem to be held by many critics of floating rates. In addition, it is of course possible to conceive of compound cases: for example, the first and second cases can be combined to yield an expectation of a partial rebound to equilibrium:

$$E(r_{t+1}) = \lambda r_t + (1-\lambda) r^*.$$

More interestingly, the second and third cases combined would yield

$$E(r_{t+1}) = \lambda_1 r_t + \lambda_2 r^* + \lambda_3 E(r_t), \quad \lambda_1 + \lambda_2 + \lambda_3 = 1. \tag{8}$$

A refinement of this that would seem to have considerable plausibility would be to pustulate a non-linear influence for r^*. Specifically, λ_2 might be thought of as an increasing function of $(r^* - r_t)^2$, with both λ_1 and λ_3 decreasing as λ_2 increased. This would represent the case in which the market had only weak opinions as to where the equilibrium rate lay, but attached increasing importance to this factor as the rate diverged from any reasonable estimate of an equilibrium zone.

The obvious question that merits consideration at this stage is that of the short-term stability of a freely floating exchange rate. This concerns the question as to whether a model consisting of (1) or (2), (3), and (5), (6) or (7) will yield an excess demand for foreign exchange that decreases as the exchange rate appreciates. Using b_t to denote the balance of payments at time t, one has short-term stability if and only if $db_t/dr_t < 0$. Consider first the model given by (1), (3) and (5):

$$b_t = \alpha_1 - \alpha_2 r_t + \alpha_5 + \alpha_6 r_t - \alpha_6 r_t - \alpha_7 K_t + u_t + v_t$$

$$\frac{db_t}{dr_t} = -\alpha_2 < 0 \quad \text{(stability)}.$$

However, the presence of a *J*-curve makes the balance of payments unstable in the absence of a capital account, and the naive assumption (5) is tantamount to excluding the capital account, since it means that the latter does not respond to the exchange rate (model (2), (3), (5)):

$$b_t = \alpha_1 + \alpha_3 r_t - \alpha_4 r_{t-1} + \alpha_5 + \alpha_6 r_t - \alpha_6 r_t - \alpha_7 K_t + u_t + v_t$$

$$\frac{db_t}{dr_t} = \alpha_3 > 0 \quad \text{(unstable)}.$$

More plausible assumptions about the generation of expectations lead to the possibility of stability, even in the presence of a *J*-curve. (All models are stable in the absence of a *J*-curve, as will readily be seen by substituting $-\alpha_2$ for α_3 in the following results.) If the market expects a reversion of the rate to equilibrium (model (2), (3), (6)):

$$b_t = \alpha_1 + \alpha_3 r_t - \alpha_4 r_{t-1} + \alpha_5 + \alpha_6 r^* - \alpha_6 r_t - \alpha_7 K_t + u_t + v_t$$

$$\frac{db_t}{dr_t} = \alpha_3 - \alpha_6 \gtreqless 0 \quad \text{as} \quad \alpha_3 \gtreqless \alpha_6.$$

Stability therefore depends on the strength of the market's expectation of a reversion to equilibrium influencing the capital account to an extent that outweighs the destabilising influence of the current account. This stabilising influence of the capital account is weakened, but not eliminated, where expectations are determined adaptively (model (2), (3), (7)):

$$b_t = \alpha_1 + \alpha_3 r_t - \alpha_4 r_{t-1} + \alpha_5 + \alpha_6 \mu r_t + \alpha_6 (1-\mu) E(r_t) - \alpha_6 r_t - \alpha_7 K_t + u_t + v_t$$

$$\frac{db_t}{dr_t} = \alpha_3 - \alpha_6(1-\mu) \gtreqless 0 \quad \text{as} \quad \alpha_3 \gtreqless \alpha_6(1-\mu).$$

The same thing is true if expectations are influenced both by an extrapolation of recent rates of change and by some notion of a reversion to equilibrium (model (2), (3), (8)):

$$b_t = \alpha_1 + \alpha_3 r_t - \alpha_4 r_{t-1} + \alpha_5 + \alpha_6 [\lambda_1 r_t + \lambda_2 r^* + \lambda_3 E(r_t)] - \alpha_6 r_t - \alpha_7 K_t + u_t + v_t$$

$$\frac{db_t}{dr_t} = \alpha_3 - \alpha_6(1-\lambda_1) \gtreqless 0 \quad \text{as} \quad \alpha_3 \gtreqless \alpha_6(1-\lambda_1).$$

If, however, λ_2 is an increasing function of $(r^* - r_t)^2$, this introduces an additional term into db_t/dr_t which will increase progressively as r_t diverges from r^*, and eventually stabilise the model even if

$$\alpha_3 > \alpha_6(1-\lambda_1).$$

The fourth element in the model concerns the intervention policy of the authorities. The literature contains essentially two suggestions as to the principles that should guide intervention policy, both of which are reflected in the Guidelines for Floating adopted by the International Monetary Fund (1974). The first suggestion, advanced by Wonnacott (1965) pp. 265–59, is that countries should "lean against the wind", by supporting their currency when it is depreciating and slowing its rise by acquiring reserves when it is appreciating. This rule is embodied in the IMF's Guidelines 1 and 2. Its logic is suggested by the analysis of possible short-run instability in the foreign exchange market in the preceding paragraphs. Using x_t to denote the foreign exchange acquired at time t through intervention, it may be described as:

$$x_t = \beta_1(r_t - r_{t-1}). \tag{9}$$

The alternative approach to intervention policy involves the authorities forming some estimate of an equilibrium exchange rate and basing intervention on the deviation of the actual rate from that estimate. Such an approach has been urged as the basis for international supervision of national intervention policies by Ethier and Bloomfield (forthcoming), who proposed that each country should establish a "reference rate" by agreement with the IMF, and would agree not to intervene in a manner that would push the rate away from a zone around that reference rate. This principle is embodied, in embryonic form, in the IMF's Guideline 3. Using $\tilde{r}$ to denote the reference rate at time t, this approach may be formalised as:

$$x_t = \beta_2(r_t - \tilde{r}). \tag{10}$$

The condition for short-run equilibrium in the exchange market is, of course, that the reserves acquired by the central bank should equal the payments surplus of the private sector, or

$$x_t = b_t. \tag{11}$$

The complete model describing simultaneously the short-run determination of the exchange rate and level of intervention is given by either (1) or (2); (3); (5), (6), (7) or (8); (9) or (10); and (11). The addition of equation (4) gives rise to a system of simultaneous difference equations that describe the evolution of the exchange market over time. For example, the combination of (2), (3), (4), (8), (10) and (11) reduces to:

$$\begin{aligned}[\beta_2 - \alpha_3 + (1-\lambda_1)\alpha_6]r_t = \alpha_1 - \alpha_4 r_{t-1} + \alpha_5 + \alpha_6\lambda_2 r^* + \alpha_6\lambda_3 E(r_t) \\ -\alpha_7 K_t + \beta_2\tilde{r} + u_t + v_t \end{aligned} \tag{12}$$

$$E(r_{t+1}) = \lambda_1 r_t + \lambda_2 r^* + \lambda_3 E(r_t) \tag{13}$$

$$K_{t+1} = \alpha_5 + \alpha_6 E(r_{t+1}) - \alpha_6 r_t + (1-\alpha_7)K_t + v_t. \tag{14}$$

Given initial conditions for r_{t-1}, $E(r_t)$ and K_t, and assuming constant values for r^* and $\tilde{r}$, this system and the realised values of the random variables u and v will determine future values of r, $E(r)$, and K, and hence also payments outcomes and reserve changes.

There are a number of questions that it would be interesting to pursue in terms of the above model. There is the question as to whether the non-stochastic model has an equilibrium solution and, if so, whether it is stable. There are the questions as to how the variability of the exchange rate and the extent of reserve use are influenced by the different expectations-generating mechanisms in the private sector and the intervention policies of the authorities. And there is the question as to how reserve use will be influenced by the change from a par value system to a floating regime.

The question of the existence of equilibrium is easy. The exchange rate of $\alpha_1/(\alpha_4 - \alpha_3)$ is an equilibrium rate provided that both the market and the authorities believe it to be $(r^* = \tilde{r} = \bar{r})$. If the private sector has a mistaken view of the equilibrium rate ($r^* \neq \bar{r}$), then (13) implies immediately that no equilibrium exists. If, on the other hand, the central bank's estimate of equilibrium is incorrect ($\tilde{r} \neq \bar{r}$), an equilibrium in terms of the model is still possible, but it is characterised by a balanced capital account and a current-account surplus or deficit matched by a corresponding reserve gain or loss. If, of course, the authorities react to a portfolio imbalance in the same way that the private sector is postulated to do, the model would need to be extended to include this fact and $\tilde{r} = \bar{r}$ would also be a necessary condition for equilibrium.

These results indicate that the present model is incomplete as a long-term model. In the long run one must also expect r^* and $\tilde{r}$ to be modified in the light of experience. However, a model intended to illuminate reserve use is essentially concerned with shorter-run questions, and so r^* and $\tilde{r}$ will be left as exogenous variables.

The question of the stability of equilibrium is far more difficult, and no general results have been obtained. The question at issue here is what may be termed medium-run stability: given short-run stability (i.e. that the exchange rate reaches a market-clearing level in each period), will the rate converge over successive periods to $\bar{r}$ given that $r^* = \tilde{r} = \bar{r}$? (Long-run stability concerns the question as to whether the rate will converge to $\bar{r}$ when r^* and $\tilde{r}$ are not initially equal to $\bar{r}$ but are adjusted in the light of experience.) It is, however, possible to demonstrate that medium-run stability can by no means be taken for granted. Suppose that at time 0 the foreign exchange market was in equilibrium with $r_0 = E(r_0) = E(r_1) = r^* = \tilde{r} = \bar{r} = \alpha_1/(\alpha_4 - \alpha_3)$, and that at time 1 this equilibrium was disturbed by a once-for-all random shock U in the current account. Substitution in (12) reveals that

$$r_1 = \bar{r} + U/H,$$

where $H = \beta_2 - \alpha_3 + (1 - \lambda_1)\alpha_6$. It will be recalled that in the absence of intervention the condition for short-run stability was that $\alpha_3 - \alpha_6(1 - \lambda_1) < 0$, so that clearly $H > 0$ is the condition for short-run stability in the presence of intervention. Further substitution in (12)–(14) reveals that

$$r_2 = \bar{r} + \frac{U}{H^2}[(1 - \lambda_1)\alpha_6\alpha_7 + \alpha_6\lambda_1\lambda_3 - \alpha_4].$$

There is no reason for supposing that

$$H > (1 - \lambda_1)\alpha_6\alpha_7 + \alpha_6\lambda_1\lambda_3 - \alpha_4,$$

which indicates that r_2 may diverge further from $\bar{r}$ than r_1 did and therefore suggests the possibility of instability.

Even if the above model is unstable in the vicinity of equilibrium, there are presumably factors such as those sketched informally in the discussion following eq. (8) which will keep exchange rates within some zone around equilibrium. (One does observe considerable volatility in floating exchange rates, but not rates that shoot off toward zero or infinity except in the wake of hyper-expansionary monetary policies at home or abroad.) The key question is, of course, how much volatility in rates and reserves would be generated by such a system when it is exposed to stochastic disturbances. One would therefore like to be able to calculate the variance of the exchange rate and the reserve change as a function of the various parameters identified in the model.

The nature of the solution may be illustrated in terms of the simplest of the above models. Consider the model described by equations (1), (3), (4), (5), (10) and (11), and assume that stochastic disturbances occur only in the current account ($v_t = 0$). If foreign investment is in equilibrium and $\tilde{r} = \bar{r}$, this reduces to

$$(\alpha_2 + \beta_2) r_t = \alpha_1 + \beta_2 \bar{r} + u_t$$

$$K_t = \alpha_5.$$

Since

$$r_t = \frac{\alpha_1 + \alpha_1 \beta_2 / \alpha_2 + u_t}{\alpha_2 + \beta_2} = \bar{r} \frac{u_t}{\alpha_2 + \beta_2},$$

$$E(r_t) = \bar{r}$$

and

$$\sigma_r^2 = E(r_t^2) - (E(r))^2 = \sigma_c^2 / (\alpha_2 + \beta_2)^2.$$

And

$$x_t = \beta_2 (r_t - \bar{r})$$

so

$$E(x_t) = 0$$

and

$$\sigma_x^2 = \beta_2^2 E(r_t - \bar{r})^2 = \beta_2^2 \sigma_r^2.$$

This model therefore possesses the most unsurprising properties: the variability of the exchange rate and of reserves depend positively on the variance of the payments flow, and negatively on the (immediate) responsiveness of payments to the exchange rate; while increased intervention increases the stability of the exchange rate at the cost of decreased stability in the reserve level (i.e. $d\sigma_x^2 / d\beta_2 > 0$).

The slightly more complex model resulting from replacing eq. (1) by (2) yields

$$\sigma_r^2 = \frac{\sigma_c^2}{(\beta_2 - \alpha_3)^2 - \alpha_4^2}.$$

Since $\alpha_3 < \alpha_4$ in the presence of a *J*-curve, an absence of intervention ($\beta_2 = 0$) would imply a negative value for the above expression. The variance would therefore be infinite, which is the stochastic equivalent to instability in the non-stochastic model. A stabilising influence, via either the capital account or intervention, is essential in order to avoid this result. The model also demonstrates that heavier intervention may reduce the use of reserves:

$$\sigma_x^2 = \frac{\beta_2^2 \sigma_c^2}{(\beta_2 - \alpha_3)^2 - \alpha_4^2}$$

$$\frac{d\sigma_x^2}{d\beta_2} = \frac{2\beta_2 \sigma_c^2}{[(\beta_2 - \alpha_3)^2 - \alpha_4^2]^2} (\alpha_3^2 - \beta_2 \alpha_3 - \alpha_4^2) < 0 \text{ when } \alpha_3 < \alpha_4.$$

Despite the absence of a capital account from this model, this result demonstrates conclusively that in the presence of sufficient instability in private-sector payments flows there is not necessarily a trade-off between exchange-rate volatility and reserve use. "Cleaner" floating, to use a particularly silly euphemism, may increase both; it may be unambiguously inefficient. This will of course seem unlikely to those economists who believe the private market to be better capable of estimating the equilibrium rate than the authorities are (i.e. that r^* is typically closer to $\bar{r}$ than is $\tilde{r}$), but this opinion rests on an empirical judgement that has never to my knowledge been subjected to test (and for which it would not seem easy to devise a test).

No similar analytical solutions have been derived for the more complex models incorporating a capital account. So long as capital flows are described by a stock-adjustment theory rather than a flow theory, such solutions would involve simultaneous difference equations and would therefore be quite complex. However, it seems safe enough to conjecture that exchange-rate variability and reserve use would both depend positively on (*a*) the strength of payments disturbances (σ_c^2 and σ_k^2), and (*b*) the inherent instability of the foreign exchange market, as measured by the size of initial perverse effects of exchange-rate changes on the current account, and the importance of extrapolation as opposed to regression in determining expectations. Stronger intervention policies would tend to dampen rate movements, but might either increase or decrease actual reserve use, depending on the degree of instability of the foreign exchange market.

Finally, the model also enables one to classify the effects on reserve use of moving from a par value system to a system of managed floating. First, the move liberates the authorities from the periodic need to treat as $\tilde{r}$ a rate which happens to be the par value but which they know perfectly well is not a reasonable estimate of $\bar{r}$. This will reduce reserve use, particularly on those occasions when r^* is a reasonable estimate of $\bar{r}$ and $\tilde{r}$ is not, which gave rise to the vast speculative flows characteristic of the adjustable peg. Second, insofar as the move leads to a weaker intervention policy (i.e. a lower value of β_1 or β_2, the latter of which is infinite at the margins under a par value system), it seems from the preceding analysis that it will increase reserve use if the foreign exchange market is unstable in the short (and medium?) run and decrease it if the market is stable. Third, it will increase reserve use insofar as a par value provides a correct focus for stabilizing speculation by the private sector, i.e. insofar as the par value and r^* are close to $\bar{r}$, and the publication of a par value increases λ_2. Fourth, the change will increase reserve use insofar as it leads to less sterilization (or other adjustment policies) that would otherwise provide a stabilizing feedback (assumed absent in the model of this paper) from payments flows to the probability distributions that generate them. The net effect of these four factors is as ambiguous as the empirical evidence.

Postscript

This paper has been left in the form in which it was presented at Stockholm. The discussion at the conference did, however, convince me that the specification of the model could have been improved: (*a*) by considering rational and extrapolative expectations-formation hypotheses as well as those actually presented, and (*b*) by using a stock ("asset market equilibrium") rather than flow ("tradeable funds") model of short-run exchange-rate determination. I see no reason for supposing that the latter change would have had major effects on the conclusions reached on the particular questions that the model was designed to illuminate, which were those analysed in the paper and not (as one participant in the Stockholm conference seemed to believe) those analysed in the other papers presented to the conference.

References

Debs, R. A.: Inflation and the economic outlook. Federal Reserve Bank of New York. *Monthly Review*. April 1974.

Ethier, W. & Bloomfield, A. I.: *The Management of Floating Exchange Rates*, Princeton Essays in International Finance, No. 112, 1975.

Girton, L. & Henderson, D.: A Two Country Model of Financial Capital Movements as Stock Adjustments with Emphasis on the Effects of Central Bank Policy, mimeo, 1972.

Grubel, H. G.: *The International Monetary System*. Penguin, 1969.

I. M. F.: *Annual Report*, 1973.

I. M. F.: *Survey*, June 19, 1974.

Makin, J. H.: Exchange rate flexibility and the demand for international reserves. *Weltwirtschaftliches Archiv*, June 1974.

Williamson, J.: International Liquidity—A Survey. *Economic Journal*, Sept. 1973.

Williamson, J.: Generalized Floating and the Reserve Needs of Developing Countries, mimeo, 1975.

Wonnacott, P.: *The Canadian Dollar 1948–62*. Toronto, 1965.

COMMENT ON J. WILLIAMSON, "EXCHANGE RATE FLEXIBILITY AND RESERVE USE"

Stanley W. Black

Vanderbilt University, Nashville, Tenn., USA and Institute for International Economic Studies, Stockholm, Sweden

John Williamson's paper investigates the trade-off between flexibility of exchange rates and the degree of intervention by authorities in exchange markets. The first part of the paper tries to measure the degree of use of official reserves before and after floating. The second part looks at the trade-off between variance in the exchange rate and variance of intervention in a stochastic theoretical model of the exchange market.

Turning first to the data in Williamson's Table 1, these measure the trade-deflated average absolute changes in published official reserves over monthly or annual periods before and after floating, for a group of nine countries.

The main conclusion from the Table is of course that reserve use has *not* ceased with the adoption of floating rates, but has only changed the rules under which it operates: from the adjustable peg system to the IMF Guidelines for Floating. This is to go from the unstable to the unenforceable. I would like to point out that the five cases of *increased* reserve use in column two are the U.K., which during this period received reserve inflows from many less developed countries that were pegged to the pound even when the pound was floating, Switzerland, where transactions between the National Bank and the commercial banks were important, Japan and Italy, which consciously intervened on a large scale, and Iceland, whose reserve use paradoxically went up on the monthly measure but down on the annual measure.

Let me now turn to Williamson's model of the determinants of reserve use. In the process of discussing this model, I will alter the expectational assumptions and adopt the hypothesis of rational expectations. The resulting simplification allows me to produce the solution that eluded Williamson.

Williamson's model is what I would call an asset market approach to the exchange market, as opposed to the strictly monetary approach. He is looking at the items *above the line* in the balance of payments. The great value in his approach is that it focusses on the problems of uncertainty and expectations that many people have been worried about. The shortcoming is that monetary and wealth variables are not treated explicitly.

Equation (1) of the model explains the *current account* as a function of the current spot exchange rate and a stochastic disturbance. I will disagree with this assumption below, on the grounds that the current flow of deliveries of goods and services is determined by *previous orders* and cannot respond in the short run to the *current* exchange rate. The *channels* through which the exchange rate affects the current account are unstated, but presumably may include relative price effects, real balance effects, and absorption effects.

The exchange rate r is measured, in the British fashion, as the foreign currency price of domestic currency, so that a rise in the rate means appreciation of the domestic currency. An alternative J-curve version, discussed below, allows for perverse short-run elasticities and stable long-run elasticities.

$$c_t = \alpha_1 - \alpha_2 r_t + u_t, \quad u_t \text{ is } N(0, \sigma_c^2) \tag{1}$$

The *capital inflow* is assumed in equation (2) to depend on a stock adjustment response to the expected rate of appreciation of the exchange rate, as well as a stochastic term. If we regard the constant term α_5 as including the interest rate differential ($\alpha_5 \equiv \alpha_6(R_d - R_f)$), the equation reflects interest arbitrage capital inflow. Note that I have written the expected exchange rate as $E_t r_{t+1}$, where $E_\tau r_t$ denotes the *conditional* expectation at time $\tau < t$ of the exchange rate at time t, based on information available at time τ. This more sophisticated concept will be utilized below to obtain the solution of the model under rational expectations, in contrast with the *unconditional* expectation Er_t formed by the adaptive, inelastic, and/or regressive expectations assumed by Williamson.

$$\Delta K_t = \alpha_5 + \alpha_6 E_t r_{t+1} - \alpha_6 r_t - \alpha_7 K_t + v_t, \quad v_t \text{ is } N(0, \sigma_k^2) \tag{2}$$

The long-run equilibrium solution of the model with no government intervention implies a zero capital account ($\Delta K_t = 0, \bar{K} = \alpha_5/\alpha_7$). The equilibrium exchange rate ($\bar{r} = \alpha_1/\alpha_2$) depends on the constant term in the current account α_1, which depends in turn on the purchasing power parity of the currency. as is argued implicitly on page 204 of the paper. We can in fact write the constant term α_1 as α_2 times the ratio of foreign to domestic prices of traded goods, if we like.

The important empirical observation from Table 1 is that floating does *not* mean that there are no reserve flows: the sum of the items below the line is not equal to zero. For convenience, Williamson assumes that these reserve flows are completely sterilized, but it is clear that in general this condition does not hold. Therefore the simplified models of floating that monetarists are offering us need to be modified to take account of the fact that the money supply is *not* independent of external factors, even in the short run.

To deal with reserve flows, Williamson introduces the central bank policy reaction function shown in equation (3). Roughly based on the IMF Guidelines, it relates central bank purchases of foreign exchange (1) to the rate of appreciation of the domestic currency and (2) to the excess of the domestic exchange rate over some *normal* value $\tilde{r}$.

$$x_t = \beta_1(r_t - r_{t-1}) + \beta_2(r_t - \tilde{r}) \tag{3}$$

Equating the private and official demands for foreign exchange to zero in equation (4), Williamson has a model which I would regard as very similar to Pentti Kouri's model presented at this seminar, except in linear form and with the long-run purchasing power and short-run interest rate arguments implicit in the coefficients α_1 and α_5. Unfortunately, he did not succeed in solving it, basically because the adaptive and regressive expectations hypotheses are too difficult to work with, in my opinion.

$$c_t + \Delta K_t = x_t \tag{4}$$

Nevertheless, he does draw a number of useful conclusions from the structure that he has laid out. For example, if the private sector's expectations are forever wrong and it cannot learn, then no equilibrium exists. Secondly, the model with regressive and adaptive expectations can have oscillations or overshooting of the exchange rate, what he calls medium-run instability. Thirdly, the variance of the exchange rate and of reserves are shown to depend on the variance of disturbances in the model and inversely on the elasticity of the balance with respect to the exchange rate.

Fourthly, intervention can increase stability of the exchange rate, but if there is a *J*-curve, there may be *decreased* variance of reserves as well. This paradoxical conclusion arises because the *J*-curve model is unstable in the absence of intervention, so that intervention actually stabilizes the model.

Let me now turn to my solution of his model under the assumption of rational expectations. The *stationary solution* of equations (1)–(4) is given in equation (5) and is identical to Williamson's result. If the authorities aim at a wrong level of the rate $\tilde{r} \neq \bar{r}$, they can keep the rate away from equilibrium, but at the cost of a permanent loss of reserves.

$$\hat{r} = \bar{r} + \frac{\beta_2}{\alpha_2 + \beta_2}(\tilde{r} - \bar{r}) \tag{5}$$

If we assume that $\alpha_7 = 1$, or full adjustment to short-run stock equilibrium on the capital account, it is possible to obtain the rational expectations solution (6) for the *conditional expectation of the spot exchange rate* at time *t*, given information available at time $\tau < t$.[1]

$$E_\tau r_t = \hat{r} + \sum_{i=t-\tau}^{\infty} \lambda^i \frac{v_{t-i}}{\alpha_6}, \quad \text{where} \quad 0 < \lambda < 1. \tag{6}$$

[1] The technique of solution is as follows. Substitute equations (1)–(3) into (4) to obtain a stochastic difference equation in r_t and $E_\tau r_{t+1}$. Take the conditional expectation E_τ as of time $\tau < t$ and solve the resulting equation by standard techniques for $E_\tau r_t$, using the boundary condition $\lim_{t\to\infty} E_\tau r_t < \infty$. The boundary condition implies that the relevant characteristic root of the difference equation is

$$\lambda = 1 + \frac{\alpha_2 + \beta_1 + \beta_2}{2\alpha_6} - \sqrt{\frac{\alpha_2 + \beta_2}{\alpha_6} + \left(\frac{\alpha_2 + \beta_1 + \beta_2}{2\alpha_6}\right)^2}.$$

The rational expectations hypothesis used to obtain this solution implies that market expectations about future exchange rates in equation (2) have the *same expected value* as a solution obtained by solving the model. I have also assumed that the expected future price path is bounded, what Pentti Kouri calls "long-run perfect foresight" and what I would call "awareness of the inevitable collapse of tulipomania".

It is easy to see from (6) that the conditional expectation at time τ depends only on disturbances to the capital account at or before time τ. Their effects on the exchange rate are softened by the responsiveness of capital flows α_6 and then distributed over the future beyond the time of their occurrence according to a geometric distribution with parameter λ depending on all of the parameters of the model. We may call λ the "elasticity of the conditional expectation". Furthermore, in the case of no government intervention ($\beta_1 = \beta_2 = 0$), if the effect of the exchange rate on the current account α_2 tends to zero, λ tends to unity and the conditional expectation behaves like a random walk.[1]

Additional disturbances at time t modify the conditional expectation at time $t-1$ given by (6) to produce the *actual* (*stochastic*) *exchange rate* given in (7).[2]

$$r_t = E_{t-1} r_t + \frac{u_t + (1+\lambda) v_t}{\alpha_2 + \alpha_6 + \beta_1 + \beta_2} \tag{7}$$

Notice that, on Williamson's assumptions about the response of the current account, the random movement in the exchange rate is softened by response from the current account, capital account, and government intervention.

The *variance of the actual exchange rate* about its long-run equilibrium value $\bar{r}$ can be decomposed into three independent components shown in equation (8): the variance of the random observed rate about its conditional expectation, the variance of the conditional expectation about the stationary solution based on government intervention $\hat{r}$, and the squared deviation of the stationary solution $\hat{r}$ from the long-run equilibrium $\bar{r}$ (due to government policy).

$$E(r_t - \bar{r})^2 = E(r_t - E_{t-1} r_t)^2 + E(E_{t-1} r_t - \hat{r})^2 + E(\hat{r} - \bar{r})^2 \tag{8}$$

This variance can be related to the parameters of the model by substituting from equations (5), (6), and (7) into (8) and simplifying to obtain (9). From this

$$E(r_t - \bar{r})^2 = \frac{\sigma_c^2 + (1+\lambda)^2 \sigma_k^2 + 2(1+\lambda)\sigma_{ck}}{(\alpha_2 + \alpha_6 + \beta_1 + \beta_2)^2} + \frac{\lambda}{(1-\lambda^2)\alpha_6^2}\sigma_k^2 + \frac{\beta_2^2}{(\alpha_2 + \beta_2)^2}(\tilde{r} - \bar{r})^2 \tag{9}$$

[1] This result contrasts with Mussa's finding of a random walk whenever disturbances are a random walk in the Appendix to his paper for the Seminar (Example 1). His finding arises because he erroneously ignores the lagged effect of a change in the exchange rate on the current account, and hence on the demand for money ($\zeta(t)$ in his model is *not* independent of lagged $e(t)$).

[2] Equation (7) is obtained by taking the conditional expectation as of time $t-1$, E_{t-1}, of the stochastic difference equation that results from substituting (1)–(3) into (4). This "conditional" equation is then subtracted from the stochastic difference equation. Utilizing (6), one obtains (7).

result it is obvious that the variance of the exchange rate is positively related to the variances and covariances of the disturbances.

Since the "elasticity of the conditional expectation" λ is related to all of the parameters of the model, the effects of changes in the parameters are not simple to evaluate, nor should they be. However, the following results can be obtained. Increased responsiveness of the current account (higher α_2) reduces λ and also the variance of the exchange rate. The same is true for increased intervention of type (2) if aimed at a "correct" target rate ($\tilde{r}=\bar{r}$). Increased mobility of capital (α_6) raises the elasticity of the conditional expectation λ and hence has a double-edged effect on the variance of the exchange rate. For small values of λ and small values of σ_k^2 relative to σ_c^2 it appears that increased capital mobility is stabilizing. On the other hand, with λ approaching unity and σ_k^2 rather higher than σ_c^2, the reverse effect can occur. Approximately the same results hold for intervention of type (1). Williamson's results on page 21 of his paper are a special case of (9) with σ_k^2, β_1 and α_6 equal zero and $\tilde{r}=\bar{r}$.

The *variance of reserves* (given by (10) in the case $\beta_1=0$) can be shown to be positively related to the coefficient of type (2) government intervention. On the other hand, increased capital mobility may either reduce or increase the variance of reserves, analogous to its effect on the variance of the exchange rate. The three terms in (10) refer to the stabilization of the conditional mean, the stabilization of the random fluctuation and the choice of

$$\sigma_x^2=\beta_2^2 E(r_t-\bar{r})^2=\frac{\lambda^2\beta_2^2}{(1-\lambda^2)\,\alpha_6^2}\sigma_k^2 + \beta_2^2\left[\frac{\sigma_c^2+(1+\lambda)^2\sigma_k^2+2(1+\lambda)\,\sigma_{ck}}{(\alpha_2+\alpha_6+\beta_2)^2}\right]+\frac{\alpha_2^2\beta_2^2}{(\alpha_2+\beta_2)^2}(\tilde{r}-\bar{r})^2 \tag{10}$$

a disequilibrium target ($\tilde{r}\neq\bar{r}$).

The *J-curve analysis* introduced by Williamson assumes that the current account responds perversely in the short run but normally in the longer run.

$$c_t=\alpha_1+\alpha_3 r_t-\alpha_4 r_{t-1}+u_t,\quad \alpha_3<\alpha_4. \tag{11}$$

The analysis proceeds much as before, but it turns out that the random part of price fluctuation (7) will be larger since it has a smaller denominator ($\alpha_6+\beta_1+\beta_2-\alpha_3$), due to the perverse response of the current account. The standard deviation of reserves in the case where $\sigma_k^2=0$ and $\beta_1=0$ can easily be calculated as

$$\sigma_x=\frac{(1+\lambda)\,\sigma_c}{1+\dfrac{\alpha_6-\alpha_3}{\beta_2}},\quad \frac{d\sigma_x}{d\beta_2}<0\quad \text{if}\quad \alpha_6<\alpha_3. \tag{12}$$

From (12) it is clear that Williamson's finding that increased intervention *reduces* the variance of reserves in the J-curve case is an artifact caused by analysis of a model that reacts perversely. As long as the capital account response α_6 exceeds the perverse current account effect, the normal effect of higher variance of reserves should be observed if intervention becomes more active.

Let me now return to my main objection to Williamson's model—the instantaneous effect of the exchange rate on the current account in eqation (1). This assumption implies a *stock-flow theory* of exchange rate determination, as is clear by the role of α_2 and α_6 in equation (7). I have previously argued on several occasions that current exchange rate movements can only affect the volume of *future* trade flows, because of the order–delivery lag. Changes in the value of current trade contracts due to exchange rate changes should enter the short-term capital account as capital gains or losses. Then the current account depends on *previous orders*, which are based on *prior expectations* of the exchange rate. Thus Williamson's model can easily be corrected by rewriting the current account equation (1) as a function of the conditional expectation of the exchange rate based on information available in the previous period, $E_{t-1}r_t$. This has no effect on either the stationary solution (5) or the conditional expectation (6), but simply removes α_2 from the denominator of the random solution (7). We then have a *stock theory* of the determination of the exchange rate, exactly analogous to Kouri's continuous time analysis. The current account is predetermined, so that the exchange rate must move, in the absence of intervention, to guarantee that *existing* stocks of assets will be willingly held.

This correction eliminates the J-curve problem, since the current exchange rate is replaced in the current account equation (11) with its conditional expectation. As a result, the current account does not respond in the very short run, perversely or otherwise, to unanticipated changes in the exchange rate. This removes α_3 from the denominator of the modified equation (7) and from the denominator of (12). Williamson's paradoxical finding of reduced variance of reserves with intervention in a perversely reacting market loses its remaining foundation.

In conclusion, let me say that while this type of exchange rate model is a useful technical device for analyzing exchange policies, it does need to be married to a macro-economic context with more fully articulated monetary and wealth variables in the manner shown by Kouri and Dornbusch.

WORLD INFLATION UNDER FLEXIBLE EXCHANGE RATES

Emil-Maria Claassen

University of Paris–Dauphine, Paris, France

Abstract

Under flexible exchange rates, world inflation is the weighted average of the national inflation rates. This paper is concerned with two categories of arguments which emphasize the higher probability of a higher inflation bias in a system of flexible exchange rates. The first category refers to a country's lower inflationary discipline when it has adopted a floating exchange rate and the second category of arguments concerns either price rigidities which become virulent qua the system of flexible exchange rates or some automatic world price level increases following the introduction of floating exchange rates. The paper leads to the conclusion that flexible exchange rates are neither inherently more inflationary nor inherently less inflationary than fixed exchange rates.

Introduction: World Inflation Rate and National Inflation Rate

In a system of fixed exchange rates the phenomenon of inflation is a world phenomenon. This statement is derived from price theoretical considerations with respect to the price formation of tradable goods in the world goods market and it is independent of any explanation of inflation, whether it be keynesian or monetarist, or of a sociological or any other type. All—relevant or irrelevant—inflation theories must have the explanation of world inflation as their target of analysis. The "national weight" in the determination of the world inflation rate is related proportionally to the relative size of the country concerned within the world economy. Consequently, inflationary impulses originating in a relatively large country have a more important impact on world inflation than those which occur in a small country. Furthermore, if the large country is simultaneously a key-currency country suffering from no external reserve constraint, it can be said that this country can—but not necessarily must—constitute the main source of world inflation. It is known that nearly all inflation theories ignore the worldwide aspect of inflation under the regime of fixed exchange rates. Haberler argues that the construction of an inflation theory for a closed economy is in itself rather difficult to attempt so that one has to abstract, first of all, from any "international complications". "This holds for 'monetarists', 'fiscalists', advocates of a Phillips curve approach, for those who distinguish between demand-pull (buyers') and cost push (sellers') inflation as well as those who deny the validity of this distinction."[1]

However, these theoreticians will enjoy their models again when there is a system of flexible exchange rates because in such a system the phenomenon of inflation is fundamentally a national phenomenon. The world inflation rate is no longer equal to the national rate, but it now becomes the weighted average of the national inflation rates. The relevant "closed" economy is no longer the world economy but the national economy. There is still the "law of one price" for a good within the world economy, but differences in price levels (inflation rates) between countries can be maintained permanently because they are corrected by a corresponding (continuous) change in the exchange rate.

If the world inflation rate under flexible exchange rates can be solved so easily, there is no need to pursue this subject any further. However, the challenge comes from the empirical side where we observe a higher world inflation rate since the introduction of floating exchange rates at the beginning of the 1970's even though there have been increasing differences between national inflation rates. Without being accused of the fallacious argument of the *post hoc ergo propter hoc*, there is nothing astonishing about its explanation because we know that floating exchange rates *can* be more inflationary than fixed exchange rates in the same way as they *can* be less or equally inflationary. If they can be more inflationary and if they can also be less inflationary, nothing precise can be said and we are again left with justifying the subject of world inflation under flexible exchange rates.

However, there are some arguments which emphasize the higher probability of a higher inflation bias in a system of flexible exchange rates. These arguments will be examined critically in the following two sections. The first argument is that of a country's lower inflationary discipline when it has adopted a floating exchange rate and the second argument concerns either price rigidities which become virulent qua the system of flexible exchange rates or some automatic world price level increases following the introduction of floating exchange rates. Because we use the monetary hypothesis, among the various inflation theories, the above arguments can be reformulated as follows. A higher growth rate of the world quantity of money could arise from the regime of floating exchange rates if there is some systematic propensity for a higher growth rate of the *national* quantity of money in certain countries (Section I) and/or if there is some automatic *worldwide* tendency towards a higher growth rate of the money supply (Section II).

---

[1] Haberler [6], p. 179.

I. The Argument of a Lower National Monetary Discipline under Flexible Exchange Rates

According to the "traditional" formulation of this argument, a country's policy of a higher inflation rate exceeding the world inflation rate will be "punished" more severely in a system of fixed exchange rates because it will be accompanied by reserve losses and a possible balance-of-payments "crisis", whereas a system of floating rates would only produce a depreciation. Regardless of the strength of the argument, the question of a higher or lower discipline is only concerned with the discipline towards the deviation of the national inflation rate from the world inflation rate where the latter can be on any level. Furthermore, the statement of a greater monetary discipline imposed by fixed exchange rates is based on the implicit assumption that a depreciation is less harmful for an economy than a potential monetary "crisis".

Even if the external constraint is less imperative for an autonomous monetary policy—in the sense of a lower as well as a higher monetary discipline—in a system of flexible exchange rates, the argument should be reformulated in terms of the specific conditions under which a country opts for a higher inflation propensity which has "technically" been made possible by the regime of flexible exchange rates. Among various conditions we have found two plausible cases. The first results from the freedom to choose any point on the Phillips curve and the second arises from a special type of an interest-rate oriented monetary policy, even though there may still be more motivations for higher monetary expansion rates (such as, for instance, the acquisition of a higher seigniorage gain, the realization of certain redistribution effects via a higher inflation rate, the monetary neutralization of excessive wage claims, etc.).

I.1. *A Lower Monetary Discipline for the Purpose of an Improvement in the Employment Rate*

The essential assumption of this case is not the existence or non-existence of a Phillips curve, but the belief held by the monetary authorities (or by the government) in the existence of the Phillips curve. Suppose that in the mind of the central banker there is a "short-run" and a "long-run" Phillips curve represented by lines I and F, respectively, in Fig. 1. As opposed to the Phillips curve discussants' traditional distinction between the short run and the long run in terms of inflation expectations, we reserve this distinction for an *open* economy where the length of the short period is inversely related to the degree of openness, the latter being defined in terms of the ratio of tradable to non-tradable goods.

Suppose that the foreign (or world) inflation rate (π^*) is 10 % and that the country's inflation rate (π) is also 10 % so that it is on its Phillips curve at point A with an unemployment rate of U_1. Suppose that the country wants

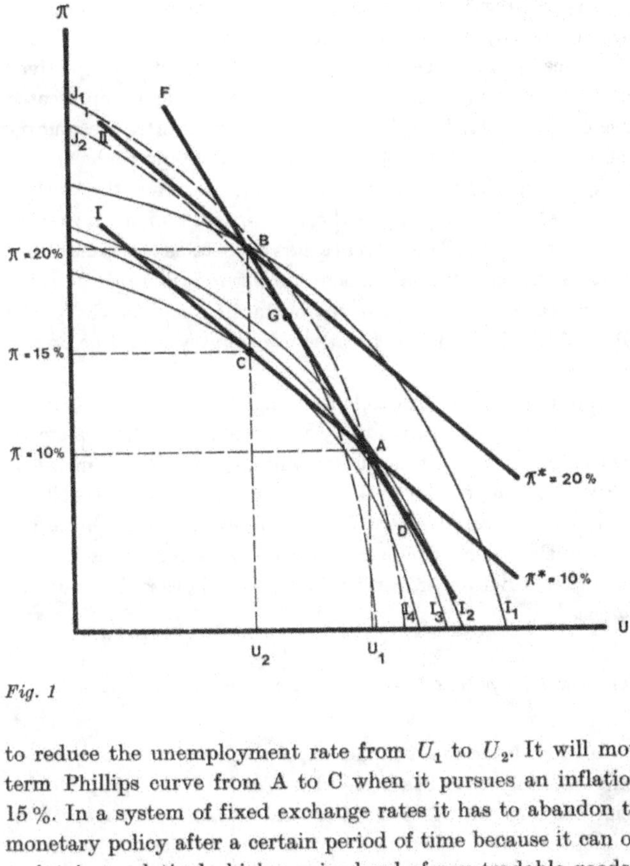

Fig. 1

to reduce the unemployment rate from U_1 to U_2. It will move on its short-term Phillips curve from A to C when it pursues an inflation policy of $\pi = 15\%$. In a system of fixed exchange rates it has to abandon this autonomous monetary policy after a certain period of time because it can only temporarily maintain a relatively higher price level of non-tradable goods and it must go back to point A because this is the only permanent point it can "choose" on its Phillips curve for a world inflation rate of $\pi^* = 10\%$. In a system of flexible exchange rates, it could choose any point on its long-run Phillips curve F. If the country still wants to reduce the unemployment rate to U_2, it has to realize an inflation policy of $\pi = 20\%$ in order to stay at point B. Under fixed rates this long-run position would only be conceivable if the world inflation is $\pi^* = 20\%$, while under flexible rates the country's exchange rate will continuously depreciate at the rate of $\pi - \pi^*$.[1]

By comparing the country's inflation rate for a system of fixed versus flexible exchange rates, one could argue that flexible rates are more inflationary

[1] The Phillips curve F is also a long-run relationship for the regime of flexible exchange rates, since in such a system a divergence between the national and foreign inflation rates does not have to be corrected *immediately* by a change in the exchange rate because of the existence of nontradable goods.

if the country wants *absolutely* the lower unemployment rate U_2 which it could realize only temporarily under fixed exchange rates.

However, this choice is not necessarily consistent with its "subjective" trade-off between the two "evils", inflation and unemployment, represented by the indifference curves I_1, I_2, I_3, I_4 in Fig. 1. Under fixed rates the country was forced at point A at which the long-run Phillips curve intersects the indifference curve I_2; during the short run it could have attained the "lower" indifference curve I_4 which is tangent to the short-run Phillips curve I at point C. However, if the system of indifference curves remains the same under flexible exchange rates, the country will choose a lower inflation rate at point D where the Phillips curve F is tangent to the indifference curve I_3; the choice of point B would be inconsistent because the country would be on the indifference curve I_1.[1]

Consequently, the introduction of flexible exchange rates can be less inflationary. But it can also be more inflationary if one assumes the system of indifference curves J_1, J_2 for which the country will improve its welfare when it moves from A (fixed exchange rate) to G (flexible exchange rate). It follows that under the aspect of an improvement in the *optimal* trade-off choice between inflation and unemployment as a consequence of a regime of flexible exchange rates, a higher inflation propensity is a plausible case, but not necessarily a strong case.[2]

I.2. *A Lower Monetary Discipline as a Result of an Interest-rate Oriented Monetary Policy*

Another possible case for an increased inflation propensity of a country when it adopts a floating exchange rate has been advanced by Melitz [10]. He assumes some special behavior on the part of central bankers with respect to the conduct of monetary policy. Their target variable is neither the inflation rate nor the growth rate of the money stock, it is only the interest rate. But this is not all. They want to fix the interest rate at the level of the international (or foreign) interest rate. Thus, for instance, if foreign countries pursue a higher inflation policy, with a resulting higher nominal interest rate, the country concerned will imitate the same policy in order to have the same interest-rate level. Such behavior of central bankers—according to some economists highly insane behavior—may arise either from a misunderstanding of the functioning of flexible exchange rates or from a solidarity conduct of

[1] Cf. Fried [5], pp. 48–49.

[2] The system of indifference curves in Fig. 1 is a static system because it does not shift during time (in the same way as the Phillips curve F is assumed to be static). There is certainly the possibility of an upward shift because people become more familiar with inflation such that they attribute a lower disutility to inflation. The result would be a higher inflation rate as compared to point D or G. But this phenomenon could also take place in a system of fixed exchange rates where the world inflation rate moves smoothly upwards due to a changing inflation mentality in the main countries of the world economy.

interest-rate conscious governors who behave in a similar way as the consumers of the relative income hypothesis. However, this special behavior does not fully explain a higher inflation rate under flexible exchange rates because central bankers behave, at least with respect to the interest rate of tradable financial assets, as if they are in a system of fixed exchange rates.[1]

An additional hypothesis has to be made which concerns the adjustment process of the internal interest rate towards the higher international level. A central bank which pursues an interest-rate oriented monetary policy also has to match temporary interest-rate fluctuations which constantly take place in an economy. If, on the other hand, the higher international interest-rate level also fluctuates, it is conceivable that the central bank, due to time-lags and to erroneous judgement of present and future economic activity, overshoots its target level so that it arrives at a higher nominal interest-rate than the international one. And if the central bank does not revise this higher level downwards, the country concerned will have a higher inflation rate than under fixed rates. Consequently, it is only after a series of specific assumptions about central bankers' behavior and the stochastic reality of an economy that a case—but certainly not a strong case—could be constructed for a country's higher inflationary bias under the regime of flexible exchange rates.

However, for the hypothesis of an interest-rate oriented monetary policy, we think we have found a more plausible case than the one proposed by Melitz for the transmission of inflation from one country to another. Suppose that a country—for instance, the foreign country—opts for a higher inflation rate under a regime of floating exchange rates because, for example, of an "optimal" lower unemployment rate as described in the preceding section. A higher inflation rate signifies a higher nominal interest rate after the inflationary expectations have kept up with the ruling rate of inflation. A higher nominal interest rate reduces the desired holdings of real-cash balances with the consequence of a higher expansion path of the price level and of lower real-cash balances by which the existing wealth is reduced. In order to restore their previous wealth level, individuals will increase their savings rate with the result of a lower real rate of interest by which the additional savings will be absorbed by an additional investment. The downward pressure of the real interest rate will be worldwide because a difference in *real* interest rates, at

[1] "If the monetary authorities do not really understand the economics of using a floating rate to achieve domestic price stability, and in particular a domestic price trend sharply at variance with other countries' inflationary domestic price trends, they will in fact simply have a fixed rate system with a little cushion of extra flexibility in the form of movements of the rate; they will therefore have pretty much the same inflationary trend as everyone else; and this in turn will build into the system expectations of continuing inflation and conventional responses to them that will make the transitions to a genuinely independent policy employing the full flexibility of rate movements a painful and prolonged process, because the public as well as the authorities will have to learn a new set of rules and a new framework for forming expectations ... It means that the monetary authority of the price-stabilizing country must expect and accept as natural a nominal interest-rate differential in favor of the other country." Johnson [7], pp. 178 and 182.

least for tradable financial assets, is not conceivable in a world of integrated capital markets, neither in a system of fixed exchange rates nor in a system of flexible exchange rates; the latter system only allows a difference in national nominal interest rates due to a difference in national inflation rates. The worldwide reduction of the real interest rate equally affects the home country. If this country pursues an unchanged inflation policy, its nominal interest rate will fall. If, however, the home country wants to maintain its nominal interest rate at the previous level—a more plausible version of an interest-rate oriented monetary policy—it has to inflate (more) at a (additional) rate which corresponds to the difference between the previous and the current real interest rate.

Fig. 2 illustrates this case. In Fig. 2*a* the equilibrium condition in the world goods market is given by the $S_w I_w$-line. For certain combinations of the real interest rate which must be the same in all countries (r_w) and the real world quantity of money (m_w), there is an equality between world savings (S_w) and world investment (I_w):

$$S_w(r_w, m_w) = I_w(r_w), \tag{1}$$

where S_w and I_w are the sum of national savings and the sum of national investments, respectively. A similar procedure can be applied for the equilibrium condition in the world money market:

$$L_w(r_w + \pi_w) = m_w, \tag{2}$$

represented by the $L_w m_w$-line in Fig. 2*a* where π_w is the world inflation rate and $r_w + \pi_w$ the nominal world interest rate. For sake of simplicity we assume stationary economies. For the special case of a zero growth rate of the world quantity of money ($\lambda_w = 0$), the equilibrium in the world goods market and in the world money market is situated at point A, producing the equilibrium values r_{w0} and m_{w0}. A certain growth rate in the world quantity of money where

$$\lambda_w = \gamma\lambda + \gamma^*\lambda^* \tag{3}$$

implies a world inflation rate of

$$\pi_w = \lambda_w, \tag{4}$$

such that the real world interest rate falls to r_{w1} and the nominal world interest rate rises to $r_{w1} + \pi_{w1}$. The coefficients γ and γ^* represent the relative size of the home country and of the foreign country, respectively, within the world economy and λ (λ^*) is the growth rate of the money stock in the home (foreign) country.

This representation is applicable for the system of fixed exchange rates as well as for the system of floating rates. The difference between both regimes

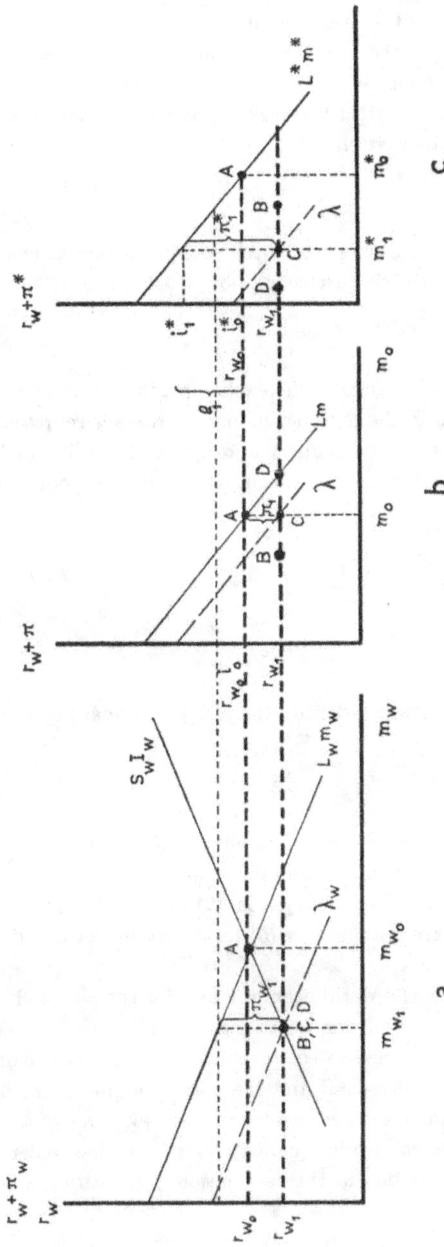

Fig. 2

consists of the interpretation of π_w, λ_w and $r_w+\pi_w$. In a system of fixed exchange rates, π_w must be identical to the home inflation rate (π) and to the foreign inflation rate (π^*): $\pi_w=\pi=\pi^*$; the same is valid for $\lambda_w=\lambda=\lambda^*$ (under the assumption of stationary economies) and for $r_w+\pi_w=r+\pi=r^*+\pi^*$. Under floating rates these rates are *weighted averages of national rates* as is indicated for λ_w in eq. (3) and as can be written for

$$\pi_w=\gamma\pi+\gamma^*\pi^*. \tag{5}$$

Differences in national inflation rates are corrected by continuous changes in the exchange rate according to the purchasing power parity:

$$\varphi=\pi-\pi^*, \tag{6}$$

where φ represents the rate of change in the exchange rate.

The equilibrium condition in the national money markets is represented by the *Lm*-line in Fig. 2*b* for the home country and by the L^*m^*-line in Fig. 2*c* for the foreign country. For instance, the equilibrium in the home national market is

$$L(r_w+\pi)=m, \tag{7}$$

where

$$\pi=\lambda. \tag{8}$$

We still lack another equation which defines the real world quantity of money as

$$m_w=m+m^*. \tag{9}$$

With these nine equations we can determine the nine variables r_w, π_w, m_w, λ_w, π, π^*, m, m^*, φ. Equations (1)–(4) determine the equilibrium levels for r_w, π_w, m_w and λ_w for a given λ and λ^*. Knowing r_w, eqs. (7) and (8) determine π and m. The remaining variables are obtained by (5) for π^*, by (6) for ϱ and by (9) for m^*.

This equilibrium system for the world economy and for the national economies will be interpreted, first of all, for inflationary equilibrium in a system of fixed exchange rates ($\varphi=0$) represented by point B in the three panels of Fig. 2. The vertical distance between B and the corresponding point on the money-market equilibrium line indicates that $\pi_w=\pi=\pi^*=\lambda_w=\lambda=\lambda^*$ and that $r_w+\pi_w=r_w+\pi=r_w+\pi^*$. The real world quantity of money has fallen from m_{w0} to m_{w1} because of the reduction in the real national quantities of money from A to B in each country.

In a system of floating exchange rates and for a given value of λ_w, many equilibrium conditions are conceivable in the home and foreign countries depending on the value of λ or of λ^*. We shall examine two situations illustrated by point C and D, respectively. C represents the special case we had in mind when the home country pursues an interest-rate oriented policy *and* when it wants to maintain a certain nominal interest rate (i_0 in Fig. 2*b*) regardless of what may happen in the rest of the world. Suppose that the foreign country moves from A to C because of its money expansion rate λ^* (see the λ^*-line in Fig. 2*c*). The real world quantity of money is reduced by $m_0^* m_1^* = m_{w0} m_{w1}$ with the subsequent fall of r_w to r_{w1}. In order to maintain the nominal interest rate at i_0, the home country has to inflate by λ (see the λ-line in Fig. 2*b* and the λ_w-line in Fig. 2*a* where λ is already taken into account by λ_w). Consequently, due to this special interest-rate policy, there is a "transmission" of the foreign inflation rate (π_1^*) to the home country (by π_1) by means of the lower real world interest rate (r_{w1}) and because of the interest target of the home country (i_0); the annual appreciation rate of the home currency is ϱ_1. However, this is only one conceivable case among many others. If, for instance, the home country does not pursue an interest-rate policy and wants a zero rate of inflation, it will be at point D (Fig. 2*b*) while the whole expansion of the world quantity of money originates in the foreign country.

In resuming the results of the argument of a lower national monetary discipline under a regime of flexible exchange rates, we can conclude that neither the (keynesian) belief in the existence of a Phillips curve nor a (keynesian) interest-rate oriented monetary policy leads *necessarily* to a higher inflation rate than the inflation rate under fixed exchange rates. The contrary is equally possible such that the system of flexible exchange rates is neither *inherently* more inflationary nor *inherently* less inflationary.

II. The Argument of Asymmetrical and Inflationary Price Effects of the Flexible Exchange Rate System

This argument is more concerned with a worldwide view in terms of the world quantity of money than the former national view in terms of the quantity of money of some individual countries even though the world quantity of money is the sum of the national quantities of money.[1] Furthermore, we only treat the possible link between flexible exchange rates on the one hand and world inflation on the other hand without discussing the opposite—and more probable—link of a higher world inflation which leads to the installation of a flexible-exchange-rate system. This latter question is important for explaining the existence of flexible exchange rates and it has to be differentiated according to the type of higher world inflation under fixed exchange rates, i.e.

[1] Plus the outstanding amount of eurocurrencies which are not analysed in this paper since we do not see any specific relationship according to which the amount of eurocurrencies should increase or decrease as a consequence of the existence of floating exchange rates (with the exception of a possible link between reserve holdings and the volume of eurocurrencies).

whether it is due to a common "inflationary" shock in terms of an increase in relative prices of certain goods with a price rigidity of other goods (e.g. the increase in food prices in 1972–1973 and in oil prices in 1974) or whether it is due to inflationary shocks originating in certain large countries through a particular expansionary monetary policy. Thus, by looking only at the possible causal relationship between flexible exchange rates and a *higher* world inflation rate, we have discovered two possible cases. The first, attributed in the press to Mundell and Laffer[1] (even though it is not clear whether they would fully subscribe to "their" argument), concludes that flexible exchange rates lead to a higher world quantity of money to the extent that there are price rigidities in the economies. The second case is concerned with the possibility of an excess supply of international reserves as a consequence of the transition from a system of fixed exchange rates to a system of (controlled) flexible exchange rates.

II.1. *The Asymmetrical Price Effect of Changes in the Exchange Rate*

The so-called "Mundell–Laffer argument" can be summarized as follows. If the system of flexible exchange rates produces a greater number of depreciations than appreciations, there will be an increase in the world quantity of money provided that the latter is expressed in terms of the currency unit of the depreciating countries. On the other hand, a change in the exchange rate causes an upward price pressure in the depreciating country and a downward price pressure in the appreciating country. If there is a price rigidity in the latter country (the so-called ratchet effect), it will pursue an expansionary monetary policy in order to avoid unemployment—a behavior which gives rise to another increase in the world quantity of money.

This argument of an increase in the world quantity of money as a consequence of a change in the exchange rate can be illustrated as in Fig. 3. Even though this model, presented by Dornbusch [3] and concerned with the devaluation effect of a country under principally fixed exchange rates, will turn out to be irrelevant for our problem, it is sometimes useful to characterize relevant cases by irrelevant models. The world economy consists of two countries of equal size which are stationary and at full-employment income (y and y^*). There are only tradable goods so that the exchange rate (e) is equal to the ratio between the internal price level (P) and the foreign price level (P^*); see Fig. 3*c*. Both countries have the same liquidity preferences (k and k^*) so that their demand-for-money functions (M^d and M^{d*}) are identical (see Fig. 3*b* and 3*d*). The world quantity of money is given, illustrated by the $\bar{M}_w\bar{M}^*_w$-line in Fig. 3*a*. It is the sum of the quantities of money at home (M) and abroad (M^*) and it can be expressed in the currency unit of the home country ($\bar{M}_w = M + eM^*$) or in the currency unit of the foreign country ($M^*_w = M/e + M^*$). The

[1] Cf. Wanniski [11].

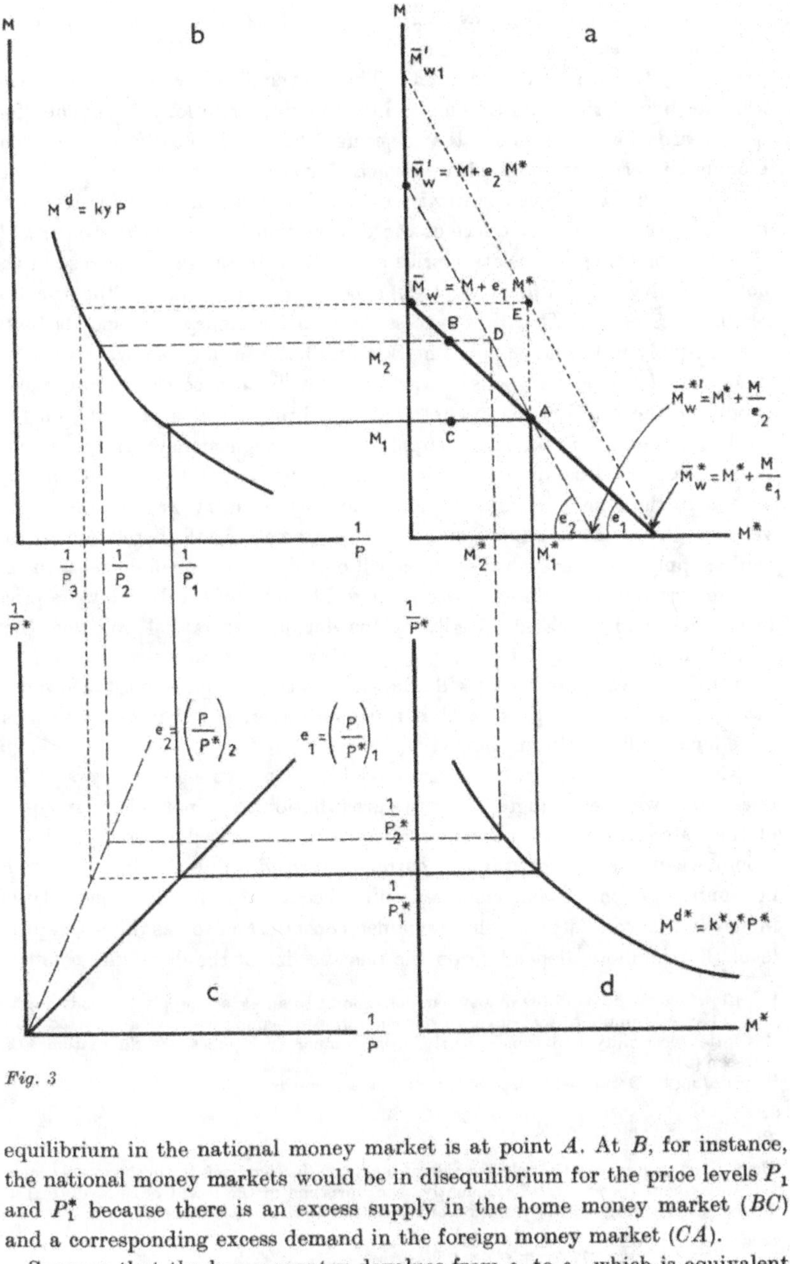

Fig. 3

equilibrium in the national money market is at point A. At B, for instance, the national money markets would be in disequilibrium for the price levels P_1 and P_1^* because there is an excess supply in the home money market (BC) and a corresponding excess demand in the foreign money market (CA).

Suppose that the home country devalues from e_1 to e_2, which is equivalent to a revaluation in the foreign country; see the dashed lines in Fig. 3*a* and 3*c*. The world quantity of money increases (by $M_1^* de$) when it is evaluated in the home currency and it decreases (by $M_1 d(1/e) = -M_1(1/e^2)$) when it is expressed by the foreign currency unit. The new equilibrium will be at D with a higher home price level (P_2) and a lower foreign price level (P_2^*). The "formal" reason for this result is that de/e must be equal to $dP/P - dP^*/P^*$. The economic interpretation of this result is as follows.

Suppose that the home country is very small in relation to the foreign country and that the impact effect of the devaluation is $de/e = dP/P$ where $dP^*/P^* = 0$, eliminating any relative price effect. Due to the price increase in the home country there will be a (stock) excess demand for money (the so-called real-balance effect). The (flow) excess demand for money corresponds to an excess supply in the home goods market and because the home goods market is a part of the world goods market, there will be a corresponding excess supply on the world goods market. This will bring about a price fall on this market giving rise to an excess supply in the foreign money market, a temporary balance-of-payments deficit in the foreign country and a temporary surplus in the home country.[1] Because the home country was assumed to be very small, its excess supply of goods is extremely small in relation to the world supply of goods such that there will be only a very small decrease in the foreign price level. The home price level will be insignificantly below its price level which had increased initially by the devaluation rate. If, on the other hand, the home country is a very large country, the main price-level adjustment (in the downward sense) will take place in the foreign country. However, in all cases, the world price level as a *weighted* average of the two countries' price levels will remain unchanged.[2]

Using this simplified two-country model we can give some answers to the question of whether changes in parities are inflationary or not. The first aspect of the "Mundell–Laffer" argument refers to an increased world quantity of money when it is evaluated by the currency of the devaluing country. There is no doubt that this is fallacious reasoning because the nominal quantity of money in the world economy has remained constant and so has the world price level. Furthermore, depending on the relative size of the devaluing country,

[1] A (flow) excess demand for money can correspond to an excess supply of goods *and* to a (flow) excess supply of securities. In our simplified reasoning we have abstracted from this latter possibility and, consequently, from temporary interest-rate fluctuations. Cf. Claassen [2].

[2] According to Dornbusch [3], p. 874, it can be shown that

$$\frac{dP}{P} = \gamma^* \frac{de}{e} \quad \text{and} \quad \frac{dP^*}{P^*} = -\gamma \frac{de}{e},$$

where γ (γ^*) represents the relative size of the home (foreign) country in the world economy and where $\gamma + \gamma^* = 1$. Consequently, the variation of the world price level (P_w) as the weighted average of the variation of the national price levels will be:

$$\frac{dPw}{Pw} = \gamma \frac{dP}{P} + \gamma^* \frac{dP^*}{P^*} = \gamma\gamma^* \frac{de}{e} - \gamma^*\gamma \frac{de}{e} = 0.$$

the world quantity of money in terms of the devaluing currency may increase, decrease or remain constant if the opposite change in the world quantity of money, now evaluated by the currency of the revaluing country, is taken into account. For instance, if the devaluing country is a very small economy in which there is only a very small fraction of the total world quantity of money, there will be an enormous increase in the world quantity of money in terms of the devalued currency. This increase is only partly compensated by the decrease in the world quantity of money expressed in terms of the currency of the revaluing country because the latter is extremely large by assumption. Complete compensation takes only place if both countries are of equal size, and an overall decrease in the world quantity of money will arise if the devaluing country is bigger than the revaluing country. Nevertheless, the "numéraire" aspect of the "Mundell–Laffer" argument remains fallacious.[1]

The second aspect of this argument is related to the ratchet effect according to which the price rigidity in the revaluing country involves an expansionary monetary policy and, through this, an increase in the world quantity of money in order to avoid unemployment. In terms of Fig. 3, this would mean that the foreign price level remains unchanged at P_1^* which is only possible if the world quantity of money increases by $\bar{M}_w^{*\prime}\bar{M}_w^*$ or by $\bar{M}'_w\bar{M}'_{w1}$ (see the dotted line $\bar{M}_w^*\bar{M}'_{w1}$ in Fig. 3*a* and the new equilibrium point E). Consequently, the foreign money supply has to be increased by more than $M_2^*M_1^*$, i.e. by more than the rate of the hypothetical price fall $P_1^*P_2^*$. The reason for this is that in our model of two countries of equal size, a devaluation of 10 % in the home country would lead to a 5 % increase in the home price level and to a 5 % decrease in the foreign price level. If the foreign price level should remain constant, there would be a 10 % increase in the home price level such that the world quantity of money has to be increased by 5 % which could be realized, for instance, by a 10 % increase in the foreign money supply. This numerical example is important particularly for the case of a very large country which devalues because the foreign country has to increase its money supply considerably and the world

[1] However, the nominal world quantity of money will increase if the devaluing country increases its money supply by the amount of the accounting gains in its initial stock of reserves. Under this aspect of the evaluation of reserves, our two-country model has to be differentiated according to the criterion of whether one of the countries is a key-currency country or not.

If there is a key-currency country and if the other country is the devaluing country, then there is the above possibility of a higher nominal world quantity of money. On the contrary, if the key-currency country is the "devaluing" country, there will be no accounting gains because the "reserves" of the key-currency country are equal to its own quantity of money. According to the usual intervention rules, it is not the key-currency country (the *n*th country) which devalues, but the other country (the $n-1$ countries) which revalues and which will have an accounting loss in its initial reserve stock. If its monetary policy maintains a direct and unchanged relationship between its outstanding money supply and its reserve stock (evaluated in its own currency), there will be a decrease in its money supply and, consequently, in the world quantity of money.

In the case where both countries are not key-currency countries (the case of the gold standard or of a special drawing rights standard), there would only be an upvaluation of the initial reserve stock in the devaluing country (because of the existence of $n+1$ currencies).

price level will increase by nearly the devaluation rate due to the size of the devaluing country.

Even though the ratchet effect argument is completely correct with respect to the world price level increasing effect of parity changes, three restrictions have to be mentioned which turn this argument into an irrelevant case. First, in an inflationary world absolute price rigidity becomes a relative price rigidity which is less probable because in the revaluing country the prices have only to rise less rapidly. Second, the ratchet effect explains a once-and-for-all increase in the world price level and not a continuous increase in the world inflation *rate;* the latter can only be explained with the help of the ratchet effect if there is continuous devaluation or if there is a cyclical devaluation and revaluation. This last remark leads us to the third and decisive restriction which focuses on the question of *why* the country concerned devalues. Our two-country model assumed an external equilibrium and a constant quantity of money before the country in question devalued. Consequently, the reasons for this devaluation could only be either an increase in the stock of reserves and/or an increase in the internal price level. The case of a higher internal price level by the means of a devaluation could only be relevant for those countries which are not able, from the point of view of technical control of the money supply, to increase the monetary base by its domestic component, that is by domestic credit. This is certainly a very limited case so that in all other cases the reason for a devaluation is just the opposite of our two-country model, i.e. instead of a devaluation which leads to a higher internal price level and to a higher nominal quantity of money in the devaluing country, it is first of all its quantity of money which increases, resulting in a higher internal price level which causes a devaluation. However, this "normal" causal link of a devaluation does not at all affect the foreign price level to the extent that the devaluation rate is equal to the expansion rate of the money supply in the devaluing country.[1]

---

[1] It should be mentioned that the above argument of the reasons for a devaluation was related to our two-country model in which both countries were stationary and in which no capital movements took place. It is evident that an external disequilibrium and a subsequent parity change do not have to be caused only by a different evolution of the price levels. They can also be caused by different real growth rates or by capital movements.

Capital movements can cause a divergence of the exchange rate from its purchasing power parity and a certain transmission of inflation from one country to another. One possible explanation has been given by Dornbusch [4]. Suppose, for instance, that the foreign country has an expansionary monetary policy with the consequence of a higher foreign price level and of a subsequent devaluation according to the argument of the purchasing power parity. A devaluation of the foreign currency is identical to a revaluation of the domestic currency. Until now nothing would happen with respect to a transmission of the higher foreign inflation rate to the domestic one. However, if a certain expectation pattern of asset holders with respect to the future evolution of the exchange rate is taken into account, the following transmission mechanism is conceivable.

The portfolio of asset holders consists of domestic and foreign assets. The expected return of their portfolio depends also on their expectations of the future exchange rate. To the extent that their expectations are "rigid" (the expected value is not based on purchasing power parity but on the past and present evolution of the exchange rate), the domestic asset holders will expect a devaluation of their currency such that there will be

Consequently, our two-country model is revealed to be completely irrelevant for the reality of parity changes. It is also irrelevant for another reason. In a world of (pure) flexible exchange rates it cannot be devalued or revalued! The central bank has an influence on the exchange rate only indirectly via its monetary policy such that the only relevant cause of a "devaluation" or "revaluation" in a system of flexible exchange rates is the case of a more expansionary or of a more restrictive monetary policy. And with this typical reason for a *depreciating* or an *appreciating* exchange rate we are back again at the argument of national monetary discipline for explaining world inflation under flexible exchange rates.

II.2. *The Inflationary Price Effect of an Excess Supply of Reserves*

The second argument of a higher world quantity of money qua flexible exchange rates is derived from the possibility of an excess supply of reserves as the consequence of the introduction of flexible exchange rates. This excess supply can be created by a reduced demand for international reserves, these being zero in the extreme case of a "purely" floating system, whereas they will be reduced less in a system of controlled flexibility.[1] In such a system an external disequilibrium is partly financed by reserves and partly eliminated by the exchange-rate flexibility (and possibly by other internal adjustment policies).

Fig. 4*a* illustrates this trade-off relationship between real reserve holdings (R/P) and the degree of flexibility (β) by the line P_1P_1. This policy combination guarantees a certain degree of external solvency (P_1). At point A the economy is under a fixed exchange rate which allows a certain flexibility, β_1, around the par value; the desired holding of real reserves is $(R/P)_1$ for a given level of its opportunity cost, i_1, which is equal to the nominal interest rate minus the interest rate paid on reserves. The demand for reserves is a decreasing function of the opportunity cost as it is shown by the demand curve $(R^d/P)_1$ in Fig. 4*b*.[2] If the country abandons the system of fixed exchange rates and opts for the degree of flexibility β_2 by maintaining the external solvency of type P_1, it will be at point B (Fig. 4*a*) with the result of a lower

---

capital outflows which effectively produce a devaluation; in the same way the foreign asset holders expect a revaluation of their currency which gives rise to a still stronger net capital inflow into their country and to a still stronger revaluation of their currency (and, through this, to a still stronger devaluation of the home currency). At this very moment our irrelevant model described above becomes relevant! In the home country the price level tends to rise *and* in the foreign country the price level tends to fall. Consequently, the home country observes a certain transmission of the higher foreign inflation rate to its own inflation rate. Furthermore, the existence of a ratchet effect in the foreign country causes an increase in its money supply and, consequently, in the world price level. Finally, this ratchet effect will be equally relevant for the home country when expectations are revised, leading to a subsequent revaluation of the home currency, etc.

[1] Machlup [9] shows that the interventions of central banks in the foreign exchange market were even more frequent during the last years of flexibility.

[2] Cf. Claassen [1].

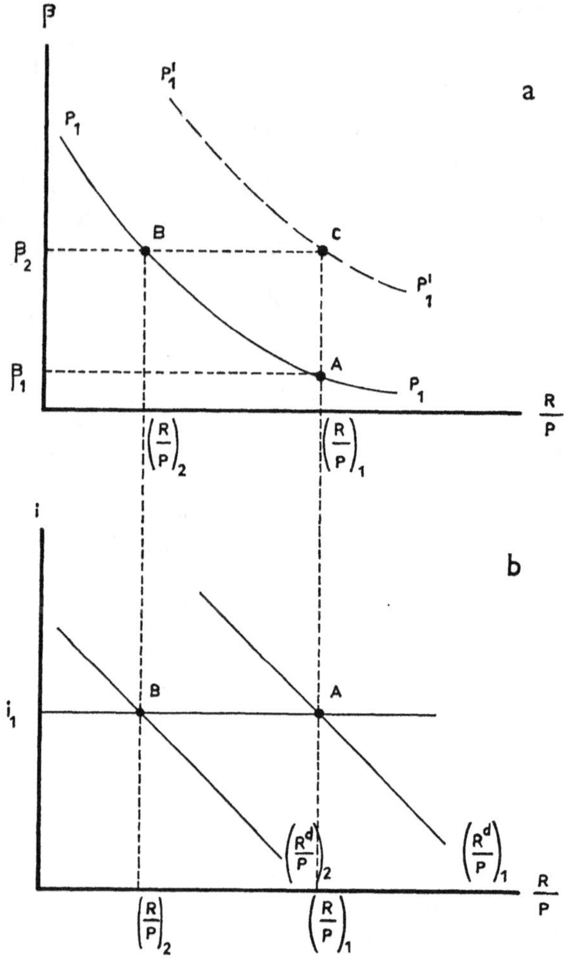

Fig. 4

demand curve for real reserves, $(R^d/P)_2$ (Fig. 4*b*); for an unchanged opportunity cost i_1 its desired stock of real reserves is reduced to $(R/P)_2$.

We now have to find the means by which the country can reduce its effective stock of real reserves to its desired level. We assume a two-country model in which one country is the key-currency country and the other country—our country in question with a reduced demand for reserves—constitutes the "rest of the world". There are two possibilities for reducing the stock of reserves to its desired level: either in real terms (an increased P) or in nominal terms (a reduced R).

The first case is not realizable. The central bank increases its money supply and, through this, provokes an increase in its price level with a subsequent depreciation of its currency *and* a corresponding gain in the book value of its reserves without affecting their real value (and without any change in the variables of the foreign country).

The second case implies that the central bank sells the non-desired part of its reserves on the foreign exchange market which involves, *ceteris paribus*, a corresponding decrease in its monetary base. The resulting appreciation of the currency, provoking a fall in the book value of the reserves of the country concerned, and the downward price movement taking place during the same period would not affect the real amount of reserves if that part of excessive reserves which had been sold on the foreign exchange market were not taken into account. It is this part of excessive reserves which has reduced the real amount of reserves of the country in question. However, the other country—the key-currency country—will observe a corresponding increase in its money supply because there will be a real transfer of goods from the key-currency country to the domestic country against the acquisition of its own currency (the excessive reserves of the domestic country). Consequently, the world level of prices will not have changed. The reason for this is the trivial fact that the world quantity of money did not change and, through this, the world price level, the real world quantity of money remained constant.[1]

In describing the first case (the illusionary reduction of non-desired reserves via an increased national price level), we have found, in this paper, a third "national" motivation of a lower national monetary discipline in a system of flexible exchange rates. The first concerned the possibility of reducing the unemployment rate by a higher inflation rate to the extent that the central bank believed in the existence of a Phillips curve and that the optimum choice in its trade-off line was a higher inflation rate. The second was related to the very particular behavior of a central banker who pursued monetary policy by aligning the country's nominal interest rate to the foreign nominal interest rate, and to the extent that foreign countries were more inflationary and that the central banker overshot the foreign interest-rate target level, he produced a higher inflation rate. The third motivation of a lower national monetary discipline is the reduction in desired reserve holdings during the *transition*

---

[1] There is another possibility of an excess supply of reserves caused by an increase in the supply of reserves. Suppose again the context of a two-country-model. One of the two countries should be the key-currency country. The latter increases its money supply, that is the potential reserves for the other country. The result will be a higher price level and a subsequent depreciation of the key-currency with the result that the nominal and real amounts of reserves remain unchanged in the other country.

On the other hand, if the additional supply of reserves consists of special drawing rights or of an increase in the price of gold, there will be an excess supply of reserves in *both* countries which can only be eliminated by a money expansion and, through this, by an increase of the price levels in both countries without necessarily affecting the exchange rate. However, these cases of an excess supply of reserves via an additional supply of reserves can occur in a system of fixed exchanged rates as well as under floating rates.

period from a system of fixed exchange rates towards a system of flexible exchange rates. However, the illusionary reduction in desired reserve holdings produces only a *once-and-for-all* increase in the world price level. On the other hand, it is conceivable that a lower demand for reserves qua flexible exchange rates is compensated by other factors which again increase this demand (take, for instance, the energy crisis which coincided with the beginning of the floating rates). Such a case is illustrated in Fig. 4*a*. The probability of a higher variability of international payments shifts the line P_1P_1 towards $P_1'P_1'$ in order to maintain the same degree of external solvency (P_1). In this particular case the demand curve for international reserves, $(R^d/P)_1$, remains unchanged (Fig. 4*b*).

It is left to the reader to find other motivations of a lower national monetary (or inflationary) discipline—but also for fair play, of a higher national monetary (or inflationary) discipline—under a regime of flexible exchange rates. This exercise is rather easy; just forget about monetary inflation theory and open the Pandora box which contains all other (national) inflation theories.

Concluding Remarks: Future Outlook

Our main concern was to show that flexible exchange rates are neither inherently more inflationary nor inherently less inflationary than fixed exchange rates. They can be more inflationary and they can be less inflationary, but the main responsibility of a possible higher world inflation rate (as the weighted sum of national inflation rates) is now shifted more to individual national monetary policies and, through this, to the degree of monetary discipline exerted by these individual countries. The relatively short period of flexible exchange rates during the last several years has revealed the possibility of a higher world inflation rate, even though this empirical argument is not completely conclusive because we do not know what would have happened to the world inflation rate if the system of fixed exchange rates had been maintained. On the other hand, for the future, the other possibility, of a lower world inflation rate than the one of the late 1960's, cannot be excluded and the possibility of zero world inflation could even be envisaged, as Harry Johnson [8] does: "... floating rates are a consequence, and not a cause, of our 'stagflation' problem. And it may even appear in hindsight that floating rates, by bottling up inflations within the borders of the inflating countries, have sufficiently stiffened national anti-inflationary resolve—in particular in the United States—to get us back to 1920s stability by the 1980s."

References

1. Claassen, E.-M.: Demand for international reserves and the optimum mix and speed of adjustment policies. *American Economic Review*, June 1975.
2. Claassen, E.-M.: The role of economic size in the determination and transmission of world inflation. In *Inflation in Small Countries* (ed. H. Frisch). Springer-Verlag (forthcoming in 1976).
3. Dornbusch, R.: Devaluation, money, and nontraded goods. *American Economic Review*, December 1973.
4. Dornbusch, R.: The theory of flexible exchange rate regimes and macroeconomic policy. *Swedish Journal of Economics 78*, No. 2, 1976.
5. Fried, J.: Inflation-unemployment trade-offs under fixed and floating exchange rates. *Canadian Journal of Economics*, February 1973.
6. Haberler, G.: Inflation as a worldwide phenomenon: An overview. *Weltwirtschaftliches Archiv 110*, No. 2, 1974.
7. Johnson, H. G.: Inflation, unemployment, and the floating rate. *Canadian Public Policy*, Spring, 1975.
8. Johnson, H. G.: Have floating rates worked so badly? *Bulletin de l'Institut Economique de Paris*, July–August, 1975.
9. Machlup, F.: Recent experiences with floating currencies. In *Recent Issues in International Monetary Economics* (ed. E.-M. Claassen & P. Salin). North-Holland, Amsterdam, 1976.
10. Melitz, J.: On the international transmission of inflation under floating exchange rates. Paper for the Konstanz Seminar on Monetary Theory and Monetary Policy, June 1975.
11. Wanniski, J.: The case for fixed exchange rates. *Wall Street Journal*, June 14, 1974.

COMMENT ON E.-M. CLAASSEN, "WORLD INFLATION UNDER FLEXIBLE EXCHANGE RATES"

Hans Genberg

Graduate Institute of International Studies, Geneva, Switzerland

The paper by Professor Claassen examines within an analytic framework some of the arguments which have led to the conclusion that flexible exchange rates imply a higher rate of inflation, on the average, than fixed exchange rates. Three types of arguments are considered. The first looks at the effect of the introduction of flexible exchange rates on the conduct of monetary policy. The second takes up the so-called Mundell-Laffer proposition which relies on price rigidities and ratchet effects. Finally, Prof. Claassen analyses the likely effect of flexible exchange rates on rates of inflation via changes in the demand for international reserves.

The main finding of the paper is that there is no necessary or even most probable relationship between the exchange rate regime and the average rate of inflation. Arguments to the contrary turn out, on closer scrutiny, to be either logically invalid or to imply an equal chance of more or less inflation with flexible exchange rates.

While I agree with Prof. Claassen's main conclusion I would like, in this note, to suggest some change in emphasis and point out some possible problems in the analytic treatment of a flexible exchange rate world. After some introductory remarks on the meaning of world inflation under flexible exchange rates I will follow the outline of the paper and treat in turn the Phillips curve and interest-rate target reasons for a less strict monetary policy discipline under flexible rates. Before my conclusion I also offer some remarks on issues related to the Mundell-Laffer proposition.

1. The Meaning of World Inflation under Flexible Exchange Rates

As Prof. Claassen notes in the introduction to his paper, inflation under fixed exchange rates is a world phenomenon. Not only can we define an index of world inflation but, with fixed exchange rates, this measure takes on *analytic* importance.[1] This is because economic theory implies that each country's inflation rate should converge to the world rate and that the *aggregate* mone-

[1] For a more detailed discussion, see Hans Genberg, "The Concept and Measurement of the World Price Level and Rate of Inflation", *Journal of Monetary Economics*, forthcoming.

tary policy of all countries determines the latter. The appropriate unit of analysis is thus seen to be the world as a whole and the concept of the world money stock is both well defined[1] and takes on a special significance.[2]

Under flexible exchange rates, on the other hand, it is not clear that we can define a world price level concept which is useful from an analytic point of view. The reason is not only that the choice of numeraire is arbitrary but also that there is no necessary link between the domestic rate of inflation and the world average we construct. I would therefore have liked to see much less reference, perhaps none, to *world* inflation in the paper which instead could have focused on possible reasons why *a single nation's* inflation policies may differ under fixed and flexible exchange rates. This would have made clear that under flexible rates, "inflation is fundamentally a national phenomenon" as Claassen puts it. The issue is not only one of language, however, since as we will see in the following sections, analytical errors may creep in when emphasis is put on world factors, and since academic reference to world inflation under flexible exchange rates may lead the unwary policy-maker into thinking that his own policies do not have to take the responsibility for controlling domestic inflation.

2. The Effect of Employment Targets on Monetary Policy and Inflation

Section I.1 of the paper contains a discussion of the effect of freeing the exchange rate on the optimal choice between inflation and unemployment on the assumption that there exists a Phillips curve type of trade-off. Prof. Claassen shows that, depending on "tastes", the inflation rate a country chooses can be either higher or lower than that which a fixed exchange rate forces it to except. Whether a simple (or weighted) average of national inflation rates (uncorrected for exchange rate changes) goes up or down cannot be easily answered with the apparatus provided in the paper since it is not quite clear how the fixed exchange-rate equilibrium inflation rate-unemployment rate point (point A in Figure 1) gets determined. One heuristically plausible argument would be that fixed exchange rates force countries to a $\pi - u$ point which is an average of the points they would choose if they were closed economies. Thus one could think of point A in Figure 1 as being the outcome of one country wanting to be at G but finding that this will lead to a balance of

[1] The reason is that with fixed exchange rates "national money stocks can be treated as components of a Hicksian composite commodity, the world money stock, since exchange-stabilization operations prevent variations in the relative values of national currencies". (Alexander K. Swoboda, "Gold, Dollars, Euro-Dollars and the World Money Stock", GIIS-Ford Foundation Discussion paper No. 2, Graduate Institute of International Studies, November 1974, p. 1.)

[2] For some empirical evidence supporting a monetary interpretation of world inflation see Hans Genberg and Alexander Swoboda, "Causes and Origins of the Current Worldwide Inflation", GIIS-Ford Foundation Discussion paper No. 6, Graduate Institute of International Studies, November 1975).

payments deficit and the other country desiring to stay at D were it not for the accompanying balance of payments surplus. The actual outcome of an inflation rate of 10 % at A is thus an average of the two optimal inflation rates which will be attained with flexible exchange rates, and there is no difference in the average world inflation rate under the two systems. A more detailed investigation how the fixed exchange rate system leads to point A may suggest reasons why the weights in the world inflation index might differ between the two exchange-rate regimes and therefore produce a different average, but this is surely a second order of small effect.

Even if we could determine that the average inflation rate unambiguously has increased or decreased, it seems to me that Figure 1 provides an excellent opportunity to show why this average is basically uninteresting under flexible rates. First of all, wherever the average lies (presumably between D and G) has no bearing on where the individual countries end up. Secondly, whether the average goes up or down does not prevent each country to be better off under flexible exchange rates in this model since each one can move to a higher indifference curve. Thirdly, the rate of change in the exchange rate between the two countries depends only on the difference between the inflation rates at D and G and is independent of the world average inflation rate.

3. Transmission of Inflation when Monetary Policy is Interest-rate Oriented

Section I.2 of the paper investigates the transmission of inflation between countries with a flexible exchange rate, the transmission being due to an interest rate pegging monetary policy. Although the main conclusion of the analysis, that inflation *is* transmitted under the described conditions, is correct, I shall argue that there are some problems with the analysis itself which stem from treating the flexible exchange rate system as if it were a fixed rate system as far as the determination of the average rate of inflation is concerned. The error comes in the aggregation of national demand functions for real money balances when rates of inflation differ between countries. It is easy to show that aggregating money demand function, like the one described by equation (7), across countries will yield a world demand function of the type specified in (2) only if a specific set of weights is used in the definition of the world inflation rate. These weights are different from those in equation (5). This means that instead of using equation (2) as one equilibrium condition we should use money market equilibrium conditions for each country separately which together with the world goods market equilibrium condition would lead to the following reduced form function for the real rate of interest

$$r = f(\pi, \pi^*) \quad \text{where} \quad -1 < f_1 < 0 \quad \text{and} \quad -1 < f_2 < 0.$$

This equation together with an assumed nominal interest rate policy can be used to study the effects of π^* on π and we would get the same results as Claassen does.

4. The Mundell–Laffer Argument

The section in Prof. Claassen's paper which deals with the so-called Mundell-Laffer argument is a good example of the difficulty of keeping the numéraire aspect of the analysis straight when exchange rates change. On page 356, for instance, a correct expression is given for the unambiguous increase in the nominal world money stock when it is measured in terms of the devaluing country's currency. On page 358 however it is asserted that the world money stock does not change at all or may increase or decrease. The clearly justified criticisms of some of the popularized versions of the Mundell-Laffer views tend to get lost in the paper because of these types of inconsistencies. The discussion of what, in my opinion, is the only reasonable interpretation of the Mundell-Laffer argument is left to a footnote (1 on p. 360) and is not sufficiently scrutinized. Relying as it does on autonomous factors moving exchange rates away from their purchasing power parity levels and a particular reaction of the monetary authorities to the consequent disequilibrium, this view could have usefully been criticized for its apparent neglect of the effects of the same autonomous changes on monetary policy and prices under fixed exchange rates.

5. Conclusion

Despite the errors I have pointed to I think that Prof. Claassen has done us a service by putting to rest the arguments that flexible exchange rates *per se* necessarily bring with them higher or lower inflation rates in the world economy. I would perhaps have liked to see a more forceful statement of the view that inflation is a national phenomenon under flexible exchange rates and that domestic policy authorities must be held responsible for controlling it. The paper also points to the danger of generalizing from the one observation we have regarding the introduction of flexible exchange rates and the near simultaneous increase in rates of inflation throughout the world.

References

Genberg, H.: The concept and measurement of the world price level and rate of inflation. *Journal of Monetary Economics*, forthcoming.

Genberg, H. & Swoboda, A. K.: Causes and origins of the current worldwide inflation. GIIS-Ford Foundation Discussion paper No. 6 (Graduate Institute of International Studies, November 1975).

Swoboda, A. K.: Gold, dollars, euro-dollars and the world money stock. GIIS-Ford Foundation Discussion paper No. 2 (Graduate Institute of International Studies, November 1974).

INFLATION AND THE EXCHANGE RATE REGIME*

W. Max Corden

Nuffield College, Oxford, England

Abstract

Is a regime of fixed or of flexible rates more conducive to inflation? In a flexible rate regime the authorities of each country can choose whatever rate of inflation they wish. In the fixed rate system countries can depart from the world rate of inflation by running payments imbalances and will trade-off the costs of accommodating borrowing or lending against the benefits from getting closer to their desired inflation rates; inflation rates are then determined in a general equilibrium system where countries "trade" their surpluses and deficits. "Inflation-prone" countries are distinguished from the "inflation-shy". Account is also taken of the special case of the reserve currency country.

Introduction

The purpose of this paper is to sort out the relationship between inflation and the exchange rate regime. Are fixed or flexible rates more conducive to inflation? The focus is not on the well-known subject of the international inflation transmission process in the fixed rate system, nor on analysing the consequences of *given* monetary expansions in different countries (a matter much discussed by "monetarists") but rather on the outcome of policy adjustments by fiscal and monetary authorities which are designed to bring about whatever transmission of, or insulation from, external inflation these authorities desire. The aim is also to show how the various inflation rates are determined in a fixed rate system when there are many different monetary authorities interacting on the rates chosen by different countries.[1]

The polar systems of rigidly fixed rates and perfectly flexible rates will be compared here. In fact the world has moved along the continuum between

* I am indebted to valuable comments on an earlier draft from Herbert Grubel and John Martin. This paper is a revised version of the paper presented at the Conference.

[1] The main paper dealing with aspects of this subject (and anticipating some of the points in the present paper) is Fried (1973). See also Mundell (1972). On the international transmission process, see Caves (1973), Turnovsky & Kapura (1974), Branson (1975), and various papers—notably those by Aukrust, Branson, Salant and Swoboda—in Krause & Salant (forthcoming).

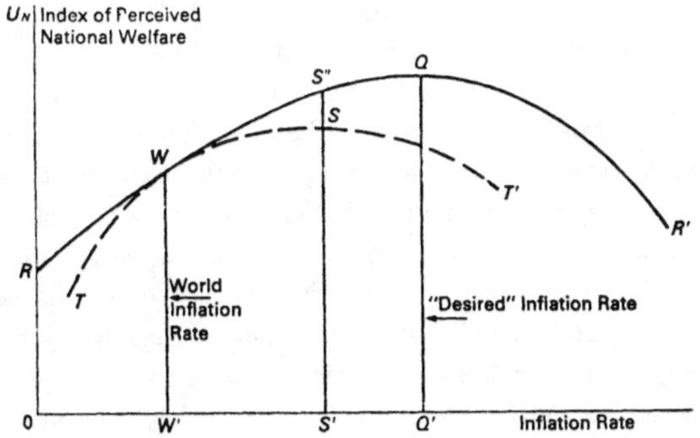

Fig. 1.

these limits in the flexible direction. Governments feel freer to alter their exchange rates under the managed floating system than under the Bretton Woods system. But most felt they had a little, occasional, freedom even under the old regime and some still do not feel complete freedom now. The polar analysis to follow would thus need to be modified if one wanted to compare the actual regimes of which we have recent experience.

I. The Fixed Rate System with Imbalances: The Inflation-Prone Country

We begin by considering the point of view of one country which is sufficiently small that it cannot significantly affect the rate of inflation in other countries. Fig. 1 refers to this country. The vertical axis shows an index of national welfare (U_N) as perceived by its monetary authorities. The horizontal axis shows its domestic rate of price inflation.

If the exchange rate is flexible, the monetary authorities can choose their own inflation rate, irrespective of what this rate is in the rest of the world. This is the well-known point that a flexible rate can insulate a country from external inflation or deflation. The curve RR' is the curve of *inflation benefit* in the flexible rate system. The benefit is maximised at an inflation rate of OQ', this being what we shall call the *desired inflation rate.*

Alternatively, the exchange rate may be fixed. The world rate of inflation–namely OW'—then becomes relevant. If the authorities do not wish the country to run a balance of payments deficit the domestic rate of inflation must then be equal to the given world rate—at least, provided there are not structural changes (which we shall assume away) that would make a different rate of inflation compatible with absence of payments imbalance. Balance of payments equilibrium is here defined as absence of "accommodating" capital movements or undesired reserve changes. With this externally-determined rate of inflation the perceived welfare level to the country is $W'W$.

We are assuming that this particular country is an *inflation-prone* country, namely a country (such as Britain) that chooses to have a higher rate of inflation than the given world rate when it is a free agent, that is, when it has a flexible rate. It is to be contrasted with an *inflation-shy* country (such as Germany) that chooses a lower inflation rate than the world rate when it has a flexible rate regime. We shall come back to the inflation-shy country later.

What is the nature of the *inflation benefit*? It is the benefit perceived by the government and monetary authorities from domestic inflation and what goes with it—i.e. from increased monetary demand for domestically-produced goods and services. This benefit may consist of an expected reduction in unemployment or avoidance of an increase (which may only be a short-run benefit) and of a desired income redistribution towards the public sector and within the private sector. One could count the various efficiency and uncertainty costs of inflation as negative benefits here. The curve refers only to *perceived* or expected benefit. The inflation benefit curve could—but need not be—derived from an orthodox short-run Phillips curve trade-off and preference map.

The curve RR' will change over time. If a given level of employment can only be maintained with accelerating inflation it is likely that the welfare level attainable at the *desired inflation rate* would fall over time, while the *desired rate* itself might rise. In any case, our approach here is short-run, so we keep the curve constant. We shall look more closely at the meaning of this curve in the next section.

Figure 1 shows that in the fixed rate system with no imbalances the government has an "excess demand" for inflation of $W'Q'$. It can satisfy some or all of this "excess demand" by running a deficit. It could, perhaps, run a deficit sufficient to bring its domestic inflation rate up to the *desired rate* OQ' The perceived welfare level that would then be attained would differ from that attained with the same inflation rate in the flexible rate system. For this time the country is running down its reserves or is borrowing, and in doing so is obtaining extra resources. Thus there is a cost as well as an additional benefit. Possible elements in the cost are the real rate of interest paid on borrowed funds, the interest foregone on funds otherwise invested abroad, an increased sense of insecurity owing to reduced owned reserves, and a political cost incurred in order to finance the deficit. The benefit is that the deficit makes available real resources to the country, absorption exceeding national output.

Now we come to an important stage in the argument. What is the *net* benefit from the deficit, excluding its effect on the inflation benefit? Suppose that before the deficit is incurred the country is borrowing abroad at an optimal rate. The real resource gain at the margin is then equal to the real rate of interest. We can include not only private borrowing but also "autonomous" public borrowing here. Any extra borrowing will be "accommodating", being the by-product of choosing an inflation rate above the world rate. There must then be a net loss on any "accommodating" borrowing, since it means borrowing above the optimum. Further, it also seems to follow that the greater the deficit and hence the greater the inflation rate, the greater the net loss.

This is represented in Fig. 1. The net loss is subtracted from the *flexible rate* inflation benefit curve RR' to yield the *fixed rate* benefit curve of WT'. The net loss increases with the rate of inflation because the deficit increases with the rate of inflation. The curve has also been continued to the left of W, to TW, to represent the idea that a surplus would also yield a net loss since foreign lending would be above the optimum. The curve TT' must also change over time. If the domestic inflation rate exceeeds the world rate by a constant amount the deficit must be steadily increasing, so that TT' must be steadily falling (but always tangential to RR' at W), gradually approaching the vertical line WW'. This is because an increasing deficit (and possibly even a constant deficit) will only be capable of being financed at an increasing real rate of interest.

If the authorities do indeed perceive the effects of payments imbalances in this way we can conclude that they will choose an inflation rate of OS' in the fixed rate system, thus getting closer to, but not actually attaining, the *desired inflation rate* of OQ'. In fact, they will have "bought" some extra inflation ($W'S'$) at a cost of what appears to be "excess" borrowing, this cost being represented by SS''. But given the fixed exchange rate constraint it is not really excess borrowing. It is excess only in relation to the optimal borrowing rate in the flexible system.

There may be constraints on the ability to borrow. In that case the curve will turn sharply down at some point, in the extreme case becoming vertical, and thus setting a clear limit to the inflation rate. But the inflation rate that maximises the perceived welfare level may be below this constraint level.

It has been supposed here that in the fixed rate system it is possible for a country to choose its own inflation rate and so to run its economy at an inflation rate different from that of the world rate, the only limitation being the cost of excess borrowing or lending abroad. This involves two assumptions.

Firstly, there have to be a reasonable number of non-traded goods. Since the domestic prices of traded goods, strictly defined, must rise with their world prices under the fixed rate regime, some goods and services have to be *non-traded* in the sense that their prices are not wholly set in world markets. This, clearly, is a resonable assumption.

Secondly, we are assuming that international capital mobility does not prevent a country from determining its own inflation rate. If there were perfect capital mobility, any one country could only bring about its desired inflation rate through fiscal policy, since monetary policy could not affect aggregate monetary demand for domestic goods and services. But in the absence of such perfect mobility, either monetary or fiscal policy, or some combination of them, could be used.[1]

Finally, it can be noted here that, conceivably, foreign borrowing may initially be below the optimum, or at least may be perceived to be. For some reason there may be a net *gain* from "accommodating" borrowing. But this raises a question about the definition of "autonomous" and "accommodating" borrowing and why the borrowing did not take place "autonomously", perhaps by the government, if there was a gain to be obtained. We shall come back to the general point of a net gain from accommodating borrowing when discussing the position of the reserve currency country, but here it need only be observed that the possibility exists and can be analysed in terms of our diagram (as is done in Fig. 3 later).

II. The Inflation Benefit Curve Further Examined

Let us look a little more closely at the *inflation benefit curve* before going on with our main analysis. There are all sorts of difficulties about this simple curve, these difficulties raising all the problems of closed-economy inflation theory which are not the main concern of this paper.

If one believed in a stable Phillips curve and a government welfare function with unemployment and the rate of inflation as arguments, there would be no problem. Indeed, one could even believe that inflation does not affect the rate of unemployment but has certain redistributive effects, and put the latter effects, rather than employment, into the welfare function. It is the instability over time of the trade-offs that is the problem. The *desired inflation rate* may maximise short-term perceived utility, but may carry within it the seeds of utility losses later, perhaps through the expectations that are generated.

Perhaps one should then redefine the inflation benefit curve as referring to the present value of discounted perceived utility resulting from various short-run rates of price inflation. This would take into account not only possible short-run employment gains from a high rate of inflation but also the unemployment to which it may give rise later.

Furthermore, the following difficulty in the analysis of the previous section has been evaded so far. The resources provided to a country by an external deficit may in the short-run improve its inflation-benefit curve.

[1] The various models of the international inflation transmission process show to what extent an external inflation is transmitted *automatically* to the domestic economy. The models attain their precision by making specific assumptions about monetary policy (constant interest rate or constant domestic credit creation), about rigidity of money wages or real wages, and so on. Here we are concerned with the outcome of *policy* adjustments that may offset or supplement the automatic processes, and that are designed finally to bring about whatever transmission of, or insulation from, external inflation the government and monetary authorities desire. We assume that the monetary authorities or governments of countries actually *succeed* in putting their countries on that point of the inflation benefit curve where they want their countries to be; thus they are able to sterilise monetary inflows or to avoid deficits or surpluses that they do not want.

We have supposed that the inflation benefit curve depends on the *domestic* trade-off between inflation, unemployment, income distribution, etc., and that this trade-off is itself invariant to the exchange rate regime and whether or not there is foreign borrowing. At the same time the net loss from a *given* accommodating payments deficit has been assumed independent of the rate of inflation, even though the amount of the deficit depends on this rate. Hence we have simply subtracted the net loss from the given inflation benefit curve. Now the point is that they *may* be related.

Suppose that the external deficit is matched by a public sector deficit and that some part of this is used not for investment but to subsidise wage-goods (e.g. food), this in turn improving the short-run Phillips curve trade-off. A fixed rate with a deficit then makes more real resources for consumption available in the short-run than a flexible rate system does. On the other hand, if we hold investment constant for this purpose, eventually consumption would have to fall relative to what would have happened without this deficit, since the deficit represents a foreign loan, not a gift. Hence in the long-run the trade-off may be worsened. On balance one cannot assume that the inflation benefit curve—which embodies both short-run and expected long-run effects—will move in a particular way. Hence one may be justified in keeping the benefit curve constant.

There is yet another complication. World inflation—and especially changes in the rate of world inflation—may be associated with changing *relative* prices. Thus a rise in the world inflation rate may, at least temporarily, raise prices of primary commodities relative to prices of manufactures. And such relative price effects may, in turn, affect the short-run Phillips curve trade-off and hence our RR' curve. One might argue that *any* significant relative price change will increase the rate of inflation for given unemployment (worsen the trade-off), or alternatively that only a rise in the prices of commodities relative to manufactures will have this effect. In any case, this complication is not explicitly incorporated in our analysis, though no doubt it could be.

III. The Inflation-Shy Country and Downward Wage Rigidity

Clearly, the whole analysis could be applied to a small inflation-shy country. This case is represented in Fig. 2. The desired inflation rate with flexible rates, OQ', is below the given world inflation rate OW', and once the possibility of a surplus is introduced, the country will "buy" a reduction in inflation of $S'W'$ with such a surplus.

In this inflation-shy case there is an additional complication. In the fixed rate system the prices of traded goods must rise at the world inflation rate OW'. The domestic inflation rate which the government perceives to be optimal is OS'. This latter rate is a weighted average of the rate of inflation of the prices of traded goods and non-traded goods. The prices of non-traded

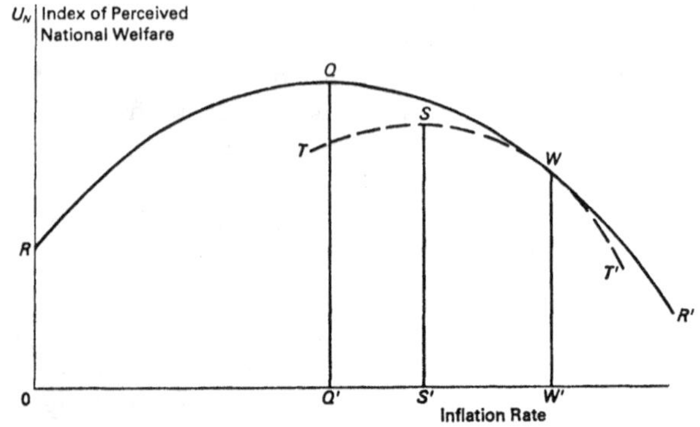

Fig. 2.

goods must then rise slowly enough for this average to be attained given the constraint on the prices of traded goods. This may not present a problem when the share of non-traded goods in the relevant domestic price index is high. Also, it does not present a problem when—as now—the world rate of inflation is high. But if the share of non-traded goods in the index is low and the world rate of inflation is moderate, it might then be necessary for the prices of non-traded goods to fall absolutely to achieve the desired result. And this presents a new constraint. If non-traded goods prices can rise, but not fall, in response to demand management policies there will then be a lower limit to the attainable domestic inflation rate in the fixed rate system, given the world inflation rate. The downward rigidity of non-traded goods may be derived from the downward rigidity of money wages. It may of course not be absolute: at a cost of sufficient unemployment it may be possible to force non-traded prices down over a range.

In Fig. 2 we could interpret the curve TT' broadly to trace out the maximum perceived welfare attainable under the fixed rate system at various inflation rates. The curve will then turn down more sharply as one moves to the left along it from W, and the optimal inflation rate OS' could (but does not have to be) higher than in the absence of this downward-price-rigidity effect. The vertical distance between TW and RW will then indicate not only the costs of excess lending but also the unemployment costs which results because all effects of demand management policies on prices have to be borne in the non-traded sector.

IV. Fixed Rates with Imbalances: The Whole System

Let us now look at "equilibrium" in a fixed exchange rate world of many countries, some inflation-prone and some inflation-shy. (The term "equilibrium" is perhaps not quite accurate since the analysis is short-term and the relevant curves must shift endogenously over time.) Since the reserve currency country might be a special case, let us postpone consideration of it. We thus suppose that there is a given quantity of reserve assets—gold and SDRs—and that there is no reserve currency country.

We start with a given uniform rate of inflation throughout the world, however determined, with optimal autonomous capital movements for all countries, and no accommodating capital movements. Now the inflation-prone countries seek to buy the opportunity of raising their inflation rates closer to their desired rates by "selling" deficits, while the inflation-shy countries similarly seek to sell surpluses (buy deficits). There is a sort of market. If many countries are inflation-prone in relation to the initial world inflation rate or if some very large country is inflation-prone, the average world inflation rate facing the typical country will rise. Thus OW' in Fig. 1 will shift to the right and less borrowing for some countries will be necessary than if the world inflation rate were given at its original level. The equilibrating factors in this market will be the inflation rates in the various countries, the rate of interest on accommodating capital movements and also any non-pecuniary elements affecting this type of capital movement.

It is clear enough that a large country will have a bigger effect on the average world inflation rate facing a particular other country than will any smaller country. And since every country will end up with an inflation rate that is somewhere between this world rate and its own *desired rate*—and may in the long run be quite close to the former—it is true that the large country to some extent "exports" its rate of inflation to the others.

But beyond this one cannot really go. One cannot say that the world rate of inflation will be determined by the inflation-shy rather than the inflation-prone or vice versa. It used to be a popular argument in Britain that the inflation-shy—the excessive deflators—determine the rate of inflation for others (i.e. force deflation on them) because they can and do impose absolute constraints on foreign borrowing by the prone. The shy can then vary their inflation rates at choice, running surpluses if they wished, while the prone are constrained. When the prone try to run inflation rates closer to their desired rates they find that their foreign exchange reserves run out, it becomes harder to borrow, and the potential lenders exert political pressure. The objection to this argument is that increasing real resource losses by the surplus countries in return for low rates of interest *do* present some constraint on continued surpluses, so that they have incentives to reduce their surpluses by inflation.

The alternative, similarly extreme, view, popular at one time in Germany, is that the inflation-prone determine the rate of inflation for the inflation-shy. In this view the inflation-shy are compelled to accept any surplus imposed on them by the inflation-prone at a given rate of interest. But the weapon of the inflation-shy is presumably the rate of interest. If they do not want to run surpluses nor to raise their inflation rates to eliminate these surpluses they can raise interest rates charged to the inflation-prone, hence discouraging the latter from running deficits and forcing them to cut their inflation rates.

In fact, neither the inflation-shy alone nor the inflation-prone alone determine the world equilibrium. Both blades of the scissors play their part.

Looking at the world of inflation-prone and inflation-shy countries together we can see that the possibility of trade imbalances brings mutual gains—in fact "gains from trade". Each can get closer to its desired inflation rate, which is the one it would choose in a flexible rate system. Each gains somewhat more freedom from the opportunity to run imbalances. But assuming that foreign borrowing and lending were originally close to optimal, neither group will actually go as far as it would in a flexible rate system. The inflation-prone country will still inflate less than in the flexible rate system and the inflation-shy country will still inflate more.

It must be stressed that at this stage we are accepting the various governments' social welfare functions. One might well take the view that increasing the freedom of inflation-prone governments to inflate may not really yield gains to countries. But that is another matter, to which we shall return at the end of this paper.

V. The Reserve Currency Country

The reserve currency country is a large country. Therefore, in the fixed rate regime it will have a bigger influence on the world rate of inflation facing other countries than most countries have. Countries that do not wish to "import" the large country's rate of inflation can insulate themselves from it, but only by running surpluses. But these surpluses involve net costs (assuming that foreign lending was initially optimal), so these inflation-shy countries will choose a higher rate of inflation than their *desired* one, this choice being the by-product of the inflation preferences of the large country.

It is a separate question whether even in the short-run it is technically possible for the inflation-shy to insulate themselves from world inflation in a fixed exchange rate regime. This has been much discussed, especially with respect to Germany. In the presence of high international capital mobility insulation through monetary policy may be difficult, so fiscal policy has to be sufficiently flexible. But the point here is that even though full insulation may be *possible* only partial insulation may be perceived by the monetary authorities as being *optimal*.

Is there anything special about the reserve currency country other than that it is an exceptionally large country? One might argue—and this has been a fashionable argument—that the borrowing which it does in its reserve currency capacity is at an exceptionally low rate of interest, lower than the world market rate applying to autonomous capital movements. The net benefit is

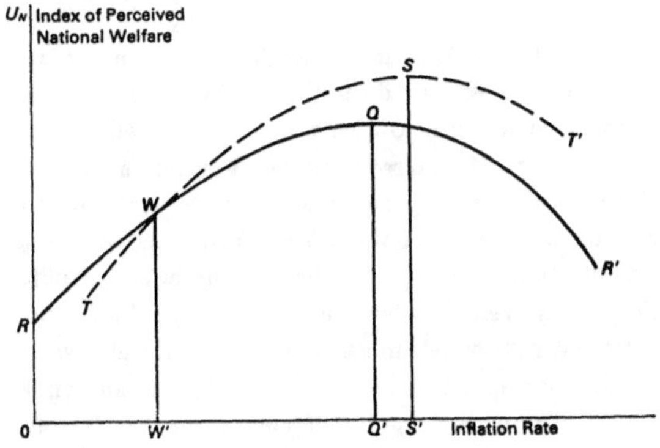

Fig. 3.

seignorage. Thus, given that it can borrow at such a low rate when it practises its reserve currency role, its borrowing is initially—in the absence of the deficit and thus of its reserve currency activities—below the optimum. Even if autonomous borrowing were at the optimum there may then be a net gain from accommodating borrowing. This represents the popular view that the U.S. has been able to obtain real resources from other countries exceptionally cheaply because she was the reserve currency country.

This case, where there is a net gain from a deficit, was referred to earlier and is represented in Fig. 3. The inflation benefit curve with a flexible rate system is RR', as before, and the rest-of-the-world rate of inflation is OW'. The benefit curve with a fixed rate system and with the opportunity to run deficits or surpluses is TWT'. This time TT' cuts RR' at W, instead of being tangential to it, the vertical distance between WR and WT', indicating the net gain from accommodating borrowing, i.e. from seignorage. The optimal inflation rate under the fixed rate regime, OS', is now actually higher than the desired rate under the flexible regime.

There is an implicit assumption in this approach. It is that the reserve currency status of this country is *given*, being quite independent of its rate of inflation. We shall come back to this assumption later.

Given this assumption, the U.S. authorities have then an incentive to engage in monetary and fiscal expansion sufficient to achieve a domestic price inflation rate above the one that would be desired with flexible rates. When there is a net *gain* from a deficit it pays to accept some "excess" price inflation. This means that the possibility of running deficits yields *two* reasons for greater U.S. monetary expansion compared with a flexible rate regime. (We are comparing points S and Q in Fig. 3 here.) Firstly, the extra monetary expansion is needed to produce the payments deficit with the given desired inflation rate OQ', and secondly it is needed to produce the greater rate of domestic price inflation OS'.

If the assumption of a net gain to the U.S. from her deficits is correct we get the interesting result that even when her desired inflation rate under a flexible rate system might have been quite low, she would rationally have chosen a higher inflation rate under a fixed rate regime. For under such a regime she benefits from the reserve currency role and has an opportunity to obtain real resources cheaply from the rest of the world. And since she is a very large economy her own inflation rate will then have a big effect in pulling up the rest of the world's. It is even possible that she pulls up the world rate of inflation above the desired rate which most countries would choose if exchange rates were flexible. In that special case the fixed rate system could be said to be more inflationary from a world point of view than the flexible rate one. But no claim is made here that this was actually so. It has been shown only that popular arguments that world inflation was generated or encouraged by the consequences of the U.S. reserve currency role in the fixed rate system *could* be fitted into the framework of the general model presented here.

Finally, let us come back to the assumption implicit in this analysis that the reserve currency status of the country is given. Presumably the willingness of other countries to hold interest-free deposits of dollars will be reduced by American inflation, but once interest payments are allowed, a rise in the nominal rate of interest can always compensate for expected U.S. inflation. Thus it is not obvious that U.S. inflation must endanger the reserve currency role nor that the real rate of interest she must pay need change because of the inflation. It is true that the continuance of a deficit and accumulation of foreign liabilities faster than general world growth will have this sort of effect (steadily moving the WT' curve in Fig. 3 down over time), but it would not be the result of inflation *per se*, but only of continuous deficits *per se*.

Nevertheless, perhaps one should allow for some kind of rigidity or lags affecting nominal rates, perhaps because market expectations lag behind reality, so that the real rate of interest at which the reserve currency country is borrowing falls the more she inflates. Two conclusions then follow. Firstly, given the reserve currency role, the gains to the U.S. from it will be greater the more she inflates since she will be borrowing more cheaply in real terms. Secondly, the reserve currency role itself will be endangered by her inflation. The first effect will cause curve WT' in Fig. 3 to be higher, encouraging U.S. inflation, while the second effect, if it operates as a threshold effect, may cause the curve suddenly to turn down at some inflation level. The latter effect could operate above or below the desired rate OQ', so that the effect of the reserve currency role could, after all, be to moderate rather than to increase the inflation rate which the U.S. would aim at otherwise. Thus this threshold effect could completely reverse the conclusion above that the U.S. authorities have an incentive to engage in monetary and fiscal expansion sufficient to achieve a domestic price inflation rate above that desired with a flexible rate.[1]

VI. Summary So Far

Can anything be said in summary so far as answer to the principal question posed at the beginning? Are fixed or flexible rates more conducive to inflation? It is clear that the answers are opposite for the inflation-prone and the inflation-shy countries and that this remains true even when one allows countries to have payments imbalances in the fixed rate system. Nothing in general can be said for the world as a whole. But the reserve currency country could conceivably be a special case. It seems possible that it would choose a higher rate of inflation in the fixed rate than in the flexible rate system even though it may be relatively inflation-prone.

VII. Which Regime Is To Be Preferred?

Finally, it seems useful to classify various common views about the relative desirability of the fixed and the flexible regime. This discussion applies also, of course, to the more relevant issue of whether it would be desirable to move along the continuum within these limits, back towards the movable peg, where alterations in exchange rates are reluctant, or foward to more flexibility in the management of the floating system. The position of various observers seems to depend crucially on the view they take about the wisdom of governments and monetary authorities. What follows is, no doubt, a rather obvious classification.

(i) If one is a Fabian and believes that governments know best (or, at least, that they are amenable to good advice) then the flexible system is best. It gives governments maximum freedom. Governments can still borrow and lend, but they can also choose their own inflation rates without having to engage in (otherwise) non-optimal foreign borrowing or lending.[2] A qualification to this

[1] In Mundell (1971) there is an elegant analysis of the relationship between inflation in the reserve currency country and holdings of its currency by other countries. The analysis is along the lines of this paragraph. U.S. inflation (actual and expected) lowers the real value of, and real return on, dollar balances held abroad, and this inflation tax affects the demand for these balances and hence the U.S. deficit. Mundell assumes that dollar balances earn a zero nominal rate for their holders. From this point of view (but ignoring the other considerations stressed in the present paper) there will be an optimum rate for U.S. inflation designed to maximise its seignorage. The argument is also expounded thoroughly in Mundell (1972) where account is taken of the domestic costs of inflation, which the reserve currency country then balances against the seignorage gain to determine the optimum inflation rate.

[2] Why do governments ever commit themselves (or say that they might commit themselves in the future) to a fixed rate regime, since in terms of their perceptions the constraint of a fixed rate seems to reduce national welfare? It is clear from our diagrams that the point Q (the best point attained with a flexible rate) always represents a higher welfare level

is that the fixed rate system may be best for the country that benefits in that system from the reserve currency role—assuming that there is significant seignorage to be derived by it.

(ii) If one believes that governments (or the parliaments that push them) generally have an excessive inflation-bias—a view common in Germany—then the fixed rate system is best for the inflation-prone countries and the flexible rate system best for the inflation-shy. In particular, the fixed rate system acts as a discipline for the inflation-prone.

(iii) Similarly, if one believes that governments have an excessive *de*flation-bias—a view that used to be common in Britain—then the flexible rate system is best for the inflation-prone and the fixed rate system for the inflation-*shy*. The fixed rate system then forces some inflation on the *shy* countries.

(iv) One might broadmindedly believe that the governments of the *prone* countries have an excessive inflation-bias while the governments of the *shy* countries have an excessive deflation-bias. In each case it is excessive from their own points of view. In that case a fixed rate system might be best since it forces each to move in the direction of the other. Of course, one of them might be forced to move too far in the other direction, since we cannot assume that the world inflation that would emerge in the fixed rate system would be just the right one.

(v) If one is an internationalist and prefers international collective decisions, explicit or implicit, the fixed rate system *may* be best. Each individual government is constrained, at least in the longer-run, but the collective governments are not. This view clearly depends on how inflation rates are determined in the fixed rate system, and is particularly relevant when there are some explicit attempts by the main governments to influence each other's policies through O.E.C.D.-style discussions. One might even hope that the system would lead to some explicit and formalised collective decision-making process. This thinking underlies some arguments for European monetary integration, the motive there, of course, being not internationalism but Europeanism.

(vi) If the common inflation rate towards which the system tends in the fixed rate system is essentially determined by a very large, or *the* reserve currency country, then one's view must depend on whether one regards the government of that country to have an excessive inflation or deflation-bias. If one feels that it has just the right bias, then presumably the flexible system would be worse for all other countries, but if the large country has the "wrong" bias, then the flexible system would be better for some and worse for others.

---

than the point S (the best point attainable with a fixed rate)—except possibly in the reserve currency country case. Perhaps the commitments of governments to exchange rate fixity are never absolute for this very reason. Perhaps official advocates of fixed rate regimes do not see the issues clearly. Perhaps some politicians or officials are trying to impose constraints on other politicians or officials, even in their own country. And, of course, there are sectional interests within a country that may at times benefit from exchange rate rigidity.

Postscript

Some time after completing this paper I realised (thanks to John Black, and after reading R. I. McKinnon, *Private and Official International Money: The Case for the Dollar*, Princeton Essay in International Finance, 1969) that there may be an unjustified implication in one of the arguments, namely that the U.S. reserve currency role goes with a fixed rate system but disappears with flexible rates. But this is clearly not so: we are now in a world of managed floating, and the dollar is as popular an international asset as ever. The main argument is simply that *given the reserve currency role* the U.S. may have an incentive to get other countries to accumulate dollars because of the supposed seignorage effect, and in a fixed rate system, but not a flexible rate one, the U.S. can encourage this by more domestic inflation.

References

Branson, W. H.: Monetarist and Keynesian models of the transmission of inflation. *American Economic Review, Papers and Proceedings 65*, No. 2, 115–119, 1975.

Caves, R. E.: Looking at inflation in the open economy. Harvard Institute of Economic Research Discussion Paper No. 286, March 1973.

Fried, J.: Inflation–unemployment trade-offs under fixed and floating exchange rates. *Canadian Journal of Economics 6*, No. 1, 43–52, 1973.

Krause, L. & Salant, W. (eds.): *Worldwide Inflation*. Brookings Institution, Washington (forthcoming).

Mundell, R. A.: *Monetary Theory*. Goodyear Publishing Co., Pacific Palisades, 1971.

Mundell, R. A.: The optimum balance of payments deficit. In E. Claassen and P. Salin (eds.), *Stabilization Policies in Interdependent Economies*. North-Holland Publishing Co., Amsterdam, 1972.

Turnovsky, S. J. & Kaspura, A.: An analysis of imported inflation in a short-run macro-economic model. *Canadian Journal of Economics 7*, No. 3, 355–380, 1974.

COMMENT ON W. M. CORDEN, "INFLATION AND THE EXCHANGE RATE REGIME"

Ephraim Kleiman

Hebrew University, Jerusalem, Israel

Appropriately enough for a paper scheduled for the close of this seminar, Corden's paper, like the one by Claassen, looks for the moral of the whole discussion: Will flexible rates result in higher inflation rates than those experienced in a fixed-exchange-rates world? Conventional wisdom of the sort expounded in elementary economics courses tells us that the answer will be positive; by abolishing the penalty of current-account deficits, reserve-depletion crises, etc., flexible rates remove a constraint on governmental behaviour. This implies that the balance-of-payments penalty constitutes the only effective constraint on the desire of governments to inflate. However, as Corden points out, given the existence of some internal constraints as well, the difference between the two regimes need not be so great. In particular, there being also a penalty—overinvestment abroad—for inflating too little under a fixed exchange rate, some countries may actually inflate less under a flexible one.

The cornerstone of Corden's argument is the inflation–benefit relationship as perceived by governments. To judge by their revealed preferences, the shape which he ascribes to this relationship is probably the right one. Nevertheless, it seems that no firm conclusions can be reached without an explicit specification of the policy objectives which underlie governmental attitudes towards inflation.

The curve OR in Corden's diagrams should be interpreted as showing inflation benefits when there are no balance-of-payments considerations (and *not* of those in an economy trading under flexible rates). And OW' is the domestic rate of inflation at which, given the world rate of inflation, there will be no pressures on the balance of payments. The greater the divergence between the actual domestic inflation and OW', the greater will be these pressures. Under a fixed exchange rate they will result in balance-of-payments deficits or surpluses, whose non-optimality as borrowing or investment is described by the curve TT' lying below OR. Under a flexible rate, this pressure will result in depreciations or appreciations of the exchange rate. These affect the domestic income distribution. Assuming the distribution at W to be regarded as optimal by the government, any departure from it will counterbalance whatever other benefits it may have ascribed to inflation. In this case, the inflation–benefit relationship under a flexible exchange rate should be described by a curve tangent to OR at W, and lying *below* it at all other points. Consequently, the difference between the optimum rates of inflation under the two regimes will be even smaller than in Corden's Figures I and II (and may even reverse its sign).

There is, of course, nothing sacred about the income distribution at W. Suppose instead that the government attaches high distributional weights to the real incomes of factors specific to the production of nontradables, and that the consumption of these factors has a high import content. Then, the more rapidly the exchange rate depreciates, the greater the worsening in the distribution from the government's point of view. If this precisely offsets the increase in the other benefits of inflation then, under a flexible exchange rate, the net benefit will be invariant to the rate of inflation up to the point OQ' in Corden's diagram, and will decrease thereafter. More plausibly, the flexible-rate curve may cut OR at W from above, so that the corresponding optimum inflation rate will be smaller than OW. Thus, under a flexible rate the government, to use Corden's term, may be inflation-shy, even if under a fixed rate it is inflation-prone (i.e., $OS' > OW'$). On the other hand, if the distributional weights attached to this group are low, exchange depreciation will be regarded as beneficial, and the same government will be inflation-prone under a flexible, as well as under a fixed, exchange rate.

Thus, the propensity of governments to inflate cannot be taken as given and invariant to the exchange-rate regime. Rather, it should be regarded as a function of the latter. The inflation–benefits relationship under flexible rates cannot really be ascertained before we know what are the factors underlying it when there are no balance-of-payments considerations. Or, to put it differently, the conclusions Corden is searching for in his paper cannot be established without answering the question which he has kept asking throughout this seminar: Why do governments inflate?

GENERAL DISCUSSION: WHAT HAVE WE LEARNED? WHERE ARE THE FUNDAMENTAL CONFLICTS OF OPINION?*

Stanley Black: Let me start by talking about what I see as the main things that we have learned. The papers of the last two days have brought us a considerable amount of understanding about (1) the relationship between *stocks and flows*, i.e. that the exchange rate is determined in the short run by equilibrium in markets for stocks of assets denominated in different currencies and in the long run by flow equilibrium in goods markets as indicated by purchasing power parity in the markets for traded goods. (2) Concerning the short-run equilibrium, we have learned about the relationship between, on the one hand, a *monetary analysis of exchange rates* focusing on the demands and supplies of different kinds of moneys, and on the other hand what has more generally been called an *asset analysis of exchange rates* focussing on the willingness to hold existing stocks of assets denominated in different currencies. The existing stocks of securities can only be changed (net) by flows of saving and investment, which take time. The existing amount of domestic holdings of foreign exchange can only be changed (net) by trade or service flows, which also take time. From the balance of payments we know that the current account plus the capital account—the items above the line—must equal the reserve flows below the line. The monetary approach observes the fact that under pure floating exchange rates, reserve movements and thus changes in the foreign component of the monetary base are zero. So the monetarists focus on the demands and supplies of moneys. The asset approach observes the *equivalent fact* that the capital account must balance the pre-determined current account, that existing stocks of assets must be held. From an analytical point of view they must give identical results. I think the papers of Rudi Dornbusch and Pentti Kouri in particular have helped us to relate these approaches. (3) I also think we have learned a lot about the relationship between the *short-run conditions of exchange rate behavior* and the *long-run conditions of equilibrium*. Kouri has demonstrated how the short-run analysis has to converge to a long-run equilibrium that is related to purchasing power parity and to the underlying monetary and real factors discussed by Dornbusch. These aspects of the discussion have, perhaps, been dominated by technical

* Edited by Lars Calmfors and Clas Wihlborg, Institute for International Economic Studies, Stockholm, Sweden

considerations: What is the proper method of analysis? How can we get our analysis straight? This is an important and useful preliminary for us in trying to deal with and understand the system of floating exchange rates and exchange rate systems in general.

There are other issues which have been raised and which are important, too. Particularly *the problem of risk* and the behavior of firms and the effects of increased exchange risk on international trade. This was raised in Aliber's paper and is clearly an important issue. Then there is the *issue of policy:* What kinds of policies do governments follow under one or another type of exchange rate system? This makes me think of Max Corden's questions and his reasons for increases in the money supply.[1] This is a large issue about exchange rate systems that need to be thoroughly explored. Corden has made some effort on that in his paper, as has Claassen.

Having tried to integrate and synthesize, let me make a few points of possible controversy. There has been something of a tendency for the monetarist participants to try to be iconoclastic. That is probably a good thing because it makes us all think. But sometimes we may go too far and just cause confusion. Let me wonder about a couple of points raised by that approach.

Let me first point out that I think that the monetary approach has a considerable value in *focusing on simple relationships* which are very useful for answering certain questions. However, these questions are not always the questions that policy makers are interested in. When they *are* the right questions, then the monetary approach—in the sense of looking at the items below the line, at the money equation itself—is the right approach. I am reminded of my conversation with some people at the Federal Reserve a few months ago, when they said that they stopped listening to monetarists when they learned that monetarists could not tell them anything about the current account or the capital account separately, i.e. that monetarists could not tell them about anything above the line. The policy makers are inevitably interested in those factors, but the monetary approach is not useful for the analysis of these questions, as many points are hidden. But I think what we have really

[1] During the seminar, Max Corden raised the issue of the determinants of the money supply, usually treated as exogenous by the monetarists. He suggested the following classification of reasons for inflationary increases in money supply:

(1) Government deficit financing through money creation because an inflation tax on money is preferred to explicit taxes.

(2) Employment stimulation involving movement along a short-run Phillips curve, which Modigliani later divided into: (2a) Active demand management at given money wages, (2b) Accommodating increases in the money supply in order to prevent unemployment from arising after high wage increases.

(3) Insufficient and lagged sterilization measures by monetary authorities when there are money flows via the balance of payments.

(4) Increases in the money supply in order to bring about an income redistribution within the private sector.

(5) Discretionary increases in the money supply in order to eliminate balance-of-payments surpluses.

(6) Intellectual fads, such as monetary expansions designed supposedly to foster growth (cf. e.g. the UK).

learned is that we can do it either way. For some questions you want to do it one way and for other questions you want to do it another way, and it is probably even wise to do it both ways.

Finally, I should like to make a more specific comment on how the model in John Williamson's paper is related to the other models, since there was considerable discussion on this point earlier. I will try to show this very quickly. The two equations below come from Kouri's paper.

$$F = F\left(\pi, Y, \frac{M}{P} + F\right)$$

$$\dot{F} = B = Y - C\left(Y - T, \frac{M}{P} + F\right) - G$$

where F = Holdings of foreign assets
π = The expected change in the exchange rate
Y = Real output
M = Money stock
P = The exchange rate
B = The current account position
C = Consumption
T = Taxes
G = Government spending

The first equation shows the stock demand for foreign assets as a function of the expected rate of change in the exchange rate, real income and total holdings of assets. The second equation shows that the rate of change in foreign holdings of assets is equal to the current account, which in turn is equal to income minus expenditure, where expenditure is a function of real disposable income and total asset holdings.

Williamson's model has two equations that are important here.

$$K = K(\pi)$$

$$\Delta K + C(P) = 0$$

where K = Net holdings of foreign assets
ΔK = Decrease in net holdings of foreign assets
C = The current account position
P = The exchange rate.

The first one is an asset-stock equation that depends upon the expected change in the exchange rate, and the second one is a balance-of-payments equation, which says that the change in the stock of assets plus the current account has to be equal to zero in the absence of intervention under flexible exchange rates. The current account is a function of the exchange rate.[1]

[1] John Williamson explains the current account as a stochastic function of the exchange rate and the capital account as a separate stochastic function of the expected exchange

I think it is fairly obvious that these two views are not too far apart. The difference is that the monetary factor is clear in the first one, whereas it is not clear in the second one, but it is *implicitly* there. That is easy to see, because one knows that this model has a long-run equilibrium where the exchange rate is equal to its long-run equilibrium value, which is clearly related to purchasing power parity. The first model has a long run equilibrium where the exchange rate is proportional to M, which also corresponds to long-run purchasing power parity, so I do not really think that this is hard to see.

Rudiger Dornbusch: This conference has shown considerable agreement in our thinking about exchange rate determination and I should like to summarize that agreement very broadly under four points:

(1) In principle the exchange rate is determined by the *general equilibrium*, stock and flow, of the relevant model.
(2) Specifically, asset markets are important.
(3) Among the asset markets it is unobjectionable to single out the money market as the center of analysis.
(4) Independent of school of thought, capital mobility and expectations are of critical importance in the determination of exchange rates.

At the level of generality at which our agreement is summarized, there is little scope for differences of opinion. The scope for disagreement arises when we make the relevant general equilibrium model operational and specific to the questions we are addressing. Here I see three major areas of disagreement or misunderstanding.

Considerable differences of opinion arise with respect to the appropriate level of *aggregation*. Specifically, the number of commodities, the number of assets and the number of countries that should be part of a "reasonable" model remains a major element of disagreement. Such disagreement reflects only in part the fact that different models are designed to elucidate different questions. More importantly, it reflects in many instances differences of opinion about the nature of the transmission and repercussion mechanism in the real world. It is not simply the fact that someone who is interested in the terms of trade is poorly served by a one-commodity model. Much more likely, it is disagreement about empirical regularities that may or not characterize the operation of the economy. Those who believe that prices are determined by wages with a constant profit mark-up will be less interested in a model that

rate. During the discussion of this paper, Mussa noted that Williamson's approach is *identical* to the monetarists' approach except that Williamson has *two independent* stochastic terms while monetarists have only *one*. The reason is that if the money demand function is stable, a drain of money via the current account must give rise to a corresponding surplus on the capital account. Therefore, only one stochastic term for the balance of payments is needed. On this, one participant noted that Mussa's conclusion rests on *perfect capital mobility*. Another participant noted that in Williamson's paper nothing prevents *any degree of correlation* and furthermore Williamson *has* introduced the possibility of such correlation. The question was left unresolved at this point.

places emphasis on the relative price of home goods than someone who believes that this particular relative price varies systematically with the level of absorption and indeed is a key link between spending and the trade balance. Such disagreement is substantive and can only be resolved by recourse to the facts. It must be distinguished from a concern for "generality" for which I have little sympathy. The useful insights we derive from theoretical structures are inversely related to their complexity. The rule should therefore be a very high level of aggregation that should only be departed from when strong empirical regularities indicate otherwise.

An important further area of disagreement arises from differences in our assessment of the *short-run operation of the economy*. In that short run we will be prepared to depart both from the behavioral equations and equilibrium properties of a full general equilibrium model. We have, however, preferences as to which particular markets we wish to clear and where we prefer to see slow adjustment. Some will want to clear asset markets, and specifically the money market, continuously. Others would emphasize that the trade supply and demand equations hold in the short run in order to use a balance of payments equation for the short run determination of exchange rates. It might be argued that there is a preference for a balance of payments equation because, under flexible rates and in the absence of intervention, the latter must be equal to zero. That argument is obviously incorrect because in the short run we may well have involuntary changes in foreign exchange inventories. There are, no doubt, similarities in the two approaches since they will have a similar treatment of portfolio preferences and expectations in their effect on capital movements. I doubt, however, that the similarities go much further and that, in fact, the alternative models could be shown to be exactly equivalent unless one of the relevant equations was a reduced form that embodied the conditions of equilibrium in all other markets.

This leads me to comment on a further source of misunderstanding, more than disagreement. Occasionally we see *reduced form equations* used in the determination of exchange rates. Their use is particularly widespread in empirically oriented work. The trouble we have with these reduced form equations is that we do not know exactly what system and what implicit set of policies gives rise to them. We *do* know that one can supplement a particular reduced form with an appropriate macroeconomic framework that allows a specific interpretation of the coefficients and reconciles the predictions with constraints placed on policies and private behavior. Failing such an explicit macroeconomic model, however, a reduced form equation for the balance of payments is really quite useless because we will not be able to identify what the coefficients mean and what policies are required to generate the effects predicted by the equation. The monetary approach to the balance of payments, or perhaps we should simply say the general equilibrium approach, owes much of its attraction to being quite explicit about the structure of the economy and about monetary policy. This quarrel with reduced form is obviously not new. In fact, it was the very point Alexander raised in his decisive treatment of the current account. The point will keep coming up for the simple reason that these reduced form models, using the Fleming shortcut, betray a very interesting and useful modeling of the conomy and of built-in policies that in the end nobody is at odds with, but that we all have to rediscover from a general equilibrium perspective.

I should like to turn next to more specific issues in the analysis of stabilization policy under flexible rates that have been thrown up at this conference. We have made some progress in thinking about stabilization policy under flexible rates. Among the ideas that were given emphasis is the notion that in the short run, because of a lack of homogeneity in the response of prices or expectations to purely nominal disturbances, there will be some potential for international transmission of nominal disturbances under flexible rates. Induced macroeconomic policies, designed to mitigate the real effects of these imported disturbances, in turn will serve to validate imported price level disturbances and cause money and prices to move together on an international level.

A second feature of stabilization policy under flexible rates and capital mobility pertains to the role of the traded goods sector in the adjustment process. The idea is that the traded goods sector is particularly sensitive to monetary policy, much like housing construction, and will therefore absorb a major part of cyclical adjustment policies. The mechanism by which monetary policy affects specifically the traded goods sector is not so much interest sensitivity of spending in that sector, but rather the effect of monetary changes on the exchange rate and thereby on international price level differentials. A monetary contraction will in the first instance induce a sharp appreciation in the spot rate and thereby cause domestic commodities to become overpriced relative to foreign goods. This applies across the board to all traded goods and therefore will immediately exert a deflationary effect on the traded goods sector. Thus, even in the absence of any interest response of aggregate demand, monetary policy does exert a strong effect on the demand for domestic output by inducing international price differentials and therefore substitution effects. While this avenue will speed up the real effects of monetary policy, it will also imply that it will tend to be quite transitory. The international price connection will exert strong pressure on the prices of traded goods and will cause changes in money to be more rapidly matched by changes in prices. In this perspective, monetary policy becomes primarily a tool for short-run management of aggregate demand or price pressure in an economy.

Four problem areas are left open for further thinking. The first pertains to the proper modeling of capital movements. Specifically, whether to treat domestic and foreign assets as highly substitutable, or on the contrary, to give emphasis to imperfect substitutability and perhaps considerable emphasis to institutional aspects of credit market policies. The second set of issues concerns the concept of capital movements, the question whether there is an independent capital flow function, or whether on the contrary, there are market equilibrium conditions for each asset with the current account specifying the equilibrium rate of capital flows. The third problem concerns the treatment of risk in modeling asset markets. That question is of considerable importance because it has implications not only for the relationship between forward rates and expected future spot rates, but also for the scope of forward market intervention by the monetary authorities.[1] A last issue to be raised concerns the very short-run pricing of foreign exchange. An interesting area here is the modeling of that pricing process including the behavior of inventory holders in foreign exchange. The object of that research would be to throw light on the considerable short-run variability in exchange rates.

Franco Modigliani: I have come here to learn about the latest fad in trade theory—the so-called "monetary" approach to the balance of payments and to figure out whether there is after all a basic difference between monetary and "non-monetary" analysis. My preliminary conclusion is that there is a high correlation between the two approaches (when used by good craftsmen), even though it is not perfect. As far as I can see, all the fuss about the monetary approach and about stocks versus flows boils down to a couple of issues. One is the question of purchasing power parity and the role of the money supply. I can hardly see that there can be much dissent among economists on this issue. Whether purchasing power parity holds precisely or not, we can agree on the very general proposition that, in the long run, the price level will be roughly proportional to the quantity of money after adjustments for productivity and population growth (and changes in money holding habits). This will be a good approximation, particularly if the money supply does nice things like multiplying by ten. I mean that if the money supply is increased tenfold, proportionality would be a good approximation for what would happen to the price level. I do not think there can be much disagreement about this, given time enough. *How long* it takes is another issue and will depend upon many other things intervening. I am inclined to think of the purchasing power parity in exactly the same vein. The foreign exchange rate, the price of foreign exchange, is a price and as all other prices it will be largely proportional to the quantity of money adjusted as before, particularly if the rest of the world is very conveniently keeping its price level constant. If it is not, then you have to adjust for *its* behavior. I think that this proposition would be roughly true even though there might be some marginal shifts in the ratio of traded goods to non-traded goods. Certainly, this will give you some idea about the long run.

[1] On this issue see Kouri, P.: Essays on the Theory of Flexible Exchange Rates. Unpublished Dissertation, Massachusetts Institute of Technology, 1975.

Now the other part of the proposition is the proposition about *stocks and flows*. It simply says that if we do have free and competitive exchange markets and free capital movements, then obviously the exchange rate cannot be determined by the value of goods exported this minute versus the amount of goods imported this minute. It will not be the case that the exchange rate is going to do wild gyrations to equate the demand and supply every second. If everybody knows that the price is going to be higher a minute later, they will be willing to hold infinite amounts of foreign exchange for one minute until the price changes. Indeed, if there is no interest rate differential, one can see that as a very good approximation, the exchange rate today must be roughly what it is expected to be tomorrow. One can introduce three months instead of a day and one can introduce interest rate differentials. Then one gets the proposition about the interest rate differential being equal to the covered spread. That relation must hold well in any kind of free market. There could be interferences, but if one operates in a free market one will get that proposition. If that is all there is in the monetary approach, then I think that is fine and I do not think there could be much controversy.

Aside from these issues, listening to the so-called monetary approach, I have noticed that there is a certain set of *pet* assumptions that they prefer to make in their models. Each of us makes assumptions in building a model. Monetarists seem to have a certain set of assumptions, such as the small country assumption, there being only *one good* or at most two goods, and the traded good being exactly the same as the goods in the rest of the world. Some of these assumptions strike some of us in the older tradition as somewhat odd, because we were used to thinking that the essence of international trade was that the kinds of things we bought were different from the things we sold, as Bill Branson reminded us earlier. In that kind of world, price elasticities become important for the balance of payments. For instance, Dornbusch is very punctilious about the effect of substitution between home goods—the lack of perfect substitution between domestic and traded goods—so that if you shift the output between the two, the ratio changes. But the older tradition was very insistent on the demand effect, the price elasticity of demand, and not so concerned about the change in the terms of trade between the domestic and traded goods. It is of course clear that in the real world both things should be taken into account and I think *ought to* be taken into account. I think Dornbusch has pointed that out very well by saying that everything really matters for the exchange rate.

The *really interesting issues* begin when we start to study adjustment paths in response to disturbances. I think we have had a number of papers at this conference which have been quite helpful. I have learned a lot from Dornbusch's paper in particular. It gives a simple, neat model for thinking about these problems. The stress on expectations in his and other people's models follows from what I said before. If today's exchange rate cannot be very different from the expected exchange rate, then what matters is in fact the expected exchange rate.

It seems to me that Dornbusch has also brought up one issue that should perhaps have received more attention in this conference. That is the question of how well flexible exchange rates work in terms of *insulating the economy* from various disturbances. In his model I found it particularly attractive that he analysed the response to a change in the outside price level. Particularly attractive, because it did show that unless speculators were infinitely wise and immediately jumped to the equilibrium rate, an increase in foreign prices would cause a rise in domestic prices. Though domestic prices have risen initially, you would eventually get back to the original price level if you held to the same money supply: the exchange rate would eventually change in proportion to foreign prices. But if there is anything less than perfect price flexibility, that process of price reduction is going to involve unemployment. I think we are going to find ourselves in the position where the Central Bank will most likely, and I suggest wisely, decide to let the money supply rise and accomodate the higher price level, at least to some extent. That really goes back to the questions that were raised by Corden about *why the money supply rises.*[1]

I have just one remark to make about what Max Corden mentioned as one of the reasons the money supply rises, namely, deficit financing. I would like to stress that in the United States there is no relation between deficit financing and money supply. There is just no reason whatever why deficit financing should give rise to a money supply increase. The Treasury does one thing and the Federal Reserve does another, so that in principle the problem is the failure of monetary policy to adjust to the fiscal policy in the right way. Of course, there are interactions to the extent that the Central Bank has interest rate targets.

Finally, in connection with the analysis of comparative systems, I think that we have had a very interesting beginning here. I think Aliber's paper is really quite important. Jaffee's discussion and the discussion that followed raised a number of issues to which I still do not have a clear answer in my mind. But, certainly, Aliber's evidence on exchange rates' variability around purchasing power parity—during floating—seemed to be quite suggestive of the fact that there are some real costs associated with flexible exchange rates. Of course, there are unfortunately also a lot of costs associated with fixed exchange rates, when the long-run equilibrium is inconsistent with the fixed exchange rate. Then one finds oneself in the painful position of having to do something about it in the form of deflationary policies.

There is one other element that is interesting. We have had a lot of talk here about the flexible exchange rates in the context of one small country.

---

[1] See the footnote on page 255.

One of the interesting things is that, by and large, small countries do not, in fact, float. If one looks around the world, one will find that what floats are blocks, but that most small countries are in fact tied to larger blocks by a more or less fixed exchange rate. No one has really analysed why this is so. In other words, the papers we have here do not throw any light on why governments and countries choose to do so. If one is willing to assume that speculators have rational expectations, and there must be some rationality in expectations, then I think that one must also be willing to assume that there must be some rationality in this choice.

Let me close with a final point about analysing alternative systems. Of course, no one need worry at the moment about fixed-forever exchange rates. It has worked remarkably well for a while—though I do not know why. But now it is over and I do not think it will come back until we are all dead and a new generation comes up that has forgotten. So I do not think we need to be concerned with that. The choice is really between various kinds of managed exchange rates, i.e. between various limitations on the rate at which exchange rates may change.

It seems to me that there is one important thing that needs to be done. One has to take into account the obligations that a system imposes on the participants. One would not suppose that the money supply would behave in the same way in a system of fixed exchange rates as it would in a system of floating exchange rates. One would not assume that it would behave in the same way if there was some limitation to the float—to the extent of variability of the exchange rates—as if there was no such limitation. In fact, one of the cases that can be made for a certain amount of fixity, is that it does tell speculators that the participants have taken an obligation to make things run reasonably smoothly. Of course, if they make impossible commitments, then speculators will and should disreagard the commitments, but if the commitments are credible I think that this might be one important element in the picture. In particular, one might hope for stabilizing speculation, helping the authority to maintain short-run stability.

Robert Mundell: As an opening comment, I would say that I do think that countries always monetize a portion of any budget—they monetize that because they do not want to see the price of government bonds go down. If they cannot sell the bonds, they cannot maintain the credibility of the government. Governments always insist upon the central bank accepting to buy up some bonds. They need something to give the commercial banks, something to support the price of government bonds. I do think that budget deficits become important in that connection in establishing the rate of monetary expansion.

Max Corden gave a list of several reasons why the rate of monetary expansion changes. I agree with them all. While he was talking, I added three or four more, a couple of which I thought were more important in some sense or at least as important as any of the others. First, one reason for monetary expansion is to *deflate away a part of the public debt*. That is the important factor in distinguishing between countries which are inflationary compared to countries that are not inflationary. Inflation-prone countries tend to be countries that have large public debts. By the increase in the rate of monetary expansion, one automatically changes the unit of account in which all debts are contracted.

I remember talking to Alexander Kafka from Brazil, who in 1966 was running for Executive Director for the I.M.F. He gave a discussion of the Brazilian inflation. The new government decided that they were going to stop inflation, but that they could not stop it at the current price level. They had to let the price level go up by 60 % before they would stabilize it, because they had just given a 60 % increase in government salaries. These had to be inflated away, before the government could stabilize. The motive for changing the value of the unit of account has to do with distribution policy, public debt policy and attempts to inflate away excessive money wage increases.

Furthermore, I think that another important factor behind monetary expansion, which has come in since 1973, is the belief in the need to inflate away the effects of the oil price increases. When the oil prices went up by four times, there was a general recognition that the result was intolerable. We were in a period of floating exchange rates during most of that period, but there was a huge jump in international monetary reserves, sufficient by and large to pay for a good part of the increased oil bills to oil countries. Now, I know that it is self-defeating in the long run, because that in turn induces anger and an attempt to raise the oil price again and that leads to more inflation in the system.

Fifteen years ago, C. P. Snow started talking about the great gap between art and science as two solitudes that could not get together and did not talk to one another. In a sense it is beginning to be a little bit true in economics too, where policy makers and scientists do not talk enough. If the economic theorist's ear is not tuned into the real world, he misses something and we get into the problem that he is not very helpful. He ceases to be listened to and loses his power because he does not contribute to the discussion.

I think that to a certain extent realism in models has to increase. We have now got an enormous proliferation of models—and they are good ones—but we have got too many models. I believe that we should have only *one* model. I think that the discussion should be based on a really strong model. What model is relevant for Sweden? What model is relevant for the United States? All countries are different, of course, but there are some general principles we can lay down about the kinds of policies that should be followed. But in the real world we have to begin to get to the question of what the policy should be.

Should we have fixed or flexible exchange rates? Here I come to a disagreement with Modigliani, who said that it is just laughable to think of fixed exchange rates in the present world. In one sense—with all the exchange rates floating—I can see why he, in looking at the world from his vantage point in the United States, does not see fixed rates as reasonable. Yet, as I look at things in my way, I think it is really eminently reasonable to contemplate that question again, because I do not look at *n* or 150 different exchange rates. I look at *one* exchange rate in the world today. Just as I would look at one or two, 50 or 75 years ago, I think. The exchange rate I would look at today would be the D mark–dollar rate. I really think that if the mark–dollar rate were fixed, almost all the other rates would fall into place. Sweden, I am sure, would like not to have to cope with the dilemma of changes in the dollar–mark parity. That creates a problem if one rate goes up and the other rate goes down. What does Sweden do? Britain has the same problem. The pound–dollar rate used to be the important rate, but in the 20th century, Germany has been a more important country than Britain, within the context here. And remember that when economic historians look back, they say that in 1925 the key thing was that Britain went back to the old parity of the pound and the dollar. I do not believe that. I believe that the important thing, even in the 1920's, was the fixing of the dollar–reichmark rate. The new reichmark had been introduced, and Germany was already beginning to be more important than Britain was. Anyway, Britain, Germany and the United States were all important in the 1920's. When the exchange rates between these countries became fixed again, there was a band-wagon effect in all countries, though from 1915 to 1924 it was a world of flexible exchange rates like today.

When one important rate gets fixed or two important rates get fixed, there is a band-wagon effect and everybody tends to fall into place. If Mr Ford and Mr Schmidt got together and decided to fix the mark–dollar rate and supported this until we got over the depression, I think that the other rates would fall back into place. I am not saying that that is necessarily a good thing, because there are many political issues. The United States can well afford to move along as a big island in this world, and whether it gives up more than it gains in some sense by having a fixed exchange rate is an open question. But the biggest country always loses more sovereignty by committing its external policy, so I think the problem is one of getting the United States to go along with fixed rates. However, if the United States would accept that amount of internationalism, the other rates would fall into place.

On the theoretical level, I have some comments to make. I agree with what Stanley Fischer and others said—and I know you all agree—that all systems are part of the general equilibrium, but that we look for partial systems that are relevant and important. *Within* that general equilibrium system we select them, by certain rationing principles, namely, Walras' Law and the homogeneity postulate.

If models depart from the homogeneity postulate, we should say so, because most people accept *that*, or at least some version of it, as a part of economic theory. But the homogeneity postulate has two children. One is the quantity theory of money, and the other is purchasing power parity on the international scene. That is an axiom so to speak, and we can all accept it. But the interpretation of the axiom is still a question. Are we going to say that we have money illusion in it? Or are there rigidities in wages, bond prices or in something else in the system? Then we have another variation. But, in my opinion, there is a far deeper implication of the homogeneity postulate, and that has to do with the difference between the Walrasian system and the Keynesian system. The most important difference from an abstract point of view is, as I see it, the homogeneity postulate or rather two interpretations of the homogeneity postulate. The Walrasian system and all calssical systems back to Ricardo have one interpretation. If you double all prices, all money supplies and all other asset supplies, no real magnitudes will be changed. *All* prices in the classical model are both spot *and* forward prices, but in the Keynesian model there are *only spot* prices. For that reason, the Keynesian system is not, and should not be, homogeneous. There are inelastic expectations and forward prices are fixed. That is the origin of the liquidity approach to the interest rate. It means that if you change prices, you can expect the prices to come back down. There is an automatic real effect that has to do with the purchasing power of money, not over present goods, but over all future goods.

The most important sentence that, I think, exists in the General Theory is: "Money is that thing which links the present to the future". The origin of that comes through Keynes' concept of the homogeneity postulate, which is that forward prices are given in the system. That is the Keynesian world, which *is* a very relevant world and *was* a very realistic world in his day. What he saw was the big downward movement of prices in the 1930's, which occurred because prices had gone up with the war in the late 1910's and also in the 1920's. They went up, and then they went down.

When prices go up, why do they tend to come down? Historically, they did not always do that. They have done that since the world went onto the gold standard, since the 1660's. But I am not taking that as a date for when the gold standard started. There is a beautiful chart that was prepared in the 1950's and later developed, which goes back 300 years. There is a steady, perfectly nonrhythmic trend of the price of gold in terms of sterling up until the gold standard ended; three hundred years of price stability until 1934 when there is a big jump. Today we are off in a new world.

I come back to what Max Corden said, and to a comment that I think Bob Gordon tried to make with regard to Corden's question. He said, "I would just change your question. Not ask why money goes up, but ask what prevents money from going up more." Well, the cost of producing money under the gold standard is the cost of producing gold. The value of money was determined by the production costs of gold. That put a lid on the monetary expansion under the gold standard. On a paper standard, on the other hand, one has to ask what prevents money from going up. For a small country, the fixed exchance rate prevented it from going up. In the larger countries like the United States, it was the Central Bank that prevented money from going up, because it did not want too much inflation. But in the world economy today, we lack, for the first time in thousands of years, something which can prevent money from going up. That, which historically always made it stop growing, has stopped making it stop growing. Even in the world of the dollar standard from 1944 to 1971, one always had *convertibility into gold*. There was, at least up until 1960 and up until 1965 in the United States, something which put the lid on the money supply. Now that lid is taken off, and we move into an anarchy where the only thing that stops the money supply from going up is Arthur Burns in the United States and the desire to avoid inflation in other countries. On the other side of Arthur Burns, there is President Ford and the pressure from the trade unions. From the international side there is the pressure to finance oil deficits and to stop the unemployment in Germany and in the United States. There is the side issue that will be a pressure upon Ford or Burns again, which is the fact that for the first time we have got two general elections coming up next year in the most important countries in the Western World: the United States and Germany. One has to sail past 1976 with a low level of unemployment, which means that the rate of monetary expansion will be high.

Finally I just want to comment on what we said about inflation and the exchange rate. What exchange rate? A small country, by virtue of being small, has *n* exchange rates. Are we talking about the average of them? Or are we talking about one or two important rates? One has to say which of those two it is and then one has to ask the question: What happens to the rest of the world? How can one explain the exchange rate by the money supply in *one* country, if the exchange rate is a relation between two monies? One does not have a full system, because in such a system one has to abandon some form of the small economy assumptions. When one gets two economies in the picture, one has to impose the question: are the countries of the same size transaction-wise? Or are they a *big* country and a *little* country? We have varying dominance relations. The dynamics will be conditioned by the size of the country, because the speeds of adjustment in the dynamic equations we are writing will be proportional to sizes. The rate of change in the exchange rate of one country *vis-à-vis* another country is proportional to the excess supply of money in one country minus the excess demand for money in the other country.

Ronald McKinnon: In view of the profusion of theoretical models, if I were an international banker or a policy maker, I would be hard pressed to come up with any clear-cut new ideas regarding how to make the system work more smoothly.

I would like to offer a pratical suggestion regarding the way in which the international capital market works, and its importance for the flexible exchange-rate system. In this respect, our attitude towards what used to be called hot money flows is very important. From their experience in the 1930's, economists such as Ragnar Nurkse were very hostile to short-term capital movements. This was more or less built into the I.M.F. charter under Bretton Woods, where convertibility was explicitly defined to exclude short-term capital movements (aside from the extension of ordinary trade credit). Many economists of our present generation, like Richard Cooper, have quite freely considered capital controls a potential policy instrument for promoting this or that domestic goal.

In contrast, I would submit that the free mobility of short-term capital is essential for the flexible exchange-rate system to work with tolerable efficiency. The flexible exchange-rate system is different in this regard from fixed rates, where the Central Bank had the ultimate responsibility of clearing international payments. We now have private commercial banks that clear forward and spot transactions and are responsible for covering and hedging. An open and unregulated capital market permits the commercial banks to undertake this function. Just by great good fortune—rather than planning—the unregulated Euro-currency market was fully developed at the time when we were forced onto floating exchange rates; and this market has become a vital institution in making the system work as well as it has. Commercial banks may now make contracts with their non-bank customers while covering themselves freely in the Euro-currency market. Without it, we would have seen a much greater escalation in the costs of clearing and, possibly, a much stronger move towards controls on current-account transactions in order to prevent exchange-rate movements.

What then does this mean for policy? First of all, I would suggest that the I.M.F. change its attitude towards short-term capital movements and try to encourage countries to permit freer short-term capital mobility. Secondly, any suggestions for regulating the Euro-currency market must account for how important it is under the flexible exchange-rate system in clearing and covering international payments. If the Euro-currency system becomes constrained in the same way that national money markets are regulated (interest-rate restrictions, credit controls and the like), the flexible exchange-rate system would become unworkable. For example, suppose the move toward floating exchange rates occurred in the 1950's prior to the formation of the Euro-currency market when most national money markets were tightly regulated with exchange controls. Then convertibility on current accounts would more likely have broken down with serious distortions in international trade in goods and services.

William Branson: We now have a lot of models with flexible exchange rates which use so-called small country assumptions. They track out what happens under various assumptions. As Modigliani noted, some of these countries are so small that it probably does not make sense for them to have an exchange rate of their own. A relevant model would be a model of blocks to which small country assumptions do not apply. This seems to be an important direction in which research should go.

The justification for using simplifying small country assumptions in cases where one might really think that they are irrelevant has to be that one is looking for a particular channel through which something works. One then assumes away all the other channels and focuses on that one. It seems to me that one of the virtues of the monetary approach is that one gets a good clear look at one channel. Most of us are perfectly happy to go along with that. But there is a slight asymmetry in that the people who are most enthusiastic about the monetary approach are not very interested in listening to cases in which other clarifying assumptions are made in order to look at some other channel. I think it would be helpful in judging which models are useful and which are not, if we looked upon these models as partial ones which make many clarifying assumptions. We should not treat them as if the writer was trying to model the whole world.

The last point I want to make is that what has been lacking here is a systematic attempt to test the new approach. We have people who seem to be willing to make statements about the world on the basis of clear and rather simple models without presenting us any evidence that it is, in some sense, the most important channel which is represented by their models. It seems to me that we have now clarified most of the channels. The interesting question would be to try to test which channels are most important and to discover how to model them into macroeconometric concepts in order to say quantitatively something about the relative importance of the different approaches to pressures on the exchange rate.

Ephraim Kleiman: My first point is a question that I raised yesterday, which I do not think I got an answer to. Granted that the exchange rate is the relative price of two monies and not the relative price of national incomes, the very best way of looking at the determination of the exchange rate is via the demand for money, including the stocks. But there is still the question: Why do people hold foreign currency as a liquid asset of the same sort as their own national currency? I think the main reason for holding money is as a store of value. You expect to be able to buy something for it in the future. I noticed that in some of the monetarist papers the arguments in the function of demand for money were represented by empty brackets. So now we have got here an empty bracket instead of the old empty economic boxes. Some of the elasticities which Max Corden is looking around for might indeed be hiding somewhere in those brackets. Because, ultimately, the reason for holding some asset is that you think you, or someone to whom you will sell it, will be able to exchange it for something else, such as a foreign good, at some future time. The amount of foreign goods you will be able to buy depends on their price, and so we are back to looking at the relative price of two national incomes. One ought to remember that looking at the exchange rate as the relative price of two national incomes was originally an attempt to explain the relative price of two national monies. So in a way we are really trying to unscramble an old omelet —and it is true that by unscrambling it one does not always get what was there at the beginning. It is, of course, quite appropriate to do so, but when doing so one should unscramble it properly and not stop at this stage.

My next point relates to the small country assumptions. I believe that there is a curious thing happening here, because most papers seem to make the small country assumptions at the same time as they include certain characteristics which are properties of big countries: a continuum of traders and speculators, perfect capital markets and so on. They seem to try to elicit policy rules for big countries from the analogues with small countries. And one should, I think, take into consideration the secondary effects which, of course, can never completely cancel out the initial effects, but which can offset them to a certain extent. Therefore, I think that the conclusions based on the small country assumptions can not really provide rules of thumb for big countries.

The last point I would like to make relates to what Bob Mundell said about the need for only one model. Now the question is: What true world do we want to explain? It has once been commented that there are very few cases where one can trace the development of economic thought to economic circumstances. Now I think that here we have a case where one can. I was wondering whether one could apply the models that were presented here today to the immediate post-war world, where endogenous capital flows were few and where capital movements were highly controlled; I do not think that we would have got very far with the help of these models in explaining the immediate post-war phenomena. In the same way the import- and export-elasticity type approach, which effectively ignores speculative motives, will not lead us far in explaining exchange-rate phenomena in the seventies.

There are two things that I would like to say on that. One is that, conceivably, the big speculative movements which we have witnessed may have represented a readjustment from a disequilibrium position which was very far away from equilibrium. In the future they *may* turn out to be of lesser importance than they were in the last few years. And that should give us some sense of proportion in evaluating how important the present approach is.

Secondly, seeing that there are two real worlds, or rather that the different models correspond to two different worlds, I would like to end with a plea to have the two of them incorporated into one model of one world.

Max Corden: I think that many of the non-monetarists here have been struggling these last few days with questions like: What is so special about the monetary approach? How do the monetarists get rid of elasticities, for example? How have we all gone wrong these years?

For this purpose, looking at Dornbusch's paper, I find that everything is in there, and that he thought of everything. But then I look at Mike Mussa's paper and he is, of course, a sitting duck. I have gone through it very carefully, line by line, and I would like to report on my conclusions with regard to the monetarist models.

First of all, it seems to be a general feature of these models that they assume that domestic assets, i.e. the domestic credit components of the money supply, are held constant. Let me take a key sentence out of Mussa's paper: "The critical element in determining the long-run cumulative effect of exchange rate changes on the balance of payments (holding the domestic credit components of money supplies constant) is the effect of the exchange rate change on the demand for money." Now, the parenthesis in that sentence is, of course, central. Then I asked myself, what have *we* been pursuing all these years in our other models. My answer, of course, is: We have supposed that the domestic credit component of the money supply is varied so as to maintain a constant level of demand for domestic goods and services at an exogenously given money wage. That is the most common sort of model, and as soon as you assume that the supply of money is being varied automatically by policy to achieve a certain result, the demand for money ceases to be a relevant consideration. Now, once you have the other model in which the supply varies so as to maintain equal demand at a constant money wage, the elasticities will come back.

Let me just say that there is no logical fallacy in the old approach; it is just that they had a different model and different assumptions, and then we could have some long discussions about which approach is the more useful.

Now let me come to another element in the monetarists' model. They do tend to assume that the money wage is flexible and maintains full employment. That seems to be more or less implicit in Mussa's paper in the end and also in Dornbusch's famous *AER* paper.[1] But, as I keep stressing, Dornbusch has of course another assumption somewhere else. Now, the classic and traditional assumption has been that the money wage is either rigid or exogenously given, or rises exogenously, and then we have built our models on that. Now, comparing those two assumptions, I could, of course, have thought of a

[1] Dornbusch, R.: Devaluation, money and non-traded goods. *American Economic Review* December, 1973.

hundred better assumptions that might have been satisfactory. The assumption that I keep thinking about is that one should assume that the *real wage* is, if not necessarily rigid, at least disagreeably inflexible. I would have thought that if we really wanted to discuss relevant models of exchange rates and advance the subject, we should focus our minds on that aspect: inflexibility or inadequate flexibility or real wages. It may not, of course, have to be one single real wage. One could distinguish between different wages, and hence income distribution effects, if one liked.

So I must concede that the old model with money wages rigid or exogenously given is not very satisfactory. I have been using it, I confess, for years. But I am not at all satisfied with the new monetarist assumption either.

Now, a related point is: why do the elasticities seem to disappear? Some of us were brought up on the ideas and the concepts of "switching" and "absorption".[1] Switching refers, of course, to elasticities. The elasticities tell us about the effects of switching devices, such as devaluation or a tariff increase. One knows that in the traditional model, with the money wage constant, the exchange rate has been the instrument of switching. But how does this switching come about in Mussa's paper or Dornbusch's *AER* paper? Well, it all comes about through the money wage being flexible. A given money wage change has particular effects on patterns of production and consumption, the extent of these effects depending upon the elasticities. The elasticities have thus not disappeared; switching happens in some sense automatically. The familiar partial elasticities are essentially the same as the elasticities along the transformation curve, say, between traded and non-traded goods, and the elasticities along the community preference map on the demand side.[2]

My final thought is: How helpful is the monetarist focus on the demand for and supply of money? In one respect it seems a good approach. It brings out the point that international issues always have domestic issues at their heart. Money supply and demand are domestic phenomena in a way, the balance of payments implications coming out as a by-product. I have found that this is so in trade theory, too. When one analyses all the issues in real trade theory, one ends up with closed-economy economics incidentally extending it to international trade. On the other hand, when one looks at the way the analysis is presented in Mussa's paper, one sees that it is beautifully neat in the beginning, everything being built around the demand for and supply of money, but that, in the last part of the paper where he gets to the interesting issues —namely *real* causes and *real* effects, which are the things that really matter —the analysis is no longer coherent. The analytic framework is simply not helpful at the points where it really counts. These are my doubts about the monetarist approach, even while conceding its elegance and insights.

[1] Johnson, H. G.: Towards a general theory of the balance of payments. In Johnson, *International Trade and Economic Growth*. Allen and Unwin, London, 1958.

[2] See Dornbusch, R.: Exchange rates and fiscal policy in a popular model of international trade. *American Economic Review*, December 1975.

David Laidler: I want to raise a point in response to Bill Branson. He said that he did not think that enough empirical evidence had been brought to bear on matters here. I really do not think that he is right. I think much of the discussion *has* focused on the theoretical models and not enough has focused on what we have learned this morning from papers which were indeed heavily empirical. Johan Myhrman gave us a framework in which both real disturbances and money disturbances logically could affect the exchange rate. He then formulated a hypothesis that monetary disturbances dominated as a matter of historical fact, and the only episode in which he found himself in some kind of difficulty was during the revolutionary and Napoleonic wars; one of the major issues in the debates of that period was whether there actually was inflation going on or not. There is a lot of solid evidence that says that monetary policies do dominate the explanation of variations in flexible exchange rates across a really wide variety of institutional circumstances.

Secondly, like Michael Parkin I was absolutely astounded by how far Jacob Frenkel could get with real numbers using very simple models. Again I think we learned something from that. We learned that there is empirical relevance in these so-called monetarist models. Now, I do not think that this morning anyone argued with Myhrman when he said that it appeared to be the case that the postulated monetary impulses dominated the explanation of fluctuations in domestic prices and exchange rates. I do not know if that means that there was consensus that this is a good way of looking at the world. But if you go to the contemporary United Kingdom, you will find that the dominant view of the interaction of monetary policy, the exchange rate and inflation, corresponds exactly to the ideas of Myhrman's "hat party", i.e. that real economic growth is to be generated by monetary expansion, but that unfortunately there is some kind of structural imbalance that drives up inflation and drives down the exchange rate, so that this poor country is thwarted in its efforts at growth by a falling exchange rate and imported inflation, which then has to be dealt with by subsidizing export industries, tariffs, quotas and so on. I think that everybody in this room has a great deal to teach the authorities of the United Kingdom. So I think that really more than some theoretical models and some mysteries about how we should analyze things have come out of this conference. There *has* been a gathering of hard evidence.

Jørgen Gelting: First, the obvious point that just as a country can be too small to have a fluctuating rate, it may be too large to have *one* rate. I think that New England, Scotland and the southern part of Italy might have been better off if they had been independent currency areas.

Secondly, if you will allow me to be completely unrealistic, let us imagine a world with freely fluctuating rates and at the same time with highly flexible wage rates. That system simply could not operate; it would lack stability. So imagine instead two extreme models: one where you have fixed exchange rates and flexible wages and another where you have completely rigid wages and completely flexible exchange rates. Now expose each system to internal and external disturbances, go through the analysis and you will reach the conclusion that the best of those two systems is the one where you have fixed exchange rates and completely flexible wages. So the conclusion is that the system of flexible exchange rates is actually a second-best solution. But now we have to put up with it. At the same time the higher rate of inflation and thus the rise in the average rate of wage increase has widened the scope for wage changes in response to changing labour market conditions. Insofar as this results in a wider amplitude of changes in the rate of increase of wages, the prospects will deteriorate for an orderly behavior of fluctuating exchange rates.

I think that Robert Mundell is right, that we may be moving towards a system where we have a few or just two currency blocks, and where all the small countries maintain fixed rates on one or the other of the dominating countries. We may then run into the problem to which Kindleberger drew attention back in 1969 that the major countries will not be able to agree on the rate of exchange between their two areas because their balance of payments targets are inconsistent.

Assar Lindbeck: I wonder, if you could hint, just a second, as to why it is impossible to have a model or a world with both flexible wages and exchange rates.

Jørgen Gelting: Primarily because a domestic disturbance would call forth opposite and cumulative changes in the wage level and the rate of exchange. Thus, domestic expansion would inflate wages and depreciate the rate of exchange. Freely fluctuating rates combined with highly flexible wages presents the standard case leading to destabilising speculation.

Alexander Swoboda: Are you just saying that one nominal magnitude needs to be fixed?

Jørgen Gelting: Yes, of course, wages or the rate of exchange.

Alexander Swoboda: First, I think that in contrast to some of the rather pessimistic or negative reactions to what was achieved at this conference, I should like to take a more positive view. In fact, I think it is quite remarkable that if we were Bob Gordon's Rip van Winkle,[1] and we had gone to sleep three years

[1] Cf. Gorden, R.: "Recent Developments in the Theory of Inflation and Unemployment". Paper presented at the I.E.A. Conference on Inflation Theory and Anti-inflation Policy", Saltsjöbaden, 1975.

ago and had been asked before what we knew about the determination of flexible exchange rates (e.g., what determines the exchange rate in the short run, how does it adjust in the long run, and so on), our answer would have amounted to very little, even in theoretical models. Now we wake up about three years later and we find a number of papers which I find basically quite successful in answering, in a very simple framework, a number of those questions.

In particular, I think we do have a much better idea, after this conference, of some of the factors that enter into the short-run determination of exchange rates. Think of what we had to say about the role of asset markets in exchange-rate determination three years ago: except for some very simple statements, very little.

We also have a much better understanding of the role of expectations in the outcome of the adjustment process. We still do not know empirically exactly what kind of expectations people actually do hold—we do not observe them directly—but at least we can test a number of hypotheses by postulating some of the implications of different expectations formulations for magnitudes which we can observe. As more contemporary data on flexible rates is being currently generated, the scope for empirical testing is widening and we can be confident that the tests will be performed.

Thirdly, I think we have advanced in our understanding of how the short run is linked with the long run: be it through some gradual adjustment to purchasing power parity à la Dornbusch or be it through the relation between the decision to accumulate wealth through the current account and the exchange rate à la Kouri. The fact that we at least have the beginnings of answers is very promising.

In fact, we have a number of models or hypotheses which are pregnant with potential policy implications. What I really would like to see worked out now are some of those potential policy implications.

In particular, the one policy implication we have been able to draw starts from a global point of view: If only the large countries in the system were to pursue a stable monetary policy, then flexible exchange rates would be much more workable, a point that Mike Mussa has emphasized. This is a most important point, but it is not enough. What policy recommendations do we make in the absence of more fundamental reform of the international monetary system? Suppose that we are concerned with a country that is neither small nor one of the major ones, and that there exists great instability in the world. Then you do not know which exchange rate you want to peg, if you want to peg one. What is then the optimal policy response to, for instance, a rise in the foreign rate of inflation? What happens if, in fact, expectations are such that this *does* get transmitted at home? Is there any appropriate response from the authorities to this kind of phenomenon or should they just try, on their side, to pursue some kind of stable monetary-rule policy?

Dwight Jaffee: I want to draw a quick comparison between what I take to be Max Corden's view of the world and Rudi Dornbusch's. Corden said before that he wants to consider the assumption that it is the real wage rate that is rigid or moves slowly. He also said that in reading Mussa's paper he was concerned about the difficulty of analyzing real phenomena; for shorthand let me call that y! I think that these things sit together: because he is interested in real y, he suspects that it is real things that influence it. On the other hand, Dornbusch is clearly looking at monetary impulses as the main thing. The variable he focuses on is p, the price, and he says, "OK, maybe y goes with it", but I do not think it is too much of a disservice to say his primary focus is on the monetary variable p.

Now, I think an interesting question is how these two things relate to each other. There are really two loops in the process. One loop is: What impact do the price effects have on the real sector? I think it is critical that we tie these two things together. The other loop is: What impact do the real things have on the monetary view? If you take the monetarist position in its extreme, it is an interesting problem, because they really say that the real sector does not have any impact on nominal variables. If you want to know what determines price levels or exchange rates, you are supposed to look at the money supplies. I think Bill Branson's point is important: *that* is really a polar view, and I do not think that anyone would really want to force it any more than the Keynesians would force their polar view.

Marcus Fleming: I want to say a few words as a more or less unreconstructed Keynesian. I have been very much impressed by the elegance of the monetarist models which I have read and I promise to use part of my retirement in studying them.

As I think about it, I do feel that I have learned something about the short-term determination of exchange rates. But like Max Corden I have difficulty in relating these models to policy problems. It seems to me that one ought to pose the question: What level of demand pressure should exist in a country? That, of course, brings in some considerations regarding the trade off between inflation and unemployment, and I do not expect much help there from monetary theory anyway. But when one has arrived at a demand target, one would like to know what monetary policy or what mixture of monetary and fiscal policies would be most conducive to getting to that objective. And nothing so far has helped me in making that type of decision.

Then I want to turn to the question of the exchange rate: I cannot help feeling that the whole question of floating rates has arisen because of the differential inflation rates in the world. An analysis which assumes wage flexibility and full employment seems to be alien to the nature of the problems that gave rise to the need for floating exchange rates.

Anyhow, having flexible exchange rates, what one wants to know is how to come to a view about what might be called the equilibrium longer term rates, from which the rates should presumably not diverge too far. I think the guidance we have had on that points to purchasing power parity in some sense. I think we have not got very far in applying this concept in practice. However, there is a little guidance there.

The next problem is, of course, to know what policies to recommend. First of all, one hopes that one of the side benefits of the floating rates would be that a freer use could be made of monetary policy. But, all the same, it would seem that in countries which use monetary policy exclusively for domestic purposes, there would probably be wide fluctuations in the rates of exchange, which might be deemed to be too disturbing. Up to a point the reconciliation of internal and external stability could, no doubt, be fostered by fiscal policies and by intervention in exchange markets. Even so, monetary policy also would probably have to be diverted to some extent from the function of attaining a domestic demand target to the function of maintaining external stability in the exchange rate.

What compromise is to be made? What sort of calculations should we make in order to determine how wide the swings in the exchange rate around the equilibrium rate ought to be? It seems to me that maybe some of these models of expectations could help in this respect. But I am a little skeptical. One thing I cannot help mentioning concerns the discussions we have had about the role of forward markets. It seems to be the assumption that at one and the same time the forward exchange rate will serve as an indicator of expectations about future spot rates and also be in line with international interest rates, because there is perfect covered interest arbitrage. Now, this seems to me to be quite unlikely. Perhaps during hyperinflation the forward rate will be a perfect indicator of expectations, because interest arbitrage is almost non-existent. But in quieter times interest arbitrage seems to dominate, especially if there is no trend in exchange rates.

Robert Aliber: The question those of us concerned with exchange markets have been worried about for the last several years is the following: Why have floating rates behaved differently from the way we were promised? It seems that there are two answers. One is that the people who were making the promises generally skipped over the history of floating rates, and the other is that the pro-floaters probably did not contemplate a situation in which we would have both general inflation and differential rates of inflation between countries, and in which there is a great deal of uncertainty and lack of confidence both in money and government.

We seem to agree at this conference that expectations are important in exchange markets. In some ways, this conclusion is an empty box. While it might be desirable to have a general theory of exchange rate expectations, my guess is that we are going to find that the formation of exchange rate expectations differs depending on the monetary environment. We have one set of exchange rate expectations in the Canadian case, a second set in the Japanese case and a third in hyperinflation.

One relevant factor we observed in the breakdown of the pegged rate system was that the expectation formation process in 1970 appears quite different from the process in 1965. Similarly, it appears quite different in 1924 than in 1922.

The expectation formation process is likely to be important in any new system if we return to price stability and go back to a system of pegged rates. We will not have had 75 years of narrow margins, as under the gold standard, and the Bretton Woods System. The expectation formation process will be different. And so one question that we should be concerned with is what have we learned under the floating rate system that will be useful when we think about designing a new pegged rate system?

Michael Mussa: Max Corden's remarks stimulate me to say something in response. It was my intention that my paper for this seminar should be general and provocative, and that it should avoid details like the small country assumption, the one good assumption, the assumption of instantaneous purchasing power parity, and all the other assumptions which we frequently put into theoretical models for purposes of analytical simplicity. I'm glad that Corden raised his questions and objections because I think that they focus on major issues.

First, concerning the domestic credit component of the money supply, it is not the case that monetarists assume that it stays constant. Indeed, one of the principal things they have to say is that if you increase it, the official settlements balance will leak or the exchange rate will depreciate.

Max Corden: You treat it as a parameter.

Michael Mussa: No, we don't treat it as a parameter in the sense that we assume that it stays constant or that its behavior is independent of the policy concerns of the central bank and the treasury. We do treat it as a parameter in the sense that we always focus specific attention on what is happening to domestic credit. This is desirable since, as Max Corden emphasized yesterday, there are a lot of reasons why the money supply might change. Hence, it simplifies discussion if we treat domestic credit as a parameter, then ask what happens when it changes, and finally ask why, in any particular instance, it changed in a particular way.

The next issue is money wage flexibility and real wage flexibility. In some simple models, full employment is assumed to be maintained by wage flexibility. But, in Dornbusch's work, in Genberg and Kierzkowski's work, and in my own work, this assumption has been relaxed.[1] In the present paper, I emphasize Modigliani's point that in the short run, the costs of domestic products tend to be fixed in terms of domestic money and that our output is not exactly the same as the output of other countries. Hence, when our currency depreciates, we expect to see some increase in the demand for our output. There is no problem in integrating this phenomenon into a monetarist model of the balance of payments.

Next, I want to comment on expenditure-switching policies and the role of elasticities. By an expenditure-switching policy, I mean a policy that switches domestic expenditure from foreign goods or tradables to domestic goods or nontradables, without affecting the level of domestic expenditure and without affecting money demand or money supply. Such a policy cannot affect the balance of payments. To affect the balance of payments we must create a divergence between amounts of all things other than money that we sell and the amounts that we buy. A switching of expenditure, by itself, does not do this.

Now, Corden means something different by an expenditure switching policy. He asks what happens in a model where the money wage is fixed and where monetary policy is used to maintain full employment if we switch expenditure toward domestic goods. Given the price of foreign goods or tradables, the switch of expenditure tends to increase employment at the given wage. To prevent employment from rising, the monetary authority must contract domestic credit and raise interest rates. The increase in interest rates reduces domestic expenditure relative to income and thus generates a balance of payments surplus. The monetary authority must sterilize the inflow of foreign exchange by continual reductions in domestic credit. The magnitude of the required sterilization operations depends on various elasticities and marginal propensities. These elasticities are calculated "along the transformation curve" because, by assumption, the level of employment is being held fixed. I think that this is what Corden has in mind by an expenditure-switching policy. There is nothing in this analysis which I find objectionable, except that I would put somewhat greater emphasis on an explicit account on what is happening to domestic credit than is usually done in the literature, and I would draw attention to the fact that the effects of the expenditure-switching policy depend on what is assumed about monetary policy.

More generally, I think that monetarists do concede an important role to relative prices and to elasticities. For instance, in analyzing the effects of devaluation, we recognize that relative prices are likely to be affected, except in a world with only one good. To determine the extent of relative price changes

---

[1] Dornbusch, R.: Real and monetary aspects of the effects of exchange rate changes. In *National Monetary Policies and the International Financial System* (ed. R. Aliber). Chicago, 1974; Genberg, H. and Kierzkowski, H.: Employment and Price Fluctuations under Flexible Exchange Rates. Mimeo, Graduate Institute of International Studies, Geneva; 1975; Mussa, M.: A monetary approach to balance of payments analysis. *Journal of Money, Credit and Banking*, August 1974.

and to know the effects of such changes, elasticities are important. But, monetarists get off the boat when it comes to use of the concepts of "elasticity optimism" and "elasticity pessimism" in discussions of the probable success of devaluation in improving the official settlements balance. Monetarists would emphasize that if the monetary authorities expand domestic credit after a devaluation, it is likely to fail; and if they refrain from domestic credit expansion, devaluation is likely to succeed.

Why should we focus attention on the demand for and supply of money? You can take the view that we have arrived at a general equilibrium model, where everything determines everything else, and we know that this is true. But, it is not very useful. Monetarists go further than that; they assert that in analyzing the behavior of the exchange rate or the official settlements balance, the demand for money and the supply of money are particularly important. Now, that might be wrong. And the fact that it might be wrong is what makes it interesting.

Suppose, however, that we are concerned with the current account, rather than the official settlements account. I would not look primarily at the demand for and supply of money. A current account deficit can be financed through the capital account as well as through the official settlements account, and usually is. If there is an investment boom in Canada, and if there is no strong reason to believe that domestic Canadian savings have changed, then since the current account reflects the difference between savings and investment, I would expect the current account to deteriorate. To determine what would happen to the official settlements account, I would want to look at the demand for and supply of money, but not for the current account.

Finally, let me conclude with a question. Look at the recent history of flexible exchange rates, particularly the wide fluctuations of the dollar–mark rate and the recent appreciation of the Swiss franc. Can we explain this behavior in terms of the standard type elasticity model focusing on relative prices of national outputs? I assert that we cannot.

Assar Lindbeck: Who has said that we can?

Michael Mussa: All right, if an elasticity model cannot explain them and a monetary model can, then I claim a victory for the monetarists on an important issue.

Assar Lindbeck: There are assets and portfolio shifts in other models as well.

I am not going to summarize at this time. However, I think this session has been quite informative. The seminar has mainly dealt with the theoretical foundations of flexible exchange rates, rather than with policy implications. I do not think that is bad. The theoretical foundations have to be straightened out before the policy implications can be drawn. From that point of view, the conference has been very fruitful. Thank you very much!

For Product Safety Concerns and Information please contact our EU
representative GPSR@taylorandfrancis.com
Taylor & Francis Verlag GmbH, Kaufingerstraße 24, 80331 München, Germany

www.ingramcontent.com/pod-product-compliance
Lightning Source LLC
LaVergne TN
LVHW021038011026
849160LV00008BA/430
9780367171827